At the Limit of the Obscene

At the Limit of the Obscene

German Realism and the Disgrace of Matter

✦

Erica Weitzman

NORTHWESTERN UNIVERSITY PRESS
EVANSTON, ILLINOIS

Northwestern University Press
www.nupress.northwestern.edu

Printed in the United States of America

10 9 8 7 6 5 4 3 2 1

Library of Congress Cataloging-in-Publication Data

Names: Weitzman, Erica, author.
Title: At the limit of the obscene : German realism and the disgrace of matter / Erica Weitzman.
Description: Evanston, Illinois : Northwestern University Press, 2021. | Includes bibliographical references and index.
Identifiers: LCCN 2020040460 | ISBN 9780810143166 (paperback) | ISBN 9780810143173 (cloth) | ISBN 9780810143180 (ebook)
Subjects: LCSH: German literature—19th century—History and criticism. | German literature—20th century—History and criticism. | Realism in literature. | Obscenity (Aesthetics)
Classification: LCC PT143.R4 W45 2021 | DDC 830.912—dc23
LC record available at https://lccn.loc.gov/2020040460

CONTENTS

ACKNOWLEDGMENTS

This book is the product of many stations, and many times that many debts of gratitude. First, I would like to express my thanks to my colleagues and students in the Department of German at Northwestern University: above all, to Peter Fenves, whose guidance, support, and scholarly acumen helped see this book through to the end, and to Sam Weber, Jörg Kreienbrock, and Anna Parkinson, for providing both intellectual inspiration and warm collegiality from the very beginning. An especial thanks is due to Eric Downing and Kirk Wetters for their generous and discerning reading of the manuscript at a crucial stage, and to Penelope Deutscher for her always on-target interventions.

This book would not have been possible without the generous support of several fellowships. A fellowship from the Volkswagen Foundation allowed me to spend a formative year at the Graduiertenkolleg "Das Reale in der Kultur der Moderne" at the Universität Konstanz, and a fellowship from the Alexander von Humboldt Foundation allowed me to spend a necessary sabbatical year at the Zentrum für Literatur- und Kulturforschung (ZfL), Berlin. I would like to thank my sponsors at these two institutions, Albrecht Koschorke and Eva Geulen, for their peerless intellectual engagement as well as logistical support, and to all my colleagues at the Graduiertenkolleg and the ZfL for providing both friendship and spurs to thought during the time I shared with them. Stefan Willer and the Habilkreis at the ZfL created a further space for questioning, support, and exchange. I also benefited greatly from an Andrew W. Mellon Postdoctoral Fellowship at the University of California, Berkeley. I would like to thank my colleagues there in the Departments of German and Comparative Literature, particularly Deniz Göktürk, Chenxi Tang, Niklaus Largier, and Karen Feldman, as well as my colleagues at the UC Berkeley Townsend Center for the Humanities, whose conversations were truly the highlight of every week. At Northwestern University, a faculty fellowship at the Alice Kaplan Institute for the Humanities, under the direction of Wendy Wall, provided me both time to write and a group of colleagues to make that time worthwhile. Finally, a grant from the Deutsches Literaturarchiv Marbach, under the direction of Marcel Lepper, enabled me to carry out invaluable research during the work's early stages.

Versions of parts of this book were presented at conferences and institutions including the University of Oregon; New York University; the University of California, Riverside; the University of Colorado, Boulder; Indiana University, Bloomington; the University of Michigan; Rutgers University; Yale

University; ENS-Lyon; and Cornell University. I would like to thank all the organizers as well as the participants of these events for allowing me to share my work with them at various stages of its development, and, even more, for allowing me to receive their observations, questions, and insights in return. Among my other interlocutors and collaborators over the years, I am lucky to have been able to count Adrian Daub, Alejandra Uslenghi, Andreas Gailus, Andrew Leong, Anette Schwarz, Anne Lagny, Anselm Haverkamp, Ari Linden, Arne Höcker, Ben Gook, Christiane Frey, Christopher Davis, C. J. Jones, Corey Byrnes, Deborah Goldgaber, Gabriel Trop, Gerrit Rößler, Ian Fleishman, Jan Behrs, Jeffrey Champlin, Jenny Willner, John Hamilton, John Namjun Kim, Joseph O'Neil, Juliane Prade-Weiss, Lauren Shizuko Stone, Michael Weinman, Nicola Behrmann, Novina Göhlsdorf, Patrick Eiden-Offe, Patrick Hohlweck, Siarhei Biareishyk, Tom Vandeputte, Tove Holmes, Tristram Woolf, Virgil Brower, and Yael Almog. Sage Anderson cast her gimlet eye over parts of the manuscript at a necessary juncture, backed up by the crack team of grammar, style, and solidarity experts Elizabeth Bonapfel, Emily Bereskin, and Ronan Crowley. Last but not least, I am grateful to Trevor Perri and Maia Rigas at Northwestern University Press for their help in making this book a reality, and to the two readers of the manuscript for their constructive and incisive comments.

An early version of chapter 2 was published as "Base Matter: Pathetic Fallacy in Gustav Freytag's *Soll und Haben*," *Colloquia Germanica* 47, no. 3 (2014, published 2017): 37–62, in the special issue "Material Worlds: Novelistic Matters of the Nineteenth Century," edited by Arne Höcker, Franziska Schweiger, and Lauren Shizuko Stone. An early version of chapter 3 was published as "'Was bedeutet der Stein?': Fetishism, Profanation, and Parody in Fontane's *Grete Minde*," *Konturen* 8 (2015): 71–98, in the special issue "What Is a Thing?," edited by Nicholas Reynolds and Jeffrey S. Librett. A further article containing elements from the introductory chapter was published as "'An Injury to Shame': Obscenity and Affect in Nineteenth-Century German Aesthetics," *Orbis Litterarum* 74, no. 1 (February 2019): 3–17, in the special issue "Materiality and the Affect of Reading," edited by Luisa Banki. I would also like to thank Klett-Cotta Verlag for permission to publish the two Gottfried Benn poems included in chapter 5.

To all these and the many others who have sustained me over the years, I owe more thanks than I can say. This book is dedicated to my parents, and to Thomas, again and always.

Introduction

✦

"Scenes that do not belong in the light of day"

> The crime consists of stating that there is in existence in the world something that is not man, that takes no notice of him, and has nothing in common with him. The supreme crime, in their eyes, is to record this separation, this distance, without trying to do anything to sublimate it.
>
> —Alain Robbe-Grillet, "Nature, Humanism and Tragedy"[1]

In the sixth chapter of J. M. Coetzee's 2003 novel *Elizabeth Costello*, "The Problem of Evil," the titular character, an established and sought-after writer, is preparing to give a talk on the theme "Witness, Silence, and Censorship" at a conference in Amsterdam. At the center of her talk is a newly published novel by a certain Paul West, a historical fiction about the failed July 20 plot to assassinate Adolf Hitler.[2] Thinking apprehensively about what she will say in her talk, Costello recalls her initial impressions of the novel: above all, her strongly negative emotions on reading one particular scene, in which the torture and execution of the plot's participants is described by the narrator in vivid and exhaustive detail. No stranger to the cruelties of the world, Costello nevertheless finds herself repulsed and outraged by the unblushing realism of the novel's narration:

> Where could West have got his information? Could there really have been witnesses who went home that night and, before they forgot, before memory, to save itself, went blank, wrote down, in words that must have scorched the page, an account of what they had seen, down to the words the hangman spoke to the souls consigned to his hands, fumbling old men for the most part, stripped of their uniforms, togged out for the final event in prison cast-offs, serge trousers caked with grime, pullovers full of moth-holes, no shoes, no belts, their false teeth and their glasses taken from then, exhausted, shivering, hands in their pockets to hold up their pants, whimpering with fear, swallowing their tears, having to listen to this coarse creature, this butcher with last week's blood caked under his

> fingernails, taunt them, telling them what would happen when the rope snapped tight, how the shit would run down their spindly old-man's legs, how their limp old-man's penises would quiver one last time? . . .
>
> That is what Paul West, novelist, had written about, page after page after page, leaving nothing out; and that is what she read, sick with the spectacle, sick with herself, sick with a world in which such things took place, until at last she pushed the book away and sat with her head in her hands. *Obscene!* she wanted to cry but did not cry because she did not know at whom the word should be flung: at herself, at West, at the committee of angels that watches impassively over all that passes. Obscene because such things ought not to take place, and then obscene again because having taken place they ought not to be brought into the light but covered up and hidden for ever in the bowels of the earth, like what goes on in the slaughterhouses of the world, if one wishes to save one's sanity.
>
> The letter of invitation came while the obscene touch of West's book was still rank upon her. And that, in short, is why she is here in Amsterdam, with the word obscene still welling up in her throat. Obscene: not just the deeds of Hitler's executioners, not just the deeds of the blockman, but the pages of Paul West's black book too. Scenes that do not belong in the light of day, that the eyes of maidens and children deserve to be shielded from.[3]

Later, Elizabeth Costello comments on her own choice of language to describe West's novel:

> *Obscene*. That is the word, a word of contested etymology, that she must hold on to as talisman. She chooses to believe that obscene means *off-stage*. To save our humanity, certain things that we may want to see (*may want to see because we are human!*) must remain off-stage. Paul West has written an obscene book, he has shown what ought not to be shown. That must be the thread of her talk when she faces the crowd, that she must not let go of.[4]

Elizabeth Costello will, however, find it increasingly difficult to hold on to this slippery yet powerful word, whose etymology, as Coetzee rightly notes, is as evocative as it is uncertain.[5] Her initial outrage at West's daring to speak about the proverbially unspeakable eventually founders on her doubts about what such "unspeakability" even means, especially for a fellow writer of realist novels still committed to art as a medium for investigation and truth. Forced almost against her own convictions into the role of censor, she embarrasses even herself with the prim moralizing of her eventual talk, all the while still unable to shake the feeling that she is somehow right, that there are somehow things both too foul and too intimate to be described for public consumption.

Coetzee's brief inquiry in *Elizabeth Costello* into the obscene is overdetermined, touching as it does not only on questions of representability but also on such issues as the dramaturgy of torture, the fascination of atrocity, the claims of the voiceless, and the "banality" of evil. Above all, however, it poses the question of an ethics of realism and what such an ethics would even look like in light of what Elizabeth Costello herself elsewhere describes as the novelist's primary task: to show, to make present, to bring to life, to expose, to feed the desire—"*because we are human!*"—to see.

It is this last consideration in particular that enables Elizabeth Costello to call West's book obscene. In a kind of fatal by-product of Roland Barthes's "reality effect," the presence of the ostensibly superfluous detail, the visually saturated narration of the scene (which Coetzee ironically allows to appear only in indirect and summarized form) here both guarantees the ability of literature to portray "reality" and makes that portrayal the source of a grotesque voyeuristic pleasure. "Sick with the spectacle," Elizabeth Costello cannot bring herself to stop returning to it, even as she comes increasingly to believe that the meticulously faithful account, the account that "leav[es] nothing out," is somehow almost as immoral as the original acts themselves. Recall that it is not so much the *fact* of the political murders that so upsets Elizabeth Costello ("not just the deeds of the blockman") as the *depiction* thereof ("the pages of Paul West's black book too"). In Coetzee's unfolding of his protagonist's thoughts, the monstrosity of the events portrayed thus begins to pale before the monstrosity of the novelist himself, who not only grants access to these events—something a news bulletin or dryly factual encyclopedia entry could, after all, do just as well—but also fleshes them out in gripping, sensuous description. Obscene is the cool directness of the abomination's reenactment, the ostentatious display of that which should only be alluded to in horror and shame. "Nothing in the book had come as a real surprise," Elizabeth Costello thinks to herself, "So what was *too much*. . . ?"[6]

"The Greeks barred representations of violence, including mutilation, rape, and death, from the stage," writes Coetzee in a section of an essay on pornography and its critics with the title "Truth and Reality." "The spirit of visual pornography," on the other hand, "is deeply anticlassical. Its ontology is the empiricism of naive realism: the real is what we can see."[7] Starting at least from the Enlightenment, there has been a long-standing relationship between "obscenity" and realism: the more shocking the representation, the more secure the guarantee that nothing has been changed or sanitized, nothing hidden to pander to conventional morality or to protect the public's delicate sensibilities. The "truth-telling trope of pornography," as Lynn Hunt has written in reference to the libertine tradition of pre-Revolutionary France, vaunts taboo-breaking as freethinking frankness, the courage to say or show outright what other forms of literature smother in sentimentality and euphemism.[8] Similarly, though working from a somewhat different corpus, Linda Williams locates the origins of modern pornography's aesthetics in "the positivist quest for the truth of visible phenomena" and the scientific or quasi-scientific efforts "to record the 'truth' of the body" through new media-technological means.[9] It is in any case no coincidence that the most famous painting of Gustave Courbet, whose precisely rendered scenes of daily life first gave rise to the word "realism" as an aesthetic term,[10] is the notorious *L'Origine du monde*, a close-up of a woman's foreshortened torso, legs spread to reveal, under a black mass of pubic hair, the provocatively parted lips of an exposed vulva. Obscenity is honesty: the sudden baring of what usually remains unseen acts not only as a nose-thumb to the censors but also, ultimately, as a metonym for the promulgation of authenticity in general, the very revelation of "the naked truth" as such.[11]

A number of studies over the past several decades have correspondingly looked at the relationship between literature and obscenity in terms of freedom, forthrightness, and changing standards of propriety, in deference to or in critical engagement with what Michel Foucault has called "the repressive hypothesis."[12] What none of these studies really investigate, however, is the theoretical underpinnings and aesthetic significance of the concept of "obscenity" itself. This is what this book proposes to do. For while "the obscene" is a notoriously unstable concept—paradigmatic here is U.S. Chief Justice Potter Stewart's infamous dictum "I know it when I see it"[13]—it is more than just a lexical placeholder or a mere synonym for pornography and blasphemy; nor is it simply to be conflated with its pragmatic use in modern and contemporary legal contexts. Rather, as I will show, the obscene has to do with the permissibility or impermissibility of sensual representation per se: that is, the artistic portrayal of the material world in its sensuous particularity and the ways in which that sensuous particularity has been considered antithetical to artistic portrayal. Particularly in the German-speaking world, where a tradition of idealist aesthetics remains dominant well into the late nineteenth century (albeit in vitiated and popularized form), realism's "thingism"[14] raises almost immediately the question of where such thingism leads: not just in terms of what kind of threat the unmediated depiction of material reality might pose to the sensitive and susceptible reader, but also in terms of whether such depiction is, strictly speaking, possible at all. For while realism, as the name implies, takes as its subject the real things of the real world, what that world is, and under what conditions its realia become thinkable, is anything but self-evident. The nineteenth-century debates about the proper form and framing of descriptive literature are thus also a debate about the form and framing of phenomenal existence as such, whose representation, in the understanding of the time, may suddenly appear to our eyes in the shape of an inadmissible alterity, a garish spectacle with no apparent connection to whatever "humanity" we might wish to save. The question of "obscenity," in other words, is the question about the decency of realism.

Art Brut

Similar to the disgusting and the abject, the obscene has historically functioned as one or another limit case of aesthetics: it is the disfigurement that forecloses the beautiful,[15] and the prurience that turns aesthetic judgment into appetitive interest;[16] it is the culmination of the sublime in voluptuous violence,[17] and the exhibitionism that compromises disclosure's purity;[18] it is the nakedness of unadorned being,[19] and the mourned-for absence of aura;[20] it is the unspeakable excrescences of formless existence,[21] and the ultra-sublime, blinding presence of the unmediated Real.[22] For this reason, most thinking on the obscene has concerned itself with discerning the *difference* between obscenity and art, usually arriving at the somewhat tautological conclusion that art is distinguishable from obscenity by virtue of the former's "artistic value."[23] Such a claim can be traced back to one of the most oft-repeated tenets of modern aesthetics, namely Kant's conception of the beautiful as "a disinterested and free satisfaction."[24] For Kantian aesthetics, beauty's self-contained logic suspends both categorial assessment and practical use, referring the beautiful object to the higher planes of apperception, understanding, and the pure play of appearances. On this view, the obscene is not just the wilderness to which the appetitive gaze is exiled; it is the deliberate perversion of aesthetics insofar as it uses appearance to solicit desire, evoking a lust for the thing while nevertheless always remaining image, not only corrupting aesthetic disinterestedness through practical reason but also bypassing practical reason through aesthetic semblance itself.

Even beyond a strictly Kantian framework, however, the premise of a definitional opposition between art and obscenity holds sway. In his 1911 essay "Das Unanständige und Kranke in der Kunst" ("The Obscene and Pathological in Art"), Robert Musil defends "obscene" art by discriminating between the representation of immoral acts and the desire for those acts themselves. To confuse the two, he writes, is to be confused about the nature of art as such: "What in reality remains fused together like a molten drop is here dissolved, untangled, interwoven—made holy, made human [verseligt, vermenschlicht]."[25] Musil's defense of the artwork as an all-but-automatic sublimation—an "intellectualized, as a chemist would say 'enriched' representation" (intellektualisierten, wie ein Chemiker sagen würde, 'angereicherten' Abbild)[26]—places him at once at the forefront of modernist anticensorship movements and in line with a tradition of media-theoretical idealism stemming back at least to Hegel's famous defense of Dutch realist painting, according to which, "instead of existing wool and silk, instead of actual hair, glass, flesh, and metal, we see only colours; instead of all the dimensions requisite for appearance in nature, we have just a surface."[27] For both Musil and Hegel, art's mediating character draws the attention away from the subject matter being represented toward the *modes* of its representation, transforming even the most profane or depraved content into beneficial spiritual expression. And yet, this apparently all-neutralizing frame of the aesthetic also exists in tension with the obscene's proverbial association with visuality as such. "What is seen," writes Jean-Luc Marion, "immediately becomes once again a ridiculous or obscene object."[28] "It is love and simple obscenity. Painting paints this," asserts Jean-Luc Nancy.[29] And Baudrillard states categorically: "Obscenity—that is to say, the total visibility of things."[30] Here, representation is not just the cure, but the poison. Whatever processes of aesthetic sublimation or humanization objects may undergo, visibility is always potentially overexposure.

This axiomatic association between visibility and obscenity has obvious repercussions for the literary mode known as realism.[31] The renewed scholarly interest in literary realism over the past few decades has led to a move away from an emphasis on narrative and theme to more trenchant questions of form, language, and rhetoric, repositioning realism as a literature not just of historical chronicle or socio-psychological observation, but also of wide-ranging epistemological, phenomenological, and psychological experiment.[32] In German studies in particular, recent scholarship on realism has tended to stress the peculiar paradoxes of an empirically oriented aesthetics and the formal strategies on which it depends: as we have known since at least Jakobson and Barthes, realism is *not* the representation of the real world, but a complex system of linguistic and narratological techniques designed to present the *illusion* of authenticity.[33] Realism, on this account, always fails to attain its goal: each attempt to grasp "reality" as a stable and comprehensible image only sets up yet another link in the chain of signifiers through which reality itself, such as it is, recedes ever farther into the distance.[34] In vain does the author or reader lay claim to the world; literature is fundamentally a system of self-referential signs, always an announcement *of* the real, never its presence.

My intention is by no means to dispute such reasoning, which I take as given. However, what sometimes gets lost in the examinations of realism's "linguistic turn" is, precisely, the question of reality—or the real—itself. Such an objection is *not* to be taken as a return to a naive empiricism, antitheoretical reading practice, or precritical notion of knowability. Rather, it should be understood as drawing attention to the fact that, for many German realists, the idea of the mimetic representation of the world was problematic in another sense than just the impossibility of literal replica. If realism, as Eric Downing has argued, is predicated on a bond of attunement or *Stimmung* between the human and the physical world, then the absence of that bond—or anyway the perception of that absence—introduces a problem at the heart of realism itself.[35] For there is not just the melancholy lament that realism can never actually arrive at "reality"; there is also the paranoid fear that reality *will* be reached, that the stony face of an impenetrable otherness will jump out from the literary work in defiance of all affective mediation. The "cold factuality"[36] of the material world repels the anthropomorphic gaze, threatening the metonymic connections between humans and things on which realist literature implicitly depends with the blank bulk of the unintelligible.

This threat, to be sure, is a phantasm. As the current body of work that goes under the name of "New Materialism," for one, has endeavored to show, the "unbridgeable chasm between life and 'crude matter' "[37] is neither simple nor inevitable, but instead the product of a long process of discursive and ideological development that establishes physical substance as the immutable and terrible truth of the world, the inertial counterpart to the dynamic forces of mind, idea, or form. Yet even if this idea of the impenetrable (but ironically still anthropomorphically menacing) otherness of matter is a historical construction, it is a construction that has had a hold on the imagination of whole generations of writers and thinkers, with consequences that go beyond realism's particular representations to the worldview these representations play no small role in shaping.

Correspondingly, one of the claims of this book will be that, in the historical process that establishes matter as "mere matter," German realism has played a crucial—if not indeed the crucial—role. If such a claim seems inflated in regard to a literature usually regarded as secondary or second-rate,[38] we need only remember that German realism also occupies an intermediate position between Kantian idealism and Husserlian phenomenology, in which, as Paul Fleming has shown, "the artist's task lies not merely in recording and archiving the ordinary [as in other national realist traditions], but also in penetrating its essence."[39] What Fleming points to as German realism's particular "aesthetics of the common"[40] is thus also what makes it decisive for the discussion of matter: for it is in the very attempt to penetrate the essence of the ordinary and the peripheral—in Hegel's words, the "intentional approach to the contingency of immediate existence, which in itself is unbeautiful and prosaic" (absichtlichen Annäherung . . . an die Zufälligkeit des unmittelbaren, für sich genommen unschönen und prosaischen Daseins)[41]—that the problem of how to portray this ordinariness and contingency in a way that would *not* be unbeautiful first rears its head.[42] In the subsequent fulfillment of Hegel's prediction for an art that makes "*Humanus* its new saint," the material world comes to be seen as that which is, precisely, opposed to "the human heart [Gemüt]"—that in which "man as such" is *in*capable of "being at home."[43]

Such suspicion of the material world is of course not exclusive to literary realism. But it is in literary realism—the poetic form of the profane world's appearance—that it reaches its apogee and crisis. For the "principle of maximum visibility"[44] that Linda Williams attributes to pornography must also be turned around: maximum visibility makes things pornographic—or rather, obscene—turning them into nothing *but* their material imminence. What Judith Butler has called the idea of " 'materiality' [as] a sign of irreducibility"[45]—gendered aspects intact—thus appears in German realism with all the strength of an anathema, to be both feared and shunned, so as not to threaten the human being's differentiation from it.[46] As the readings in this book will demonstrate, much of German-language literary realism can be understood as a series of strategies to eliminate or in some way mitigate that irreducibility, to prevent a dead and inhuman nature from emerging within what ought to be the consummate showplace of human reason and feeling, the work of literature itself. Mimetic fidelity inverts into antiaesthetics at the fulcrum of things' signification. Those scenes that do not belong in the light of day, that the eyes of maidens and children deserve to be shielded from, are the scenes that shine a spotlight on the darkness of matter.

Adult Books

Friedrich Schlegel throws down the gauntlet in a fragment from 1797. "Every perfect novel should be obscene" (Jeder vollkommne Roman muß obscön sein), he declares; "it should also offer the absolute in voluptuousness and sensuality" (er muß auch das Absolute in der Wollust und Sinnlichkeit geben).[47] Leaving aside for the moment exactly what Schlegel might have meant by this,[48] it seems fair to say that German literature in the wake of Romanticism was far more concerned with reining in such "voluptuousness and sensuality" than in offering anything like its "absolute." In reactionary backlash against the *Vormärz*'s combination of philosophical materialism and radical politics—and with a watchful eye turned toward the corrupting influences of French boulevard literature—nineteenth-century German writers are increasingly on their guard against precisely the kind of sybaritic style that Schlegel seems to recommend. Thus Julian Schmidt, coeditor of the prominent literary and political journal *Die Grenzboten* (*The Border Heralds*) and one of the leading voices of *Nachmärz* culture, in his three-volume *Geschichte der deutschen Literatur seit Lessing's Tod* (*History of German Literature since Lessing's Death*), warns:

> There is something holy that inheres in morality, such that the brazen injury to shame [die freche Verletzung der Scham], against which one cannot defend oneself, is nevertheless inevitably avenged. . . . If the heat of passion distorts the spirit, bringing to the fore the physical, animalistic, unfathomably murky aspect of the soul, the dark power of nature, in which no light shines: . . . there art can do as little as the law [so hat auch die Kunst nichts mehr zu thun, so wenig wie die Justiz].[49]

Schmidt's critique, drawing on the legal language of the day, is primarily aimed at the representation of emotional excesses (here specifically, in the dramas of Friedrich Hebbel): "the fever of sexual desire, rut, the monomania of pregnant women, madness."[50] However, for Schmidt and his intellectual cohorts, the other sense of "the dark power of nature" (die dunkle Macht der Natur) is never far away: the portrayal of the human being as a creature driven by its lusts corresponds to a "materialist" or (more or less synonymously) "cynical" idea of what Schmidt elsewhere calls "a soulless nature, that descends into a chaos of dirt and stone" (eine seelenlose Natur, die zu einem Chaos aus Schmutz und Stein herabsinkt).[51] Only the "intimation of the whole" (die Ahnung des Ganzen)—Schmidt quotes the *Gründerzeit* art historian Herman Grimm—"counterbalances the monstrous fragmentation into individual symptoms into which all life dissipates as soon as we would examine it in its smallest moments. It allows us to grasp the world, which threatens to dissolve into dust as soon as we reach our hands out for it, so firmly that not an atom of its infiniteness is lost."[52]

Thus, in multiple registers and with varying degrees of vehemence, writers and thinkers of the mid- to late nineteenth century decry the "naked reproduction of everyday life" (das nackte Wiedergeben alltäglichen Lebens),[53] the "representation of an incommensurable nature, that engages only curiosity, not sympathy,"[54] the "immediate appearance" (unmittelbare Erscheinung), which "present[s] itself . . . as the real and the true, although the truth is in fact contaminated and concealed by the immediacy of sense" (sich selbst . . . als das Wirkliche und Wahre [gibt], während doch das Wahrhafte durch das unmittelbar Sinnliche verunreinigt und versteckt wird).[55] Evidently, the times are no longer propitious for voluptuaries. Yet the new literature is also to be a worldly and an *empirical* literature, a literature in which, in Schmidt's words, "law, constitution, morality is no longer exhausted in general formulas, but rather is expressed in particular representations, grows into immediately present life" (Gesetz, Verfassung, Moralität erschöpft sich nicht mehr in allgemeinen Formeln, sondern es explicirt sich in bestimmten Vorstellungen, es wächst in das unmittelbar gegenwärtige Leben hinein).[56] In a Hegelian gesture of which Schmidt himself appears to be unaware,[57] the universal must be the actual, or it does not deserve the name of universal at all. But the actual must also be the universal, lest it reemerge as a mere aggregate of disconnected data without order or meaning: "For the realism of literature does not consist in the fact that it sees and depicts every detail, but that it sees and depicts every detail in the correct proportions."[58] Only the "spiritualization [of the material], the transfer of everything material into the spiritual realm" (die Vergeistigung [des Materials], die Uebertragung alles Materiellen ins Seelische)[59] provides the condition for a new, "serious" art,[60] an art of human being in the world, which metabolizes the volatile particularity of objective data into an expression of general spiritual truths.

Thus emerges what Downing has called "the paradox of a realist program that appeals directly to the sensible world and yet fears the sensual one, the paradox of a program that would ground itself precisely on that which it would also deny."[61] However, it would not therefore be quite correct to speak of an "obscene" subtext in realist literature—much less, to claim with Jean Baudrillard that "realist art [falls] into a kind of obscenity by becoming descriptive, objective or the pure reflection of the decomposition—the fractalization—of the world."[62] Rather, the aesthetic necessity of the spiritual transformation of the material, such as not only Schmidt demands, establishes the conditions by which such "decomposition" or "fractalization" comes to be seen as "obscene" in the first place. The risk of the *in*correct proportion of detail to idea threatens the presumed coherence of existence itself, transforming the not-yet- or never-to-be-spiritualized appearance of the material world from a neutral object of phenomenological observation to an exhibitionistically defiling residue.

What is clear, in any case, is that the traditional conflation of "obscenity" with sexual or scatological acts does not exhaust the full range of the term's significance. Tracking the development of obscenity law in nineteenth-century Germany, the historian Sarah L. Leonard observes that early definitions of "obscene and immoral" (obszöne und unsittliche) or "indecent" (unzüchtige) publications are concerned "not strictly (or even primarily) [with] sexuality," but with all potential threats to public order and decorum, "a vision of immorality focused . . . on a vague set of infractions and shortcomings associated with the lower echelons of society"[63] that also includes such things as criminal tales, quack science manuals, and antiestablishment tracts. Even later, when the jurisdiction of obscenity law begins to shift toward more narrowly sexual infractions, the emphasis is still on the affective and political risks of obscenity more than on questions of personal virtue. Hence the long-standing definition, alluded to above, of obscenity as, in the words of the 1838 Criminal Code of Saxony, "the injury to morality through indecent, publicly offensive acts" (die Verletzung der Sittlichkeit durch unzüchtige, zum öffentlichen Ärgernis gereichende Handlungen)[64] or, still more pointedly, in the 1841 Criminal Code of Hesse, the "injury to modesty [Schamhaftigkeit]."[65] In the antiobscenity statutes of nineteenth-century Germany, shame or shameability thus becomes a vital public good, to be secured against harm for the preservation of states' social cohesion and the emotional well-being of their citizens.

Yet despite such affective specificity, these legal definitions still leave open—insofar as they take for granted—exactly what one should be ashamed *of*.[66] The Hegelian aesthetician Karl Rosenkranz provides a provisional answer to this question in the section on the obscene in his 1853 compendium, *Ästhetik des Häßlichen* (*The Aesthetics of the Ugly*). Taking his cue from the language of the law, Rosenkranz declares, "The obscene consists in the intentional injury to shame" (Das Obszöne besteht in der absichtlichen Verletzung der Scham).[67] From this definition, however, Rosenkranz goes on to elaborate the anthropological conclusions that the laws themselves do not: "Shame is holy and beautiful, for it expresses the spirit's feeling of being in its essence over and above nature; it [spirit] cannot be without nature [naturlos], but it should be free from it [naturfrei]."[68] Shame is thus the revelation of human exceptionality at its most metaphysical: the human being, fashioned in God's image, suffers the ignominy of the flesh in which that image is manifested. In this sense, shame must remain, if not necessarily injured, than at least always potentially *injurable*: similar to how the sublime in Kant saves the subject from the shock of the infinite through the possibility of thinking that shock, shame raises the subject out of its brute nature by countering it with the horror thereof. The feeling of shame in the face of nature is the proof that one has transcended it.

Rosenkranz's examples of obscenity are largely the expected ones of antique phalli, pornographic novels, and French dances. However, it quickly becomes clear that content alone, in Rosenkranz's assessment, is not enough to make something obscene. This becomes particularly evident in his discussion of the erotic frescoes of the recently excavated sites of Pompeii and Herculaneum, to which Rosenkranz devotes a substantial part of his analysis. Here Rosenkranz contrasts the "obscene-chaste" (obszöndezenten) scenes of nymphs and satyrs, which receive his cautious approval, to the more blatantly pornographic frescoes of men and women engaged in sexual intercourse that Rosenkranz, following the scholarship of the time, attributes to the "cubiculis Veneris" of Pompeian brothels.[69] In the first set of images, the ambivalence of the sex act is neatly divided in two: on the one side, a leering and tumescent satyr, "lost in the rigidity of sensuous intoxication" (in der Erstarrung des Sinnenrausches verloren), and on the other, a half-clad nymph, "stretched out in all the splendor of her snowy limbs on the mossy pillow" (sich in aller Pracht ihrer schneeigen Glieder auf den moosigen Pfühl hingebettet), oblivious to the violation about to befall her.[70] Rosenkranz's description of the picture thus presents it as a kind of salutary *Kippbild*: though the image depicts a moment of graphic and indeed violent sexuality, as a mythological and allegorical scenario, it both allows for the possibility of spectatorial disidentification (lust as grotesque) and situates its image within a recognizable narrative context. The ethical "softening" (Mildern) of the obscene that Rosenkranz observes in the image is more than just a function of its idyllic fantastical setting; as something possessed of a larger background and external interpretative framework, the image bears a meaning that transcends the visual presentation of mere sexually aroused and arousing bodies.[71] The pictures redeem their own pornography, so to speak, in telling its story.

No such redemption is to be found, however, in the second group of paintings, "those erotic scenes . . . where lovers in manifold positions perform the work of nature, and usually a slave stands by who has served the aphrodisiac potion and whose presence is what really first evokes the vivid feeling of the obscene. Disgusting! [erst recht lebhaft die Empfindung des Obszönen hervorbringt. Ekelhaft!]."[72] Clearly, part of the problem in these paintings for Rosenkranz is their transfer of erotic desire from the realm of fantasy and allegory to that of the actual and the everyday (including, not least, the representation of women as active sexual participants rather than slumbering rapeable objects). However, as Rosenkranz's remark makes clear, far more problematic than the images' everydayness is the inclusion of the servant in the picture, whose presence, as a specifically *non*aroused, *non*participating body, throws the couple into relief and makes the scene obscene "erst recht lebhaft." Like the plaster fig leaves glued to the genitals of antique statues, which, Rosenkranz says, "already generate obscene effects [bringen schon obszöne Wirkungen hervor], for they draw attention to them [the genitals] and isolate them,"[73] the servant not only implicitly facilitates the lovers' actions with his proffered erotic aids, but also marks out the image *as* image. With his phlegmatic gaze, now trained on the lovers, now looking discreetly away, the servant introduces a position with which it is no longer possible to dis-identify, because it is the position occupied by the viewer him- or herself.[74] Stand-in for the prurient spectator and the pandering artist all at once, the servant, drawing attention to the lovers' ostensible absorption, confirms the frescoes' complete and thoroughgoing theatricality.[75]

This connection between theatricality and obscenity makes intuitive sense to us, and not just because of the false etymology of the "ob-scene."[76] But what is so problematic about theatrical display? Why *is* physical exhibition a source of shame and/or shameful pleasure? What, again, is one ashamed *of* in the shame of one's self-exposure? Jurists and aestheticians of the nineteenth century might well have taken such questions for granted, insofar as the answer, or at least a possible answer, is as old as the oldest story of Judeo-Christian history itself. In Eden, go the well-known lines, Adam and Eve "were both naked . . . and were not ashamed";[77] however, after eating from the Tree of the Knowledge of Good and Evil, "the eyes of them both were opened, and they knew that they were naked; and they sewed fig leaves together, and made themselves aprons."[78] For Augustine, perhaps the most consequential of all this story's interpreters, the reason for this shame and the primary result of Adam and Eve's disobedience is the postlapsarian separation of the body (that is, certain parts of the body) from the will: "Wherein could be found a more fitting demonstration of the just depravation of human being by reason of its disobedience, than in the disobedience of those parts whence nature herself derives subsistence by succession? For it is by an especial property that those parts of the body are designated as *natural*."[79] In the automatism of erection, the body reveals itself first *as* a body, defying the soul that should be master over it just as Adam and Eve defied the God who should be master over them.

In his commentary on this interpretation, Giorgio Agamben notes that Augustine here follows in a long-standing tradition of attributing the shame attached to such naturalness to Adam and Eve's loss of their previous "garment"—the garment of God's grace. As Agamben goes on to argue, grace (*gratia*), thus conceived as an "ineluctable supplement" to the human body, renders the human body itself always already corrupt: "Original nudity immediately disappears underneath the clothing of grace, to then reappear as *natura lapsa* only at the moment of sin, that is, the moment of denudation."[80]

Henceforth, human nakedness is no longer simply nudity, but always a stripping bare. (Or, as Rosenkranz puts it, "Nature does not know shame and the dear beast, as one says in German, is never ashamed.")[81] "The uncontrollable nudity of the genitals," Agamben paraphrases Augustine, "is the cipher of nature's corruption after sin."[82] Grace, in this sense, is the "chimerical" identity between the soul and its incarnation;[83] shame—the first emotion of a fallen humanity—is the knowledge of (the) difference.[84]

This idea of grace as a tenuously held identity between soul and flesh clearly has consequences for more than just Christian theology. In his influential take on Kantian aesthetics, "Über Anmut und Würde" ("On Grace and Dignity"), Friedrich Schiller elaborates an idea of grace as "the beauty of form under the influence of freedom" (die Schönheit der Gestalt unter dem Einfluß der Freiheit), that is, beauty as a natural harmony of motion in contrast to the static forms of what he calls "architectonic" beauty.[85] Grace, for Schiller, is the speaking body, the "expression of the soul in volitional movements [willkürlichen Bewegungen]":[86] the elegant gestures of the human figure as the sensuous manifestation of the will that moves it or indeed as the sensuous appearance of sentience as such. But there is a corollary to this: "Volitional movements alone can be graceful, but . . . only those that are an expression of moral sentiments [ein Ausdruck moralischer Empfindungen]. Movements that have no other source than sensuality, whatever their volitionality, belong only to nature, which can never ascend to gracefulness on its own [die für sich allein sich nie bis zur Anmut erhebet]."[87] During these merely sensual movements, even the presence of the will is not enough to prevent the human being from falling back into a natural state—or rather, from allowing nature to suspend the will entirely:

> When a person, prey to desire, lets the natural impulse rule over him without restraint, his inner self-sufficiency disappears along with every trace of it in his physique. Brutishness alone speaks from his blurry, deadened eyes, from his lecherous, open mouth, from his choked, quaking voice, from his short, rapid breathing, from his trembling limbs, from the whole of his languishing frame. . . . The dead forces of nature [Die toten Naturkräfte] begin to get the upper hand over the living forces of organization, form is subdued by mass, humanness by base nature [gemeiner Natur].[88]

Schiller thus portrays the human body as a theater of war, in which the rationality of the will battles for control with the automaticity of drives and the natural irrationality of matter itself.[89] In the throes of passion, the human being forfeits the freedom that is its birthright; now "sensuousness [arrogates freedom] *to itself*" (die Sinnlichkeit [nimmt die Freiheit] *sich selbst*).[90] However, it is not just in moments of passion and desire that nature emerges victorious:

> The universal powers of nature, as we know, wage an eternal war with the particular or organic ones, and the most artful technique will eventually succumb to *cohesion* and *gravity* [*Kohäsion* und *Schwerkraft*]. For this reason, the beauty of physique, as *mere product of nature* [*bloßes Naturprodukt*], has its determined period of blossoming, ripening, and decay . . . and its customary end is that *mass* gradually gains control over *form*, and in the *accumulated* material, the living formative impulse prepares its own grave [daß die *Masse* allmählich über die *Form* Meister wird, und der lebendige Bildungstrieb in dem *aufgespeicherten* Stoff sich sein eigenes Grab bereitet].[91]

In the gradual deterioration to which all flesh is heir, a de-formed materiality gives the lie to the body's structure, exposing, as it were from behind its beautiful appearance, the shapeless masses of an original substance:[92] "The freedom of forms, which the ethical will had merely restricted, is overpowered by coarse matter [der grobe Stoff], which always gains as much ground as is seized from the will."[93] Only in the ethereal movements of grace is a temporary truce declared; otherwise, "Nature takes back what she has given":[94] the body is no longer a battlefield, but a tomb.

A century and a half later, this antithesis between expressive physicality and dead matter will reappear in a seemingly unlikely but in fact directly related context: the analysis of sadism in Jean-Paul Sartre's program statement of existential phenomenology, *Being and Nothingness*. As it was for both Schiller[95] and, in a different way, for Augustine,[96] grace for Sartre is the living performance of human freedom that temporarily suspends the shamefulness of physical presence: "In grace the body is the instrument which manifests freedom. . . . Facticity then is clothed and disguised by grace; the nudity of the flesh is wholly present, but it can not be *seen*."[97] Gracefulness, in other words, is the body as the immediate expression of the will that moves it, a body, in Sartre's phrase, "in situation."[98] A temporary disjuncture or maladaptation between will and body, on the other hand, results in "awkwardness" (le maladroit): "Where we expected to seize a key to the situation, spontaneously emanating from the very situation, we suddenly encounter the unjustifiable contingency of an unadapted presence; we are put face to face with the existence of an existent."[99] The sadist's aim, then, is to radicalize this awkwardness, to reveal the flesh as an "unjustifiable contingency" by removing the freedom that ordinarily veils it, forcing the body into "postures which entirely strip it of its acts and which reveal the inertia of its flesh"[100] and thus "to incarnate the Other through violence."[101] "As for the type of incarnation sadism would like to realize," Sartre continues, "this is precisely what is called the Obscene."[102]

This much, however, is easily said—near to tautology. (What is more "obscene," after all, than the Marquis de Sade?) But Sartre's examples of obscenity are not limited to the sexually compelled and objectified body of the sadist's victim. The incarnation of the other also extends to "certain involuntary waddlings of the rump" and "the proliferation of the fat cells," which, in a way precisely analogous to the tortured body, "[exhibit] a superabundant facticity in relation to the effective presence which the situation demands."[103] Schiller in fact already singles out corpulence in "Über Anmut und Würde" as an antithesis to grace, in a footnote appended to the above-cited passage on mass versus formal beauty:

> For this reason, one often finds that such physical beauty becomes indeed noticeably coarsened in middle age by obesity, and that instead of the tender, barely visible lineaments of the skin, furrows sink in and sausage-shaped folds push out [daß, anstatt jener kaum angedeuteten zarten Lineamente der Haut, sich Gruben einsenken und wurstförmige Falten aufwerfen] such that, imperceptibly, the weight gains influence over the form, and the charming and varied play of beautiful lines over the surface is lost in a steadily swelling cushion of fat.[104]

Fat yields naturally, so to speak, what the sadist must work to produce: the morbid appearance of matter as mere thereness. If grace is the effective invisibility of the flesh in beautiful expressive movement, then obscenity is the flesh's reappearance as unfree expression*less*ness: in Sartre's words, an "unjustifiable facticity . . . *de trop* like every contingent,"[105] whose material presence, frozen in the deformations of torture or the inertia of flab, can no longer not be seen.[106]

Understood in this way, "the obscene" encompasses much more than the mere depiction of taboo acts and/or objects, more even than the theatrical ostentation of sensual forms: it is the name for the fear of the radical alterity of matter, a response to the perceived excess of phenomenal appearance beyond or outside that which can be assimilated into a framework of meaning. "Had I dreamed of this enormous presence?" writes Sartre earlier, in the famous climax of his philosophical novel *Nausea*; "I was not surprised, I knew it was the World, the naked World suddenly revealing itself, and I choked with rage at this gross, absurd being. . . . I shouted 'filth! what rotten filth!' and shook myself . . . , but it held fast and there was so much, tons and tons of existence."[107] If for the ancient Greeks, according to Schiller, "nature is never *simply* nature [*bloß* Natur], thus they need not blush to honor it,"[108] for those living after such pagan enchantments, it is a different story. What James I. Porter has called the "disgrace of matter" in post-Socratic aesthetics—the Platonic dismissal of the physical "so that Being in its translucent essence can shine through more purely, untarnished and untainted"[109]—thus returns in the modern age in the form of matter's opaque *in*essentiality: in Schiller's words, a "sensuousness [Sinnlichkeit] . . . without soul" that, fallen from grace and gracefulness alike, no longer expresses anything but itself.[110]

Indecent Exposure

Obscenity, however, clearly refers to something more than just the presence of sensuous matter as such. For if *shame* is an anthropological or affective phenomenon, in which the fleshy materiality of the self is suddenly experienced as other,[111] the *obscene* must be understood as an aesthetic concept, that is to say, a mode of presentation by which such othering is facilitated and carried out. Thus the philosophical anthropologist Max Scheler (whose 1913/1926 study of the phenomenon of shame closely maps onto Rosenkranz's analysis) speaks of the difference between lovemaking and mere copulation: "Intercourse," he writes, "should no doubt not function as an action or movement of a purpose [einer Zweckhandlung oder Zweckbewegung], but should be a *movement of expression* [*Ausdrucksbewegung*], i.e., an expression of *love* uniting two individuals."[112] "Any isolated observation of the sexual organs and their apperceptive *breaking out* of the whole of the person," however, "deprives the sexual parts of their erotic value and reduces them to organs of excretion and objects of disgust."[113] In the transport of lovemaking, the other's body is perceived as the physical manifestation of an integrated being, a body *ensouled*; to perceive the other *as* body, on the other hand, is as it were to fall out of love, to regard the other as a mere aggregate of parts without subjectivity or expressive potential. What Eric Santner has described as the shameful creatureliness of one's own flesh—"an uncanny, somehow material excess experienced as both intimate and foreign to oneself"[114]—turns, in the dehumanizing observation of the other, into the shame*less*ness of exhibitionism: the "absolute mediality," to speak with Agamben, of a material excess *without* intimacy, "the brazen-faced indifference [of showing] nothing but the showing itself."[115] (Another way of saying this is "presentness is grace": but presentness is, precisely, not *presence*.)[116]

What these and countless other examples suggest is that "obscenity" is dependent on a kind of radical realism, the presentation of the sensible object outside either subjective reference or mitigating context. This is the problem famously addressed by Georg Lukács in his seminal essay "Erzählen oder beschreiben?" ("Narrate or Describe?"), in which he lambastes the "lifeless, fetishized things" (erstarrte, fetischisierte Dinge) of the "descriptive style" as something contrary to the very principles of literature, a betrayal of the *human* needs that literature is all but definitionally obligated to serve.[117] Following on Lukács's critique, several scholars over the past few decades have examined the phenomenon of "detail-fetishism" in nineteenth-century literature and culture, often within a Freudian or Marxian framework.[118] As such studies show, the detail comes to troubling prominence in nineteenth-century literature and art, appearing at once as an index of reality and (particularly in the context of nineteenth-century imperialism and the growing trade in both commodities and ethnological knowledge) a seductive diversion from real concerns, a shiny partial object in place of an absent or unrecognized whole.[119] Thus, as Naomi

Schor has suggested (in an argument *against* the detail's devaluation), "What is perhaps most threatening about the detail [is] its tendency to subvert an internal hierarchic ordering of the work of art which clearly subordinates the periphery to the center, the accessory to the principal, the foreground to the background"[120]—wherein the center and the foreground emerge most often as the experience of European masculinity and the clean lines of the sublime style. The detail thereby emerges as a "vehicle for pollution,"[121] contaminating art's ideal forms and general essences through the naive fascination of the particular.

Or as Lukács puts it: "description provides no true poetry of things but transforms people into conditions [Zustände], into components of still lives."[122] Lukács's complaint, informed though it is by the art and politics of his own time, nevertheless repeats what was already a commonplace of nineteenth-century literary criticism. Thus the novelist and theorist Friedrich Spielhagen, for example, in his 1864 essay "Ueber Objectivetät im Roman" ("On Objectivity in the Novel"), laments the difficulty of epic narration in the modern age:

> The poet of antiquity was in the fortunate position of being confronted with a primitive humanity, in which only the major general features were apparent. . . . But we! Good gods! with our modern microscopic eyes we see a world of the most diverse, heterogeneous individuals, where the ancient bard saw only one uniform mass. How are we to give an impression of this kaleidoscopically multicolored world [dieser kaleidoskopisch bunten Welt], indeed, even the most superficial sketch [die äußersten Umrisse], if we maintain the cumbersome method of objective representation [die schwerfällige Methode der objectiven Darstellung].[123]

The sheer complexity of experience and knowledge in the contemporary world makes it all but impossible to capture that world through mere phenomenal description. Hence Spielhagen insists, counterintuitively but paradigmatically, on realism as a form of idealism: "Wherein does the objectivity of the artist consist? Therein, that he applies himself entirely to what is his first and only task: to make his work the expression of the idea he wishes to represent," adding in a footnote: "I notice that I am using 'idea' in the Platonic sense of an archetypal image [eines Urbildes]."[124] Realism is here the revelation of order out of seeming chaos, a distillation of the world to its essential elements that reflects the truth of things far more than ever could the "objective representation" of the empirical world itself.

It is in this same vein that Julian Schmidt praises contemporary work in the natural sciences—in particular, Alexander von Humboldt's *Kosmos*—for having brought the "infinite multiplication" (unendliche Vervielfachung) of nature together with "the greatest pleasure of spiritual life, the understanding of the interrelatedness of the universe [das Verständnis für den Zusammenhang des Weltalls]."[125] For Schmidt, previous eras had regarded the natural world only as an object to be used or a fantasy to be daydreamed about; "Now, however, science has enlightened us as to how, in each natural object, a life of its own prevails. The world has filled itself with individualities, each of which holds its justification in itself."[126] But it is not only in the natural sciences that such a view of the world should prevail. The "immersion of thought in the essence of nature"—the understanding of the world as an infinite yet ultimately coherent totality—"also gives a new content to our art":

> Our most modern realism . . . is not just a return to our ownmost German nature, but also the necessary expression for the transformation of our senses [die Umformung unsrer Sinne]. The art of showing nature in its ceaseless movement, its pulse, as it were, corresponds to the visual training of our modern eyes [entspricht der Uebung unsers modernen Auges, zu sehn]: how strange certain chapters of "Laocoon" now appear to us! The travel writers and the poets compete with the landscape painters: they understand not only how to make the outlines of things clear to the senses of touch and sight, but also how to abstract, so to speak, the waves of light that, in their evanescent movement, grant those things color and radiance.[127]

Just as in the sciences, the newly discovered immensity of material nature contributes to a recognition of its essential lawfulness, a newly mature plasticity of description in literature reveals not the described thing itself so much as the conditions of its describability. Thus, Schmidt enthuses, "our modern poets have truly learned to make sensual nature into a mirror and echo of the spirit" (unsre modernen Poeten haben wirklich gelernt, die sinnliche Natur zu einem Spiegel und Wiederhall des Geistes zu machen).[128] The Lessingian separation between static and temporal representation is overcome in the protophenomenological understanding of the world as apperception and temporal becoming. The visible face of nature, once so alien, becomes representable by becoming internal. Description *entails* narration.

This is the sense of the much discussed notion of "Verklärung," which served as a kind of byword for German realist writers and theorists of the nineteenth century. In the words of Theodor Fontane, with whom the term is most often associated:

> It is not the task of the novel to describe things that happen or at least *could* happen . . . : the point is that, in the hours that we devote to a book, we have the feeling of continuing our real life, and that between the lived life and the fictional one there is no difference besides the one of that intensity, clarity, lucidity, and roundedness [jener Intensität, Klarheit, Übersichtlichkeit und Abrundung], and consequently, of that intensity of feeling [Gefühlsintensität] that is the transfiguring task of art [die verklärende Aufgabe der Kunst].[129]

"Verklärung" thus refers not simply to an idealized or sanitized reality, as has sometimes been assumed,[130] but rather—befitting its biblical provenance—to a reality invisibly transformed by reference to an overriding form of meaningfulness, more specifically, to the meaningfulness of the human experience of reality itself.[131] In other words, "Verklärung" transforms realism from a mimetic to a psychological and phenomenological model: from the appearance of the things themselves to the event of their appearing. Realism, in this sense, is *not* naive mimesis, mere simulacrum—as the critics of the time never tire of repeating. Rather, realism is the representation of the world as the expression of human beings' reflection *on it*, a "*poetic* realism," in the words of the term's popularizer, Otto Ludwig,[132] that "recreates the world," not as a "so-called fantastical . . . that is . . . disjointed [zusammenhangslose]" world of mere physical objects, but instead as a world as it is *re*-presented in the minds of those that inhabit it, and thus as a world "that contains all its conditions and consequences within itself," "in which the coherence [of things] is more apparent than in the real one" (in der der Zusammenhang sichtbarer ist als in der wirklichen).[133]

Again, neither the suspicion of sensual appearance nor the attempts to find ways of containing it is anything new. But the particular dilemma of realism is that it is compelled by its own logic to display the sensual and the material, at the same time as it continues to regard the sensual and the material with mistrust and horror. Indeed, more troubling even than the detail of which Schor et al. speak may be the appearance (or, rather, the idea of the appearance) of materiality as such, in comparison to which even the most random of concrete objects is already a form of idealization. What Hegel, in the *Aesthetics*, memorably calls "the hard shell of nature and the ordinary world" (die harte Rinde der Natur und gewöhnlichen Welt)[134] emerges more and more as the flip side to the human sphere of activity and ideation, which presents that sphere with a blank wall, a failure of sympathy and an embodiment of *non*knowledge beyond which thought cannot pass. In this context, the seemingly automatic slide of nineteenth-century attacks on "materialism" in literature between a critique of content and a critique of style, between accusations of immorality and complaints about tediousness appear as something more than mere intellectual laxity. For what the meticulous recording of sensual particulars excludes is precisely all that which would make the world more than sensual presence: a form, order, intention, idea, emotion, or interpretation that would have the power to turn even the most vulgar of individual elements into necessary parts of a larger whole. If this form, order, intention, idea, emotion, or interpretation falls away, however—if the historical, perspectival, and psychological frameworks for phenomenal appearing are removed—it is only a short step back to what Rosenkranz calls the "common tickling" (gemeinem Kitzel) of bodies on display,[135] a "profanation of the holy mysteries of nature"[136] in the "meaninglessly 'out there'" figures of sensuous showing.[137]

It is in this sense that Slavoj Žižek speaks of the "obscene object of postmodernity": "a certain real, traumatic kernel" that "resists symbolization, but is at the same time its own product."[138] Contrary to Žižek's claims, however, this obscenity is not an ontological given (nor, in the end, is it something particularly "postmodern"). But Žižek is correct to observe that this unsymbolizable real is a product of the very symbolic order that it seems to repel: for to be experienced at all, the radical otherness of the apparently meaningless requires a notion of transcendent meaning against which that meaninglessness can be measured.[139] (As Downing states: "The 'real' is the uncanny and opposed to the 'realist' "[140]—but, it must be added, only within the representational economy of realism itself.) Why *does* Elizabeth Costello find Paul West's description of the torture of the political prisoners so repulsive? Not so much because of the torture as such, but because the relentless particularity of the narration—indeed, much like torture itself—disassembles the scene's human significance into the innumerable parts of its physical composition. As a last insult to the victims' dignity, their would-be historically and personally significant deaths emerge as just another collection of contingent bodies, an empty spectacle of mere physical stuff shamelessly on display.

We therefore need to add a refinement to our previous understanding of the obscene. In the section of *Totality and Infinity* titled "The Phenomenology of Eros,"[141] Emmanuel Levinas—in an unstated but nevertheless clear rejoinder to Sartre's account of sadism—insists on the necessity of the *human* in order for obscenity to occur.[142] "The non-signifyingness of the wanton [lascif]," Levinas stipulates, "is . . . not equivalent to the stupid indifference of matter."[143] "Elements and things remain outside of respect and disrespect";[144] in contrast, the "exorbitant ultramateriality"[145] of the eroticized other occurs as a specific "inversion"—which Levinas, for his part, terms "the feminine"—of the ethical demand of human being itself:

> It is necessary that the face have been apperceived for nudity to be able to acquire the non-signifyingness of the lustful [lascif]. . . . In this inversion of the face in femininity, in this disfigurement that refers to the face, non-signifyingness abides in the signifyingness of the face. This presence of non-signifyingness in the signifyingness of the face, or this reference of non-signifyingness to signifyingness—where the chastity and decency of the face abides *at the limit of the obscene yet repelled but already close at hand and promising*—is the primordial event of feminine beauty.[146]

Erotic desire for the other—that is, for woman as other[147]—then takes place at the membrane-like border between the "expressive" face of interpersonal communion and the "disfigured" and "exposed," object-like and objectified countenance. The "event of feminine beauty"—which is to say, the limit-event of the obscene itself—is the moment when the other's face, ordinarily "the manifestation of the height in which God is revealed,"[148] reverts to the expressionless opacity of its physical surface, in which the face, so to speak, temporarily *becomes* body (a reversion that can moreover be "inverted," for Levinas, in the "weightless grace" of the work of art).[149]

In this sense, Levinas's description of the erotic encounter "at the limit of the obscene" is singularly to the point. For the obscene not only represents the limit of eros, beyond which sexual play tips over into repulsion or contempt; the obscene is *itself* a limit case or borderline condition, situated at the precise moment where that which should have the capacity to signify seems to reverse into its opposite. For Levinas, moreover, such reversal requires no special sadistic tortures or physical defects, but only the situational "renunciation of expression and speech [parole], that sinks into the equivocation of silence, a word that bespeaks not a meaning but exhibition."[150] If eros is "inverted signification,"[151] the kittenish play with nonsignifyingness within signifyingness, then the obscene is the interpolation of a *true* meaninglessness into something supposedly invested with meaning, the presence of nonsignifyingness in that which seems to ought to signify.

What this means, however, with all due respect to Levinas, is that "elements and things" can indeed be obscene: to the extent, that is, that they are understood *as manifestations of human meaning*. Such an understanding is precisely what is at stake in German realism. The "perspective of interiority,"[152] by which German realism "displays less the social and historical world in its 'objectivity' [than] the world as it presented itself within a particular individual's way of perceiving and experiencing, acted on his inner experience, and referred him back to himself,"[153] establishes the conditions for a modern secular mimesis—but, in doing so, also revives the taboo against it. In other words, the nineteenth century's attempt to solve the growing ambivalence about the representation of the sensual and the phenomenal by relocating meaning from the phenomenal world to the human experience thereof increasingly becomes an agent of that ambivalence itself, separating the phenomenal world from the perceptions and interpretations of which it is still necessarily the object.[154] In this sense, the obscene is not merely incidentally or circumstantially bound up with realist literature, but inherent to it. If nature's countenance is to be, in Schmidt's words, a "mirror and echo of the spirit," then the literary representation of this countenance reintroduces the "presence of non-signifyingness" within the signifyingness of spirit itself: the hard core of the hard shell of nature that German realism never ceases attempting to get around.

Earthly Matters

"What is the business of the novelist, after all," asks Elizabeth Costello, "what has been her own lifetime business, but to bring inert material to life . . . ?"[155]

It is precisely in this idea of the bringing-to-life of "inert material" that "the obscene" as an aesthetic category emerges. In the subsequent chapters of this book, I examine some of the stages of this emergence in the works of six exemplary realist (or rather, *realistic*) writers of the long nineteenth century. The first two chapters examine German-language realism's early efforts to regulate the representation of matter in the novels of Adalbert Stifter and Gustav Freytag. In Stifter's idiosyncratic masterwork, the 1857 novel of education *Der Nachsommer* (*Indian Summer*), Stifter's much praised, and much criticized, attention to material detail is perhaps only matched by the novel's striking leitmotif of trash, disorder, decay, and chaos. While trash and decay are often seen—not least, by Stifter himself—to represent matter at its most *non*human and *non*aesthetic, I argue that Stifter uses the then-contemporary painting style of the picturesque to prophylactically recuperate for practical as well as aesthetic purposes precisely that which seems most irrecuperable. Through an examination of Stifter's multifaceted deployment of picturesque techniques within the literary work, I demonstrate how Stifter both dramatizes the redemption of trashed objects from their disuse and writes his novel as an example of that redemption, reintegrating apparently irredeemable matter into the novel's world as the paradoxical epitome of purposiveness and holistic order. Though on the surface Freytag's 1855 mercantile potboiler *Soll und Haben* (*Debit and Credit*) would seem to have very little in common with Stifter's rarefied world of epicurean stasis, it too deploys prophylactic strategies against the danger of a materiality that threatens to outstrip its human use. Specifically, Freytag plays a double game with anthropomorphic tropes, to at once distinguish between ways of relating to the material world and establish hierarchies of value among them. Drawing on nineteenth-century discourses of animism and fetishism, I show how Freytag carefully manages the symbolism attached to material things: on the one hand, through a subtle personalization of goods and objects, and on the other, through a selective and tendentious use of pathetic fallacy, especially in the characterization of the novel's primary villain, the Jewish speculator Veitel Itzig. In this way, Freytag shores up the logic of an (in all senses) bourgeois realism, which casts out what does not give itself to be humanly handled as an uncanny and dangerous excess.

The book's third chapter considers the realist representation of materiality from a slightly different aspect: the materiality of the image itself. In Theodor Fontane's 1879 historical novella *Grete Minde*, set against a background of the Reformation era's *Bildersturm* polemics and bans on the theater, Fontane subtly dramatizes the question of the legitimacy of sensual representation in both the early modern and the contemporary age. In particular, the novella contains a muted but insistent leitmotif of the representation of the material object and its precarious position between transcendence and profanation, idolatry and disenchantment, whose stakes, for the novelist who wants to portray the world in its reality, could hardly be higher. Using Fontane's scattered but insightful theoretical writings as basis, I read *Grete Minde* as Fontane's early-career reflection on the difficult position of realist literature between mimetic taboo and object fetish—for which Fontane's influential middle position of a "verklärte," or "transfigured," realism, while bearing witness to Fontane's shrewd understanding of the issues at stake, only complicates the paradoxes of the "naked, prosaic realism"[156] that Fontane seeks with such a middle position to resolve.

Such paradoxes come to a head in the fourth chapter of this book, which takes on the topic, inevitable in this context, of German naturalism—whose fleetingness in the history of German literature is belied by the heat of the controversies it engenders. Following a brief reading of Émile Zola's controversial masterpiece *Nana*, I turn to the work of that most committed and pugnacious of the German naturalists: the dramatist, essayist, poet, and self-styled revolutionary Arno Holz. In Holz's early fictional works, particularly the cowritten prose vignette *Papa Hamlet*, as well as in programmatic aesthetic tracts such as *Die Kunst: Ihr Wesen und ihre Gesetze* (*Art: Its Essence and Its Laws*) Holz dogmatically insists on precisely that which poetic realism had rejected, a "consistent realism" of perfect sensory replication. However, as I show, in this very attempt at provocative directness, Holz's own work displays a fear of the material world that is even more pronounced than that of his predecessors, which then reemerges in his late work as a kind of performative hyperrealism, tamed, if at all, only by Holz's fantasies of artistic omnipotence.

My final two chapters move beyond the history of realism proper to examine the afterlives of its debates and polemics in the works of Gottfried Benn and Franz Kafka. Benn, a doctor by trade, was heavily influenced by naturalism at the start of his writing career, but quickly turned away from what he came to see as its naive positivism toward a far more vexed view of material representation and the mind/body relation. Thus, in his early work—particularly his breakthrough poem cycle *Morgue* and the series of short prose texts *Gehirne* (*Brains*)—Benn turns realist discretion on its head to present a world of literal dead matter or meaningless nature, in a frontal attack against nineteenth-century materialism and nineteenth-century antimaterialism alike. Like Benn, Kafka, too, engages directly with the aesthetic and ontological legacies of literary realism. Unlike Benn, however—in whose antihumanist provocations the presumptions of humanism persist all the more strongly—Kafka's writing takes aim at the presumptions of humanist aesthetics themselves. I read the last of Kafka's three novel-fragments, *Das Schloß* (*The Castle*), as his response to the aesthetic controversies of the mid- to late nineteenth century around the representation of the sensual and phenomenal world. With *Das Schloß*, Kafka writes a "realist" novel, but removes the realist novel's logical supports, converting an ostensibly verisimilar poetics of description into a narrative that constantly undermines its claims to both emotional consistency and referential truth. What is left over in this process is just that appearance of bodies, dirt, mass, and matter that nineteenth-century German realism had most feared. Yet this appearance is no longer a singular source of horror, to be transformed into history and experiential meaning, but instead a dryly comic travesty of just such transformations and a potential basis of a new aesthetics beyond questions of decency and obscenity alike.

Most of the above texts, of course, contain very little that is comparable to the scenes of Paul West's novel in *Elizabeth Costello*, not to even speak of other, more typically "obscene" works. Coetzee's protagonist could read most of them with an untroubled conscience, free from the sense of being party to an indiscretion: of being made complicit, as voyeur, in a barbarism of more than just historical dimensions. However, in their distinctive stagings of the conflict between "our humanity" and the "things that we may want to see," they prepare the ground for the charge of obscenity that Coetzee's fictional reader is compelled to level at the scenes in her own book, "the talismanic word"[157] of a wanton and inhumane material representation. What Schlegel had hoped for at the dawn of the German novel comes to pass—but not in the way he imagined. Realism's "absolute in voluptuousness and sensuality" finally arrives, but less as a celebration than as a predicament: the imagined fall from grace of a world whose seductive alterity will not be so easily overcome. The obscene emerges as the name for this fall, the flip side of realism's humanist premises, the outrage at the world's otherness at the moment of its supposed appropriation.

Chapter 1

✦

Against Nature

Adalbert Stifter

> The eye is pleased with the tuftings of a tree: it is amused with pursuing the eddying stream; or it rests with delight on the broken arches of a Gothic ruin. Such objects, independent of composition, are beautiful in themselves. But the rock, bleak, naked, and unadorned, seems scarcely to deserve a place among them.
>
> —William Gilpin, *Observations on the River Wye*[1]

> I love this kind of shame.
>
> —Adalbert Stifter, *Feldblumen*[2]

In the crucial midsection of Adalbert Stifter's 1857 novel of education, *Der Nachsommer* (usually translated as *Indian Summer*), Stifter's protagonist Heinrich Drendorf, having recently turned his attentions from the natural sciences to the study of fine art, suddenly learns the lesson of the aesthetic gaze: "The mountains stood before me now in a charm and a totality [im Reize und im Ganzen] in which I had never before seen them. For my scientific research, they had always been just parts. They were now images where before they had been mere objects [Sie waren jezt Bilder so wie früher blos Gegenstände]."[3] This is a revelation. Although Heinrich had also drawn rocks, plants, landscapes, and man-made objects in his naturalist studies, his sketches had always remained mere reproductions of isolated elements, judged according to their accuracy and instrumentalized for the purposes of scientific knowledge. Now, however, the whole picture begins to come into view; in contrast to the flat data of natural history, "one could immerse oneself [sich versenken] in the pictures, because they had a depth to them; the objects always lay there spread out for contemplation [die Gegenstände lagen stets ausgebreitet zur Betrachtung da]."[4] Aesthetic experience grants a meaning to things that mere information had not been able to provide; "for here, what mattered was to capture a spatial reality [ein Räumliches], not just in its physical dimensions and natural colors, but so to speak as the soul of a larger whole [gleichsam als die Seele eines Ganzen]."[5]

This ideal of artistic wholeness is one that Stifter himself, at least in the eyes of his critics, did not always achieve. In the infamous and oft-discussed pan of *Der Nachsommer* by Stifter's contemporary Friedrich Hebbel, Hebbel exemplarily charges Stifter with the propagation of a "doltish realism [stumpfen Realismus], that takes the wart to be as important as the nose upon which it sits."[6] Aiming for completeness, Stifter proceeds by trivialities; his writing thus "tears itself increasingly away from the all-constraining, but also all-connecting center" (vom alles bedingenden aber auch alles zusammenhaltenden Zentrum), moving, in its pedantic infatuation with detail, from the "breakdown of form" to the "disintegration and crumbling of matter"[7] until it succeeds, finally, in "losing sight of Man entirely."[8]

Stifter was no admirer of Hebbel, whom he appeared to consider a purveyor of cheap sensation.[9] Still, if knew of Hebbel's review, he must have found it vexing. Indeed, Hebbel is merely repeating a point that Stifter had already addressed several years previous in the preface to his 1853 story collection *Bunte Steine* (*Multicolored Stones*), which begins, with uncharacteristic archness, "It was once remarked of me that I only portray small things, and that my characters are always only ordinary people [gewöhnliche Menschen]. If this is true, then today I am in the position of being able to offer my readers something even smaller and more insignificant [ein noch Kleineres und Unbedeutenderes an zu bieten]."[10] For once, Stifter is being ironic: as has frequently been emphasized, for Stifter, it is precisely the small and the insignificant that is the true source of greatness, insofar as the aggregation of small, seemingly insignificant details is what makes up the invisible and overarching order of the world—Stifter's famous "gentle law" (das sanfte Gesez)—itself.[11] Thus Eric Downing summarizes: "As both scientist and realist artist, the investigator sees only discrete, unconnected pieces and fragments,"[12] but an idea of the whole, such as that which Heinrich finds in his paintings, "guarantee[s] that the pieces and fragments function *as* pieces and fragments, as signifiers of a common, but empirically absent, reality."[13] The dissolution and disintegration of which Hebbel accuses Stifter is thus the very thing that Stifter's "overrated talent for the diminutive" (überschätzte Diminutiv-Talent)[14]—his patient and painterly descriptions of the phenomenal world—is originally intended to rectify. Just as nature's design only becomes knowable through the multitude of in themselves trivial manifestations (at the same time as these manifestations are only cognizable as parts of nature's grand design), so too must created works both draw on the profusion of sensory data and organize it into a comprehensive whole, the regulative unity of the all-encompassing, all-representing artwork as such.

In fact, what both Stifter's preface to *Bunte Steine* and *Der Nachsommer*'s aesthetic meditations attempt to address is one of the main challenges facing German-language realist literature of the mid-nineteenth century: how to square the demands of art with new and potentially incompatible developments in the physical and natural sciences. Thus Julian Schmidt compares what he sees as the previous age's false alternative of materialism versus Romanticism to the current comprehensive and holistic worldview, in which "every spot of earth discovers its own physiognomy, and the double infinity that the telescope and the microscope disclose to us is filled with varied, unique, and richly animated life [die doppelte Unendlichkeit, die uns das Fernrohr und das Mikroskop eröffnen, füllt sich mit buntem, eigenthümlichem und reichbewegtem Leben]."[15] Such a "double infinity" of the incomprehensibly great and the imperceptibly small is one for which, according to Schmidt, Stifter bears the standard.[16] For Schmidt, both programmatically and performatively, Stifter evinces a "marvelously clear eye for the minute features in the life of plants, stones, animals."[17] In contrast to earlier writers, who either instrumentalized the material world or cast it in a mystified haze, Stifter succeeds in portraying the world as something empirical *and* universal, physical *and* transcendent, in which everything that is part of the universe is for that reason worthy of the most careful aesthetic attention. "He literally hears," remarks Schmidt with uncharacteristically hyperbolic praise, "the grass growing."[18]

And yet, as in Hebbel's critique, attentiveness to detail alone is not enough. "The true ideal of both life and poetry is not to be found in grass and weeds, not in ruins and quarries, not in fanciful cloud drifts and airy elven figures, but rather in the world of men and the whole seriousness of its moral relations,"[19] outside of which even the patient attentiveness to the natural world falls into eclecticism and "incongruity" (Zweckwidrigkeit).[20] "Stifter forgets," admonishes Schmidt, "that God is not the writer's intended audience."[21] This idea of the alienating quality of pure visual description will be repeated time and again in debates on realism, culminating in Georg Lukács's categorical assertion, in "Narrate or Describe?," that "a 'poetry of things' independent of people and of people's lives does not exist in literature."[22] More recent approaches to Stifter's work, of course, have challenged such convictions. Thus Eva Geulen speaks of Stifter's "verbal-realist law," according to which "the minimalization, or better, eradication of the distance between representation and represented" finally leads to a new form of language in which words "do not signify what happens; they are what happens."[23] Meanwhile, Elisabeth Strowick has argued that Stifter's details are not as static as they have often been made to seem but, rather, effect a "dynamization of description,"[24] concerned less with the objective depiction of the empirical than with the (depersonalized) process of perception itself: in Strowick's Lacanian formulation, "an uncanny, *other scene* [*anderer Schauplatz*]" of reality *effects* for which Stifter is both the most relentless and most foresighted of advocates.[25]

Such analyses have rightly rescued Stifter from his reputation as mere miniaturist and pedant. Yet, as Schmidt's ambivalent praise of *Der Nachsommer* already suggests, Stifter's infamous "antianthropocentrism"[26] is not so much *opposed* to the humanist project as in despair of it. Heinrich's thoughts on the unifying power of artistic representation vis-à-vis scientific study do not just mark an incidental shift in his choice of pastime; they arrive as the epiphanic solution to that which had so troubled him in his earlier explorations: how to reconcile the seeming incoherence and impenetrability of the material world with the ideals of order, form, and meaning that govern—or ought to govern—human civilization? How to understand the multitude of individual objects as more than a chaos of random ephemera? For the natural world does not always reveal "the soul of a larger whole" so easily as in Heinrich's landscape drawings (and even in those, he admits, "the first attempts were a complete failure [mißlangen gänzlich]")[27]—indeed, most of the time it actively repulses the attempt. Thus Heinrich muses at one point in the course of his participation in that most Stifterian of occupations, the scavenging of scrap material for the construction of new furniture:

> When I looked at those pieces of inanimate bodies [unbelebter Körper] that I had gathered for my cabinet, I had to think about how some of these bodies were lying here, others elsewhere, that enormous masses of the selfsame substance [ungeheure Mengen desselben Stoffes] were piled high somewhere in huge mountains, and that again and again small stores of material [Lagerungen] intermittently changed places with one another. Where did they come from, how did they pile up like that? Are they arranged according to a law, and how did this come about? Often there are pieces of a larger body, alone or in a group, in places where the body itself is not to be found, where they are not supposed to be, where they are strangers [Fremdlinge].[28]

Such a gathering up and repurposing of neglected, foreign bodies is what Stifter's writing in general—and *Der Nachsommer* in monumental particular—puts to work. This repurposing however, is not simply the fussy rage for order of the obsessive-compulsive; nor is it merely the melancholic corrective to the ever-present specter of political and social unrest.[29] Rather, it is a strategy by which Stifter attempts to heads off the threat of "mere" materiality that haunts realist literature at its inception. By narrating a series of rituals of restoration at the same time as it performs a form of restoration through that narrative, Stifter's novel establishes a world in which nothing ever actually goes to waste, in which even its "Fremdlinge" may—must—be made to signify. For it is only in the expectation of the world's immanent meaningfulness that one can be anxious about its lack. *Der Nachsommer* represents an attempt to satisfy this expectation at the very beginning of the realist style, in the face of the challenges posed to it by the alien contingencies of the natural world as much as by the limitations of naturalistic representation itself. For Stifter's thoroughly material poetics, nature and art alike must be saved from the ruin that an art of nature seems to entail.

Degenerate Art

Stifter's oft-discussed enthusiasm for collecting and connoisseurship, coming to semiautobiographical fruition in *Der Nachsommer*, has long been seen as the complement to the accretive quality of his poetics, and for good reason: collecting, like describing, comprehends the multifariousness of the physical world and orders it according to meaningful aesthetic and cognitive principles.[30] What is less often remarked upon, however, is the extent to which these objects of collecting and connoisseurship in Stifter are—or rather, *were*—trash.[31] Where this is noted, the first point of reference is usually the early descriptive essay "Der Tandelmarkt" ("The Flea Market") from the 1841–44 collection *Wien und die Wiener* (*Vienna and the Viennese*). In this essay—a droll and, for Stifter, surprisingly conventional portrait of the Vienna junk market—Stifter owns up to a particular affection for old-fashioned and forgotten objects, such as those sold at the various stalls in the titular marketplace. The first reason he gives for this affection is, typically, humanist and narrative: such objects, though fallen into disuse, continue to bear the trace of their past owners' lives; to the half-forgotten histories of our forebears, Stifter writes, they provide the "penetratingly concrete commentary" (sinnlich eindringende Commentar).[32] However, Stifter's affinity for old objects "also extends to completely useless, medieval stuff and all kinds of lost junk whose language we no longer at all understand" (erstreckt sich aber auch auf ganz unnützes, mittelalterliches Zeugs und auf jeden verschollen Trödel, dessen Sprache wir gar nicht mehr verstehen).[33] Though Stifter's language in this passage remains humorous, in keeping with the piece's overall tone of breezy bonhomie, what he expresses here, albeit only in nascent form, is no matter for joking: that even those more recognizable material objects, whose recollective "speech" Stifter still finds so poignant, might one day, in the course of time, *also* fall silent. Old objects are the archives of our lives and desires; but those things whose language "we" are no longer able to interpret are things that have lost their connection to human meaning entirely, indeed, to the point where we can no longer even say what they once had been or were supposed to be at all.

Despite such intimations of ephemerality, in the "Tandelmarkt" essay Stifter still presents his predilection for "leftover junk" (übriggebliebener Plunder)[34] as no more than a harmless eccentricity and charming mild diversion. However, if Stifter's predilection for discarded and superannuated objects begins as a raconteur's curiosity about these objects' former lives,[35] by the time of *Der Nachsommer* this idiosyncrasy will be transformed into an aesthetic program whose consequences could not be more in earnest. "What waste and functionlessness were to [Heinrich's father] the merchant Drendorf," writes Carl E. Schorske (in a reading of *Der Nachsommer* as a precursor to fin de siècle aestheticism), "the abuse of beautiful things and the loss of the treasures of the past were to the new aristocrat Risach. Property and *objets d'art*, both painstakingly acquired, deserved to be protected against the inroads of human carelessness and the erosions of time."[36] And yet the particular care, bordering on fanaticism, with which the objects of *Der Nachsommer* are tended to is more than just a protective measure against potential future loss on the same level as mercantile profit margins. As Tove Holmes has argued, one of Stifter's aims in *Der Nachsommer* is, through the presentation of the training of Heinrich's visual sensibilities, to mimetically offer his readers a literary-pedagogical program by which those readers will likewise learn to see and be at home in their world, working in consort with a nature that gives itself over to be contemplated, collated, and known.[37] Such homely harmony, however, is wrested from the jaws of chaos. If, in the preface to *Bunte Steine,* every phenomenon is meaningful insofar as it forms part of an integrated and rationally ordered universe,[38] in *Der Nachsommer,* the attention shifts to precisely that which has fallen out of or threatens to fall out of this ordering. For, as Heinrich's aforementioned meditations on natural decay already indicate, it is loss alone that cries out for recuperation:

> "Here," said my companion, "things that were produced long before us, indeed, sometimes several centuries before our time, and have fallen into disrepair [in Verfall geraten sind], are restored, at least insofar as time and circumstance ever permit. In old furnishings and objects resides a charm of the bygone and the faded [ein Reiz des Vergangenen und Abgeblühten] almost as much as in old paintings, which a person experiences ever more strongly the older he becomes. Such a person therefore seeks to preserve whatever belongs to the past, just as he himself has a past that no longer quite fits with the fresh present of those growing up all around him. This is why we have founded a workshop for antique objects [eine Anstalt für Geräte des Altertums], which we endeavor to wrest from decay, to put back together, to clean, to polish, and to reintroduce into daily use [die wir dem Untergange entreißen, zusammenstellen, reinigen, glätten und wieder in die Wohnlichkeit einzuführen suchen]."[39]

Of course, it almost goes without saying that restoration can only take place on the condition of prior damage or dispossession. But it is also clear that for Risach it is above all this damage and dispossession itself that gives his conservation efforts purpose and meaning. On both the thematic and the narrative level, Heinrich's tutelage at the home of his mysterious friend dramatizes an ongoing process of reclamation, from the repurposing of discarded scraps of raw material to the setting right of formerly abandoned hopes for domestic bliss. Thus it is not simply the case that Risach is leveraging the traces of an idealized past against a dreamed-of future; nor does he prize tradition for its own sake, or for the sake of its exemplarity and norm-establishing power. While all of these factors may be present in *Der Nachsommer*, the true value of Risach's restored objects is constituted, precisely, by their "charm of the bygone and the faded," that is, by their *having been considered obsolete or worthless*. Restoring damaged artifacts offers Risach the opportunity, not just to create beautiful things, but to rescue them from the material disorder by which they are inherently menaced—and thus also, to add his own value of recognition and redemption onto whatever value they might otherwise possess. The erstwhile abuse and neglect of objects becomes the precondition for their future safekeeping. The Asperhof's cultivated proprietor is not just any collector, but a garbage collector.

Such a thematization of the revaluation of other people's trash, perhaps unmatched in the history of the novel (with the possible but telling exception of Huysmans's *À Rebours*),[40] is also the cornerstone of Stifter's own, new and improved, renewing and improving aesthetics. Sean Ireton has observed that the nature representations in several of Stifter's short stories follow a "tripartite schematic of *order—disruption—reinstated order*," by which natural catastrophe is followed by a denouement of peacefulness and elegiac repair.[41] Such a schematic is not only additionally present in *Der Nachsommer* (albeit in a somewhat more understated fashion than in the short stories), it is also the very process of the life cycle of trash itself. In his groundbreaking study *Rubbish Theory*, the sociologist Michael Thompson explains that commodity objects may be classified according to one of three categories: transient, durable, and the "covert" category of rubbish.[42] As Thompson shows, objects are constantly moving between these categories; however, that movement itself takes place in a highly restricted fashion. While transient objects can easily turn directly into trash (e.g., through disuse or decay), they can never move immediately into the category of the durable. It is only once objects have *passed through a phase* of being trash that they can be reclassified as durable, prized by the antiquarian and the connoisseur for their rarity, esotericism, or nostalgic cachet. While Thompson, for his part, wholly excludes the idea that something once counted as durable could ever reenter the category of trash,[43] his own examples for durability, such as antiques and historically protected buildings, already make clear that durability requires structures of power and consensus that perpetuate the conditions for creating durable value in the first place.[44] Outside of such structures, however, value can falter. Thus Martin and Erika Swales argue that, while Stifter's "litanesque style" may have the effect of "mak[ing] us stay as long as possible with the being of things,"[45] his "poetry of clutter" is also "balanced on a knife edge": "For, without an inherent meaning to them, such objects are a dead and deadening presence. Once our assent to the sacramentalism of things is disturbed, then the clutter threatens to congeal into junk. . . . One man's collection may be another man's rubbish."[46]

It is precisely this "assent to the sacramentalism of things" that *Der Nachsommer* seeks to compel. Granted, the first motive Risach gives for his work is not reparatory, but historicist and archivistic. Musing in strikingly

Hegelian terms on the history of art, Risach laments how much of the cultural heritage "still awaits a future revelation" (harrt noch der zukünftigen Enthüllung),[47] expressing the almost postapocalyptic (or perhaps merely post-Anthropocene) hope that "after the completion of the human [nach Abschluß des Menschlichen], some mind will be able to summarize and survey the entire art of the human race from its origins to its end,"[48] to which Risach's friend Mathilde meaningfully comments, "That would be doing on a large scale what you now do on a small one" (Das wäre ja im Großen, was du jezt im Kleinen thust).[49] But such a love of the forgotten and the antique is not simply the diligence of an amateur historian looking out from the vantage point of the end of art; nor is it merely a reactionary taste for the good old days of quality craftsmanship and a flight from modern life.[50] As Stifter's comments in the "Tandelmarkt" essay already indicate, Risach's restoration efforts are also a way to make sure that these cultural artifacts, saved from oblivion, will never fall silent again, that, even if they themselves go out of style, their presence will forever fit into a history and a larger meaning. And even more, it is a way to answer the question that a scientifically sensitized realist poetics inherently entails: How do nonhuman things acquire (or can be made to acquire) human meaning, when they are nothing but perishable matter? What is the difference between the object's existence and its appearance to the human being? And what is the human being, if it is ultimately made of the same perishable, fleetingly visible stuff as the objective world itself? making restoration finally not simply a means of recuperating lost value, but an aesthetic and indeed an ethical good in and of itself. In *Der Nachsommer*, in other words, there is a direct line between *salvage* and *salvation*.

Such questions about the material perishability of the human being are already vividly posed in another section of *Wien und die Wiener*, the reportage "Ein Gang durch die Katakomben" ("A Tour through the Catacombs"). Just as in the "Tandelmarkt" essay Stifter emphasizes the connection between the market's abandoned objects and these objects' past status as human possessions, in this piece Stifter emphasizes the contrast between the piles of neglected corpses and the souls that had once filled them:

> Out of the gap protruded a welter of coffins, piled up one on top of another fathoms high, jutting out in horrible slivers and splinters from the vault's darkness [mit gräßlichen Trümmern und Splittern herausragend aus der Finsternis des Gewölbes]—time had dislodged some of the boards and joints so that a whole confused heap of them lay on the ground, and above, in the opening they had left, the naked feet and limbs of the dead protruded out into the air, abandoned by the protecting and sheltering wall of their coffins and, like these, destined to slide forwards down the sloping boards and eventually tumble onto the ground below. It was a sight even more harrowing than that in the vault of the mummies, because it opened more

> directly onto the realm of decay and destruction [weil er unmittelbarer das Reich der Verwesung und Zerstörung aufthat], and was nearer to the time when all these bodies still walked and lived.[51]

Stifter's necropolis is the terrible mirror image of the city above it, the reduction of its denizens and all their striving to a heap of broken furniture and desiccated flesh. Indeed, for all Stifter's sentimental meditation in this essay on the "unfathomable life of human beings" (des unbegreiflichen Lebens der Menschen),[52] his description of the catacombs is a shockingly secular memento mori, in which not the biographical content of a lived life, but the "worthless mass" (werthlose Masse) of the body that had once contained it is the final truth of human existence.[53] If, according to Walter Benjamin, the production of the corpse in the German baroque drama is the condition for the body's transfiguration into the sanctification of allegory,[54] Stifter's quizzically profane corpses seem to emblematize nothing but the spectacle of their own physical impermanence, returning, in their obsolescence and deformation, to the muteness of their material presence.[55]

For the intolerable thing is this: just because something cannot be understood does not mean it cannot be seen. At least part of the horror in the passage of the catacombs essay is the way in which the body parts of the corpses poke out of their coffins, disturbing the usual discretion of the tomb and forcing the viewer to acknowledge the implacable inhumanness of their lifeless presence. "It was an inexpressible relief," Stifter writes on coming across a pile of children's caskets, "that none of the tender little limbs could be seen sticking out of the coffins" (daß man von den Särgen keines der zarten Glieder hervorragen sah).[56] The unbearable sight of the bodies in the catacombs is the visual manifestation of the triumph of matter over spirit: a spectacular exhibition of literally soulless bodies as the deformed form of ensouledness itself.[57] But even this exhibition, in the end, is only a synecdoche for the "sheer nakedness" of *all* matter, in which, as Joseph Vogl has put it, "the violence of death . . . scatters the anthropomorphic 'figure' and buries it under the irreversible mutations of its material."[58] Seen in this light, the restoration work that goes on in *Der Nachsommer* is much more than an act of aesthetic nostalgia as a reaction to cultural and political turmoil: it is also a metaphysical intervention against the loss of legibility of the phenomenal world and its ceaseless transformation into decay and desuetude, in the context of a scientistic and—a perhaps surprising but not inaccurate word to describe Stifter's enterprise—journalistic literature dependent on the sensual description of the concrete and the this-worldly.[59] What Catriona MacLeod has called *Der Nachsommer*'s "peculiar combination of quasi-religious aesthetic spectatorship and a voyeurism that borders on obscenity" is thus not only a question of the repressed sexual appeal and/or grotesque florescence of particular objects (for MacLeod specifically: the sculpted female body and the phallic cactus);[60] it is also a question of the potential indecency of all objects whatsoever, in the context of their inevitable reversion to a materiality that no longer has a form by which to evoke even the fetishistic pull of visual desire.[61] If the corporeal yet idealized sculpture is, as MacLeod suggests, Stifter's "antidote to death,"[62] the potential perishability of even such idealized forms—not to mention the perishable human body itself—threatens the viewer with more than just the illicit force of libidinous wanting. Decay crosses over the border that separates fetishized object from senseless sensuous appearance. Before the decomposition of the merely material, the order of realist representation itself breaks down.

Waste Management

The task that Stifter sets himself is thus to reclaim this dispersed and mutated material, to make out of decay and trash itself something of such permanent and unassailable value that the human being can never again fail to recognize itself within it. As the aforementioned criticisms of Stifter's antihumanism already indicate, however, the mode according to which Stifter attempts this reclamation is not yet the social and psychological mode of bourgeois realism, which imbues objects with meaning to the extent that they are used and reflected on by the characters that encounter them. Rather, befitting Stifter's transitional status in the history of German literature,[63] Stifter takes recourse to an at once more scientific and more straightforwardly formalist strategy of artistic mediation, which can be summed up in the curiously both proto-naturalistic and self-consciously constructed mode, proper to the time, of the *picturesque*.

The picturesque is itself a kind of transitional aesthetics, "enjambing," in the words of the art historian Arnold Maillet, the "fundamental rupture between the classicism of the eighteenth century and the modernity of the nineteenth," that is to say, between an aesthetics of neoclassical formalism and an aesthetics of naturalist veracity.[64] William Gilpin, the British priest, artist, and essayist who is commonly credited with introducing the term "picturesque" into aesthetic discourse, defines the mode his 1792 essay *On Picturesque Beauty* primarily through the idea of "roughness" (or sometimes "ruggedness").[65] Classical regularity may be desirable in real life, writes Gilpin, but within the composed stillness of a painting it can appear "insipid."[66] What the spectating eye really wants is not uniformity but contrast, not symmetry but movement, not evenness but texture, not static unities but a dynamic vision "uniting in one whole a variety of parts"[67]—which only a *prior* roughness and unevenness facilitates.

Such an essentially early Romantic, anticlassical mode of art seems at first diametrically opposed to Stifter's Biedermeier sensibilities, which tend to an obsessional, indeed pathological symmetry.[68] Yet not only was Stifter himself well acquainted with the picturesque style, as both his own myriad paintings of craggy rocks and swirling clouds and his professional art criticism attest;[69] the aesthetics of the picturesque also appears in multiple ways within his literary work—not least, in the plot and representational strategies of *Der Nachsommer* itself. It informs the Asperhof residents' predilection for touristic pleasure-hikes in the foothills—whose "rapid variation and yet . . . similarity of terrain" Heinrich first finds boring but eventually learns, with Risach's guidance, to appreciate.[70] And it governs Heinrich's aforementioned decision, midway through the novel, to abandon the technical precision of his earlier drawings for "indefiniteness" (Unbestimmtheit) and a more atmospheric, emotive style.[71]

Above all, however, the picturesque resonates in *Der Nachsommer* in the aforementioned attentiveness the novel pays to that which has fallen into disuse and neglect. Paradoxically enough, for Gilpin and later aficionados of the picturesque, no subject matter leant itself more readily to this modern artistic mode than that of old and dilapidated buildings. ("Is there a greater ornament of landscape," Gilpin asks at one point, "than the ruins of a castle?")[72] This is no less the case for Stifter. Indeed, given the atmosphere of frankly claustrophobic immaculateness that ordinarily reigns in *Der Nachsommer*, in which whole parts of a house are "not actually meant for living in but rather for looking at,"[73] and even the plant life is free from all signs of blight,[74] it is striking to note how frequently and insistently the motif of ruins and of the painting of ruins returns in Stifter's novel. This motif is associated above all with the minor character Roland, an artist and artisan in the Freiherr von Risach's pay and the closest thing *Der Nachsommer* has to a "temperamental artist." (On making his acquaintance, Heinrich describes him as a "very fiery man of strong resolve and intense desires").[75] Roland's very first appearance in the novel, toward the beginning of its second volume, finds him already at work on a particularly telling project:

> Not far from Lauterthal there was namely a lonely farmstead, or actually more of a solid stone castle-like house, which had once belonged to a family that had become wealthy through trade in mountain products and through an increasingly extensive commerce with many parts of the world, and then had become poor again through the degeneration, imprudence, and wastefulness of their descendants [durch Entartung ihrer Nachkommen durch den Leichtsinn derselben und durch Verschwendung]. It was one of the members of this family who had built the great stone house. . . . In the house there were beautiful architectural elements, beautiful stonework, and beautiful woodwork, partly in the ceilings, doors, and floors and partly in the furnishings. Woodworking must once have flourished much more in the mountains than at present. None of these objects were allowed to be removed from the house, and nothing was to be sold. Roland had received permission to draw whatever might seem to him worthy of drawing [zeichnungswürdig].[76]

Stifter's description of the ruined house as potentially "worthy of drawing" effectively translates Gilpin's circular definition of the picturesque as the representation of things that "please the eye from some quality, capable of being illustrated in painting" (as opposed to beautiful things, which merely "please the eye in their natural state").[77] Though the house's furnishings are repeatedly described as "beautiful," the pleasure that the house gives, as in Gilpin, is ultimately not derived merely from its formal attractiveness, nor even from its uniqueness and commodified rarity. To the contrary, Stifter makes clear that it is precisely the semidecay of the house itself and the formerness of its former glory that constitute the larger part of its aesthetic appeal. That is, the obsolescence of the farmstead's objects make them more than just classically beautiful—they are now also visually *interesting*. (Indeed, the picturesque may be the moment when "interestingness" overtakes "beauty" as aesthetic criterion.)[78]

In this sense, the definition of the picturesque as a quality "capable of being illustrated in painting" turns out to be perhaps not so tautological after all: for what the picturesque shows more than anything is the aestheticizing power of the human gaze and its amazing capacity to convert even decay and formlessness—by certain accounts the very opposite of the aesthetic[79]—into a source of pleasure and lively sensual charm. This, in any case, is how Heinrich summarizes his experience a of group trip through the countryside—a veritable textbook illustration of Gilpin's "picturesque travel"—at the end of the ninth chapter:

> Everything on this trip was quite delightful and amiable, . . . each thing, an old church, in which the faithful had once prayed, a crumbling span of wall [Mauertrümmer] on the crest of a mountain where mighty and formidable people had once made their home, a lone tree standing on top of a hill, a little cottage along the path on which the sun was shining, everything took on a peculiar gentle charm and a meaning [alles gewann einen eigenthümlichen sanften Reiz und eine Bedeutung].[80]

This passage—which will return in the novel's final sentence, as Heinrich asserts that "everything, even my scientific efforts, now had simplicity, purchase, and meaning" (jedes selbst das wissenschaftliche Bestreben hat nun Einfachheit Halt und Bedeutung)[81]—epitomizes the picturesque ethos of Stifter's novel. It is hardly incidental that the "gentle charm" (sanften Reiz) attained by the old and half-preserved in the mellow light of touristic contemplation echoes the "gentle law" (sanftes Gesetz) of the preface to *Bunte Steine* (published just four years before *Der Nachsommer*), with which, as noted above, Stifter attempts to counter a *Sturm und Drang*–ish taste for sensation and intensity with the quieter marvels of everyday natural events. Paul Fleming has traced this predilection for the ordinary and the everyday in part to the sociologist Adolphe Quetelet and his pioneering studies of statistical regularity in human behavior, by which "the chaotic manifold phenomena of everyday life" gradually organize themselves into a comprehensive and comprehensible image.[82] One of Quetelet's names for this image—the image of the subsumption of irregular parts within the statistically average whole—is, precisely, "the picturesque." As David Martyn argues in this context, "The picturesque gives us striking and interesting singularities—but singularities which, when combined, obey the law of the statistical mean. The result—in theory—is an art that is true precisely to the extent that it gives us an aesthetically affecting representation of the common."[83]

Such an "aesthetically affecting representation of the common" is also present in Stifter's own descriptions of the picturesque, for example in his review essay "Ausstellung des oberösterreichischen Kunstvereins (1860)" ("Exhibition of the Upper Austrian Artists' Association [1860]"), where he contrasts the tendency toward "monumental subject matter" (gewaltige Stoffe) in newer landscape painting with the subtler motifs of earlier work: "In his ideal compositions Claude [Lorrain] has beautifully combined trees, gossamer expanses, glittering streams, and shimmering air; Ruisdael's more realistic paintings have an austere Nordic tree or forest, a bit of earth from which a little spring flows forth, or often just the simplest forms of grass, the earthen wall of a hut, and air."[84] The commentary Stifter appends to this is much in the vein of his earlier remarks in the preface to *Bunte Steine*: "The great and profound artist can also see in small things the myriad delicate relationships and nuances [die vielen zarten Beziehungen und Abstufungen]; they provide him with his riches, and it is these riches he seeks to convey."[85]

From this art of minor motifs, a "sublimity of regularity"[86] is born. And yet, the equalizing and harmonizing power of statistical averages notwithstanding, it is clear that the picturesque—in practice—is not so much the erasure of irregularity as its paradoxical valorization. Thus, while it is true that Gilpin writes that "the province of the picturesque eye is to *survey nature*; not to *anatomize matter*. . . . It examines parts, but never descends to *particles*,"[87] this commonplace of eighteenth-century aesthetics fails to fully capture what distinguishes the picturesque from its more established art-historical counterparts. For what characterizes the picturesque, in the end, is in fact not an interest in the typical, the reconciled, and the whole, but instead a counterintuitive and almost touching attraction to the atypical, the irreconcilable, and the broken: precisely that which, at least for a classically trained eye, holds no interest, that which—fallen into the dustbin of history or simply into the dustbin—has literally been *over-looked*.[88]

The picturesque therefore does not merely offer a middle ground between the inhuman grandeur of the Burkean sublime and the beguiling calm of the beautiful: it also offers a middle ground between the use value of the past and the musealization of the future: a space, to speak with Thompson, in which the rubbished object turns into treasure qua rubbished object. Heinrich's diverting excursion through the Austrian countryside is also an excursion through time, as he imagines the former perfection of now obsolescing objects while luxuriating in both the recuperative power of new aesthetic constellations and the poignancy of those objects' evanescence. Such a revaluation of the obsolete and the evanescent, moreover, has more than just aesthetic implications. For as Stifter himself was all too aware, the process of falling into the dustbin that enables the picturesque gaze is also no less than the basic process of nature itself. Thus Heinrich wonders: "How did the form of the mountain in general [im Großen] come to be? Is it still there in its original purity, or has it undergone changes, and is it still undergoing changes even today? How did the shape of the earth itself come to be what it is, how did these furrows become etched in its countenance, are its gaps great, are they small?"[89]

It is in light of such meditations that W. G. Sebald has described Stifter's landscapes as "not . . . documents of sentimental nature description, but examples of a diagnostic insight, well ahead of the scientific knowledge of his time, into the entropic tendency of all natural systems."[90] More accurate, however, would be to say that Stifter attempts to sentimentalize entropy *itself* through the "diagnostic insight" of its universality. If decay is the law of nature, then the representation of nature's decay must be an art of the most perfect and consummate lawfulness.[91] Stifter's desire for scientific truth leads him inexorably to the paradoxical principle of an aesthetics of waste, for which his own art and writing must thenceforth be both fulfillment and redemption. In this way, the picturesque emerges as something more than just a minor sublimity or pseudo-pastoral nostalgia: rather, it is at once a precursor to naturalism and a proto-antiaesthetics, a quixotic attempt to reclaim for and within art that which is traditionally the *in*aesthetic per se.[92] In the picturesque—"a form of recycling proper to kitsch"[93]—the debased and disordered matter whose extreme form Stifter encounters in the Viennese catacombs is refashioned, not merely as mood and visual interest, but as the entropic-teleological principle of all existence, the perversely unlawful law of the natural world itself. Beauty and trash come together under the rubric of aesthetic truth. Stifter's picturesque emerges as the uncertain mediation between naturalistic fidelity and neoclassical sublimation, between "purity" and "impurity,"[94] between dead matter and dynamic form. It is an alibi for realism before realism's time.

Frame Story

Nowhere is Stifter's thematization of the picturesque more apparent than in the landscape painting that Roland shows to the Asperhof crowd toward the end of the novel. Heinrich's first impression of the still-unfinished work betrays a kind of nonplussed ambivalence:

> In this desolate space was represented neither mountain nor rivers nor plains nor forests nor a smooth sea with handsome ships, but instead rigid rocks, not standing upright in ordered formations, but rather thrust into the earth as if by accident, so to speak, as strangers [Fremdlinge], like those Norman settlers on the ground of the island that did not belong to them. But the ground was not like the ground of that island, [but instead] jagged and irregular without tree or bush and with parched grass and luminous white crevices in which innumerable slabs of quartz were heaped up, staring, along with the rubble and ruins that were everywhere strewn about, up at the scorching sun.[95]

No object in Stifter conforms more perfectly to Gilpin's "forms / Of tufted woods, and beetling rocks, and tow'rs / Of ruin'd castles," that "from the smooth expanse, / Shade answ'ring shade, inverted meet the eye."[96] But though the finished version of Roland's picture will later be met with (cautious) approval, the ambivalence with which this first version is received also indicates the point at which Stifter's ideas begin to diverge subtly from Gilpin's aesthetic program. As Roland's subsequent explanation of his painting reveals, the doubtful quality of his work is a result of his having committed two major aesthetic sins. First, he has aimed not for artistic insight but for mere sensation and flash; as he himself remarks, "I'd also like to try out oil painting, which has always appealed to me more than my watercolors, and in which it ought to be possible to portray powerful and passionate things [Gewaltiges und Feuriges]."[97] Second, and perhaps even more seriously, he has taken his subject not from nature, but from his own imagination, that is, he has bypassed the gathering and reshaping of already existing ruins to create as it were a fantasy vision of *new* ruins ex nihilo.[98] As Heinrich's jeweler friend (whose own art, significantly, entails showing off the raw material of the earth to its best advantage) comments on Roland's work: "He can become an important artist, or else an unhappy person, that is, if the fire in him, which now flows toward his art, turns away from its object and directs itself toward the young man's inner self."[99] Or, as Risach himself dryly comments on leaving Roland's studio: "He should travel" (Er sollte reisen).[100]

What becomes clear, through Roland's painting, is that the picturesque—*even* in pictures—has its limits. The picturesque may be the aesthetic redemption of decay and devastation, but Roland's valorization of the ruins for their own sake—or, rather, for the strong passions that their irregularity and "roughness" evoke—risks fetishizing decay and devastation as such.[101] In effect, it risks approving of the "degeneration," "imprudence," and "wastefulness" that leads to the production of ruins in the first place. "A piece of Palladian architecture may be elegant in the last degree," writes Gilpin. "But," he continues, "should we wish to give it picturesque beauty, we must use the mallet, instead of the chisel: we must beat down one half of it, deface the other, and throw the mutilated members around in heaps. In short, from a *smooth* building we must turn it into a *rough* ruin."[102] This extraordinary description, verging on the comic, lets slip the fact that the aesthetic reclamation of entropy and waste may forget its own purpose and tip over into a dangerous love of entropy and waste itself, dissipating the ordering gaze of the picturesque within the very excess it was originally designed to contain.[103] Thus Roland himself speaks at one point of a country estate owned by a potential suitor of Heinrich's eventual love interest Natalie, "one of those men," he comments with undisguised contempt, "who always have to be inventing and building things":[104]

> "On the Randek he has a disintegrating castle [ein zerfallendes Schloß]," Roland continued, "in which there are splendid doors that may even date back to the sixteenth century. The steward advised him not to get rid of the doors, and so they've been gradually falling into ruin. They are contained in our drawing-books, and would be a wonderful enhancement to rooms built and furnished in the style of that time. Even if they couldn't serve as doors any more, they could easily be used for tables or other things. I've also sketched some extraordinarily beautiful corbels in the Randek chapel, which is in an extremely dilapidated state."[105]

The picturesque thus emerges in Stifter as a highly paradoxical aesthetic mode, in which an appreciation for the beauty of the outmoded and the pathos of decay is mixed with a schoolmarmish disapprobation of its cause. Roland's attraction to the castle's crumbling structures, on the border between superannuated splendor, antiquarian value, and future disappearance, cannot quite make up for the scandal of their novelty-infatuated owner's neglect. In the context of a "reawakening time"—implicitly, a time not far from that of the novel itself—"that has shaken off its darkness, but hasn't yet broken through to comprehensive action" (die ihre Verdüsterung abgeschüttelt hat, aber zum allseitigen Handeln noch nicht durchgedrungen ist),[106] the neglect of the once beautiful is the impetus for aesthetic attention; but in a future time, a time that *has* broken through to action, such neglect must be foreclosed.

It is against this background of the future of restoration that the picturesque in *Der Nachsommer* makes its claims. Speaking of his successful repair of a Renaissance Madonna and Child that Roland discovers crumpled up on the floor of a neighbor's attic, Risach says, "What inspired us was not merely the feeling of creating something, but rather the far more elevated feeling of bringing something back to life that would have otherwise been lost forever" (so war es nicht blos das Gefühl eines Erschaffens, das uns beseelte, sondern das noch viel höhere eines Wiederbelebens eines Dinges, das sonst verloren gewesen wäre).[107] The rescue of objects from the state of trash provides an even greater pleasure than the creation of beauty alone, combining the perfection of aesthetic beauty with that in which—at least if Kant is to be believed—beauty can have no part: namely, the *practical* perfection that asks of an object "what sort of thing it is supposed to be."[108] For Kant, beauty's freedom from ends means that its only concept is this freedom, in which the teleological or interested question of the "what" becomes counterproductive. With the lost or damaged artwork, however, an entirely different dynamic comes into play. For what the lost or damaged artwork is "supposed to be" is, precisely, a beautiful work of art. Art restoration—and art restoration alone—thus achieves what for Kantian aesthetics is strictly impossible, a "supposedly formal but also objective purposiveness"[109] in which the aesthetic and the teleological, the beautiful and the good, exceptionally, overlap.

Such a pattern of restoration as teleology is also mirrored in the narrative of *Der Nachsommer*: Risach's youthful erotic disappointments with Mathilde, whose story Risach recounts to his protégé toward the end of the novel, not only serve as the literal precondition for Heinrich's eventual union with Mathilde's daughter Natalie, but also thereby transform this union from what would otherwise be an ordinary marriage plot into a well-nigh soteriological redemption. In Heinrich and Natalie's domestic happiness, the metaphorical "trash" of Risach's love life is recovered and turned into something of lasting meaning. Happy endings notwithstanding, however, the primary incentive in the novel for the transformation of yesterday's rubbish into tomorrow's durables remains the fear of the incongruity and inassimilability of matter itself. For if dirt, according to Mary Douglas's influential analysis, is "a residual category, rejected from our normal scheme of classifications,"[110] the first result of this is a rejection of dirt and dirtied things from the category of classifiability as such. Heinrich's retelling of Roland's discovery of the painting of the Madonna and Child, for example, aptly illustrates how trash falls, not just out of monetary and social value, but out of human meaning entirely:

> The painting was unmounted [ohne Blindrahmen], not even rolled up, but rather folded together like a piece of cloth, and lay in the dust. Roland couldn't tell exactly if it was of any value and bought it from the man for a paltry sum. A soldier . . . had used it as a simple bindle cloth and had put in it the dirty linen and old clothes that he brought home to be mended. That was why there were cracks in the painting where the canvas had been folded, in which there was no more paint to be seen, having flaked off from the force of the creasing. . . . Besides those cracks, there were also other places where the paint had rubbed off through the ravages of time [die Mißhandlungen der Zeiten], such that not just the background of the painting, but here and there even the mere naked threads [die lediglichen nackten Fäden] of the old canvas could be seen.[111]

The painting thus comes into Risach's possession as a literal rag among rags, "mutilated" (verstümmelt) and covered in "ineradicable dirt" (unausrottbaren Schmuz).[112] A kind of Turin Shroud in negative, it remains indifferent to both the divine image it bears and the human divinity of its creator. The result of such double indifference is that "Roland couldn't tell exactly if [the painting] was of any value" (Roland konnte nicht genau erkennen, ob es einen Werth habe), which is as much as to say that he cannot make out what the painting is—or, to speak again with Kant, what it "is supposed to be"—at all. As Douglas specifies: "Perceiving is not a matter of passively allowing an organ—say of sight or hearing—to receive a ready-made impression from without. . . . In a chaos of shifting impressions, each of us constructs a stable world in which objects have recognizable shapes, are located in depth, and have permanence."[113] Once outside of this artificially stabilized world, however, things revert to their sheer material presence, the "mere naked threads" of their imageless and idea-less matter.

What Thompson calls the "invisibility"[114] of rubbish is therefore also its un*recognizability*: its failure to be made to fit into the accepted order of things, to be understood *as* something able to be named and represented in the first place.[115] The specific genius of the picturesque, then, is to devise a way to make representable all that which seems most to resist representation: "In short," writes Gilpin, "every form of life, and being may have its use as a picturesque object, till it become too small for attention [i.e., literally imperceptible]."[116] In this way, the picturesque in Stifter is more than just the subsumption of the exception and the irregularity within a reassuring wholeness; it is the attempt to restore visibility to that which has been cast out of the perceptual and historical order, and thus, to restore meaning to that which has been cast out of the economy of human meaning itself. What scarcity and nostalgia are in the realm of commodities, the picturesque is in the realm of the aesthetic: the agent of transformation from trash to durable as a consequence of a recontextualization.

Unlike the assiduous residents of the Asperhof, of course, the picturesque gaze does not seek to literally restore artworks and artifacts, much less, to tidy up natural irregularities. But it does restore artifacts and irregularities in another sense: in framing them and thus making them thinkable again as something visually coherent—in other words, as a *picture*. Thus Arnaud Maillet speaks of the compositional imperative created by the late eighteenth century's "'rediscovery' of nature,"[117] in the context of which was developed what came to be known as the "Claude mirror" or "Claude glass": the handheld, slightly convex black mirror that enabled amateur aesthetes to view nature "picturesquely," for example as in a painting by Claude Lorrain.[118] "As aids in the realization of views and sketches," Maillet writes, optical instruments like the Claude glass "will enable the eye and the hand of the artist and the tourist to become accustomed to the production of landscapes. In fact," Maillet continues, "a reversal occurs: up to then, the landscape engendered the painting; with the fashion of the picturesque . . . the painting comes to condition the landscape."[119] In a stunning inversion of mimetic principles, art is no longer the reproduction of nature, but its condition of visibility; the aesthetic gaze makes the landscape comprehensible *as* something looked at.

Stifter, again, was aware of the latest aesthetic trends, and makes passing reference to Lorrain and other "picturesque" artists in both his art reviews and his literary works. (Lorrain is among those artists listed, for example, in Heinrich's father's art collection.)[120] But the instrument of the Claude glass also makes a literal appearance in one of Stifter's earliest works, the 1840 epistolary novella *Feldblumen* (*Wildflowers*). Specifically, the device of the Claude glass figures prominently in the crucial scene of the novella—which anticipates many of *Der Nachsommer*'s thematic obsessions—in which Stifter's narrator, Albrecht, first catches sight of his future object of desire. As Albrecht writes to his friend and interlocutor, Titus:

> I don't know whether, at the time when we were both in Vienna, a black convex mirror [ein schwarzer erhabner Spiegel] had already been installed on a pedestal in the middle of the Paradiesgarten . . . anyway, now such a mirror is there and a piece of the city—a few green trees, a plot of grass in front of them, and a part of the surrounding suburbs—stands in exquisite smallness [in niedlicher Kleinheit] within its borders, all swimming in a kind of twilit gloom in the mirror's black glass. Before this mirror there stood . . . a woman, whose build, which I could only see from behind, promised great beauty, and was gazing into it. . . .
>
> As she kept standing there, I pictured to myself the ridiculous group we formed, and this gave me the courage to force her to turn to face me, so I suddenly said, "A truly underworldly light hovers over this little image." She turned around—and I nearly fell backwards.[121]

Never again will Stifter be so frank. The appearance of the beautiful woman effects a "tear" (Riß) in the "circle of my mental images" (Kreis meiner Vorstellungen): a break in the otherwise all-encompassing symbolic order that is all but literalized in the domed surface of the mirror itself.[122] As Albrecht goes on to state, his coup de foudre is emphatically *not* the Claude glass's comforting pleasure of the aesthetic, but something much more dangerous and uncanny: "Is it an impression of beauty [Schönheitseindruck] that I am merely failing to recognize? . . . But I've seen Raphaels, Guidos, Corregios—they were all wonderfully beautiful, but different. . . . It was not beauty that was operating here; . . . the entire image lies on them [the nerves of my brain] as if burned into the mirror of my eyes [das ganze Bild liegt auf ihnen, wie eingebrannt dem Spiegel meiner Augen]."[123] It is only when the woman has been introduced as a friend of some of Albrecht's friends and has given evidence of both her intellect and her purity that Albrecht's shock can be neutralized and the woman's image reinscribed—not least, as potential wife and mother—within the "erhaben" but also "niedlich" framing that the black mirror represents. As Albrecht writes, in a philosophical digression in the chapter directly preceding his scene of encounter: "Before the curved mirror of our senses hangs but the phantasm of a world; the true image is possessed by God alone" (Vor dem Hohlspiegel unsrer Sinne hängt nur das Luftbild einer Welt, die wahre hat Gott allein).[124] The suddenly unmediated appearance of the woman's face, however, is neither divine true image nor even the darkened reflection thereof, but an object of sheer sensual fascination *without* pattern, purpose, or meaning, a beauty, in the words of Peter Fenves, no longer underwritten by a transcendent order and thus a presence "helplessly exposed to shame."[125]

This thematization of the framing device of the Claude glass in *Feldblumen* has its analogue in *Der Nachsommer* in the motif of the (literal) frame. While the frame is in some ways more restricted than the Claude glass, since it does not directly affect the image itself, what it shares with it is the power to delimit and compose the prodigious wilderness of the world for tranquil aesthetic consumption.[126] The mirror in *Feldblumen* not only allows Albrecht to safely focus on the image of the beautiful woman's back, but also enables him and any other passersby to comprehend a whole swath of Vienna and its suburbs "in exquisite smallness" within the mirror's circumference. It is no coincidence, then, that talk of frames and framing recurs in *Der Nachsommer* with almost the same insistence as the theme of ruins that might well be considered its pendant.[127] Only once Roland's finished picture is framed and exhibited properly (in an event given disproportionately prominent placement in the fifth to last paragraph of the novel) does its threateningly anarchic aspect begin to diminish, and the picture itself becomes, if not quite yet a completely successful work of art, at least a harbinger of future artistic achievement.[128] Similarly, in the narrative of the found Madonna and Child, it is the painting's lack of a frame that, more than anything else, signals its abject status, such that it is the eventual framing of the picture—and indeed *not* the restored image of the picture itself—that constitutes the crowning glory of Risach's restoration:

> When after a long time, after much trouble and several interruptions, the painting finally stood before us in a handsome gold frame in the antique style, it was a kind of celebration for us. . . . It is not true, as it is often said, that a beautiful woman is more beautiful without jewels than with them: and in the same way it is not true that a painting has no need of a frame to be shown to its best advantage. For our Madonna, I had ordered a frame to be made according to drawings of medieval models, and supervised its construction when my business dealings or my inclination brought me to the city. The frame arrived at the Asperhof long before the picture itself was finished,

> and thus had to wait in the meantime packed inside its box. Indeed, we didn't even attempt to fit the picture in the frame before it was finished, so as not to weaken the final impression. In the case of new pictures, of course, placing them in a frame can reveal that there are still things to add and change, and many things can be fixed in such paintings only once one has seen them framed. In the case of old, restored paintings, however, things are different, particularly if they are restored using our methods. According to these, it is what already exists that guides the restoration process: one cannot paint any differently than one paints, and the depth of passion and the brilliance of the colors is determined by that which is already to be found on the canvas. What the picture will look like in its frame then no longer depends on the restorer, and whether it looks more or less splendid in its new frame is to the credit or blame of the original master, whose work must not be altered. When our Madonna, which had not yet even been given a coat of varnish, finally looked out from the frame's antique form, which fit the canvas perfectly, it was a marvelous sight, and only now did we see how much tenderness and force the old master had displayed in his painting.[129]

Though Stifter is not exactly known for his descriptive restraint, the repetitive emphasis on the frame in this passage is extreme even for him. Indeed, by the end of Risach's account, the image of the Madonna and Child, ostensibly the whole point of the anecdote, has all but disappeared, effectively effaced, despite Risach's own claims, by the very furniture chosen to enclose it:

> Although the frame contained raised carvings of flowers, ornamental shapes, and even aspects of the human form, all emphasized to the same powerful effect, the picture itself did not appear busy, indeed it dominated the frame, and transformed the frame's opulence into a graceful multifariousness, at the same time as it asserted itself through its own power, its brilliant colors enthroned in dignified adornment [in den erhebenden Farben von würdigem Schmucke umgeben thronte]. A faint cry escaped the lips of all those present, and I was glad that I had not been mistaken when I, counting on the picture's power, ordered such an opulent frame for it.[130]

It is as if, in all these narratives of framing, Stifter were reenacting the trauma of his tour through the catacombs, placing the threateningly perishable human figure, sprung from its casing, safely back inside its wooden box. Indeed, it would not be too much to read the entirety of *Der Nachsommer* as Stifter's attempt to work through his encounter with the necropolis in *Wien und die Wiener*, mediated by the mirrored image of the beautiful woman in *Feldblumen*. Another passage in *Der Nachsommer*, a description of a landscape

Heinrich comes across during one of his excursions, demonstrates almost all too well Stifter's compulsion to revisit this primal scene of his aesthetic education: "I found dead forests, as it were charnel houses of forests [todte Wälder, gleichsam Gebeinhäuser von Wäldern], only that here the dead limbs were not amassed in some hall, but still stood upright in the ground. White peeled clean dead trees in great numbers, so that one could only presume that in this place a forest had once stood."[131] As in the catacombs essay, such a vision also gives rise to thoughts on mortality and transience in general: "Will many things, will everything change completely all over again? At what rate will this happen? If the mountains are steadily eroded by the weather and their own streams, if the debris [Trümmer] falls down into the valley, if it is broken down into even smaller pieces and finally washed out by the current into the lowlands as sand and rubble [Geschiebe], how far will this go?"[132]

In other words, the lesson that Stifter receives in the catacombs is the double one of *the corruptibility of form* together with *the permanence of matter*. That all is vanity is a familiar, even a comforting idea: what is unbearable, however, is that there would be something that remains *after* everything disintegrates, a mere substance that falls apart into an ever more amorphous, ever more unrepresentable yet still present facticity. In this context, the disappearance of the center in favor of the frame in *Der Nachsommer* is not merely an incidental stylistic weakness on Stifter's part, but the neuralgic point of his whole literary project. Just as the picturesque's all-encompassing and yet circumscribing gaze transforms the mass of brushy landscape and artifactual detritus into an aesthetically valid image, the presence of a frame (even if only an implicit or imaginary one) allows one to distinguish the orderly landscape from the field of rubble, the valuable antique from the canvas rag, the divinely ordained givenness of the world from its alien, anarchic presence. In short, the frame (including the framing gaze of the picturesque) is both an allegory for and a defense against what Hal Foster, drawing on Lacan, has called the aesthetics of "the obscene": an excessive form of realism in which "the object-gaze is presented as if there were no scene to stage it, no frame of representation to contain it, no screen."[133] In this new twist on the spurious etymology of the "ob-scene"—no longer either off- or of the stage, but *without staging*—things appear, or rather are imagined to appear, as pure presence, a subject- and object-annihilating "pulsatile gaze" of the visible beyond or beneath the ordering realm of the symbolic.[134] Foster describes this aesthetic as a development particular to European and American late twentieth-century art. However, the consideration of Stifter's waste management strategies in *Der Nachsommer* makes it clear that what Foster calls "the real as a thing of trauma" (as opposed to the classically mimetic "reality as an effect of representation")[135] begins far earlier than Foster's own points of reference would indicate. For what one sees in *Der Nachsommer*, as well as in many of Stifter's other works, is less a "realist" aesthetics of symbolic verisimilitude than an attempt to ward off a traumatic real through symbolic verisimilitude itself, to frame and shape that which is represented as a way to bind the "obscenity" that perpetually threatens to break through it.

Such a dynamic, moreover, is not just the result of Stifter's historical circumstances, private quirks, or even proto-postmodern prescience.[136] Rather, the impulse to bind the traumatically real through realist framing is a direct function of realism's own humanizing impulses: for as soon as literature gives itself the task of representing the world through human eyes, any aspect of the world that does *not* give evidence of human relationality or activity begins to become a problem. Thus Heinrich (in an uncanny anticipation of contemporary theories of prehuman ontology and deep time)[137] ruminates on the history of the natural world as

> a history in which Man is but an afterthought [Einschiebsel], and who knows what a trivial one, since even this history might be dissolved by the histories of still greater beings. . . . Who will be able to finally see this history with clear eyes? Will such a time ever come, or will it only ever be known by the one who has already known it from all eternity?[138]

"From such questions," Heinrich continues, "I fled to the poets."[139] In the absence of the capacity to view the natural world from the standpoint of eternity, literature provides Heinrich with an anthropocentrically circumscribed lens through which to focus the terrible immensity of the world around him. Tellingly, Heinrich favors those authors who, in contrast to what he calls the "poets of bombast [Schwulstes]," present "things and events . . . securely within the framework of their own inner greatness (in einem sicheren Maße in dem Rahmen ihrer eigenen inneren Größe), or, alternately, those who "offered emotions with a beautiful moral force, that made a deep impression on me."[140] In Heinrich's judgment (which does not differ greatly from Stifter's own), literature serves one of two exemplary functions: to trim the phenomenal world to human cognition, or to subordinate the phenomenal world to human feeling. For these services, concludes Heinrich, "I loved the words [I read], and I loved the men [who wrote them]."[141]

Every work of art, of course, and indeed every act of perception, necessitates a process of ordering, framing, and self-limitation.[142] What sets Stifter's work apart, however, is how conscious he is about this process, how unremittingly he puts it to work, and how clear-eyed he is about the nature of the process itself:

> "A jewel in its case," said a voice, "is like a picture without a frame, or rather, like a frame without a picture."
>
> "So it is," replied Risach, "one can only judge each thing in its proper setting [man kann jedes Ding nur an seinem Plaze beurtheilen]."[143]

The unnamed voice's aphoristic comment in this passage is perhaps less strange than it initially seems: the "picture" that the piece of jewelry is to "frame" in this instance is the woman, whose beauty is then set off by her accessories in the same way that the picture is set off by its encasement.[144] But not only does the aphorism thereby imply, in a way entirely consonant with the novel's poetics, that without its frame the image is effectively invisible; it also contains the whispered suggestion that image and frame might, in the final count, be wholly interchangeable, or even that the frame might turn out to be more valuable than that which it is intended to enclose. What Jacques Derrida has called "the deterioration of the *parergon*, the perversion, the adornment" appears in Stifter's picturesquely ruined landscapes and elaborate picture frames all too clearly as "the attraction of sensory matter": the waste products of phenomenal existence that the sublimating protocols of classical-idealist and Romantic-picturesque aesthetics are both, in their different ways, designed to overcome.[145] If art transforms the material chaos of nature by virtue of its framing activities, when the frame becomes the whole of the image, the borders drop away again; the frame itself becomes a form of perverse presence, a surface every bit as unfathomable as that which it was supposed to have contained.

What all of this this suggests is that the shift between "reality as an effect of representation" and "the real as a thing of trauma"[146] is in fact no shift at all, but instead coterminous within the development of realism itself. Stifter writes his novel as a Claude glass made of words, a verbal analog of the picturesque gaze in the deliberate effort to make out of the limitless "Fremdlinge" of the natural world a durable and graspable whole. If this effort ultimately ends up seeming almost as limitless as that world itself, it is then only a logical conclusion.[147] Long before naturalism's pseudoscientific ambitions elevate epistemological exactitude into an aesthetic principle, *Der Nachsommer*'s restoration efforts raise the specter of the world's essential unknowability: not only in terms of its empirical magnitude and temporal continuity, but also in the sense of its tendency to fall away from human understanding and usability, or, in another register, to possess a plumbable depth and deeper meaning below the brazen display of its material surface.[148] For the *world* picture, we will never be able to "tell exactly if it [is] of any value." As the indignation his work has evoked since its publication attests, Stifter is no anomaly, but the bad conscience of realism, who writes the allegory of obscenity in the attempt at its purification.

Chapter 2

Base Matter

Gustav Freytag

But for adults only
there's something special to see, how money multiplies,
anatomical,
not just for entertainment: money's genitals,
all of it, right there, the whole process—, educational,
and guaranteed to increase
your potency . . . .

—Rainer Maria Rilke, *Tenth Duino Elegy*[1]

In his 1835 philosophical novella *Wally, die Zweiflerin* (*Wally, the Skeptic*), the *Junges Deutschland* author Karl Gutzkow has his eponymous heroine put the dilemma of realist epistemology succinctly: "Rationalism held to the impossibility of recognizing the thing in itself; supernaturalism to the possibilities that might lie behind it. The thing in itself was as negative as it was mystically positive: within it lay the vast chaos of doubt every bit as much as the chaos of emotions. . . . It was an argument about the start of a circle."[2] As Gutzkow's words bear witness, in the aftermath of the Kantian critique, the question of how to think a material world whose essence has been deemed inaccessible to human knowledge reopens the conflict between subject and object that the Copernican turn had originally been intended to bypass, calling forth diametrically opposed solutions that, in their different ways, bespeak the pain of being repulsed by what one had previously thought to be able to understand. "The Kantian philosophy . . . seemed to possess the key to every secret . . . but the consequences . . . were of the opposite kind."[3] Humanity may well have achieved well-nigh godlike heights in science and art, "but the Godhead still sits behind a curtain and hides its brittle face [ihr sprödes Antlitz] and refuses to come and unveil itself. What have we done to it? [Was haben wir ihr getan?]"[4]

Gutzkow's heroine resolves her difficulty through the expedient method of a dagger in the breast. For the more pragmatic advocates of programmatic realism, however, the better solution was to decide that the question itself was badly posed. Thus, instead of the increasingly unsustainable extremes of subjectivism and objectivism—in which, in Gutzkow's words, people "waltzed their debates around and exhausted themselves in practical and theoretical concessions"[5]—programmatic realism propagates what the early realist novelist Otto Ludwig calls "a world positioned between the objective truth of things and the law that our mind is called on to bring to it."[6] "Our poetic goal," Ludwig writes, is "no longer to preach about and reflect on our ideals, but rather to embed those ideals within active life, give them concrete representation" (nicht mehr Predigen von unseren Idealen, Reflexionen darüber, sondern Vertiefung derselben in das handelnde Leben, concrete Darstellung derselben).[7] Epistemology takes a backseat to psychology and sociology; Gutzkow's crisis of objective knowledge is exchanged for a practical *dialectic* of things and persons, a world that is filled with meaning as a consequence of the human relation to it.

Ludwig's description of a literature of "active life" (das handelnde Leben) is not only an apt motto for, but also likely as not at least partly in mind of Gustav Freytag's bestselling 1855 novel *Soll und Haben* (*Debit and Credit*).[8] Appearing twenty years after Gutzkow's metaphysical romance (which was incidentally banned throughout the German states), Freytag's tale of the young Anton Wohlfahrt's danger-fraught rise from son of the petite bourgeoisie to head of an established trading house appears to keep programmatic realism's dual promise in exemplary fashion: first, to seek out fit subjects for literature in the actual and the everyday, and second, to present these subjects as significant in themselves, rather than as allegorical sounding boards or backdrops for philosophical musing. In both the financial and the poetical sense, the novel rejects speculation in favor of what Russell Berman has called "the commodified currency of the literary economy":[9] a controlled exchange of things and meaning that "aims at material objects, but . . . never fully identifies reality with them."[10]

Among the several things such a literary economy entails, one is a change in the relation to the phenomenal world as such. As we have already seen, for early programmatic realists such as Freytag and his friend and collaborator Julian Schmidt, realism's attention to the things of the world must not involve a concern with material things for their own sake, but should always subordinate these things to their meaning for the human beings who encounter them. An attention to things per se—or worse, an idea of things' independent inner life—is no more than a belated animism, a revival of primitive nature religion under the strain of its obsolescence. Nowadays, Schmidt chides, such representations are the stuff of children's stories, or at best a device for comedy.[11] But they can have no place in a modern, serious, grown-up literature, for which the "dissemination and consolidation of ethical ideas in the detail of real life" (diese Ausbreitung und Vertiefung der sittlichen Ideen in das Detail des wirklichen Lebens) is "the necessary, the only basis of a true poetry."[12]

Thus realism radicalizes the Copernican turn—by taking it for granted. (As an unsigned 1849 review of new literature in Schmidt and Freytag's journal *Die Grenzboten* [*The Border Heralds*], probably by Schmidt himself, declares: "We overcome the opposition [between ideal and real] by dismantling it" [Wir überwinden den Gegensatz, indem wir ihn zerlegen].)[13] And yet the problem still remains of how to connect material objects to reality, if "reality" is not to be identified with material objects as such. In other words, what Berman observes as programmatic realism's "[restructuring of] the physical environment . . . according to a bourgeois logic [of] particular appearance as the expression of the general essence"[14] also raises the question of how essence comes to be attributed to appearance in the first place, without reducing reality to an outgrowth of consciousness or attributing consciousness to physical reality.

Again, at the time of its publication, *Soll und Haben* could be considered the preeminent expression of such views, marrying a largely dialogical, scenic narrative to a story whose moral lies in the proper management of goods and assets and the virtues of a stable German middle class in a politically and economically expanding German state. However, Freytag's novel also remains haunted by the very ontology that both it and programmatic realism disavow. For while works of realist literature, as Eric Downing has argued, "teach us to look for meaning in the signs of resemblance and sympathy between the human and the nonhuman world,"[15] such resemblance is nevertheless conditioned by a hierarchy that places the human world solidly at its apex. Therefore, if the first threat to literary realism is objects' slide into a mute chaos of undifferentiated matter, the second is their acquisition of a liveliness or agency beyond anthropocentric subordination. What Jane Bennett has called "the narcissism of humans in charge of the world"[16]—the primary narcissism of the nineteenth-century novel—has its flip side in the thought of a secret life of things, a lurid world in which objects possess agency independent of human understanding or control. However, as Freytag's novel also shows, far more effective than the mere avoidance of this world—which, like all repressed things, always risks a return in force—is the attaching of it to particular characters and situations, coding them with specific affects at the same time as this coding is made to reflect back on those characters and situations themselves.[17] The material thing (with or without the "in itself") thus reemerges in *Soll und Haben*, not in the form of its inaccessible or perishable presence, but in the idea of its uncannily independent existence, of a form of life that defies the priority of human experience to the point of supplanting the human (or what gets to count as "the human") entirely. Just as in *Der Nachsommer* Stifter narrates the aesthetic restoration of discarded objects, in *Soll und Haben*, Freytag tells a story of the victory of practical anthropocentrism over empathic noumenalism, poetically reestablishing the order of human and nonhuman worlds on which realism implicitly depends, and in the perversion of which both alike forfeit their rights to sympathy.

Persons and Things

In their cowritten statement of intent upon taking over the editorship of *Die Grenzboten*, Schmidt and Freytag waste no time in announcing the new era:

> The old *Grenzboten* belonged to the period of restoration, a period in which public life was in such a sorry state that speculative literature [die abstracte Literatur] predominated, that the questions of the day were more often than not treated as a mere pretext for pretty representations, that politics was only to be seen in belletristic garb.
>
> That era is over. Literature is justified only to the extent that it immerses itself in life, that it devotes itself to it warmly and unreservedly [als sie sich in das Leben versenkt, sich warm und ohne Vorbehalt ihm hingibt]. . . . The new age has cast off all dainty forms, all concern for graceful exteriors, and we, her sons, do not want to dishonor the robust nature of our mother [wollen der robusten Natur unserer Mutter keine Schande machen].[18]

Freytag and Schmidt's demand is, in part, a political one: in the wake of the social instability and revolutionary enthusiams of the *Vormärz*, the task is now the (implicitly right-Hegelian) "reconciliation of the contradictions within Germany" and the "brotherhood of all the German tribes" (Verbrüderung aller deutschen Stämme) under the collective aegis of the new bourgeois-conservative regimes.[19] But the demand is also an aesthetic and epistemological one: the literature that expresses such reconciliation should no longer take flight in speculation and fairy tale (including and perhaps especially the fairy tale of radical political transformation). Rather, it must turn its attention to the existing conditions of the real world, cut to man's measure on the evidence of the senses and the ideological consensus of the age. Writers have always described the world in various ways—the point, now, is *not* to change it.[20]

One of the things that should not be changed, for Schmidt and Freytag, is the idea of that "life" itself in which literature should be immersed. Thus the British art critic John Ruskin—writing from a different vantage point than Schmidt and Freytag but in much the same spirit—begins his essay "Of the Pathetic Fallacy" (from his critical opus *Modern Painters*) with an attack on the Romantic tendency, announced in the title, to project internal perceptions onto external objects. "German dullness," Ruskin complains, "and English affectation, have of late much multiplied among us the use of two of the most objectionable words that were ever coined by the troublesomeness of metaphysicians—namely, 'Objective' and 'Subjective.' "[21] What follows from this opening is a somewhat tongue-in-cheek attack on Kantian epistemology: Ruskin mocks the notion, supposedly propagated by German philosophers of the day, that positive claims about the world are now passé, that from now on one is permitted to make claims about things only insofar as they appear to one's individual awareness. However, this humorous critique of Kantian epistemology (or rather, its Schopenhauerian elaboration) is only a prelude to Ruskin's true concern: namely, the overuse of anthropomorphic description in eighteenth- and nineteenth-century literature, to which Ruskin gives the name, now long since entered into common usage, of "pathetic fallacy." For Ruskin, writing just one year after the publication of Freytag's novel, pathetic fallacy is a kind of debased by-product of the critical method: the Kantian tenet that we can only know that which we perceive ends up misrepresented as the idea that the empirical world is identical to our perceptions thereof. Pathetic fallacy is the bastard child of Enlightenment epistemology and premodern animism, a failure of imagination and a sentimental recourse to half-believed fantasies whose use is but the resort of certain "morbid and inaccurate" poets "too weak to deal fully with what is before them or upon them."[22]

Given this state of affairs, realist literature would seem to preclude anthropomorphism from the outset. Yet surprisingly, works of nineteenth-century realism do not renounce anthropomorphic tropes, but, to the contrary, make use of them with some regularity. As the writer and critic F. C. Delius, for one, has shown (in an overlooked monograph on realist weather-personification), realist literature especially employs anthropomorphism to establish a "reciprocal determination" between the hero of the novel and his environment, confirming the moral rectitude of the one through its reflection in the other.[23] Such a "reciprocal determination" is already on display, however ironically, in Freytag and Schmidt's editorial statement: its ostensibly no-nonsense message of realist objectivity is pitched on the covert anthropomorphism of a literature giving itself over to life "warmly and unreservedly," and the age as a formidable matriarch for whose "robust nature" her doughty sons should be no cause for shame. Yet there remains a crucial difference between the realist use of anthropomorphism and its Romantic counterpart. In his reading of Baudelaire's late Romantic sonnet "Correspondances," Paul de Man notes the paradox that "anthropomorphism seems to be the illusionary resuscitation of the natural breath of language, frozen into stone by the semantic power of the trope. It is a figural affirmation that claims to overcome the deadly negative power invested in the figure."[24] Anthropomorphism, for de Man, breathes life back into the killing metaphor, which turns world into mere language—but anthropomorphism is also the metaphor *of* this breathing back of life, taking away as it were with one hand what it has given with the other. The liveliness of the world turns out to be just another ruse of language, for whose overcoming that liveliness had first been invoked. With the transition to realism, however, a different dynamic comes into play. For if anthropomorphism is always doomed to disappoint insofar as it figures the natural world's ensoulment only *as* figure,[25] for the explicitly anthropocentric poetics of realism, such disappointment is not to be lamented, but *desired*.

Hence what is at stake in the realist novel is not even the success or (for de Man, inevitable) failure of the anthropomorphic trope, but rather the degree of conspicuousness in its deployment: the anthropomorphization that does *not* call attention to itself, that appears as if it were natural, is the return of the Romantic repressed in its most mystified version and thus a threat to the system of relations between human and world on which bourgeois realism depends.[26]

In this way, however, realism's application of the pathetic fallacy also represents a change, not just in the nature of its use, but in the very meaning of the trope itself. No longer is the objective world imagined as a source of vitality and an agent in its own right (be it only as a form of nostalgic reenchantment); rather, things are brought forth as the mirror of human actions, a projection screen for characters' dispositions, fortunes, and emotional states. As Georg Lukács insists: "Objects come to life poetically only to the extent they are related to men's life, that is why the real epic poet does not describe objects but exposes their function in the mesh of human destinies, introducing things only as they play a part in the destinies, actions and passions of men."[27] Though probably not quite what Lukács intends, anthropomorphism is one way to effect such relatedness, allowing inanimate objects to "come to life" indeed as the lightly ironic externalization of those "human destinies" themselves. Realist anthropomorphism is thus also a form—albeit an equivocal one—of that "humor" that, in the words of Wolfgang Preisendanz, "saves narrative literature from prostituting itself as a mere inventory or representation of existing prosaic reality."[28] By always presenting the external world as it is *filtered through* a particular standpoint, humor keeps the focus on the human subject even in the midst of factical abundance. Henceforth, the novel's claim to reality is guaranteed by the modesty of its scope: meaning is no longer looked for *in* the world, but in what human beings make *of* that world and the ways in which they represent it. Accordingly, whereas Romanticism deploys anthropomorphism as an inherent feature of poetic language itself (all the way to the radical anthropomorphism of the lyric I),[29] realism *saves* the trope for particular moments of lyrical introspection or heightened dramatic intensity. When realism wants to advertise its realness, the language is expository and clinical. When a "Romantic" intensity of feeling is demanded, realism reaches for the language of Romanticism. In other words, realism makes use of anthropomorphism not performatively but mimetically: no longer to conjure a real homology of subject and world, but to represent a particular character's thoughts under the sway of an idea of this homology.[30] Rather than seeking to bridge the gap between the subject and reality, realism's "humor" thematizes that gap and reinstates it as *style*.

For this reason, however, realism demands a degree of control in its use of figurative language that exceeds even the lyric poetry for which such language is supposedly constitutive.[31] Freytag, therefore, takes no chances. Many readers of *Soll und Haben* have pointed out how the novel mobilizes a new aesthetics of the material, an aesthetics in which things are not merely described as part of a milieu-establishing detail realism, but attended to precisely to the extent that they embody human values and practices: Lukács's "destinies, actions and passions of men"[32] embedded directly in the articles of their use.[33] As in most realist works, this endowing of objects with human significance in *Soll und Haben* is accomplished above all through the novel's plot and the myriad opportunities it provides for its characters to interact with their environment. What is perhaps unique to *Soll und Haben*, however, is that the endowing of objects with human significance is also realized within the novel's subject matter itself. Julian Schmidt's proclamation that "the novel must seek the German people where they are at their best, namely, at work" (Der Roman soll das deutsche Volk da suchen, wo es in seiner Tüchtigkeit zu finden ist, nämlich bei seiner Arbeit)[34] is one that Freytag takes not just as epigraph, but as directive: the world of *Soll und Haben* is the world of work, business, and trade, an unending nexus of international exchange that charges objects—in a way not dissimilar to the Marxian commodity fetish[35]—with the entirety of their history from origin to consumption. More effectively than Stifter's recuperative antiquarianism, the demonstration of how commodities literally accrue value on the open market elevates the multitude of objects to a greater, transcendental whole, tying them to an expanding network of domestic and international trade in which, moreover, as Kristin Kopp has observed, Germany itself (together with the virtuous Germans of Freytag's novel), emerges as the local "nerve center" of the new global imperial economy and the fulcrum of the political and historical world at large.[36]

Indeed, if at first it is the romance of exotic goods—"palm oil from the eastern coast of Africa," "tallow from Poland"[37]—that appears to the young Anton, in Freytag's formulation, as "the source of a peculiar poetry, one at least as worthy as those poetic sensations deriving from that fairytale allure which the strange and the foreign call forth in the soul of Man,"[38] such objects will eventually cede their place to a more down-to-earth—so to speak, realist—kind of lyricism, as Anton progresses from a fascination with these goods' qualities to a desire "to achieve through study a clearer picture of the land from which they came and of the people who had gathered them."[39] Objects are anthropology: from the borderline mystifications of the commodity fetish we move to a representation of "the great relationships of work," to quote from Schmidt's summary, which combines the "historical seriousness" of the business world "with a humorous delight, in which a warm German nature can be glimpsed" (mit einem humoristischen Behagen, durch welches ein warmes deutsches Gemüth blickt).[40]

But Freytag does more than merely narrate the interaction between humans and their world; he also makes it integral to his poetics. There is little ekphrasis or description for description's sake in *Soll und Haben*, still less that kind of unmotivated detail that constitutes the proverbial "reality effect" of nineteenth-century literature.[41] Rather, more often than not, the thingly details of *Soll und Haben* possess a subtle but intrinsic allegorical value, in which the specific objects, however unspectacular in themselves, consistently bear a larger, symbolic significance.[42] Such moderate allegory, to coin a term, is established right from the novel's first sentence: "Ostrau is a small provincial capital not far from the Oder, famed all the way to Poland for its school and its sweet gingerbread cakes, which are still baked there with an abundance of real honey" (Ostrau ist eine kleine Kreisstadt unweit der Oder, bis nach Polen hinein berühmt durch ihr Gymnasium und süße Pfefferkuchen, welche dort noch mit einer Fülle von unverfälschtem Honig gebacken werden).[43] What here first appears to be a straightforward presentation of local color is, on closer inspection, nothing of the sort. Indeed, this seemingly innocuous opening is no less than a preview in miniature of the novel's central themes. Tradition, *Bildung*, bourgeois comfort, uprightness—the contrast between the Ostrauer bakers' "unverfälschtem Honig" and the future counterfeiting skills of the novel's Jewish villain Veitel Itzig is crying—material prosperity, local pride, eastward expansion, not to forget good old-fashioned German home cooking: Freytag's opening sentence contains it all.

This moderate allegory, and the use of lyrical language in general, occurs most often at the beginning or end of a chapter, where Freytag steps out in full raconteur mode and allows himself a rare moment of magniloquence as a way of setting the scene. "Never had the flowers bloomed so luxuriously and the birds sung so cheerfully as during that summer on the Baron's estate,"[44] begins one chapter; "Happy the foot, that strides over the broad expanses of his own land," another.[45] That both of these poetic flights occur in the context of descriptions of the novel's aristocratic milieus is no accident; as several critics have pointed out, Freytag's depictions of the landed gentry are tinged with imagery and language borrowed from Romanticism and its sometime models, the fairy tale and the medieval romance.[46] Such lyrical holdovers are precisely the mannerisms that Ruskin excoriates as the sign of those poets who "feel strongly, think weakly, and see untruly,"[47] though it would perhaps be more accurate to describe them as those who feel and think according to conventionalized affects, as the contrast between Ruskin's criticism of Pope's translation of the *Odyssey* and his qualified praise of Coleridge's *Christabel* makes clear. Pope's flowery metaphors, when spoken by the practical-minded Ulysses, are in fact "not a *pathetic* fallacy at all, for they are put into the mouth of the wrong passion. . . . Therefore, we see that the spirit of truth must guide us in some sort, even in our enjoyment of fallacy. Coleridge's fallacy has no discord in it, but Pope's has set our teeth on edge."[48]

In the case of *Soll und Haben*, however, more essential than the poetic efficacy of its anthropomorphic images is the question that Christine Achinger has posed, namely, "what, in the contemporary world of the novel, such bygone myths and conceptions are incorporated *as*."[49] As Achinger goes on to suggest, the incorporation of such language in *Soll und Haben* is to be taken neither as a "true" pathetic fallacy (in the sense of the expression of genuine subjective passions that Ruskin attributes to Coleridge) nor as a fussy and contrived mannerism (such as that of which Ruskin accuses Pope). Rather, Freytag's use of pathetic fallacy is a "conscious play with traditions *as* traditions," a quotation of prior poetic modes with "hyperbolical and metaphorical function."[50] Though Achinger expresses her conclusions only circumspectly, her supposition of the citational and intentionally incongruous character of such passages is thoroughly supported by the novel's own depiction of the aristocracy as itself a cultural archaism. In the schematic sociology of Freytag's world, the members of the landed gentry are certainly not the villains; but they remain nonetheless products of an earlier era, for all their glamour unsuited to the new, hardworking, mobile, capitalist society growing up all around them. (Though for this reason they are also eminently suited—as the happy match of the heedless and charming Lenore von Rothsattel to the equally heedless and charming Fritz von Fink illustrates—for a position at the vanguard of German colonialism, where their chivalric dash and feudalistic know-how will come in exactly handy.) The point of Freytag's "false" pathetic fallacies in these instances is thus precisely their falseness; whatever its fascination, a literature that still believes in the affective life of things is as silly as an insistence on agricultural idyll in a rapidly industrializing Germany. The attachment of a floridly expressive, "Romantic" language to the novel's aristocratic milieu consigns both to a past that, while not without its charms, no longer fits the reality of the times.

It is in contrast to this pretty but ultimately outmoded form of poeticizing, then, that Freytag posits the by now oft-discussed concept of the "poetry of commerce" (Poesie des Geschäfts).[51] Certainly, this poetry—or, rather, the bourgeois sphere with which it is identified—also contains its anthropomorphizing and fairy-tale moments, most notably in those passages describing a certain plaster cat statuette belonging to Anton, which springs to life from time to time as a kind of whimsical extradiegetic commentary on Anton's life and adventures.[52] "One Sunday morning," begins one such passage, "Anton was absorbed in his reading of Cooper's Last Mohican, while outside the window, the first snowflakes danced their war dance and attempted in vain to infiltrate the yellow cat's sanctuary."[53] Here, the allusion to James Fenimore Cooper's *Last of the Mohicans* all but states outright the literary conventionality of the passage's personifications: in a particularly modern twist on Ruskin's idea of affective states, the trope is a direct result of Anton's losing himself in American adventure novels, to the point that he envisions Cooper's exotically bellicose Indians in the prosaic German snowflakes at his window. Such fantasies, however, will gradually fade away, in direct proportion to the gradual fading away of Anton's callowness. As he matures, Anton comes to learn to prefer the poetry of commerce: not, indeed, as something opposed to literature's pleasures, but as their most perfectly realized form. For commerce, too, stirs the emotions, connects parts to wholes, and elevates the spirit—and no longer merely out of the faraway and the make-believe, but out of the reality of the here and now.[54]

In this poetry, *all* material objects are potentially raised up in the light of their anthropocentric appropriation, at the same time as this anthropocentric appropriation thereby reveals itself to be the modern, pragmatic adaptation of Romantic transcendence itself. However, for an accurate assessment of Freytag's poetics, this claim must be met with an important qualification. For whatever fetishistic enchantment Freytag's "magic of the commodity"[55] implies, it is still only insofar as commodities act as mediators that they are enchanted: only, that is, insofar as things are *handled* by human beings, who, for all the auratic coruscation that objects may present, alone possess selfhood, consciousness, and agency. And while it is one thing to insert into one's novel anthropomorphic interludes about protecting spirits and talismanic statuettes, or to celebrate the commodity as the concrete symbol of human activity, it is quite another to tacitly assume that the inanimate, material world actually bends to the moods of its human inhabitants—much less, could possess its own independent ideas and affects. (It is significant, for example, that even Anton's infamous *Gipskatze* reverts to an inanimate object in its owner's absence.) If, in the words of Barbara Johnson, "personification and anthropomorphism endow the world with meaning centered around the representation of human being,"[56] the anthropomorphic trope that points to itself *as* trope is sign for nothing so much as the mediating consciousness of human being itself, which reshapes the world in its own image. Thus anthropomorphism, as a "mere" figure of speech, is divested of its power, transferred to the realm of fantasy and to rhetoric in the weak sense of the term. But the quieter, slipperier, and above all *self-naturalizing* trope of pathetic fallacy returns to anthropomorphism its performative force, positing a *Dingwelt* that, unlike the pliant world of exchangeable goods, needs no human actors to quicken it to life.

Dark Arts

Therefore, if for Ruskin pathetic fallacy is a poetic defect and slightly risible category error, for Freytag, pathetic fallacy is a real representation, so to speak, of a danger that is no less than existential in character. In Freytag's review essay "Ein Dank für Charles Dickens" ("A Note of Thanks for Charles Dickens"), published in the Spring 1870 issue of *Die Grenzboten*, Freytag defends Dickens's work from charges of artificiality or exaggeration, contrasting it positively to an idea of realism as the mere "daguerreotype of reality." "What [Dickens] gives us," argues Freytag, "may well appear in its details very different than it does in real life. Yet in terms of what really matters, he and only he has discovered the highest truth that is vouchsafed to man to represent. He has reinterpreted the monstrous, terrifying, incomprehensible world in human terms [Er hat die ungeheuere, furchtbare, unverständliche Welt ins Menschliche umgedeutet], in accordance with the needs of a noble and yearning mind."[57] Freytag's main point here is merely the long-standing one of artistic truth versus factual documentation, updated to account for the new elision of the two. But the anxiety that underlies Freytag's claims should not be ignored: outside of fiction's expressive reinterpretations, the real world is "monstrous, terrifying, incomprehensible." It is *not* human, but must be *made* so by authorial selection and mediation, by giving to the impersonal chaos of existence a new, intimate meaning. For the contrary does not merely lead, bad enough, to a soulless empiricism; loosed from human context—and from human dominion—objects potentially take on a life of their own, usurping for themselves an agency and a freedom that should be the human being's privilege alone.

Again, however, Freytag does not ban such fantastical or supernatural aspects from his novel; to the contrary, he *stages* them as essential elements of the novel's plot, in a conflict of literary styles that directly mirrors the social conflicts they are used to represent. It has become a commonplace of *Soll und Haben* scholarship to describe its Jewish characters in general—and its indisputable villain, the parvenu, usurer, and, eventually, murderer Veitel Itzig in particular—as stand-ins for the "materialist" ontology and aesthetics bluntly rejected by the advocates of programmatic realism.[58] Certainly, one does not have to be an especially careful reader of *Soll und Haben* to notice that the character Veitel Itzig does not exactly receive a positive treatment in the novel. Far more, even, than the novel's other Jewish figures (who are nevertheless all in one way or another incompatible with German society),[59] Veitel is a pure villain out of melodrama: a back-alley Shylock lacking both the latter's eloquence and dignity, physically as well as morally ugly, ignorant of any attitude beyond servility, guile, and the abject bitterness of the inherently unlovable. With his insinuating, inescapable presence, he is the very embodiment of what the contemporary philosopher Alain Finkielkraut has called, with tart irony, the "visible Jew": "an obscene creature, indecent; morality as well as personal hygiene demanded that such an exhibitionist be shunned."[60] However, Veitel's "obscenity" goes beyond his status as archetypical object of antisemitic revulsion. For one, it is a surprising fact that, even more than the novel's depictions of its aristocratic milieu, the sections devoted to Veitel are overwhelmingly marked by long passages of sensuous description and a portentous, strongly figurative language. Granted, the first reason for this is elegant in its obviousness: Veitel is a schemer, and schemers scheme alone. Unlike the novel's other characters, who are constantly in commerce with one another—in both senses of the word—Veitel's machinations take place in a solitude of exposition. But there is perhaps another reason for Freytag's attaching of such passages to the novel's primary antagonist. What Eric Santner has described as the problem of "creaturely" exhibition—"the mute 'thingness' of nature . . . beyond our capacity to endow it with meaning"—is epitomized in the sinister lyricism of Veitel's world, which emerges indeed as "a piece of human history that has become an enigmatic ruin."[61] Just as Veitel's cunning manipulation of financial documents destabilizes the relationship of sign to value on which the realist novel depends,[62] Veitel's presence perpetually blurs the border between thing and human, not only inverting the hierarchy by which things are subordinated to human needs, but making it unclear where the human ends and the thingly begins in the first place. Even Veitel's speech, evincing "more larynx than higher grammar" (mehr Kehlkopf als höhere Grammatik),[63] reduces the human to its physical parts, degrading language itself—the very vehicle of spirit—to its crude somatic basis.

Veitel, in short, is less a figure for materialism than a material figure, a grotesque specter of half-humanity by which Freytag transforms the uncanny familiarity of the material world (including the materiality of the human being itself) from universal condition into active threat.[64] Thus, while Veitel clearly evinces none of that "warm German nature" with which, according to Julian Schmidt, Freytag's novel ennobles the world of global capitalist exchange, to uphold the typological pattern of "materialist" naturalism versus "humanist" realism is in some sense to replicate the novel's own aesthetic ideology (if also rejecting its political one); for all *Soll und Haben*'s schematicness, there is something more going on in the novel than such a neat correspondence would allow. Of course, given that *Soll und Haben* is not just an exemplary work of German bourgeois realism, but also *the* paradigmatic novel of bourgeois mercantilism, everyone in the novel moves in what is very much a material world. Yet Veitel Itzig evinces a kind of complicity with things that makes him unique—and uniquely uncanny—in Freytag's universe. Such a complicity with things already characterizes Veitel's first entrance in the life of the novel's hero, as the narrative recounts in flashback:

> In earlier times, Anton had had the opportunity, through the valiant use of his tongue and his little fists, to save the young Jew from ill-treatment on the part of certain impertinent schoolmates and to acquire for himself a sense of being a defender of oppressed innocence. To wit, in one dismal school scene, in which a knackwurst was used to evoke in Itzig feelings of despair, Anton had advocated for Itzig so heroically that he himself came away with a gash in the head, while his opponents, crying and bloody, ran away behind the church and ate the knackwurst themselves. Since that day, Itzig had displayed a kind of devotion to Anton, which he proved by allowing himself to be assisted by his protector in difficult school assignments, and occasionally by helping himself to a piece of Anton's butter roll.[65]

The "feelings of despair" (verzweifelte Empfindungen) that the threat of eating *treyf* evokes in the young Veitel is not far from the affects of disgust that his own figure will later evoke in good Christian society: the taboo—confirming Julia Kristeva's insight about the uncanny reflexivity of the abject—rebounds metaphorically on its observer.[66] However, not only does Veitel's disgust reciprocally signal his own disgustingness (much in the sense of the children's taunt "It takes one to know one"), it also grants the innocent piece of ground pork a sinister power that the reasonable German omnivores—bullies and rescuer alike—know that it does not, in fact, possess.[67]

In a pair of essays on the rhetorical contradictions of Ruskin's pathetic fallacy (which, like Veitel's orthorexia, calls up more problems than it solves), J. Hillis Miller points out that both anthropomorphism and its avoidance are dependent on covertly religious premises, albeit from opposing denominations. As Ruskin himself concedes, anthropomorphism can have a purpose in certain forms of prophetic writing to express the idea "that God and his workings in the world are so far above man as to be namable only in catachrestic personifications."[68] But "the renunciation of the pathetic fallacy as idolatry," for which Ruskin ultimately advocates, depends on a conviction no less religious in nature, namely, "that only God has the right to give personality."[69] True religion, then—and that means, for both Ruskin and Freytag, Protestant religion—lies not in attributing personality and emotion to material things, but in recognizing the God-given personality and emotion within *oneself*. However, the religion to which Veitel Itzig belongs (even if Freytag presents it more as race than belief system) is a false, unredeemed religion, a religion *without mediation*. Fetishistically fixated on the letter and the flesh, Judaism fails to understand that it is through the human being alone that the material world acquires significance; its world, cast into the semipagan darkness of an unknowable God, remains fatally caught between materiality and magic, a complex of sacred and profane objects with agency but without spirit. The pathetic fallacy of everyday phenomena, in other words, is the fallacy of a people *without grace*.

Again, most readers of *Soll und Haben* have overlooked such aspects to focus on Veitel as a figure of icy modern calculation. Thus Achinger, for example, describes the "Jewish" relation to things (the scare quotes are also hers) as one of an "excessive . . . coolness, that strips all things of their luster and reduces them to their material value."[70] Where Anton experiences, Veitel merely appraises; where Anton envisions a world with its innumerable interpersonal interconnections, Veitel sees only the abstract figures of his balance sheets. (One might express this by saying that Veitel's understanding of "Soll" and "Haben" reduces the terms to their literal financial definitions, whereas Anton also understands their ethical and emotional connotations.) Thus is the true poetry, not only of trade, but of realism as a whole so to speak foreclosed. Again, though, this description of Veitel's worldview as one of the cold pragmatism of the bottom line is only half the story. For behind Veitel's disdain for the human worth of goods and commodities (to say nothing of his disdain for people themselves) hides a *premodern* idea of the occult life of things independent from human beings entirely.[71] This return of the repressed premodern appears already in the novel's very first conversation between Veitel and Anton, where Veitel expresses his faith in the power of "the science, what's written on papers" (die Wissenschaft, sie steht auf Papieren geschrieben), whose mere possession is sufficient to transform its owner into "a powerful man."[72] But this implied black magic of trade secrets has a still blacker provenance, as the lines of dialogue that precede this remark make clear:

> "There is a formula, what for to force someone you want something from, even if he doesn't want." ["Es gibt ein Rezept, durch das man kann zwingen einen jeden, von dem man etwas will, auch wenn er nicht will."]
>
> "Do you have to give that person a potion," asked Anton contemptuously, "or a magic herb?"
>
> "Centaury [Tausendgüldenkraut] is the name of the herb, what you can do with a lot in the world," Veitel replied. . . . "Whoever has the secret will become a great man like Rothschild, if he lives long enough."
>
> "If he doesn't get arrested before then," Anton interjected.
>
> "Arrested nothing!" answered Veitel. "When I go to the city to learn, I'm going to look for the science, what's written on papers. Whoever finds the papers becomes a powerful man; I'm going to look for these papers until I find them."[73]

Such beliefs, observes Ulrich Kittstein laconically, "at first call up associations with magical-alchemical practices; however, they play out in the course of the novel in highly modern form."[74] But to speak of mere "associations" with occult practices here is not only a gross understatement: as the above passage makes plain, it is not the difference from, but precisely the *affinity between* these practices and Veitel Itzig's dark financial arts that is at issue.[75]

Indeed, in his ignorance of the true value of things in favor of a lust for money per se, Veitel embodies that perversion of natural economic processes that Marx attributes to the "hoarder" (Schatzbildner), in whose hands "the liquid form of wealth and its petrification, the elixir of life and the philosophers' stone are wildly mixed together like an alchemist's apparitions [spuken alchymistisch toll durcheinander]":[76]

> Since money does not reveal what has been transformed into it, everything, commodity or not, is convertible into money. . . . Circulation becomes the great social retort into which everything is thrown, to come out again as the money crystal. Nothing is immune from this alchemy, the bones of the saints cannot withstand it, let alone more delicate *res sacrosanctae, extra commercium hominum*.[77]

Money hoarding is the ne plus ultra of the capitalist economy, the worship of "the fetish of gold"[78] so fearsome it has the power to absorb all other fetishes within it. Freytag, it hardly needs to be said, does not share in Marx's distrust of the liberal market. For that very reason, however, Veitel's financial chemistry must be made to appear all the more dubious, all the more unnatural. Like so much else in *Soll und Haben*'s binary universe, the occult aura of Veitel's business dealings serves as a foil to the Schröter company's far more concrete form of commerce, protecting the latter from the suspicion of indecency that inevitably falls on the practice of moneymaking as such. In the concluding words of Schröter's daughter (and future Frau Wohlfahrt) Sabine: "Property and wealth [Wohlstand] have no value . . . without the beneficial force that maintains dead metal in life-giving motion [welche das tote Metall in Leben schaffender Bewegung erhält]."[79] By juxtaposing Veitel's sinister profiteering with the Schröter house's honest mercantile trade, Freytag thus implicitly underscores what Marx elsewhere makes explicit: "A commodity as a use-value has an eminently material function" (Als Gebrauchswerth wirkt die Waare ursachlich),[80] but the speculator and the hoarder, holding fast to money's "metallic corporeality" (metallischen Leiblichkeit), "vaporizes it [wealth] into a mere phantom" (verdunstet ihm zum bloßen Hirngespinst).[81]

Even Veitel's first step up the social ladder as a part-time dry goods peddler entails a form of esoteric substance conversion, a petty alchemy of the con artist variety:

> He possessed the skill of using mica to make old brass gleam and to give the highest polish to old silver; he was always eager to buy discarded old suits,—something regarded by all those in the know as the symptom of a bold and audacious nature,—he knew, by means of a peculiar brushstroke, how to give their pilled cloth an appearance of newness that lasted just long enough to fool his buyers, whom he strove to find among poor schoolmasters, gangly confirmation students, and tradesmen just released from their apprenticeships.[82]

Such sham renovations are the diametrical opposite of the Freiherr von Risach's restoration work in *Der Nachsommer*: instead of returning things mistakenly deemed worthless to their true value, Veitel's huckster wizardry envelops actually worthless things in the mere illusion of luxury, the better to turn a quick profit from his unsuspecting marks. But Veitel's overpolished brass and brushed-up suits are only training for the shady transactions with which he will later seek to make his fortune:

> Thus he endeavored to secure his capital . . . until the great day came when he would use that capital to put the whole estate in his hands. . . . He would broker purchases and sales as so many others

> did, the poor devils who begrudged each other their half percent as much as the elegant gentlemen with impressive titles who drove up real estate prices and made hundreds of thousands through cunning, bribery, and hidden paths.[83]

Lead takes on the shine of gold in Veitel's underhanded entrepreneurship, which eventually reveals itself as no less than the model for market speculation—high *and* low stakes—per se.

For this reason, even if certain aspects of Veitel's portrayal mark him as a modern character, it would be mistaken to consider him as a simple personification of the cold rationalism of the contemporary age. Writing on Stifter, Walter Benjamin speaks of a "rebellion and darkening of nature" in his work, which on occasion "swerves into the horrifying and demonic" (ins höchste Grauenvolle, Dämonische umschlägt).[84] For Benjamin, this swerve is manifested above all in Stifter's female characters, "where [nature's] perverted and subtly disguised demonic force assumes the innocent aspect of simplicity."[85] What for Stifter, then, is incarnated in the woman—the alien face of nature—is for Freytag incarnated, less typically but also more unambiguously, in the Jew. For Veitel is more than just an ordinary swindler and arriviste: he is a kind of *Erdgeist*, a bogeyman, who, like Dickens's would-be parvenu Uriah Heep,[86] exerts a repulsed fascination and a not entirely latent erotic hold over his potential victims.[87] What Veitel embodies is thus not the modern attitude of a rationalized and soulless nature, but rather the fatal sympathy that exists between this nature and the never-quite-extirpated traces of an ancient animistic past, an uncanny and excessive cosmos from whose weird materiality idols may emerge indeed.[88]

The point here, however, is not that Veitel is not properly materialist *enough* in his dealings. The point, rather, is that materialism itself is never quite materialism; insofar as the material object is seen to resist human consciousness, the materiality of matter is always uncanny, always in excess of itself. And this idea of a material existence of things in excess of rational necessity is not only the specter haunting modern finance; it is also the specter haunting realist fiction, whose legitimacy and above-board status, like the legitimacy of modern finance itself, are secured only on the condition of the former's exorcism. Therefore the autonomy of the inorganic *must* be placed on the side of evil, so as to differentiate the trade in real goods—the *Handel* that signifies (in the Grimms' *Wörterbuch*) "in the most general sense, that which is carried out and accomplished with one's hands [was mit den händen betrieben und ausgerichtet wird]"—from those immaterial-material financial dealings that seem nevertheless to revitalize all the thaumaturgic possibilities of a more primitive age. Veitel's traffic in anthropomorphism provides Freytag with a way to control, to contain, and, ultimately, to banish the "monstrous, terrifying, incomprehensible world"[89] once and for all, freeing the realist novel from both the alterity of matter and its animistic reinvestment through the shoring up of the border between human *Handlungen* and the *Handeln* of things eerily animated to life.

The Devil Incarnal

And yet, realism is also constantly crossing the border it sets up between persons and things, not only shaping the material world according to the perception of its human inhabitants, but allowing that world to reflect back reciprocally upon them.[90] In his classic analysis of Balzac's description of Madame Vauquer's boardinghouse in the opening passages of *Père Goriot*, Erich Auerbach demonstrates the way in which Balzac makes scenic description do double duty as character portrait, in an "atmospheric realism"[91] that Auerbach, for his part, attributes primarily to the combined influence of nineteenth-century biology and historiography. "What confronts us," Auerbach writes, "is the unity of a particular milieu, felt as a total concept of a demonic-organic nature and presented entirely by suggestive and sensory means."[92] Auerbach's use of the word "demonic" in this sentence is clearly meant primarily in the Greek sense of the term: Madame Vauquer is the spirit of the place, her soul but the effluvium of the objects that surround her, at the same time as her presence animates these objects with character and significance. In the context of a postanimist, post-Cartesian worldview, however, the other sense of demon as evil spirit is never far away: malignance inheres in the agency of things without human soul.[93] While Auerbach may have chosen his example simply on the basis of its prominence in Balzac's text, it can be no accident that the passage he selects is precisely one in which the character's "mixture of stupidity, slyness, and concealed vitality," emanating from her environment, "gives the impression of something repulsively spectral,"[94] in which the primary consequence of a character's atmospheric "synthesizing" of her milieu is precisely to "[deepen] the impenetrability and baseness of her character which is constrained to work itself out" within it.[95] Auerbach's "demonic" fusion of character and milieu thus bespeaks more than just a desire to capture the typology of the times; it also bespeaks realism's uneasy negotiation between the world of things and human beings—whereby the refusal on the part of certain characters to respect the terms of this negotiation moves them beyond mere unsavoriness into the realm of the diabolic.

This, at any rate, is very much the case in *Soll und Haben*. In the same way that Veitel is constantly surrounded by things that he both manipulates and seems to merge with, he is also characterized by his surroundings in a way different from almost every other character in the novel. From the very first scenes, Freytag establishes a pattern of identification between Veitel and his settings that marks him as something more and yet less than human, at the same time as it endows the nonhuman environment with a spectral and sinister agency. "Veitel Itzig . . . had a curious predilection for crooked side streets and narrow walkways":[96] the cramped alleys of the Jewish ghetto are the veritable physical manifestation of Veitel's being, the mirror image of his own crooked and narrow soul. As Veitel arrives for his first fateful meeting with the doomed Jewish tradesman Hirsch Ehrenthal, "on the first floor [of Ehrenthal's house] gleamed white frames enclosing great slabs of mirrored glass; under the roof the windows were blackened, dirty, here and there a shattered pane. There was no good character in that house; it had the look of an old gypsy woman who had thrown a new colored shawl over her old beggar's habit."[97] Though this house and its "character" are admittedly not Veitel's own, it is no accident that this description is offered at the moment of his approach, as if his standing gave him the power to summon all of the novel's other *genii loci*. Indeed, directly after this meeting, the novel finds Veitel sitting in a corner of the boardinghouse where he is living, "with his restless mind calculating and devising business schemes, from time to time flapping his hands and swinging his legs in animated cogitation, until the darkness of night broke in through the door and the small oil lamp began to crackle and give signs [Miene machte] of going out."[98] Here, Freytag effectively dismembers the person Veitel into his constituent parts, a puppetlike composite of twitchy mind, hands, and legs barely more human than the pantomimic expressiveness of the oil lamp beside him, while the darkness that "breaks in" (eindrang) through the guesthouse door not only foreshadows Veitel's own invasion of genteel society, but also grants the night itself a threatening, slinking physical force that represents the thoughts as yet only abstractly playing out in Veitel's imagination in vividly material form.

Other scenes establish the identification of Veitel with his environment still more plainly—for instance the conclusion to the episode in which Veitel begins his tutelage with the alcoholic lawyer Hippus, where Freytag, taking a page from the tradition of the gothic novel, urges his prose to its most purple expression:

> The lamp had gone out, the little squire had emptied his refilled brandy bottle and, worn out from talking, lay sleeping on his straw sack, and Veitel still sat there on his footstool. This night, he wasn't thinking about his customers, about the money he had paid out, but was instead writing promissory notes [Schuldscheine] to the black walls. . . . Finally he opened the door to the wooden balcony, leaned over the railings and looked out into the twilight at the water below, which flowed by like an enormous river of ink. And still he wrote promissory notes in the black shadows of the houses opposite and wrote receipts on the dark water's surface until his weary body collapsed, exhausted [bis sein müder Leib erschöpft zusammenbrach], and he fell asleep in a corner, his hot head propped up against the wooden wall. The night wind drove over the waters in cold gusts, while below the river gurgled plaintively [klagend] against the wooden posts and ledges of the old houses. What he had drawn in the

> shadows slid off, and what he had written on the water washed away, and yet that night his soul had issued a promissory note that would one day be demanded of him with interest and compound interest. The wind howled, and the storm wailed, wild augurs of guilt, avenging messengers of the law [Was er in die Schatten gezeichnet, das verrückte sich, und was er auf das Wasser geschrieben, das zerrann, und doch hatte seine Seele einen Schuldschein ausgestellt in dieser Nacht, der einst von ihm eingefordert werden sollte mit Zins und Zinseszins. Der Wind heulte, und der Sturm klagte, wilde Mahner an die Schuld, rächende Boten des Gerichts].[99]

Tzvetan Todorov singles out the "questioning of the limit between matter and mind," or the "collapse of the limit between subject and object," as the fundamental principle of fantastic literature.[100] This is precisely what takes place in the above passage. The pathetic fallacies of the "plaintive river" and the "driving wind" and the apostrophizing of natural phenomena as "wild augurs" (wilde Mahner) and "avenging messengers" (rächende Boten)—also recalling the world of finance—paint an image of Veitel's environment surging around him with untamable, uncanny life, while the verbs "slide off" (sich verrücken) and "wash away" (zerrinnen) not only refer to the literal shadows and water on which Veitel writes his imaginary bonds, but also imply the illusoriness of those bonds themselves and the madness they will bring in their wake. Meanwhile, Veitel himself is reified into a mere "body" (Leib) that "collapses" (zusammenbrach) into sleep, leaving, in the place of a person, only a dismembered head slumped against a wall. Such ontological disorder is only further exacerbated by the ambiguous grammatical agency of the passage: through a kind of pronominal amphibology, Hippus, the "little squire" (der kleine Herr) who teaches Veitel Itzig about the business of debt collection and who will later become one of Veitel's most tragic victims, turns, as if in cinematic dissolve, into Veitel himself. Later in the passage, a similar technique makes it unclear where the night wind ends and Veitel begins ("Im kaltem Zuge fuhr *der* Nachtwind. . . . Was *er* in die Schatten gezeichnet . . ."). Not only are object and subject, matter and mind allied, they are all but grammatically indistinguishable, creating a protean, nightmare world antithetical in every way to the daylight world of differentiated persons and things.

In this context, it is helpful to look at another moment in the novel where Freytag makes use of anthropomorphizing language, an early passage describing the young Anton as he makes his way to the capital:

> Everything around him was bright, fragrant, billowing, as if in electric fire; he drank in the intoxicating fragrance [Wohlgeruch] that arose from the blossoming earth in deep gulps. . . . In the field, the heads of wheat leaned toward him on their swaying stalks, nodding and greeting him, and in their shadow countless crickets hummed their song:

> Merry, merry in the sunshine! On a willow tree sat a little colony of sparrows [ein Volk Sperlinge]; the tiny barons of the field did not fly off as he stopped and stood before the tree [als er vor dem Stamm stehenblieb], indeed, they bent their necks and called out to him: "Good day, wanderer, where to, where to?" and Anton said quietly, "To the big city, to life."—"Good luck," called the sparrows, "Godspeed!"[101]

Just as the dark and stormy night of the "Schuldschein" passage is meant to signal similar qualities in Veitel's person, here the pleasant weather and the well-wishing fauna symbolize, or rather, reflect Anton's own optimistic disposition, in each case binding environment and character together within a single affect. Yet more important than the similarities of these two passages are the differences between them. For, unlike Veitel, Anton does not actually meld with the environment that represents him; his environment inclines to him, but he remains the subject surveying and passing through it. It is thus an important point of distinction that, while Veitel eventually falls asleep in the "Schuldschein" passage, Anton remains active and awake. This fact, seemingly trivial, allows Freytag to suggest that Anton's anthropomorphisms are but figures of his imagination, knowingly projected into the world around him, whereas the anthropomorphisms of the "Schuldschein" passage are presented as things as it were outside Veitel's consciousness, substantivized as "real" paranormal phenomena rather than sentimental ironic projections. In the end, it is thus Anton's sympathetic *distance* from the objects around him that allows him to endow them with meaning and value, while Veitel's attempted integration into the world of things results almost immediately in those things' limitless power over him. In contrast to the calm proprietary glow in which the objects of Anton Wohlfahrt's world are bathed, Veitel's *Schauerroman* universe swarms with a life of its own.[102]

In other words: once again, outside of its citational and sentimental usages, anthropomorphization steps over the boundaries of what realism sanctions and renders it suspect. But the suspect use of anthropomorphization can thus be used *for* suspect cases all the more effectively. Freytag's unmarked anthropomorphizing reaches its indisputable climax in the climax of the novel itself (of which the "Schuldschein" passage is clearly a foreshadowing), where Veitel, attempting to flee from what he imagines to be the ghost of the man he has recently murdered, falls ignominiously to his death:

> A violent shudder shook his limbs, he descended unsteadily, step by step. As he set his foot in the water, he heard a pitiful groan. He held on to the wooden wall, as the other had done, and gazed down. Again a deep groaning sounded, he realized that he was the one breathing so laboredly. . . .
>
> Dark was the night, rain still dripped down through the heavy air, a fog covered the houses and balconies along the river, only here and

> there did a set of steps, a pier, or the gabled roof of a house emerge obscurely from the dark gray mass. The water pooled against the old posts, the stairways, and the ledges of the houses and murmured monotonously. . . . He clung to the slippery wood of the posts, so as not to sink. . . . With a cry, the criminal jumped back, his foot slipped from the walkway, he fell into the water up to his neck. Thus he stood in the river, above him howled the wind, in his ears the water roared [rauschte] ever more wildly, ever more threatening. . . . Slowly, the strange figure detached itself from the beam, it rushed [rauschte] along the same path he had taken, the phantom drew nearer, again the hand stretched out toward him [das Gespenst trat ihm näher, wieder streckte sich die Hand nach ihm aus]. He jumped back in horror, deeper into the current. Another stumble, a loud cry, the brief struggle of a drowning man, and it was over. The current rolled on and took the body of the dead man with it.
>
> The banks of the river began to come to life. Torches shone along the water's edge, weapons and uniforms covered in cloaks flashed in the glow of the lights. The calls of search parties could be heard, and at the foot of the stairs a man waded along the riverbank and shouted up: "He was carried away before I could reach him, tomorrow we'll find him at the weir."[103]

Here Freytag derives maximum benefit from the use of what might be called *covertly pathetic* adjectives (similar to what I. A. Richards calls "projectile adjectives"),[104] adjectives that have both an objective and an affective valence. The river that sounds "monotonously" (eintönig) and then "ever more wildly, ever more threatening" (immer wilder, immer drohender) is at once an ordinary catachresis and an expression of the increasingly panicked disorder of Veitel's own mind; the "slippery wood of the posts" (schlüpfrige Holz der Pfähle) is no doubt *actually* slippery from slime and water, but it cannot fail to evoke Veitel's own moral duplicity and veiled sexual creepiness, his ingratiating glibness and eager slide into vice, trickery, and crime.

If such affect- and judgment-laden adjectives still remain within permissible usage, however—an example of Ruskin's "temperament . . . borne away, or over-clouded, or over-dazzled by emotion"[105]—other aspects of this passage make use of a less common procedure. This procedure is already signaled in the very first lines of the above passage, where Veitel, exceptionally, checks his own imagination: as he steps into the water, he first thinks he hears it release a groan, only to realize, in a last moment of lucidity, that it is he himself who is groaning. As Veitel's fear takes over, however, so too does his fantasy: from the *Hirngespenster* of a guilty conscience is conjured a "real" ghost who pursues him to his actual doom, at the same time as Veitel himself, designated now only with the substantives "the criminal" (der Verbrecher), "a drowning man" (eines Ertrinkenden), and finally "the dead man" (des Leblosen), gradually slips into the realm of objects over which he no longer maintains control. Thus does the logic of pathetic fallacy become self-fulfilling prophesy: Veitel has indeed discovered the "formula, what for to force someone you want something from," but, like the Sorcerer's Apprentice, discovers to his horror that its power is turned against him.[106] More than just the subjective truth of his inner panic, Veitel's animistic *Judenblick*[107] catalyzes the world around him, in a failure of ontological and tropological propriety whose chief and last victim is himself.

Veitel's death by drowning is thus at once the complement to and culmination of his life by pathetic fallacy: the unstable element, on which what is written is washed away, also finally covers over the head of *Soll und Haben*'s sinister financial magus, who conjures money out of nothing and in whose presence the material, inanimate world, over which a humanist epistemology has only recently established its dominance, threatens once again to come to life. With Veitel's death, however, the pathetic fallacy also dies; where once the inanimate had assumed the characteristics of the human, now the human assumes the characteristics of the inanimate, this time for good. A "stumble, a loud cry, the brief struggle of a drowning man" (ein Taumeln, ein lauter Schrei, der kurze Kampf eines Ertrinkenden)—the penultimate sentence of the paragraph piles up an inventory of disconnected nouns to describe the last gasp of thingly life. The first line of the next paragraph marks the dawn of the new era: "The banks of the river began to come to life" (An dem Rand des Flusses wurde es lebendig). Life returns to its proper place, first tentatively and synecdochally, then literally with the reintroduction of actual human voices and forms. Even the very last paragraph of Freytag's novel, in which the evocation of "industrious house spirits" (fleißigen Hausgeister) might seem to revive the rhetoric of pathetic fallacy, in fact registers its end: "The poetic dreams that the boy Anton had nursed in his parental home . . . have turned into real ones" (Die poetischen Träume, welche der Knabe Anton in seinem Vaterhaus . . . gehegt hat, sind ehrliche Träume gewesen).[108]

The pathetic fallacies of *Soll und Haben* are thus neither ornamentation nor stylistic lapse on Freytag's part—a last hectic flare-up, so to speak, of difficultly relinquished Romantic tendencies. Rather, Freytag deploys the trope of pathetic fallacy *homeopathically*, in order to link together epistemological uncertainty, thingly life, and racial otherness and thereby to expel all three, all at once, from the modern novel's purview. With Veitel's end, Freytag exchanges the fevered nightmares of ontological speculation for the "real" dreams of a modern, pragmatic, socially and morally edifying literature. The life that counts, human, German, productive life, requires the death of the uncanny life of things and matter, the transformation of its corpse into so much bloated flotsam. And Veitel Itzig must die, not merely because he is a Jew and a usurer with no proper role in the new bourgeois economy, but because he is—or is made to become—the avatar of the obscene autonomy of the material world that a realist literature must foreclose in order to be.[109]

Chapter 3

✦

Iconolatry and Iconoclasm

Theodor Fontane

> If the papists have any shame, let them no longer use this subterfuge, that images are the books of the illiterate; which is so clearly refuted by numerous testimonies from Scripture. Yet, though I should concede this point to them, it would avail them but little in defence of their idols. What monsters they obtrude in the place of Deity is well known. But what they call the pictures or statues of their saints—what are they but examples of the most abandoned luxury and obscenity? . . . Even prostitutes in brothels are to be seen in more chaste and modest attire, than those images in their temples, which they wish to be accounted images of virgins.
>
> —John Calvin, *Institutes of the Christian Religion*[1]

> The beautiful epitaphia
> Are crumbled and no longer there;
> And whatever else of art and charm
> One once could see with pleasure warm
> Has come to ruin in the flames
> And of my church nothing remains.
>
> —Caspar Helmrich, *Annales Tangermundenses*[2]

> Detail-nonsense doesn't do any harm, as long as the whole thing is properly filled and thought out.
>
> —Theodor Fontane to Maximilian Ludwig, May 2, 1873[3]

Though it retains a dubious canonicity as a text of the right size and sentimentality to be foisted on high school students, Theodor Fontane's 1879 novella *Grete Minde*, while a bestseller in its day, is no longer one of his better-known works. Based, so the subtitle tells us, "on an old chronicle of the Mark" (nach einer altmärkischen Chronik),[4] the novella tells the story of Valtin and Grete, only children and half-orphans who live in neighboring houses in the Brandenburg town of Tangermünde at the beginning of the seventeenth century, in the years just before the outbreak of the Thirty Years' War. As the novella opens, Grete, the daughter of a Tangermünde patrician and a Spanish Catholic woman (by way of Bruges), is treated with neglect and scorn by her sanctimonious sister-in-law, Trud, and Trud's husband, Grete's surly half-brother Gerdt. After her father's death deprives her of her one true protector, Grete—described, like her late mother before her, as a great beauty—finally reaches the limits of her endurance and, together with Valtin, runs away from home. When the narrative rejoins the pair after an ellipsis of several years, it finds Grete and Valtin members of the traveling acting troupe that had previously fascinated Grete as a young girl and the unmarried parents of an infant child—and Valtin himself lying fatally ill in the attic of the inn where the actors are currently lodging. As his dying wish, Valtin makes Grete promise to return to Tangermünde and throw herself on Gerdt's mercy. When Grete returns home to honor her promise, however, her half-brother refuses her not only the sanctuary she asks for, but also the inheritance that she proudly demands in its stead. Thus thwarted, Grete decides to take her case to the Tangermünde council, hoping that they, at least, will recognize her claims. But when Gerdt, who also happens to be one of the councilmen, lies under oath about Grete's right to her share of their father's money, Grete realizes that she has no chance of a fair hearing and exits the hall with words of contempt. Finally, forsaken, insulted, and alone, Grete takes justice into her own hands and sets fire to the town of Tangermünde, holding Gerdt and Trud's young son aloft as she tumbles with him from the church's bell tower into the flames below.

In the scant critical literature devoted to it, Fontane's novella is usually read as a fable of injustice and revenge in the vein of Kleist's *Michael Kohlhaas*,[5] a minor tragedy of familial ties and small-town relations,[6] a melodrama of the failed search for individual emancipation in a repressive society,[7] or a parable of bourgeois self-interest and criminality in the manner of Fontane's own *Unterm Birnbaum*.[8] Yet Fontane's novella encompasses more than such plot-based approaches would suggest—more, certainly, than the simple "genre picture and character sketch" (Sitten- und Charakterbild) Fontane himself once disingenuously claimed it to be.[9] In what follows here, therefore, *Grete Minde* will be approached less in terms of its thematic content than in terms of its formal poetics—or rather, in terms of how Fontane uses its thematic content to work through the questions that its formal poetics raises. For what is on the surface a simple tale of exclusion and revenge in seventeenth-century Brandenburg and a seeming anomaly in Fontane's oeuvre is also a sustained reflection on the task of the novelist in the modern age and the corresponding charges of idolatry, blasphemy, indecency, and, indeed, obscenity the modern novelist risks incurring, in the context of the portrayal of what

Fontane names at one point, with as much fascination as reproof, "the merely material world" (die bloße Sinnenwelt).[10]

Already from his early career as a journalist and art critic, Fontane was acutely aware of the vexed relationship between sensual representation and discursive content.[11] In his 1853 review essay "Unsere lyrische und epische Poesie seit 1848" ("Our Lyric and Epic Poetry since 1848"), Fontane joins the growing chorus of critics of mere illusionism with his warning that realist art should not be mistaken for the naive mimesis of everyday life: "Life is always only the marble quarry in which the raw material for infinite sculptures is contained. . . . The marble block as such, merely torn from a larger whole, is not yet an artwork."[12] Such an awareness of the necessity of artistic reworking is clearly reflected in Fontane's own fiction, which not only mines its details for symbolic import, but also continually foregrounds, far more than the description of the external world itself, the ways in which people *talk* about that world and the thoughts, sensations, and actions that it facilitates.[13] Thus, as Gerhart von Graevenitz has observed, Fontane's images are "not resolvable into a simple opposition between the real and the unreal"; rather, they show "that media and signs . . . always appear in mediatic and semantic *contexts*, . . . that realities are shaped and constructed through collective phantasms, then suddenly to fall out of their imaginary roles into sheer factuality, that objects are merely objects and at the same time points of intersection for memories and auras."[14]

Yet such an attunement to the associative, constructed, context-dependent nature of reality is also perpetually shadowed by an ambivalence toward those same "mere objects," which, *without* the supplement of memory and aura, threaten to reappear in the nakedness of their "sheer factuality" indeed. This ambivalence is what *Grete Minde* dramatizes. If for Fontane the real world is a perpetually shifting aggregate of perceptions and associations—making depiction itself, as Eric Downing has put it, "as much a matter of exceeding a representational realm as achieving it"[15]—such exceedance must be understood within the context of realism's troubled relationship to the "representational realm" per se. Meanwhile, the confessional disputes of the Protestant Reformation that linger in the background of *Grete Minde* are the same disputes that will reemerge, in altered form, within German realism—where Fontane's consistent practice of using "realistic details as a source of the ideational and the symbolic"[16] is also his way of attempting to close the gap opened up long ago by such disputes between the idea and its material incarnation, and which Fontane moreover allows to play out in his novella in complex and subtle ways. That which Stifter tries to circumscribe, in other words, and Freytag to expunge—the autonomy of materiality in realist representation—Fontane, at the beginning of his career as novelist, speculatively performs, staging the aesthetic controversies of the past as a way to explore the artistic possibilities and prohibitions of his present.

The Flesh Made Word

For a novelist whose name is so synonymous with German realism,[17] it is more than a little surprising to realize that Fontane's second longer published work of fiction in fact constitutes a turn away from the representation of contemporary life and toward the outmoded genres of ballad, chronicle, and romance.[18] Loosely based on actual events—albeit ones far more scurrilous than the tale Fontane eventually makes out of them[19]—the text conjures up the seventeenth century out of an assortment of archival material (in particular, Caspar Helmrich's *Annales Tangermundenses* and Andreas Rittner's *Alt-Märckisches Geschichtbuch*), sometimes even in the form of direct borrowings and quotations. Fritz Martini reads such archival practices as Fontane's feel for the "popular imagination" (Phantasie des Volkes), which poetically reweaves historical facts and events into the "fabric of a historical-natural-nationalist whole."[20] More recent scholarship, on the other hand, has tended to stress Fontane's use of historical sources as a modern or indeed postmodern "recombinant poetics,"[21] a "mix of mixed media that determines the new collective imaginary, a mixture in which technologically and mass-produced images begin to hold sway over perceptions."[22] Almost all critics, however, have noted the peculiar anachronistic quality this archival method gives to Fontane's novella, whose characters' attitudes, motivations, and behavior, more often than not, have a distinctly modern cast.[23] Such anachronicity is evident, for example, in the passage describing the appearance of Trud and her cousin (and Valtin's young stepmother) Emrentz at a town feast for the visit of the local prince-elector. In the middle of the account of the assembling crowd, the narration pauses to note that both women are "dressed with an unusual opulence and splendor [absonderlich reich und prächtig gekleidet], in necklaces and high ruffs, and Emrentz, in spite of the July heat, had not been able to bring herself to forgo her little ermine-trimmed jacket [und Emrentz, aller Julihitze zum Trotz, hatte sich ihr mit Hermelinpelz besetztes Mäntelchen nicht versagen können]."[24] Here the descriptive precision of the passage—not "Mantel" but "Mäntelchen"; not "Hitze" but "Julihitze"—and, even more, the muted irony of its voice firmly register the gap between the literary conventions of the early modern period and those of Fontane's own.[25] Despite Fontane's occasional (spurious) use of archaisms,[26] the reader is never allowed to forget that the novella's characters would not recognize the language in which they themselves are brought to life. In applying a contemporary style to seventeenth-century events, Fontane makes the nineteenth century loudly heard.

Yet the historical setting of *Grete Minde* is more than just a way for Fontane to highlight the self-aware contingencies of his own poetics, or a wellspring of material on which he can exercise his synthetic and empathic imagination, but also a thematic element in its own right.[27] It is of course impossible to overstate the impact of the Reformation and its ensuing wars on the political and cultural landscape of Europe. In his *Geschichte des Dreißigjährigen Kriegs* (*History of the Thirty Years' War*), Friedrich Schiller, while lamenting the extent of the war's devastation, nevertheless appeals to something like the cunning of history in his assessment of its outcome:

> Terrible and destructive indeed were the first effects in which this general political sympathy announced itself. . . . But Europe emerged free and unsubjugated from this dreadful war, through which it learned for the first time to see itself as a interdependent community of nations, and this fellow feeling between the nations . . . would be in itself enough of a benefit to reconcile the world citizen to the war's horrors.[28]

For Schiller, in other words, the main lesson of the Thirty Years' War is the birth of national self-determination and the establishment of a modern European order as laid out by the Peace of Westphalia. Indeed, Schiller does not hesitate to describe the religious aspects of the war as a historical ruse through which the cause of national sovereignty is set in motion: "The most urgent motives drawn from reasons of state fail to move the ordinary subject [lassen den Untertan kalt], who seldom understands, and still more rarely cares. In such circumstances, the only course of action left to a politically astute ruler is to bind the interests of state to some other interest nearer to the people's heart."[29] Sectarian fervor allows heads of state to mobilize private individuals disinterested in political matters to political action, channeling personal passions and in-group identification for the greater good of all.

For the more skeptical Fontane, however, the lesson to be drawn from the theological and political battles of early modern Europe is rather a different one. Fontane focuses precisely on what Schiller, in his concern for matters of state and nation, largely leaves out: the effects of such world-historical events on the lives of those individuals themselves.[30] Many of the characters in *Grete Minde* comment ruefully on the changing times. "Yes, child, I've lived through many different ages" (Ja, Kind, ich habe viele Zeiten gesehen), explains the prioress of the now expropriated Arendsee cloister to Grete, "For, you should know, I'm almost ninety-five years old, and I was already born and baptized when the doctor from Wittenberg went to Worms and stood before the Emperor Charles V."[31] The head of the itinerant acting troupe recollects, "And all that [the state seizure of church property] was done by your previous prince-elector, your Herr Joachim, who I even got to see get buried. Was the first time my dear departed father came up from Wittenberg. '71, and I was still a child."[32] Meanwhile, the human cost of the coming wars is darkly prefigured in the thoughts of the town's pastor, Gigas, on the occasion of the visit of the recently converted Kurfürst Johann Sigismund: "How was he to face the noble prince? The apostate, who perhaps wanted to drag everything in town and country down to ruin and perfidy! And as brave as Gigas was, he was overcome by a wave of fear and weakness [Und so mutig Gigas war, es kam ihm doch ein Bangen und eine Schwachheit an]."[33]

As the descendant of French Calvinist Huguenots who sought refuge in Lutheran Prussia, the theme of confessional conflict was already, so to speak, Fontane's birthright.[34] In fact, the theme of differences in religious belief and praxis—as well as, often, the difference *between* belief and praxis—is a not infrequent one in Fontane's work: one thinks, for example, of the lapsed Catholic Roswitha in *Effi Briest*, or the mixed-faith marriage of Graf Adam and Franziska in *Graf Petöfy*.[35] Yet it is only in *Grete Minde* that the theme of denominational difference plays a central role in the plot itself.[36] The lines in the sand are drawn, literally and figuratively, already in the very first scene of the novella. When the young Valtin scratches out Grete's name in the dirt of the ground where they are playing, Grete's inability to read the letters of her own name reminds her of the fact that Valtin has recently begun to take lessons with Gigas, whose weird looks and stern manner, Grete says, she finds frightening. Valtin immediately dismisses Grete's qualms—but not, however, without raising some of his own:

> "It's all right," reassured Valtin. "Gigas is good. So long as you're not a Calv'nist or a Cath'lic. Then right away he gets mad, and all fire and flame."
>
> "Yes, see, that's just it . . ."
>
> Valtin kept on drawing lines with the stick. Finally he said: "So is it true your mother was a Cath'lic?"[37]

Although Gigas will prove to be a far more tolerant clergyman than the thirteen-year-old Grete imagines, Grete is not wrong to suspect that her mother's Catholicism will turn out dangerous for her in the long run. Grete's exotic parentage marks her from the beginning as an outsider, whose religious and racial otherness makes her an object of suspicion and contempt even within her own family. Even before she runs away from Tangermünde, Grete is treated as a heretic and a wanton—in Trud's words, the bearer of "a dead obedience [ein toter Gehorsam], of which the heart knows nothing"[38]—gradually sowing in her the seeds of a justified resentment and leading to the "fire and flame," indeed, of her savage end.[39]

But perhaps the biggest problem with Grete's ancestry, at least in terms of the novella's thematics, is, once again, the problem of the *image*. As is well known, the conflicts over the representation of the divine image and of the incarnated presence of God flared up dramatically in the years following the Protestant Reformation, with consequences not just for fine art, but also for the idea of representation as a whole.[40] In his 1522 polemic "Von Abtuhung der Bilder" ("On the Removal of Images")—the text that would rekindle the iconoclastic debate in the German-speaking world—the Protestant theologian Andreas Karlstadt rebuts Pope Gregory I's widely influential claim that religious images are defensible as teaching tools for the illiterate: in Gregory I's words, the "books of the laity" (bucher der Leyhen).[41] "How can a piece of wood or a lump of stone teach?" (Wie kahn ein holtz oder stein lerenn?), Karlstadt counters, quoting from the prophet Habakkuk, "It may well be decorated with silver or gold, but there is no spirit in it" (Ehr ist woll mit silber oder golth getzyrtt / aber keyn geyst ist yhn yhm).[42] For Karlstadt, as for other Protestant iconoclasts, the religious image is not merely an unreliable expedient to Christian teaching, but a wholesale travesty of God's true nature: "For we call the crucified image [das gecreutzigt bild] a lord god and . . . venerate it as though Christ himself were present. . . . Thus we give the images the same name as the things God loves, and prove our guilt with our words and deeds that images are our gods."[43] For all the potential guidance that certain images might bring, one must not confuse the signifier with the signified, the cause with its effects. The true presence of God, the proper object of devotion, is the Word; "our pictures," by contrast, "are things with which our eyes commit whoredom [mit welchen / vnßere augen bulen / vnd puben]."[44]

Fontane himself was both aware of the history of Protestant *Bilderstürmerei* and sensitive to its ravages. Already in his 1860 Scottish travelogue *Jenseit des Tweed* (*Beyond the Tweed*), he makes passing reference to the lasting cultural consequences of iconoclastic destruction:

> Taste and comfort found a home here very late. When Scotland entered into close political relations with France during the sixteenth century, the country's conditions were still so poor and desperate that there was not the least thought among the population of any competition or emulation. Puritanism took care of the rest; whatever remained of treasures and models of good taste, it burned them to the ground or stripped them of their beauty. Seclusion, poverty, and the purely inwardly oriented religious life of the Scottish people combined to make it difficult for both art and its never-failing companions, comfort and luxury, to establish themselves in the land and gain the rights of residence [Bürgerrecht]. Here the house remained but a plain stone building with small doors and few windows, a bulwark against wind and weather, a fortress, solid, close, warm, but—bare.[45]

Fontane is far too equanimous a tour guide to take a strong position on the Scottish Reformation, but it is nevertheless clear from the above passage that his sympathies lie more with the lovers of "comfort and luxury" (Komfort und Luxus) than with the preachers of militant asceticism. Indeed, Fontane makes a point of praising art and beauty, not just for their own sakes, but as the very preconditions for human happiness, pleasure, conviviality, stability, and civil society at large. And yet, the fact that Fontane almost immediately turns the conversation from "treasures and models of good taste" (Schätzen und Vorbildern guten Geschmacks) to domestic questions of house and home means that Fontane is not completely insensitive to the pull of the iconoclastic argument. Images are neither sinful nor useless for Fontane, but they are still *ancillary*, valuable primarily insofar as they promote the greater goals of sociality, pleasure, and communal well-being.

Fontane directly addresses these problems in *Grete Minde* in the fifth chapter of the novella, in the narration of Grete's first visit to the pastor Gigas. When Gigas asks a testing question about the nature of her prayers, Grete guilelessly recites a pious little song that she has learned from her nursemaid Regine, a Catholic just as Grete's late mother had been. Gigas wastes no time in reproaching Grete, gently but firmly, for the song's implicit espousal of the anathematized doctrine of good works.[46] But the real heresy is yet to come:

> "For you see, all our good works are nothing and mean nothing, for all our actions are sinful from the very beginning. We have nothing but faith, and there is only one thing that can atone for us and that has value [sühnet und Wert hat]: the Crucified One."
>
> "Yes, sir . . . I know . . . and I have a sliver from his cross." And in happy agitation she pulled a golden capsule from her bodice.
>
> Gigas recoiled for a moment, and his red eyes seemed to have become even redder. But he gathered himself again quickly . . . and said calmly: "That is idolatry, Grete."[47]

The main significance of this dialogue, of course, lies in its character-establishing function, allowing Fontane to set up the combination of innocence and otherness in Grete that will be the source of so many of her troubles. But it also sets up the leitmotif that will be pursued throughout the novella: the worship of the material object and its implications for (realist) art. "The maker of images makes an image" (Der bildmacher mach eyn bilde), writes Karlstadt, referencing Isaiah 44:18, "and bows before it. . . . Thus, they have forgotten that the eyes of the image do not see and that they have no understanding in their hearts [das die augen der bilder nicht sehen und das sie in yrem hertze nicht verstehnd]."[48] Karlstadt's ostensibly faithful quoting of Isaiah in this passage in fact contains a significant reinterpretation. For in Isaiah, it is not the idols who are blind, as Karlstadt has it, but, more expectedly, the idolaters in their ignorance: "They have not known nor understood: for he hath shut their eyes, that they cannot see; and their hearts, that they cannot understand" (Sie wissen nichts und verstehen nichts; denn sie sind verblendet, daß ihre Augen nicht sehen und ihre Herzen nicht merken können).[49] That is, where the prophet's condemnation is based merely on the idol's materiality—"I have burned part of it in the fire; yea, also I have baked bread upon the coals thereof; I have roasted flesh, and eaten it: and shall I make the residue thereof an abomination? shall I fall down to the stock of a tree?"[50]—Karlstadt's abjuration rests on the material idol's failure to *be* the divinity that it promises, to open the eyes and the heart that it still seems, all too vividly, to possess. Karlstadt's silent rewriting of the biblical passage thus reinscribes the livingness of the inanimate image into the very effort to establish its deadness. What for the prophet is a mere absurdity, is for Karlstadt the disgust that arises from disappointed love.

Karlstadt himself is surprisingly candid about the ambivalence of his position. In a remarkable and oft-commented passage, he admits that the violence of his repudiation of the image is only matched by the violence of his desire for it:

> Now I want . . . to confess my secret thoughts to the whole world with sighs and admit that I am faint-hearted and know that I ought not to stand in awe of any image and am certain that God expects of his people that they should not stand in awe of images [olgotzen]. . . . But (I lament to God) from my youth onward my heart has been trained and grown up in the veneration and worship of pictures [erbiethung vnd wolachtung der bildnis]. And a harmful fear has been bred into me from which I would gladly deliver myself and cannot. As a consequence, I stand in fear that I might not be able to burn idols. I would fear that some devil's joker [der Teuffels narr] would do me injury. Although, on the one hand, I have Scripture and know that images have no power and also have neither life, nor blood, nor spirit, yet, on the other hand, fear holds me and makes me stand in awe of the image of a devil, a shadow, the noise of a small leaf falling, and makes me flee that which I should confront in a manly way. . . . Had I not heard the spirit of God cry out against the idols and read his Word, I would have thought: I do not love any image; I do not stand in awe before any image. But now I know how I, in this case, stand toward God and images, and how strongly and deeply images are rooted in my heart.[51]

While it would be simplistic to claim Karlstadt's ambivalence as the source of iconoclastic movements in general, his argument in this passage is nonetheless revealing. On the one hand, as Karlstadt stresses, the sinfulness of idolatry has less to do with the image per se and more to do with the image's ability to take on meaning in *excess* of its materiality, seducing the observer away from spiritual divinity to its sensual imitation. However, the rejection of the image's spiritual content demanded by the iconoclastic position—and indeed, by any depotentiation of symbolic representation—results in the image being in excess in a different sense: as a *mere* image or empty sensuous appearance, a meaningless presence all the more meaningless for the meaning once attributed to it. This is the double bind of the iconoclastic position: if the enchanted image is wicked, the disenchanted image is godforsaken. And this double bind is not only at odds with the homey aesthetic pleasures that Fontane misses in Scottish interiors (not to mention the homey aesthetic pleasures of realist description), but also bears upon that most fundamental of Christian beliefs, the doctrine of the Incarnation itself. "And the Word was made flesh, and dwelt among us, . . . full of grace [Gnade] and truth":[52] *this* was a dogma that few but the most radical of sectarians wished to reject. What changes, then, between the Hebrew prophet and the Protestant theologian is the idea that the true divinity could *ever* take visible form. As Karlstadt's fellow iconoclast John Calvin writes: "Daily experience teaches, that the flesh is never satisfied, till it has obtained some image, resembling itself, in which it may be foolishly gratified, as an image of God. In almost all ages, from the creation of the world, in obedience to this stupid propensity, men have erected visible representations, in which they believed God to be presented to their carnal eyes."[53] But for Christian thought, God *has* appeared to "carnal eyes," in a form that can, like any other sensate body, be represented and reproduced.

More effective than destroying the idol, then, is to split it in two. Therefore, as Jennifer Waldron has argued, "Protestant iconoclasm was founded on a double theological investment": on the one hand, the glorification of the human being as a "motivated" carrier of meaning, and on the other, the abjection of the inanimate thing as something for which the attribution of meaning is entirely arbitrary.[54] The "lingering vibrancy of matter in the early modern period" entails a compensatory insistence, in contrast to the sanctified immateriality of human vitality, "that nonliving matter was in fact 'dead.' "[55] Iconoclasm perpetuates itself, not only in the disappearance of representation (all the way to the "end of art") but also in the simultaneously empty and excessive presence of the images and artifacts that remain. Art's sensuousness loses its soul: "In the pure, cold light of the Reformation, everything the church holds takes on a hideous and obscene shape."[56]

Vera Icon

Naturally, by the time Fontane sits down to write *Grete Minde*, the violent repudiation of the image is long since a thing of the past. However, German realism's "return to materiality" (Rückkehr zur Dinglichkeit),[57] with its interest in signifying objects, reanimates the iconoclastic debate with a fervor unseen since the Reformation's hylephobic purges. "Idol worship doesn't get any better just because you put a freshly dressed up fetish on the altar" (Der Götzendienst wird darum nicht besser, wenn man einen neu aufgeputzten Fetisch auf den Altar stellt), remarks Julian Schmidt in a polemic against the so-called *Märzpoeten*.[58] If religion, as W. J. T. Mitchell argues in a gloss of Lessing's aesthetics, "fetters painting by removing it from its proper vocation, the representation of beautiful bodies in space, and enslaves it to a foreign concern, the expression of 'significance' through 'symbolic representations,' "[59] such fettering is, from another perspective, precisely the point. That is, for the post-neoclassical humanism of the nineteenth century, the problem is less the semantic supplements that are added to images than the presence of images *without* such supplements. No matter how beautiful, the representation of bodies in space for their own sake results in nothing but an eclectic, "meaningless" (inhaltslos) art, in which artists "stored up the pagodas of Japan, the vases of Pompeii, the icons of the Rhenish-Byzantine school, and the new-fashioned abstractions in a great heap of curiosities, and delighted in these motley images with childish joy [sich in kindischem Behagen an diesen bunten Bildern ergötzte]."[60]

For the programmatic realists, at least—among whom Fontane may, with qualifications, be included[61]—the challenge was thus to find the universal idea within the particular manifestation and to establish, in contrast to both allegorical belaboredness and pagan allotria, a necessary reconciliation of world and spirit. In this context, it is anything but incidental that Fontane rewrites *Grete Minde*'s story partly as a religious conflict: for such reconciliation was conceived of not only as a modern, but also as a *Protestant* accomplishment. Schmidt formulates this idea succinctly at the end of the first volume of *Geschichte der deutschen Literatur im neunzehnten Jahrhundert* (*History of German Literature in the Nineteenth Century*):

> Protestantism gathered together the contraries of the divine and the earthly within the human heart, where they unfolded in concrete fullness; whereas in both the old Church and the new Jesuitism, heaven and earth were two worlds, which opposed one another in a completely external way [sich ganz äußerlich bekämpften]. For the true Protestant poet, life, character is a continuity, the soul an organic whole.[62]

To wit: the doctrinal problem of how to worship the incarnate God without worshipping incarnation as such maps directly onto programmatic realism's epistemological-aesthetic problem of how to deal with the phenomenal world such that one neither prostrates oneself before the indiscriminate fantasies of an enervated Romanticism, nor succumbs (in what for Schmidt and company is but a logical consequence) to a vulgar fascination with the merely sensual.[63] The fatal error made by both materialism and Catholicism is that of separating the material and the spiritual worlds, and then worshipping matter in spirit's stead (in materialism deliberately, in Catholicism so to speak merely as by-product). When it is then realized—as it will always be realized—that the spiritualization of this matter is not intrinsic but arbitrary, what is left is matter alone, dead substance, the idol as corpse.

Thus it is neither chance nor antiquarianism nor local historical interest that leads Fontane to adapt the story of Margarete von Minden for his second longer work of fiction. Conrad Wandrey's early complaint that, "if

[Fontane's] intention [in *Grete Minde*] was to bring the historical background to life through these allusions to the bitter wars of religion, then he went too far"[64] gets it exactly backward: the religious conflicts of *Grete Minde* are not an ornamental backdrop to the novella but its thematic core, the motive force of its plot and the reason for its telling. What Gigas accuses Grete of in her childish naïveté is also what was perceived as the main danger of a realist literature in the German-speaking world: the investment of objects and bodies with a meaning that they do not actually possess. Yet this same act of investing objects and bodies with meaning is also one of the main tasks of the realist writer, who is obliged to portray a world both concrete and coherent, insofar as it is the concrete world in which the coherency of life unfolds. Thus, where Friedrich Schlegel had once demanded that the novel offer "the absolute in voluptuousness and sensuality,"[65] Fontane, half a century later, stresses the insufficiency of *mere* sensual presence in literature, which "relates to true realism as crude ore to metal: the refinement is missing" (verhält sich zum echten Realismus wie das rohe Erz zum Metall: die Läuterung fehlt).[66]

As noted in the introduction, the refinement that Fontane demands here can be summed up in his corresponding concept—borrowed from the language of the Gospels—of "Verklärung."[67] For Wolfgang Preisendanz, "Verklärung" is that authorial distance or stylistic remove (similar to Hegel's "objective humor") through which the literary work marks itself as a literary work and, hence, as something distinct from real life.[68] But Fontane's own idea is actually both more specific and more comprehensive than this. With his dialogue-driven, inference-heavy novels—in which what exposition there is occurs almost entirely through the characters' own observations and perceptions—Fontane does more than just emphasize the *author's* role in the mediation of reality; he shows how reality is always already mediated, always already inevitably shaped by the thoughts and contexts of those living within it.[69] Indeed, as Thomas Pfau has demonstrated, Fontane not only consistently draws the reader's attention from the object to the character's perception of the object; he also (in what Pfau sees as an anticipation of Husserl's theory of image consciousness) draws the reader's attention from the character's perception of the object to the awareness of the experience of that perception, sketching out a "process of 'pictorialization' ['Verbildlichung']" in which image and understanding occur simultaneously, so to speak, as a function of their mutual constitution.[70]

In this way, even the most seemingly trivial or incidental detail is raised up into meaning (in an engagement with the phenomenal world far more natural than Freytag's person/thing dialectic): no longer for its own sake, nor for the meanings it might betoken, but, now, for the *consciousness* that it facilitates. Fontane's position might thus seem to recall Schelling's Schillerian description of grace (*Anmut*) as "the soul of form, or nature's soul" (die Seele der Form, oder die Naturseele).[71] However, for Fontane, the point is "to give nature, not a soul, but . . . language."[72] In other words, instead of an idea of the inner vitality of the object, Fontane emphasizes the object as a site of *discourse*. (This is also why the object in Fontane need not only mean the art object, because the focus is less on the image's creation than on its being apprehended.) Thereby is the phenomenal world as it were automatically transformed into the articulation of human activity and ideas, "if we may be allowed this facetious expression, a '*representation of interests*' ['*Interessenvertretung*'] in its own fashion."[73] In place of the impossible access to the Real enters a real*ism* of psychological and sociological verisimilitude: the *conditional* glory of a world that matters insofar as it is illuminated by those who live it.

Again, Fontane's objections to a purely naturalist or naively mimetic art are well known. What is less well known, however, is the pull exerted by such mimesis on Fontane himself. As Fontane puts it in a 1854 letter to Theodor Storm: "My inclination and—if I may be permitted to speak thus—my forte is description [Schilderung]. My depictions of internal states may occasionally be deficient, external things I have in my power [Am Innerlichen mag es gelegentlich fehlen, das Äußerliche hab' ich in der Gewalt]."[74] Thus it is clear that the much lauded subordination of description to narrative in Fontane's work is not natural but, to the contrary, hard-won. "Only when I have history as a basis do I have powers at my disposal that are otherwise foreign to me, like one who regains his strength as soon as his feet once again touch native soil":[75] without the ballast of historical event, however, the connection between visual description and spiritual phenomena remains—at least, in Fontane's self-assessment—elusive.

In this light, Fontane's work as a whole—and *Grete Minde* in particular—can be read as an attempt to stake out a moderate Lutheran (so to speak, Gigasian) position between an antiquated idolatry and a fanatical iconoclasm, between the fetishistic adoration of the image and its wholesale rejection. Here, however, the moderate position is also the riskiest one: for it admits the necessity of both the sensual world and its representation, but is unable to guarantee that this representation will not usurp that for which it should, at best, be only an instance. Such riskiness can be seen, for example, in the description of Grete's gold reliquary that forms the midpoint of the aforementioned dialogue with Gigas (elided in the previous quotation of the scene):

> Gigas recoiled for a moment, and his red eyes seemed to have become even redder. But he gathered himself again quickly and took the capsule and looked at it. It hung on a little chain. In the top section of the capsule was a Holy Mother of God, etched in fine lines, but underneath was a little piece of red silk, and inside that, the sliver of wood. The old man snapped the lid shut . . .[76]

The ekphrasis embedded within this passage—just as Grete's Virgin is embedded in her capsule—momentarily brings the action to a standstill, fixing the reader's attention, along with Gigas's, on the static presence of the idolatrous image. To be sure, such a double fixation is already a kind of narrative privileging: in a typically canny move, Fontane uses the shock of ekphrastic description to yoke the reader's fascination to Gigas's own, and thus to draw attention *away* from the passage's ekphrasis back to character, story, and affect. Yet such a move still takes nothing away from the ambivalent attraction of the sacred/taboo image itself—suspended, as so often, on the exemplary thingliness of the female figure.[77] Indeed, the ambivalent attraction of the portrait is only further emphasized by the description of Grete's Virgin as being "etched in fine lines" (in feinen Linien eingegraben); the not merely homophonic relationship between engraving and the grave is here made all but literal by the fact that Grete's capsule is also a heirloom from her late mother: "the only thing I have from her" (alles, was ich von ihr hab').[78] And underneath this dead image, problematic enough, lies the truth of the picture itself: the fetish object, the same bit of wood that Karlstadt, evoking Isaiah, reminds his readers is also used to cook meat and warm bodies, tucked suggestively into the forbidden depths of the capsule's "little piece of red silk" (rotes Seidenläppchen). In other words, what for Grete is the signifier of faith and motherly love is for Gigas only a seductive and scandalous bit of debris: at best, the memento mori of itself, a symbol for the always potential petrification of a merely sensual belief and art. Grete's relic—in both senses of the word—figures the process by which things come to reveal the suspect nature of their own meaningfulness.[79]

This theme of the process of the disappearance of the meaningfulness of things, their slide into obsolescence and illegibility, forms no less than the hidden leitmotif of Fontane's novella as a whole. In the pivotal chapter "At the Wendish Stone" ("Am Wendenstein"), in which Grete makes her fateful resolution to run away from home, Grete and Valtin climb up on a hill outside of town to get a look at the festivities surrounding the visit of the local prince-elector (the aforementioned Johann Sigismund). Before they can reach a proper vantage point, however, the children tire out and turn into the deep grass, where they come suddenly upon an old earthwork:

> On top of this earthwork there was an oddly shaped boulder [ein Feldstein von absonderlicher Form], so thickly covered over with lichens that only a few half weathered-away characters could be laboriously made out. This boulder was then what they sat on.
>
> "What does the stone mean?" asked Grete.
>
> "I don't know. Maybe it's a Wendish grave."
>
> "How's that?"
>
> "Don't you know? This is the field where the great battle of Tanger was. Heathens and Christians. And the heathens won. And on either side of this earthwork we're sitting on, in front of us right up to the woods and behind us all the way to the river, they lie in the thousands."[80]

Fontane's *Wendepunkt am Wendenstein* thus turns, not just on a material object, but on a material object that has been overgrown, worn away, eroded to the point where it cannot really be decided if it ever had a significance at all. A merely potential pagan fetish, it rises up doubly dead above the thousands of corpses to which it fails even to bear proper witness. Grete's question about what the stone "means" not only echoes Gigas's words about the doctrine of works years earlier; it also repeats his message: letters, stone, works, and relics all "mean nothing," but only refer in their lack of signification to the signification they can no longer promise.[81]

At times a strange fetish quality even attaches to Grete herself, indeed from her very first appearance:

> Only now did her figure [Gestalt] come into view. She was a half-grown girl [Es war ein halbwachsenes Mädchen], very delicately built, and her fine lines, but even more the oval and the color of her face, indicated a foreigner [eine Fremde].[82]

As in the lesson scene between Grete and Gigas, here a short descriptive passage brings a temporary but precipitous halt to the novella's flow of dialogue, forcing the reader to linger on static appearance rather than being carried along by dramatic action. But it is not only this fact that binds these two moments together: in one of Fontane's many internal allusions, the "fine lines" (feinen Linien) of Grete's physiognomy are the precise words that will later be used in the scene with Gigas to describe the image of the Virgin in Grete's reliquary. One way of reading this connection, of course, would be to see it as a pointed identification on Fontane's part—against the opinion of conventional morality—between the innocence of the Virgin Mary and that of Grete. But another way of reading it is to note that, in allying the two images, Fontane presents Grete herself proleptically and from the beginning as an effigy, an idol, in the vignette-like oval of her face already en-capsulated as an object of adoration, of desire, and, indeed, of death. Greta's delicate prepubescent beauty (the *other* thing she "has" from her mother) is to the novella as her icon is to her: an object that draws the attention away from spiritual matters and holds it instead within the idolatrous fascination of pure surface.

The troubling implications of such a connection are only strengthened by Fontane's barely latent sexualization (or rather, genitalization) of Grete's locket, with its silky red lining half concealing the tiny salvific sliver. One does not have to have had read one's Freud here to notice a certain connection between ekphrasis, the female genitals (more specifically, the phallic female genitals), and the sexual or religious fetish. Indeed, the ambivalent voyeurism that for Freud is the very condition of the fetish's creation is also the problem of ekphrastic description and religious idolatry alike: the gaze that comes to a stop, "half-way, as it were,"[83] between the progressively revealed features of the mother's body and the simultaneously feared and desired sight of her nonexistent penis is the same gaze that causes Grete to reverently carry her locket as a piece of the True Cross, the gaze that fixes on particular images and objects as a pathological surrogate for a never-to-be-reached whole. Whatever one thinks of the psychological truth of the female phallus, it is not too difficult to see that the concept functions in part as a metaphor for an idea of physical and ontological completeness as a defense against the disaggregated segments of the "castrated" and "wounded" body. And it is also not too difficult to extend this idea of physical and ontological completeness to that of the completeness of meaning in general—something Lacan later only makes explicit in his description of the phallus as "the signifier that is destined to reveal meaning effects as a whole, insofar as the signifier conditions them by its presence as signifier."[84] The fetish is the figurative protection against the loss of those "meaning effects," a preemptive compensation for the lack where a fullness of signification should be.[85]

But just as the creation of the fetish does not extinguish the premonition of the lack of that for which it offers compensation, the disenchantment of the fetish does not make the fetish itself disappear. It persists—but now as the remnants of itself, a merely material presence with "neither life, nor blood, nor spirit" (weder leben / bluth / nach geist).[86] And such a lifeless presence is not limited to gold, silver, and wood, as Karlstadt would have it, but extends—as the parallels between Grete's physiognomy and the image of the Virgin in her mother's locket make clear—to that ultimate bearer of signification in the age of humanism, the human face itself. In defiance of the realist emphasis on the transfiguring power of the human "heart," Grete's exotically beautiful face already shows up from the beginning as something sensually "dis-figured,"[87] as foreign and unreadable as the heathen stone about which she will later inquire. In the icon-like oval of Grete's face, as in the idolatrous bit in Grete's locket and the "half weathered-away characters" (halb verwitterte Schriftzeichen) of the Wendish megalith, Fontane registers the fear that is, so to speak, the flip side of Achilles's shield: if the image can be spurred to life through narrative and affect, the loss of narrative and affect might return the image to its alien physical presence, to a material signifier with nothing any more to signify. And though Fontane is no iconophobe, his paired descriptions of Grete's reliquary and Grete's face still function as a plangent warning against the adoration of the image—including the human image—as a substitute for more "real," intangible forms of signification. As Fontane's own genially ironic attitude toward the preoccupations and conventions of the past already shows, in the end *any* image may be exposed as an idol, a fashion, a "meaning effect"—a fetish in whose innocence only children and heathens believe.[88]

In the Puppet, or in the God

Nowhere are the repercussions of such disenchantment more apparent than in the subplot of the "traveling people" (fahrende Leute), the itinerant actors whom Grete and Valtin join after their elopement and whose performances of "The Last Judgment" and "The Fall"—in that order—effectively bookend the novella. With this subplot, Fontane evokes the Reformation-era campaigns against the theater, for which Trud's Cromwellian comment "It disgusts me to see God and the Devil as mere puppets" (Es wiedersteht mir, Gott und Teufel als bloße Puppen zu sehen)[89] is only the most explicit of the novella's many references. While Fontane's sympathies clearly lie neither with Trud nor with her theatrophobic (and xenophobic)[90] convictions—"That's just something Trud drummed into your head" (Das hat dir Trud ins Gewissen gered't),[91] says Emrentz to Grete when she wonders aloud about the performance's permissibility—Trud's critique is nevertheless allowed to resonate uneasily in the novella, which shrewdly equivocates on both the aesthetic value and the moral propriety of the puppeteers' art. "They're only puppets" (Es sind ja Puppen), Valtin reassures the young Grete just before the first curtain rises, whereupon Grete responds, in an observation that could stand as motto for the novella as a whole: "But they mean something, and I don't know if it's right" (Aber sie bedeuten was, und ich weiß doch nicht, ob es recht ist).[92]

Indeed, in many ways, the novella does not contradict, but actually corroborates Trud's critique, portraying the puppeteers' work as a gaudy popular spectacle, in which not only the sublimity of religion but also the spiritual content of art has been all but eradicated:

> The Last Judgment! Dramatic spectacle in three acts, with Christ and Mary, including the reward for the virtuous and the damnation of the wicked. Also angels and devils, and a fireworks extravaganza, but without any banging or shooting and suchlike hazardousness [ohne Knall und Schießen und sonstige Fährlichkeit] in order to not, so we hope, be in any way troublesome or displeasing to "the lovely ladies."[93]

Such pageantry brings the Last Judgment dangerously close to the profane processions of the medieval carnival, in which holy images were intentionally degraded—in Mikhail Bakhtin's phrase, made to undergo "a transfer to the material level"[94]—in a humorous and holiday mood.[95] The ambivalent status of theatrical presentation is then emblematized in the disaster that takes place during the performance: when a lit bit of paper falls into a vat of fireworks, the simulated hellfire of the "Last Judgment" turns into real flames, causing a series of explosions that clears the theater and sends Grete into a nervous swoon. "I knew it," Trud comments, hearing the blasts from afar, "God doesn't allow Himself to be mocked" (Gott läßt sich nicht spotten).[96] Yet this apparently divine sanction of what Jonas Barish calls "the antitheatrical prejudice"[97] is not quite as clear-cut as Trud's gloating would have it. For what the explosion in the theater demonstrates is in fact less the blasphemous falseness of the theatrical spectacle than the seductive realness of its effects:

"And then, where the play had been, everything was smoke and fumes and fire" (Denn da, wo das Spiel gewesen war, war alles Rauch und Qualm und Feuer), Grete says upon waking from her faint, "and I thought that the Last Day had come" (und ich dachte, der Letzte Tag sei da).[98] Unlike the level-headed Valtin, whose disbelief in the reality of the performance also allows him to pull Grete away from the fire in time and save the day, Grete observes the performance with a naive mixture of credulousness and awe. But if this reaction puts her at odds with her skeptical friend, it also puts her strangely in line with the opinions of her narrow-minded stepsister: Trud's conviction that the fire is a divine judgment on the troupe's performance means that, for all her puritanism, she too believes, in her way, in the literalness of the theatrical incarnation. Grete's awe and Trud's contempt are two sides of the same icon: the one a faith in the potency of the signifier as the thing it represents, the other a faith in the potency of the signifier as the evil of its own emptiness.

Fontane dramatizes the problem of theatrical signification in the dialogue between Trud and her more tolerant—indeed, hedonistic[99]—father-in-law:

> "You're too severe, Trud, and the reason is that you only know our Tangermünde ways. And in Alt-Gardelegen it's the same. But out there in the world, in the great states and cities, there art dares to represent the highest and most holy [da wagt sich die Kunst an alles Höchste und Heiligste], and there are pious and esteemed masters who have neither thought nor wrote nor painted nor sculpted anything but the glory of Heaven and the horrors of Hell."
>
> "I know all about that, father," said Trud dismissively. "I've seen those kinds of pictures in our church in Gardelegen, but a picture is different than a puppet."
>
> "Picture or puppet," smiled the old man. "They want the same thing, and that makes them the same."
>
> "And yet, father, I believe there's a difference if a pious and esteemed master, as you put it, paints a picture to the glory of God, or if an unchristian man traipses around the countryside with a Turk woman and a Merry Andrew for profit's sake and fills the taverns with his play and empties the churches."[100]

Trud's dislike of the theater seems at first to rest merely on the dissipation of the actors' lives and the unfairness of their box office advantage (an observation that leads the cynical Gerdt to remark that the fire and brimstone of Gigas's sermons, too, has no other goal than to fill the seats and the tithe box). But her comments also contain a more fundamental critique. For the theater is more than just a copy of a copy, that bugbear of all iconophobia since Plato. What Christopher Wild has called "the erotic mediality of the theater" means that even the most pious of theatrical performances is compromised from the beginning, "insofar as the act of watching is an expression of desire for the watched object *as* object on display."[101] Like the prostitution to which it was often compared,[102] the theatrical performance is a public display of flesh, a "moment of public exposure of something that should remain private, that is to say, hidden."[103] If the image is always potentially idolatrous, then the theater, dependent on the living embodiment of that which it represents, not only heightens the seductive verisimilitude of the image itself, but also exacerbates the confluence of sacred content and profane form to the point of intolerability.[104]

However, it is not merely the public display of private flesh that makes the theater inherently suspect. For the theater is, so to speak, the better fetish, whose images, unlike the dead matter of the icon and the relic, appear to move with the vivid force of life itself. It is thus instructive that Fontane—in a detail otherwise essentially irrelevant—specifically remarks on the transition in the latter half of the novella from puppets to live actors. Such a transition accurately (if anachronistically) reflects the history of German theater: in the theater reforms of the eighteenth and nineteenth centuries, the puppet theater in particular was targeted for elimination as a form of low popular spectacle, whose existence put the bourgeois theater's claims to aesthetic legitimacy into question.[105] In this sense, it would be easy to read *Grete Minde*'s theater reform as Fontane's symbol for art's progress toward an ever greater naturalism, in which the stock characters and schematic plots of the past are increasingly fleshed out with realistic human psychologies and differentiated, three-dimensional presences. Fontane presents just such a view in the naively bemused conversation of two farmworkers: "''N ye know, Hanne, they don' jest play no more wi' strings 'n puppets. Now they do all 'a that themselves.' 'Aye, I heard 'bout it too. Real people . . . Lawd, what all ye don' see now'days!' " ("Und weet'st all, Hanne, se speelen joa nicht blot mihr mit Zocken un Puppen. Se kümmen joa nu sülwer rut." "Joa; so hebb ick't ook hürt. Richt'ge Minschen . . . Jott, wat man nicht allens erlewen deiht!").[106] Despite what one might expect, however, the replacement of marionette figures with real human beings in *Grete Minde* does not lead simply to a greater humanization or true-to-lifeness of the theater. To the contrary, it results in a kind of marionettization of its human actors, in which they become mere fungible bodies fitted into their roles, no more than the living copies of their "wooden likeness" (hölzernen Abbild).[107] "Played twice every day," boasts the head actor to the innkeeper, "first the puppets and then us" (erst die Puppen und dann wir selber).[108] Or, as the novella's penultimate sentence relates, with heavy irony, on the "Turk woman" Zenobia's replacement of Grete in the performance of the "Original Sin": "No one noticed the change in the lineup" (Niemand achtete des Wechsels, der in Besetzung der Rollen stattgefunden hatte).[109]

Thus, if part of the sinfulness of the theater is that it travesties the notion of the human being created in God's image, the replacement of puppets with human actors does not solve, but only redoubles the theater's medial problem. For instead of displaying mere models of living form, now the theater puts real live human beings themselves on the stage. The "Turk woman" (Türkenweib) and the "Merry Andrew" (Pickelhering) come to life as the profane materialization of God's Word, superficially transfigured within their roles: a change of costume, but not of heart. The theater is thus no less than the effective perversion of the Incarnation, in whose anthropomorphic role-play both the human nature of Christ and the human being made in God's image are burlesqued for public amusement. Like the fascinating lineaments of Grete's face, the live theater turns the very thing that should be the counterpoint to idolatrous worship into an empty idol: the "motivated sign" of the human form itself.[110]

But this is perhaps not even the worst of it. As Wild argues, the problem with the theater's inherent *Schaulust* is not only that it obscures the distinction between seeming and being in its display of real human bodies with counterfeit souls, but also that, in doing so, it restages—again and again and again—the act of being seen and of seeing oneself being seen that is, as it were, the original sin of original sin itself.[111] This perpetual restaging of the Fall is carried out literally by the actors in *Grete Minde*. "'Member, Gret', 'ere's still 'nother play today" (Denk, Gret', 's gibt noch a Spiel heut'), Zenobia tells Grete, in what are, in fact, her only spoken lines; "They want the 'Rig'nal Sin.' Them folks don' give us no peace" (Den 'Sündfall' wollen's. Das Leutvolk laßt uns ka Ruh' nit).[112] Or again, in the loaded words of the head actor: "Played twice every day, first the puppets and then us. And always a full house and not an apple on the ground [Und immer voll, und kein Apfel zur Erde]."[113] Such repetition makes a mockery of the "origin" of original sin, turning representation (as a copy of an ur-image) into perpetual iterative performance. But it also makes the point that the theater, *as* performance, renews the eye-opening, self-denuding moment of the Fall each time it puts itself on, displaying the actors' bodies in an act of representation all the more brazen in this case for the symbiosis between medium and content.

Grete's own tale, of course, is itself a story of the loss of innocence and the birth of shame—so much so, in fact, that it is easy to overlook its theological and aesthetic implications in favor of the more evident drama of her social transgressions. These are not only concretely manifested in the form of her nameless infant child, but also linked to both the theater troupe and to Grete's final crime by Gerdt's vulgar double entendre to the Tangermünde aldermen: "I've got nothing in common with females who light their fires between hedge and ditch" (ich habe nichts gemein mit Weibern, die zwischen Heck und Graben ihr Feuer zünden).[114] Indeed, Fontane goes out of his way to emphasize the sexual aspect of Grete's shame in the response of the farmer who gives Grete a lift on her way back to Tangermünde, after she attempts to pay him for the trouble: "Naw, naw, miss, tha' won' do. Er are ye a missus?" (Nei, nei, Deern, dat geiht nich. O'r bist ne Fru?).[115] Grete's reaction to the farmer's question—all the more conspicuous because narratively unnecessary—makes its implications clear: "She turned red, but he noticed nothing and made a right onto the road through the field" (Sie wurde rot, aber er hatt es nicht acht und bog nach rechts hin in den Feldweg ein).[116]

However, if the connection between the loss of virginity and the fall from grace, fixed etymologically in the German word *Unschuld*, is only all too apparent in *Grete Minde*, the implications of Grete's shame also extend well beyond her violation of sexual norms. As Wild has shown, there is a connection between the early modern theater's desire to see and its myriad dramas of virginity tested, sullied, and put on trial. The truth of virginity, which is invisible to the eye—hence the farmer's question—is translated on the baroque stage into the violent mutilation and dismemberment of the female body. But, to the extent that its aim is to reveal the soul by destroying the body, torture fails: "The act of breaking open the shell of the body reveals only a purely material interiority, an interiority abandoned by the spirit. The secret of the body, its meaning, therefore lies hidden, not behind the veil of its border, the skin, but rather in the opaque depths of fleshliness itself."[117] Thus emerges the other aim of torture: the theatrical presentation of these "opaque depths of fleshliness" themselves as punishment by exposure. In lieu of an unavailable knowledge, the body is forced to show itself in its most inexorable materiality, displayed as a pile of degraded yet graspable parts where an integral but ungraspable person used to be.

"Original sin: the failure to be clothed in an essence."[118] As in the looping performances of *Grete Minde*'s players, in the martyred flesh of Gryphius's Catharina and Lohenstein's Epicharis is repeated, albeit in particularly drastic form, the aftermath of Adam and Eve's eating from the Tree of Knowledge: stripped of self-identity and self-evidence, the human body becomes a thing like any other, unconcealed in the fact of its material thereness. Of course, unlike either the heroines of the baroque theater or the historical Margarete von Minden, Fontane's Grete is neither tortured nor gruesomely executed for her crimes.[119] But the traces of her namesake's shameful end nevertheless remain: in the blush that spreads across her cheeks on the way to Tangermünde; in her nameless natural child tucked under her coat; in the daily exhibition of her body on the theatrical stage; in the homology between her own face and the fetishized face of the idol; and, not least, in her final appearance (in what is an unmistakable echo of the real Margarete's death at the stake) atop the burning beams of the church tower.[120] And this shameful exposure, or exposure as shame, to which Grete is repeatedly submitted is not only an evocative residue of baroque poetics or a criticism of hypocritical sexual mores, but also a commentary on the novella's own artistic methods. The shame of exposure is the obverse of *Verklärung*: in place of the transfiguration of the material world through the living human being, the human being is reified into lifeless matter. Realism's own "original sin" lies in its susceptibility to that reification, to the display of bodies of all kinds in the attempt to get at some essence, some tangible manifestation of an intangible grace that was once the world's birthright. Grete's fall—all her falls—is the mark of a guilt from which not only she, but literature itself must be saved.

The Devil's Joker

Given the convention of using artist figures as authorial stand-ins, it should come as no surprise that the plainest commentary in *Grete Minde* on the sociohistorical conditions of Fontane's novella is provided by the leader of the theater troupe—the "unchristian man" of Trud's aspersions—in the aforementioned tavern interlude. Remarking on a passing allusion to the nuns of Arendsee in an improvised drinking song, the actor exclaims:

> But where do you get the nuns? [Aber woher denn Nonnen?] There aren't any nuns any more. I mean, in this country. Down below, in the Empire, they've still got plenty. . . . But here! Everything abolished, what they call "secularizing" [Aber hier! Alles aufgehoben, was sie "säkularisieren" nennen].[121]

On the most literal level, the actor's words refer to the state seizure of church lands and property practiced throughout Europe from the Reformation to the nineteenth century: a bit of historical background that will be brought into the foreground in the very next chapter as Grete goes to petition the old abbess, now living almost alone in a slowly crumbling cloister, to provide Valtin with a Christian burial.[122] The actor's remarks, apparently incidental, both prefigure this scene and reinforce the importance of the novella's theme of religious tensions as a foreshadowing of far grimmer and more world-altering conflicts. Here, the "aufgehoben" of the above passage can be read with all its Hegelian connotations intact, as the decaying old order—Catholic, premodern, feudal—eventually gives way to the bourgeois Protestantism of Fontane's Prussia. But this is no simple triumphal history, and not only because the tactfully averted argument that threatens to break out between the actor and the innkeeper hints at the approaching decades of war, expulsion, and terror that remade Europe and upended the lives of, among others, Fontane's own ancestors.[123] As the ironic but rueful spokesperson for ecumenical tolerance, Fontane's actor also gives voice to what is lost in the process of "secularization" in the metaphysical as well as the juridical sense, recognizing, even as he acknowledges that the age of Catholic hegemony is over and done, the faded charm of its culture and the claims to dignity of its adherents: "As you like. Let's let the Junkers and the nuns be. Nuns have a right to exist too" (Meinetwegen. Lassen wir die Junker und die Nonnen. Es muß auch Nonnen geben).[124]

It is on the basis of such sentiments that Georg Lukács describes Fontane as a "wavering figure,"[125] critical of bourgeois values but unwilling to take a strong stance against the system that enables them. However, the disagreement in the tavern also suggests another interpretation of Fontane's ambivalence, one that touches on a cultural transition perhaps even more fundamental than that which interests Lukács. For the words of Fontane's actor also refer obliquely to his own art, which, born in the sacred spectacles of the medieval mystery play, now stands as a testament to the theater's commercialization and deritualization, that is, to its transformation from cultic practice to secular aesthetic activity. This shift, moreover, is one ushered in by Protestantism itself. Indeed, for the Reformation iconoclasts, it is primarily the religious aims of art, and not artistic representation per se, that is the source of its blasphemousness. "I am not so scrupulous as to think that no images ought ever to be permitted," writes Calvin,

> but since sculpture and painting are gifts of God, I wish for a pure and legitimate use of both; lest those things, which the Lord hath conferred on us for his glory and our benefit, be not only corrupted by preposterous abuse, but even perverted to our ruin. . . . We conclude, therefore, *that nothing should be painted and engraved but objects visible to our eyes*: the Divine Majesty, which is far above the reach of human sight, ought not to be corrupted by unseemly figures.[126]

Such a prescription would be at home in the strictest of realist programs—and not only because the rejection of the idea that sensual matter could ever serve as a representation of God leads to the grudging concession that it *may* represent the sensual world. As Hegel already saw, the essential mismatch in Christian art between spiritual content and concrete form eventually leads to the increasing arbitrariness of that form itself: "Romantic art leaves externality to go its own way again for its part freely and independently, and in this respect allows any and every material, down to flowers, trees, and the commonest household gear, to enter the representation without hindrance even in its contingent natural existence [auch in der natürlichen Zufälligkeit des Daseins ungehindert in die Darstellung einzutreten]."[127] The removal of a ritualistic role for sensual representation leads to an art in which any subject matter is available, insofar as anything can now potentially represent interior life. But the further consequence is an emptying out of the force of that subject matter, which, revealed as no more than a metaphor for something actually *un*able to be represented, reappears now as *true* contingency. What Gerhard Neumann has remarked in terms of the commodification of art in Fontane's *L'Adultera* goes double for the religious image in the age of its disenchantment: "The reservoir of images . . . no longer possesses authenticating force."[128]

In this way, even if the repertoire of *Grete Minde*'s acting troupe remains strictly scriptural in content, its performances confirm Walter Benjamin's insight into the melancholy immanence of the baroque *Trauerspiel* vis-à-vis the eschatological transcendence of the medieval mystery play. For Benjamin, the loss of a horizon of redemption in the baroque drama results in a shift from a *temporal* to a *spatial* model:

> The baroque knows no eschatology; and for that very reason it possesses no mechanism by which all earthly things are gathered in together and exalted before being consigned to their end. The hereafter is emptied of everything which contains the slightest breath of this world, and from it the baroque extracts a profusion of things which customarily escaped the grasp of artistic formulation and, at its high point, brings them violently into the light of day, in order to clear an ultimate heaven, enabling it, as a vacuum, one day to destroy the world with catastrophic violence.[129]

The baroque theater loses control over the objects it marshals against ontological emptiness. But the disenchanted theater of *Grete Minde*—once again befitting the strategic anachronicity of Fontane's text—also indicates something decidedly contemporary: for the worldliness that to the mystery play is unknown and to the *Trauerspiel* is a source of affliction is for the realist novel *formally necessary*. If the transition from mystery play to *Trauerspiel* results, for Benjamin, in that allegory whose function "is not so much to unveil material objects as to strip them naked,"[130] then the transformation from the melancholic ontotheology of the baroque mourning play to the compulsory secularism of the realist work implies the presentation of the material object as always already potentially naked, always already potentially deprived of the meaning that lies anyway outside it.

Thus, and with all due respect to Fontane's actor, what takes place in *Grete Minde* is less a secularization than a *profanation*, in the sense that Giorgio Agamben gives the term. For Agamben, secularization involves a change of focus, but not a change of quality. Profanation, by contrast, "neutralizes what it profanes": it strips away the charmed field that surrounds the phenomenon and "returns [it] to common use" in the form of deritualization and play.[131] But such profanation, for Fontane, is not merely (or not yet) the emancipatory practice that Agamben sometimes portrays it as. As Agamben himself writes, in a passage uncannily evocative of Karlstadt: "No one knows better than children how terrible and disquieting a toy can be once the game it forms a part of is over. The instrument of liberation turns into an awkward piece of wood; the doll on which the little girl has showered her love becomes a cold, shameful wax puppet."[132] And it is not just dolls that can turn cold and shameful: any object invested with meaning reverts to a dead presence as soon as that investment can no longer be sustained. Fontane therefore depicts profanation, not as a solution, but as a danger lurking within the disenchanted representations of realism itself. The ban on the representation of the divine leads to the resettlement of divinity in the inner life of the human being—but with this sanctification of human inner life returns the temptation to the idolatry of the sensual world in which that life unfolds, and which could at every moment cast off the meaningfulness it was supposed to have taken on and stand exposed again in its bare materiality. In the words of Samuel Weber (glossing Benjamin),

> From the moment when, in the spirit of the Reformation, all works are declared to be intrinsically empty, . . . the world of appearances . . . can no longer be taken for granted. The light that illuminates it no longer comes from within, . . . is no longer a *lumens naturale*. It comes from elsewhere, an elsewhere that bears no intrinsic relation or affinity to that which it illuminates. Like a *spotlight* . . . it casts a harsh glare, violating everything it thereby renders visible.[133]

From the inner illumination of *Verklärung* to the cold light of obscenity is but a short distance, crossed as soon as the faith in a greater power behind the "world of appearances" is lost. Just as the puppeteers' performances present biblical history as a constant iterative loop, the profane theater of Fontane's novella—both the theater presented within the novella, and the "theater" of the novella itself—performs the iconoclastic controversy as eternal return, in which, moreover, the repressed penal theater of the historical Margarete von Minden's tortured and dismembered body and the fetishized physicality of the disgraced Grete reappear as the all-too-vivid proof of the severability of material part from spiritual whole that the modified iconoclasm of "poetic realism" was designed precisely to circumvent.

It is thus no exaggeration to claim the anachronistic anomaly that is *Grete Minde* as the foundation of Fontane's realism, the novella in which not only Grete, but realism itself is put on trial. "Nothing but heathens and Turks" (Heiden und Türken sind's),[134] sneers Trud on the occasion of the traveling actors' appearance. However, such words do more than just bear witness to Trud's personal xeno- and iconophobia; they also hint at Fontane's own anxieties about the potential idolatry of mimetic representation, in which even the humanist phenomenalization of the image and the object fails to fully expunge the threat of their material presence. The compromise formations of poetic realism, which were to have laid such controversies to rest, in fact constitute their return: "And the heathens won" (Und die Heiden siegten).[135] But this victory, too, is a highly ambiguous one, shadowed from the beginning by forgetting, by sin, by travesty, by reification, by torture, and by death. In this way, Fontane's reinterpretation of the terrible fate of Grete Minde presents his tentative exploration of iconoclasm as a kind of tragedy in its own right, the difficulty of poetic realism to sustain the delicate equilibrium that is the condition of its existence.

Chapter 4

✦

Presence as Profanation

Arno Holz

> There is no Redemption of the object. Somewhere there is a "remainder," which the subject cannot lay hold of, which he believes he can overcome by profusion, by accumulation, and which in the end merely puts more and more obstacles in the way of relating.
>
> —Jean Baudrillard, *Passwords*[1]

> OPHELIA: You are as good as a chorus, my lord.
> HAMLET: I could interpret between you and your love if I could see the puppets dallying.
>
> —William Shakespeare, *Hamlet*[2]

Thus far, this book has argued that "the obscene" forms a hidden leitmotif within German realism, shaping authors' thematic and aesthetic choices at the same time as these choices work to usher the concept itself into being. Yet for all the criticism of a "lopsided realism, which repudiates the ideal" (der einseitige Realismus, der das Ideal verleugnet),[3] the intolerable breaking through of what Schiller once called "sensuousness without soul"[4] usually remains no more than a latent and subterranean threat, successfully contained by techniques of contextualization, allegory, and psychological perspective (not to mention the plain fact that any work of language is opposed to asemantic presence by definition). The three previous chapters have shown how this threat, the product of a post-Romantic intensification of the divide between matter and spirit, nevertheless emerges from time to time symptomatically, as a product of its repression (or, sometimes, conscious examination). For the most part, however, whatever "obscenity" is, it must be said that German writers of the mid- to late nineteenth century manage, by and large, to avoid it.

With naturalism, however, the discourse around obscenity becomes crystal clear. In innumerable reviews and commentaries, Émile Zola, the Goncourts, and their German epigones are charged with having "replaced . . . reality with the obscene or grotesque visions of [their] overheated imagination";[5] with promoting a "pathology of the body" (Pathologie des Leibes);[6] with creating a "*littérature de boue et de sang*, which must instill horror in every temperate, purity- and cleanliness-loving nature."[7] For the shocked humanists of the late nineteenth century, Heinrich Heine's call for an "emancipation of the flesh" (Emanzipation des Fleisches)[8]—his own contribution to the debates over literary sensualism set off by Friedrich Schlegel—returns in the form of a hyperbolic realism, practiced by writers whose "relationship to actuality," in the words of one critic, "can be summed up in the idea that they regard dust, dirt, mud, and excrement as realities, . . . whereas they prefer to hold the bright, the luminous, the fresh, the dust-clearing, the dirt-rinsing, that for us is no less 'real,' for a 'fantastical whitewashing' ['phantastische Schönmalerei'] and an 'outdated concept' ['abgedienten Begriff']."[9]

Of course, the naturalists themselves saw their work not as a pathological distortion of reality, but merely as its most advanced likeness. In the well-known passage from Émile Zola's programmatic essay "The Experimental Novel":

> Our work is to go from the known to the unknown, to make ourselves masters of nature. . . . If our work, often cruel, if our terrible pictures needed justification, I should find . . . this argument conclusive: "You will never reach really fruitful and luminous generalizations on the phenomena of life until you have experimented yourself and stirred up in the hospital, the amphitheater, and the laboratory the fetid or palpitating sources of life. If it were necessary for me to give a comparison which would explain my sentiments on the science of life, I should say that it is a superb salon, flooded with light, which you can only reach by passing through a long and nauseating kitchen."[10]

Zola's motivations remain basically moral and pedagogic, trained on the far horizon of a future knowledge. But it cannot be denied that the "long and nauseating kitchen" (in Zola's quotation from the physiologist Claude Bernard) soon comes to appear less as the means of naturalist representation than as its ends. This fact, however, is due perhaps less to a depraved taste for sensation, as naturalism's critics were quick to decry, and more to the moral and scientific impulses of naturalism itself. In the words of Wilhelm Bölsche, one of the foremost defenders of naturalism in Germany: "A relentless necessity will force [the realistic writer] to the most severe consequences, and if he includes unhealthy elements [das Ungesunde] in his experiment, which is anyway not to be avoided, then he is obliged to carry it out completely to its logical conclusion."[11] In other words, if the realist writer "should describe life as it is,"[12] then this "as it is" must extend to *all* aspects of life, even its most shocking, unpleasant, or disillusioning. Meanwhile, with the debasement of Enlightenment aesthetics into a vapid *Bildungsbürgertum*, the art of idealization is reproached as being mere weak-mindedness and kitsch, subordinate to the harder, masculine principles of clarity, accuracy, and positive fact. "Truth" and "beauty" begin to part ways; "that which cannot be said" becomes that which must be said: the gritty, the graphic, and the unsentimental come to stand in metonymically for the real, a guarantee in and of itself of artistic legitimacy.

Thus emerges what one critic has called the "tenuous alliance between the notions of 'realism' and 'art for art's sake,' which . . . uneasily coexist[] in the history of modern 'obscene' literature."[13] Still, in this dance of ideologies, the obvious question is rarely posed: Why were earlier works of art, which deal every bit as much with objectionable and unpleasant topics, *not* deemed threats to public decency? Writers of the nineteenth century might be forgiven for thinking they were permitted to talk about sexual desires and acts, crime, violence, disease, drunkenness, poverty, putrefaction, etc., given that such themes had already been part of the standard fare of literature from Homer to Goethe. By the mid-nineteenth century, however, the portrayal of such things has become, in the words of Karl Rosenkranz, only the "aberrations of a time that, out of its morbidly pathological interest in corruption, considers the misery of demoralization to be something poetic." "Literature," adds Rosenkranz, in a telling metaphor, "prostitutes *itself* when it represents such matters."[14]

What changes, once again, is not the topics of art so much as the way in which these topics are portrayed. Naturalism's sin is not that it turns its attention to lifeless objects, sexual drives, or social ills, but that it fails to portray these things on a human scale, the "Copernican point of view," according to Max Nordau's infamous screed *Entartung* (*Degeneration*), without which "we lose the right, and also the desire to apply to Nature the measure of our logic, our morals, and our own advantage."[15] As Hans Blumenberg has argued, however, in his essay "The Concept of Reality and the Possibility of the Novel," such a loss of "the Copernican point of view" may also be a paradoxical consequence of the Copernican epistemology of the classical realist novel itself. As Blumenberg shows, realism's portrayal of an infinitely expanding, always potentially knowable but only ever partially known world eventually leads to a sense that the *real* reality must be located elsewhere; the idea of truth shifts to one *not* governed by human beings, "that which is totally unavailable, which cannot be relegated simply to the level of material for manipulation, but can only occasionally appear to be processed by one technique or another, then to reveal itself in the full potency of its overwhelming autonomy as a '*factum brutum*.'"[16] The autonomy of alterity, which poetic realism worked so hard to surmount, ironically reappears as aesthetic principle in naturalism's emphasis on the transcendent status of empirical knowledge as such. Worse, this autonomy of alterity is extended to the very thing that, for poetic realism, was supposed to militate against it: the human being itself. If from the perspective of its defenders, naturalism's interest in the poor and working classes represents an enlightened broadening of literature's scope, such an interest also blocks the readerly identification of its bourgeois audience (and indeed, its bourgeois authors) that realism had always implicitly relied on, turning its protagonists into case studies rather than characters, less proxies for the reader than exotic subjects for examination.[17] For poetic realism's defenders, such a blockage of idenfication then leads almost as a matter of course to a literature of "coprolalia" (Mist-Rede),[18] "sexual psychopathy,"[19] "a perversion of the olfactory sense which make the worst odours, especially those of all human excretions, appear . . . agreeable and sensually stimulating,"[20] in short, to an "obscenity without circumlocution" (Schweinerei ohne Umschweif),[21] which holds out the promise of objective truth as a cover for lurid fascination.

Such a perverse combination of attraction and abhorrence finds what is no doubt its consummate expression in the opening chapter of Zola's most scandalous novel, the 1880 *Nana*. In that chapter—*pace* Lukács, a tour de force of narrative technique—the audience members of the cabaret theater in which Zola's novel opens wait with bated breath for the début entrance of the title character, whose enigmatic virtues have already been touted in the theater director Bordenave's aggressive word-of-mouth publicity, in the yellow posters hanging "in the garish illumination of the gas lamps, in the washed-out nakedness of that room" (dans la clarté crue du gaz, sur la nudité blafard de cette salle),[22] and, of course, in the lengthy scene-setting descriptions of the theater in the chapter itself, lambasted by Lukács as a "literature for specialists."[23] Toward the end of the chapter, however, at the beginning of the third act of the evening's tacky neoclassical burlesque, Bordenave's—and Zola's—withholding techniques finally pay off. Nana reemerges, but for a thin veil completely in the nude:

> The three knocks sounded; the usherettes, weighed down with furs and overcoats, exerted themselves to give them back to the returning crowd. . . . In the previous scene, Diana had come to an agreement with the god, who would pretend he was going away on a trip to clear the way for Venus and Mars. As soon as Diana was alone, Venus entered. A shiver ran through the room. Nana was naked. . . . No one was laughing any more, the faces of the men were strained, serious, their nostrils contracted, their mouths parched and inflamed. It was as if a breeze had passed through, very soft, charged with silent menace. All of a sudden, from within the coquettish little girl, the woman had stood up, troubling, bringing with her the frenzy of her sex, opening up the secret of desire.[24]

An intradiegetic, psychologically naturalistic reading of this scene—a reading that Zola's text certainly encourages—would emphasize that the sight of Nana's naked body sexually arouses the theater's (mostly male) audience, leaving them dry-mouthed with desire and ready to fork up more cash for the next performance. Sex sells; pornography advertises; Bordenave's three-act commercial for his newest ingénue's *chatte* turns his theater not just figuratively but literally into the "bordello" he insists on it being called. But it does not require all that much hermeneutic finesse to see that what is at stake in this opening scene—the scene of a theater, after all—is not just sexual desire, overwhelming and all-powerful as that may be. It is also visuality, exposure, spectacle as such. Not only does the delayed gratification of the revelation of Nana's sex all too clearly parallel the delayed gratification of the revelation of Nana herself; the entire chapter, and indeed the entire novel, plays out as an allegory of the phenomenon of the desire to see, to possess, to know, "to make ourselves masters of nature" that is at the very heart of Zola's—and not just Zola's—project. Nana's ostentatious visibility (all the more so in the scenes where she is peered at from behind, that is, when she is not aware that she is on display) is no less than the exposure of exposure itself, in which the gratification obtained in viewing and inspecting is higher than any other gain of pleasure.

Or almost. For whatever "new and autonomous realm of the sensory"[25] is unleashed in Zola (and whatever its ideological ramifications), this is not the motivation he gives for his method. For Zola, again, the point of naturalist observation is not simply the lubricious pleasure of observation, but rather the technical insights that such observation allows:

> Here is our role as intelligent beings: to penetrate to the wherefore of things, to become superior to these things, and to reduce them to a condition of subservient machinery. . . . We are, in a word, experimental moralists, showing by experiment in what way a passion acts in a certain social condition. The day in which we gain control of the mechanism of this passion we can treat it and reduce it, or at least make it as inoffensive as possible. . . . In this way we shall construct a practical sociology, and our work will be a help to political and economical sciences. I do not know . . . of a more noble work, nor of a grander application.[26]

Zola thus provides a motivation for his writing every bit as humanistic as that of the poetic realists: not only will the examination of individual parts allow us to understand the workings of the whole, but this understanding, in turn, will allow us to eliminate the parts that threaten the whole in its collective health. The peculiarity of *Nana* in Zola's social-diagnostic novel cycle, in this case, is that Nana herself—the keeper of "the secret of desire" (l'inconnu du désir), the very incarnation of scopophilic longing—is the "passion" to be identified and gained control over. Given this state of affairs, it is a curious fact of Zola's novel that, as Peter Brooks has noted, "Nana naked is strangely veiled."[27] Not just in her appearance on Bordenave's stage, where a bit of gauze acts as a sop to ideas of artistic value, but also in private, the depths of her sex remain hidden, first by her labia,[28] and then by Zola's own nervous swerves into lyricism, allegory, and myth. Writes Brooks: "The visual inspection of Nana leads to a certain denial of what is seen, a turning away from the truth."[29] "Forces" may be intimated "in their effects,"[30] but for all Zola's analytic efforts, the "mechanism" of the "passion" driving society, the "origin of the world," the thing in itself remains, in the end, invisible. Despite being examined from every angle and put in every possible position, Nana—the whore of Saïs, the epistemological bitch who refuses to give it up—somehow escapes his grasp.

In this way, *Nana* is both Zola's bitterest and his most melancholy novel: at once a violent revenge fantasy on the body and person of Nana as the incarnation of a knowledge over which he cannot, in fact, "gain control,"[31] and a self-aware, even world-weary demonstration of the hubris of thinking that he could have ever controlled it. When Zola writes of Nana at the end of her opening night that she "remained victorious with her marble flesh, her sex strong enough to destroy all those people and remain itself unscathed [son sexe assez fort pour détruire tout ce monde et n'en être pas entamé],"[32] this is either irony, or kitsch: for Nana (to contain ourselves to the textual evidence) will indeed end up destroyed along with the world in which she lives, dying grotesquely of smallpox as outside France marches in blissful ignorance toward the disaster of the Franco-Prussian War. "Venus was decomposing" (Vénus se décomposait):[33] Nana's sex, with all its proffered promises of possession and revealed knowledge, does not just close; it collapses.

Zola's ambivalence and, in a way, his discretion in regard to Nana is thus in part an unconscious recognition that his project "to penetrate to the wherefore of things" is, in the end, an impossible one. "Zola takes fright at his own creation" not just because the understanding of Nana, the "motor force of the narrative,"[34] is "more difficult than understanding a coal mine or a locomotive,"[35] but also because in Nana he has created a paramount symbol for a nature that mocks its observer with the impenetrable materiality of its surfaces. (Indeed, with all respect to Brooks, the "motor force of the narrative" is not Nana—however much Zola's own words would try to convince one otherwise—but rather the male desire that is again and again projected onto her.) In Nana, mystery and obscenity go hand in hand: outside the untold secrets the hollow of her sex is imagined to contain, she is, even before the pox destroys her beauty, a figure of pure carnality, an almost inhuman mass of flesh, hair, and skin coalesced into one single object of obsession. That Zola, for all the boldness of his rhetoric, regularly averts his eyes from the spectacle of this flesh to enter the safer confines of mythology and allegory (including, as Jameson has shown, the allegory of fleshly affect itself)[36] is a mark of his ultimate circumspection as an author, his rueful admission that the thing he keeps trying to get a closer look at will, in the end, always evade his gaze.

Peep Show

Such circumspection is precisely what Arno Holz would overcome. As "the most consistent realist" (der consequenteste Realist)—in the possibly ironic title bestowed upon Holz by Gerhart Hauptmann in the dedication to his play *Vor Sonnenaufgang* (*Before Sunrise*) and subsequently entirely unironically adopted by Holz himself[37]—Holz claimed to have achieved that which even Zola was too cowardly or too conventional to carry through: an art of total objectivity, from whose pitiless frankness and perfected mimetic technique there would, henceforth, be no going back. Most of Holz's contemporaries, alas, were of a different opinion. Despite a handful of nominations for the Nobel Prize and a multivolume edition of complete works published in his lifetime, the world denied Holz the success that he thought was his due: a fact that was at once a source of real material distress—Holz remained financially dependent on odd jobs and handouts from friends for the majority of his adult life—and further fuel for his sense of aggrieved brilliance and righteous contempt for his age. Like his model and elder contemporary Friedrich Nietzsche (though with somewhat less justification), Holz presented himself as the martyred inaugurator of the new era, a revaluator of aesthetic values who receives naught but scorn and neglect for his pains.[38]

Posterity has not been much kinder to Holz than his peers, usually confining him to a footnote of a footnote, the lesser contemporary of Gerhart Hauptmann in the short-lived history of German naturalism. What scholarship there has been on Holz over the past few decades seems to be split into two camps: on the one side, those who would condemn Holz as the Judas of naturalism, who betrayed its social commitments for the false consciousness of the heroically lonely self,[39] and on the other, those who would exalt Holz as the John the Baptist (if not indeed the Christ) of German modernism,[40] the unsung harbinger of twentieth-century literature and the liberator of German poetics from its classical shackles.[41] The latter position, of course, requires a willful forgetting of Goethe, Hölderlin, Whitman, Mallarmé, Ibsen, and anyone else Holz conveniently leaves out—or dismisses as a mere novice—in his claims to have invented quantitative meter, *vers libre*, free indirect discourse, regionalist dialogue, the problem play, and the modern verse epic. The frequent parodic thrust of Holz's work is already an indication of the extent to which it exists in reaction to—and in antagonistic relation with—previous literary history. Even Holz's vanguardist gestures, the one constant in his genre-spanning body of work, are basically poses borrowed from Heine, Nietzsche, Zola, and all the other true and less true prophets of the age. Holz felt himself to be a latecomer; he compensated by presenting himself as the first man.[42]

And yet, Holz fascinates: not only for the dumbfounding spectacle of his logo- and megalomania, but also for the way in which his work, in the very fanaticism of its aims, brings German realism's troubled relationship to materiality to its spectacular head. In Holz's avant-garde, though never quite avant-garde enough, poetics, Holz carries the mimetic premises of realism to their most extreme conclusion, attempting to create a literature in which no detail is left out, in which each thing is trotted out on the stage of its literal presence. The outcome is not only what Winfried Menninghaus has called the "hyperreality of disgust"[43]—revulsion as the acid test of anti-Romantic veracity—but also the disgust of hyperreality, the rapt horror of the phenomenal world as uncomprehended sensual presence, in a conscious inversion of poetic realism whose consequences extend beyond even the outsized ambitions of Holz himself.

It is no accident that the opening scene of *Nana* takes place in a theater, and not only because the theater provides a ready metaphor for naturalism's veridical ambitions. Particularly in Scandinavia, where Ibsen's groundbreaking dramas set the tone, and in the perpetual latecomer Germany, the theater was one of the preeminent venues of naturalism, fertile soil for the cultivation of the new art.[44] In the last decade of the nineteenth century, organizations such as the *Freie Bühne* and the *Freie Volksbühne* in Berlin, and the naturalist organ *Freie Bühne für modernes Leben* (*Free Stage for Modern Life*, soon to be renamed the *Freie Bühne für den Entwicklungskampf der Zeit*, or *Free Stage for the Contemporary Struggle for Progress*) propagated works of German and international naturalism through performances, publications, translations, book and theater reviews, and polemical essays on culture, politics, and aesthetics.[45] Despite the valid objections of contemporary critics that even the most true-to-life performance can never be more than a "translated nature,"[46] German naturalism found in the stage both a favorable medium for its kitchen-sink perspectives and a useful foil against which to foment its aesthetic revolution.

Holz delivers his own verdict on the theater in the preface to his 1896 play *Sozialaristokraten* (*Social Aristocrats*), later reproduced in the essay *Evolution des Dramas*. For Holz, while all genres must bear responsibility for the misconceptions that have occurred in the pursuit of artistic truth, the theater, for reasons of both medium and custom, has been particularly guilty of offenses against aesthetic honesty. Not only in Schiller or Goethe, but even in Ibsen—yea, even in the revered Shakespeare—a dependence on contrived, trivial plots and a fusty, poeticizing language fails, time and again, to deliver the really real of the real world. Thanks to the recent exertions of Holz and his sometime collaborator (and later, rival) Johannes Schlaf,[47] however, "it is from the exact opposite standpoint . . . that today's young men proceed." For them, Holz proclaims,

> the language of the theater is the language of life. Only of life! . . . Their goal is clear: to reduce to a minimum all the inevitable side-effects arising from the respective medium of reproduction and thereby increasingly present, in place of the mannered life that has been handed down up to now, the nearly real [statt des bisher

überliefert gewesenen posierten Lebens damit mehr und mehr das nahezu wirkliche zu setzen], in a word, to gradually expel the "theater" from the theater.[48]

On one level, what Holz means by his intention "to gradually expel the 'theater' from the theater" (aus dem Theater allmählich das "Theater" zu drängen) is nothing particularly esoteric: in lieu of the classical stage's bombast and simper, the new theater will offer plain language as it is spoken; in lieu of conventional farces and melodramas, it will stage the real everyday problems of real everyday people; in lieu of sublime destinies and tidily resolved plots, it will present lived life in all its squalor, banality, pettiness, and irresolution.

Even if Holz himself consistently rejected any intimation that his ideas might be anything less than sui generis, this sentiment was one shared by many of Holz's contemporaries. In the words of Holz's (for a while) fellow naturalist August Strindberg:

> It is true that we who have been raised on French comedy in our national court theatre have gained the impression that people are not presentable unless they have twenty thousand francs in interest income. . . . We have lost faith in the social ideals of low-cut starched shirts and six yards of train. These things have taught us to despise the kind of beauty that exists at the expense of others.[49]

The new theater, then—Strindberg quotes *Hamlet*—will "hold as 'twere the mirror up to nature; . . . show virtue her feature, scorn her own image, and the very age and body of the time his form and pressure."[50] It is in this same spirit of mimetic fidelity that Holz praises his early collaborations with Schlaf as "small, completely spontaneous studies directly from nature, without giving a thought, so to speak, to God and the world" (kleinen, völlig absichtslosen Studien direkt nach der Natur, ohne uns sozusagen um Gott und die Welt zu kümmern),[51] and their play *Die Familie Selicke* (*The Selicke Family*)—praised by the publisher Wolfgang Rothe as "perhaps the only real play of the naturalist era, precisely that 'experiment' in the sphere of drama that Zola had proclaimed in his aesthetic writings after 1880"[52]—as a drama "through which one looked in on a slice of life as if through a window" (durch die man in ein Stück Leben wie durch ein Fenster sah).[53] In line with naturalism's basic tenets, Holz announces the transformation of the stage from a place of boulevard entertainment and high-toned kitsch into a venue for a radically quotidian, radically true-to-life art, which will now offer, in place of artistic falsification, "life with an immediacy . . . , with an accuracy which today we may hardly even be able to imagine" (das Leben in einer Unmittelbarkeit . . . , in einer Treffsicherheit, von der wir heute vielleicht noch nicht einmal eine entfernte Vorstellung haben).[54]

Yet Holz's wish to replace theatrical affectation with a more down-to-earth aesthetic also contains a far more radical rethinking of the theater as medium: indeed, one that would do away with the notion of a "medium" altogether. The tradition of *Theaterfeindlichkeit* is, of course, a long and storied one. What distinguishes naturalism's particular antitheatrical vogue from its predecessors, however—as Jonas Barish argues in his classic study *The Antitheatrical Prejudice*—is that it is no longer propagated, as before, by philosophers or theologians, but now by the creators and producers of the theater itself. Barish attributes this change mainly to the theater's increasing division of labor, in which playwrights and directors come to experience a growing distrust of the actors and artists of whose ranks they are no longer part.[55] Such an observation goes a long way toward explaining the lengthy stage directions of much naturalist drama, which specify not just details of setting, blocking, and costume, but also physiognomies, verbal inflections, and even atmospheric conditions, effecting what is at times a veritable novelization of the dramatic stage.[56] In the case of Holz, however, whatever practical concerns he might bring to his aesthetics, more to the point than the potential waywardness of professional actors is the idea of the theater as ossified bourgeois institution, serving up cliché sentimentality for an escapism-addicted public. And beneath this idea lies a still older ground for Holz's antitheatrical sentiment: that is, the distrust of artistic imitation itself.

Holz elaborates such distrust most fully in his 1891 manifesto *Die Kunst: Ihr Wesen und ihre Gesetze* (*Art: Its Essence and Its Laws*). In this work, Holz—whose faith in the brilliance of his own ideas appears never to have required outside confirmation—imagines himself to have resolved the problem of art's relationship to life that has troubled aesthetics ever since Socrates banned the poets from the Republic. Holz lays out his theory anecdotally, in the form of a series of epiphanies. One day, he relates, after having long cudgeled his brains over aesthetic conundrums (around 108 pages long, in the original printing), he comes upon a young boy who shows Holz a drawing he has just made. Holz, unable to identify the subject of the drawing, asks what it is supposed to be. Only on being told by the boy what the drawing represents—a "Suldat"—does Holz then recognize the blob as a torso, the diagonal line as a sword, etc. This recognition leads Holz to what he styles as the eureka moment of his aesthetics, the discovery of his infamous formula "Art = Nature – x."[57] Critics have debated what Holz actually intends by this formula, none of whose terms are in fact self-explanatory. The basic intention, however, seems clear: if art's task is the presentation of truth, and if truth, according to the positivistic teaching that Holz adopts from Zola, Taine, and Mill, is identical with empirical reality, then the aim of art can be nothing other than the maximally faithful replication of that reality. Since no copy can be a perfect copy, however, the little differential x enters in, not as a positive recommendation but as a regrettable inevitability, the "re-" of representation as the corruption of mimesis itself.

In this way, at least, Holz's theory constitutes an interesting shift in emphasis. For Holz, art is not a refinement of reality, as it was, for example, for the humanist advocates of poetic realism. Rather, art is *privative*, and what it is privative of is presence, existence, material fact. In an intuition almost Greenbergian in character, Holz defines art as a kind of reduction to abstraction—"real soldier" minus the soldier's physical facticity—all the way to the point of pure nonrepresentationality.[58] But whereas Greenberg notably champions such a notion, Holz's ambition is to reduce this differential *x* as much as possible, to progress from a rudimentary—indeed, a childish—impressionism to full-on trompe-l'œil illusion. Holz's formalist naturalism, which basically dispenses with the movement's political and reformist motivations, thus forms a kind of perversely deconstructive response to Plato's critique of representation: with Plato, Holz maintains the badness of the copy vis-à-vis the original; against Plato, however, Holz places the original, not in the idea, but in the phenomenal appearance of the world itself. This is what Holz means by the corollary that he appends to his formula a few pages later: "Art's tendency is to become Nature again. It does so in accordance with its respective conditions of reproduction and the methods of their use" (Die Kunst hat die Tendenz, wieder die Natur zu sein. Sie wird sie nach Maßgabe ihrer jedweiligen Reproduktionsbedingungen und deren Handhabung).[59] Holz is so pleased with his formula that he repeats it nearly word for word a sentence later, punctuating it for good measure with a "Yes! That was it!":[60] "If this proposition is true, that is to say: if the law that it expresses is a real one, one present in *reality*, and not merely one that I foolishly imagine, one in my *skull*, then it overthrows everything that up to now goes by the name of 'Aesthetics.' And for good."[61] To others, of course, the logical inevitability of such a conclusion may be somewhat less obvious. In fact, Holz's formula has the form of a paradox: if art is defined by its deficiency vis-à-vis reality, and if progress in art means correcting this deficiency, then the best and most advanced artwork would be—no art at all. Even if Holz elsewhere denies that naturalism aims at mere reproduction,[62] the technical thinking behind such an axiom is clear: all art strives after the condition of replica, held back only by lack of skill and the limitations of the medium. The little boy's drawing means to be a soldier, but only manages, so to speak, to be art.[63]

As most critics have noted, Holz's actual literary works, even his most orthodoxly "naturalist," inevitably fall short of such iconomachic goals. However, this fact does not prevent the paradoxes of Holz's aesthetics from emerging in other, even more consequential ways. These paradoxes are already apparent in Holz's earliest and best-known work (cowritten with Schlaf), the narrative sketch *Papa Hamlet*.[64] First published as a "translation" from the Norwegian under the pseudonym Bjarne P. Holmsen—at once a joke on the literary establishment and a barefaced attempt to cash in on the Ibsen craze—*Papa Hamlet* presents a day in the life of the washed-up alcoholic actor Niels Thienwiebel, which climaxes in Thienwiebel's accidental killing of his infant son and his own demise, in a coda eight days later, from exposure and drink. Thematically, the piece is a loose adaptation of Schlaf's previously published sketch *Ein Dachstubenidyll* (*A Garret Idyll*), though the two works actually have little in common outside of a few details and the sentimental motif of an infant's death. Stylistically, the piece is an experiment, albeit an inconsistent one, in what the nineteenth-century critic Adalbert von Hanstein disparagingly termed Holz and Schlaf's "Sekundenstil" (second-by-second-style): the ostensibly real-time description of a scene without embellishment or authorial intervention, an attempt to approximate the saturated immediacy of lived experience in written form.[65] In *Papa Hamlet*, this approximation is accomplished in one of three main ways: the foregrounding of direct speech without speech tags; the meticulous descriptions of physical minutiae such as the onomatopoetic representation of melting ice ("Tipp . . . Tipp . . .")[66] and the extended leitmotif of a sputtering oil lamp;[67] and the presentation of minimally commented action through what can only be called stage directions, such as "Amalie nodded. Somewhat tiredly,"[68] or "Long pause . . ."[69]

Whatever pretentions the piece makes to artless objectivity, then, it is already clear from the above list that neither stylization nor authorial bias is in fact excluded from Holz and Schlaf's sketch. The title of the work alone gives away its authors' polemical intentions: Shakespeare's melancholy Dane will be unceremoniously transformed into a melancholy daddy, gnawing on the remnants of his former glory and saddled with all the trivialities of family life in an underclass existence. Indeed, in their desire to take the Bard of Avon down a peg, Holz and Schlaf lay on the irony everywhere extra thick. Their pitiful protagonist is unfailingly referred to as "the great Thienwiebel" (der grosse Thienwiebel); his sickly, carping wife Amalie is "the charming Ophelia" (die reizende Ophelia); his squalling, pacifier-sucking baby bears the name—what else?—Fortinbras. The second section of *Papa Hamlet* shows Thienwiebel at home, still in his pajamas, attempting (and failing) to deliver that most famous of Hamlet's monologues:

> "To be or not to be, that is the question:
> Whether 'tis nobler in the mind . . .
> Ah, rubbish!!"
>
> With a jerk, the copy of Shakespeare that he had just only taken from his dressing gown pocket flew onto the table, where it found itself in the company of a spirit stove, a brown clay milk jug without a handle, a glass lamp, and a photograph of the Great Thienwiebel in a mora-wood frame.[70]

Such deflationary citationality is perhaps the most prominent stylistic feature of *Papa Hamlet*—more so, indeed, than the descriptive exactness Holz and Schlaf laud in their "translator's preface" (attributed to "Dr. Bruno Franzius"). A steady stream of direct quotations from Shakespeare's drama (in

August Schlegel's translation), mostly from the title character's better-known lines, turns up, not only in the form of Thienwiebel's recitations, but also as decontextualized scraps of language with which Thienwiebel peppers his speech, and as points of ironic commentary in the passages of third-person narrative.[71] Regardless of their placement, however, in each case the point of the citations is the unsubtle contrast between the dramatic grandeur of the Shakespearean tragedy and the petty shabbiness of the Thienwiebel household. The drunken, showboating Thienwiebel is clearly not Prince Hamlet (nor was meant to be), and his compulsive, senseless quoting of the play in which he once played the starring role serves not to express his reality, but only to further alienate himself from it. But Shakespeare too, Holz and Schlaf imply, is just as much a phony, crafting pretentious, high-flown utterances that no one would ever actually speak and that bear no relation to actual people or real life. Indeed, even if Thienwiebel's existence were a less obviously ignoble one, the satirical force of *Papa Hamlet* would still hold, for the mere fact of showing the actor behind the role necessarily destroys the dramatic illusion. Insofar as actors are professionals in pretense, the unemployed actor is the consummate metaphor of the real, pulling back the curtain, as it were, on the curtain itself. Holz and Schlaf's sketch is effectively a parabasis without a play, a sustained breaking of the fourth wall in a strikingly literal-minded parable of the falsity of theatrical seeming as such.

Here a further valence to Holz and Schlaf's title comes into view. For "Papa Hamlet" not only refers to the Prince of Denmark's entrance in his new role of deadbeat dad; it also points to the appearance of Shakespeare's *Hamlet* as the literary Oedipal father that must be killed: the overdetermined primogenitor of modern drama and the source from which, arguably, the entirety of modern German literature springs. In this sense, *Papa Hamlet* can be read as one giant raspberry blown at Goethe's exultation "And I cry Nature! Nature! nothing so natural as Shakespeare's characters" (Und ich rufe Natur! Natur! nichts so Natur als Schäkespears Menschen).[72] Against Goethe's celebration of Shakespeare as a "true nature-devotee" (wahre[r] Naturfromme[r]),[73] Holz and Schlaf submit that the immortal Bard is simply one of that tribe of "Nature's journeymen" of whom Hamlet himself, in his speech to the players, says "[have] made men and not made them well, they imitated humanity so abominably."[74]

A discussion of theatrical motifs in *Hamlet* is clearly well outside the scope of this chapter. Suffice it to say here that if the metatheatrical elements in *Hamlet* form a subtle and multifaceted argument about seeming and being, public persona and private person, performance and belief, life and art, these subtleties seem largely to have escaped the attention of Holz and Schlaf. *Their* metatheatrical references, by contrast, would appear merely to make the point that the theatrical performance—and, by extension, all art—is always and inherently a romanticizing deception, a fiction for the benefit of weak-minded idealists that Holz and Schlaf's intrepid unmasking is intended to "reform altogether."[75] Holz's stated desire to take "theater" out of the theater is thus not simply a notion of a more and better theatrical illusion; rather, it is a rejection the idea of theatrical illusion per se, an ultra-Platonic attack on artistic representation that is in direct tension with Holz's own insistence that things' appearances *are* their reality, that the statement "The essence of art does *not* consist in the exact reproduction of nature" is a mere "dogma"[76] ripe for debunking. The result is a love-hate relationship with phenomenal appearance itself: the resurgence of mimetic taboo out of realism's radicalization.

The Body without Origins

After the eradication of "theatrical" language and performance, Holz's second demand in *Evolution des Dramas* (for him, but a logical consequence of the first) is the end of the Aristotelian prioritization of dramatic action over theatrical character.[77] Holz's reasoning for this idea, which he calls the "fundamental law of all drama" (Fundamentalgesetz alles Dramatischen),[78] is not much more cogent than most of his other arguments. His main point is essentially one of genre specificity: if novels are based on plot, then the theater, in contrast, must be based on characters. To each his own: "The one is held back by his methods [Mittel], the other sustained by them. That is the difference."[79] Such an argument, however, does not hold up for very long: even leaving aside the fact that literary genres can indeed overlap, it must be admitted that novels, after all, have characters too. Holz's insistence on character as something unique to the dramatic medium would thus hardly be worth mentioning, if it did not at the same time illuminate something vital about the place of the theater within Holz's (and not just Holz's) naturalism. For while theater and prose lay equal claim to both plot and character, there is something that the theater has that prose fiction does not: namely, *real, live, speaking bodies in real physical time and space.* This is the paradox of the theater: that it is at once the epitome of inauthenticity, and the most "real"—or at least, the most four-dimensional—of all classical artistic media. Unlike in prose, in which even the crassest materiality must be selected, temporalized, and linguistically mediated, the theater can show everything, all at once, in concrete actuality. Indeed, one possible reason for the traditional suspicion of the theater over all other forms of art is that in the theater, the reality is simultaneous with the simulacrum: the appearance of the actor *is* the appearance of the character, the stage is a real physical space *and* the place it represents, the prop is both real tangible object *and* its symbolic function, and so on. Such a simultaneity of embodiment and simulacrum makes the theater the exemplary form of naturalist literature, which can thereby at least theoretically sidestep the selecting and ordering mechanisms of narration and put reality on stage in living, breathing concreteness—even if only always as the self-conscious exhibition of itself.

If the theater is thus a kind of allegory of realism, however, then *Papa Hamlet* is the allegory of that allegory, in which Holz and Schlaf attempt to signal a hypertheatrical realism more authentic and immediate even than the theater's mediated unmediatedness. The first element of such allegorization in *Papa Hamlet* is the sustained emphasis on dirt, corporeality, and physical squalor throughout the piece. Thienwiebel's aforementioned failure to complete the "To be or not to be" monologue, for example, is implicitly blamed on his view of his son's drying diapers:

> "Whether 'tis nobler in the mind to suffer
> The slings and arrows of outrageous fortune, or . . .
> or . . . ? Atrocious!"
> The great Thienwiebel paused again.
> "I can't take it! I can't take it!" ["Nicht zum Aushalten das! Nicht zum Aushalten!"]
> The five small, yellow rags, hung up to dry on a clothesline behind the stove, had made him completely lose his train of thought.
> "Disgusting!"[80]

This passage is representative. Throughout *Papa Hamlet*, the blowsy physicality of the Thienwiebel household is presented as a deidealizing challenge to the presumedly hypocritical daintiness of the classical stage. Time and again, material filth enters in to destroy the dramatic illusion and bring Thienwiebel rudely back to a fortune that is, indeed, everything other than "noble." Such a valorization of corporeal frankness is sometimes even promoted by Thienwiebel himself, for example in his sudden panegyric—perhaps the first of its kind in German literature—on the practice of breastfeeding:

> "You know what? We're using the completely wrong methods to feed the kid, Amalie!"
> "Oh, go on!" . . .
> "Trust me, Amalie! I'm telling you, the most natural method is always the best! Think about it: what do Negro women do? They don't have bottles! They feed their children themselves, you see . . . and, and—well! and they thrive that way! Thrive! Am I right?"[81]

This conversation—incidentally one of the few passages that *Papa Hamlet* reproduces more or less intact from Schlaf's *Ein Dachstubenidyll*[82]—will later take on decidedly sinister implications in the piece's climax, as Thienwiebel accidentally manhandles his infant son to death. At the same time, Thienwiebel's insistence in this scene "that the most natural things are always the most reasonable" (daß das Natürlichste immer das Vernünftigste ist)[83] echoes many of Holz's own statements on art and culture, for example his declaration, in the essay *Evolution der Lyrik*, that "the great way back to Nature" in literature has been "one of the most noteworthy happy accidents of our era."[84] Everything else is, like bottle feeding, merely "a *perverse* method" (eine *verkehrte* Methode),[85] a product of the perverse values of "today's culture . . . the culture of the European world."[86] The portrayal of the body in all its ingesting and excreting materiality is a necessary condition for a literature that has left Romantic squeamishness definitively behind.

The second technique by which *Papa Hamlet* attempts to model a more-than-theatrical immediacy is the effort, already noted, to bring literary language as close as possible to natural speech. Again, what elevated style there is in *Papa Hamlet* is present only in the form of travestied *Hamlet* quotations, whose aim is not to imitate Shakespearean eloquence but precisely to annul it through parodic decontextualization. Otherwise, the bid is clearly to reproduce everyday spoken language as accurately as possible, in what the contemporary critic Franz Servaes approvingly called Holz's "kinesics of speech" (Mimik der Rede).[87] In *Papa Hamlet*, this kinesics means above all the incorporation of those pauses, non sequiturs, interruptions, elisions, tics, and anacolutha that a traditionally oratorical literary language would inevitably leave out. Even cries, stammers, slurs, grunts, coos, and sobs are rendered with loving precision: "Hoo, hoo, hoo, hopp!! Hoo, hoo, hoo, hopp!! Bumm!!!";[88] "Grrr . . . grrr . . . grrr . . . äh!";[89] "a! Na?! a—a—a . . .";[90] "Du! Sag a . . . a . . . Nun? Wird's bald! . . . Na? . . . A! . . .";[91] "Ach Gott, ja! So'n . . . Ae!! . . ."[92] In a way that almost anticipates Artaud—albeit with the exact opposite motivation—Holz and Schlaf push language to the limits of articulateness.[93]

It is along these lines that some critics are led to praise Holz as an early practitioner of psychological realism, constructing a language, not of discursive meaning, but of "emotional, atmospheric, and auditory effects, . . . the way one speaks and how this speaking brings buried half-conscious layers to expression."[94] However, Holz's concern is not really for the hidden layers of his characters' psyches, most of whom remain, indeed, little more than stock figures. Rather, his concern is for language's surface textures and tones, a bravado display of acoustic simulation on the same level as the imitative rendition of infantile gurgles and the drip of melting ice. What emerges from this bravado display is then not the liberation of language from its "theatrical" misuse but the isolation of the voice qua voice: in Mladen Dolar's words, an "extra-linguistic element which enables speech phenomena, but cannot itself be discerned by linguistics."[95] In Holz and Schlaf's cultivation of a quasi-onomatopoeic "intimacy of vocal tone" (Intimität des Sprechtons),[96] the voice thus emerges as a form of sensual appearing—indeed, of bodily emission—that puts the spiritual content of verbal expression itself into question. The voice becomes, in Dolar's apt phrase, the "excrement of the signifier,"[97] the waste product language leaves behind in meaning's wake.

Such an "excrement of the signifier" is everywhere visible—or rather, audible—in *Papa Hamlet*. The voice in Holz and Schlaf's sketch is anything but the presence of self-identical logos; to the contrary, it is a physical voice, a voice of tongues, lips, larynxes, voices blurred by drink, deformed by dialect, choked by shock, a voice obedient not to the will but to the mindless automatism of speech and the alterity of the body that produces it. In other words, Holz and Schlaf's "phonographic"[98] style establishes an excessive materiality within language itself, of the same kind that is found in the threadbare tips of Thienwiebel's house slippers,[99] the dust-covered tube of rash cream fallen behind the stove,[100] or the medicinal stench of Amalie's vapor baths.[101] And yet, despite the evident disgust for the physical voice that runs through *Papa Hamlet*, its premise remains that of an absolutely authentic vitality: in Holz's formulation, a "language of life, that we set against the previous paper language" (die Sprache des Lebens, die wir an die bisherige von Papier setzten).[102] What stands out above all in Holz's works, then, is the spectacular failure of this premise: *Papa Hamlet* invokes the voice as the unmediated taking-place of language—but what emerges is only either the word-salad citationality of the empty-headed actor, or the voice, "acoustically present in nauseatingly unsettling corporeality,"[103] as pre- or asemantic thereness.

Such a potent combination of linguistic melancholy and linguistic disgust might seem to resemble that of Hofmannsthal's Lord Chandos (written only thirteen years after *Papa Hamlet*), for whom, famously, "the abstract words, of which the tongue must necessarily avail itself in order to bring forth any sort of judgment, crumbled in my mouth like moldy mushrooms."[104] However, as the above quotation already makes clear, what repels Chandos is not the materiality of language so much as the breakdown of its semantic promise, the failure, in the wake of Baconian empiricism, of words to correspond in a necessary or sufficient manner to the things they designate. Holz, too, feels the breakdown of language's connection to lived reality, as his jeremiads against the theater's "paper" language demonstrate. This feeling will eventually lead Holz to the satirical pastiches of *Dafnis* and *Die Blechschmiede* (*The Tinsmiths*) and, finally, to the logorrheic omnivorousness of his multivolume poem *Phantasus* (to be discussed, along with *Die Blechschmiede,* below), in which Holz claims to have created a language where "['things'], which had once lain indistinct and as if behind veils, are now vividly expressed" (["die Dinge"] drücken sich plastisch . . . aus, die noch verschwommen und wie unter Schleiern lagen).[105] In *Papa Hamlet*, however, Holz's attempted solution to the problem of language's arbitrary relationship to signification is not yet to parody or to transcend it; instead, his solution is to bypass the problem of linguistic meaning entirely, establishing a correspondence of language to reality not through semantic reference but through pure acoustic mimicry. But this mimicry, styled as corporeal product, is still implicitly set against a normative idea of disembodied meaning that turns the physical voice into something even more repugnant than the theatrical poeticizing it purports to attack. If for the more socially engaged naturalists the representation of rough physicality among the lower classes ostensibly served the purpose of bringing the misery of their living conditions critically to light, for Holz, the dirt of the *Lumpenproletariat* is but a metaphor for the dirt of vocal utterance itself—and hence, of any sort of material presence in excess of expressive meaning.[106] The excrementality of the voice is the property of a fallen language, a waste matter expelled from logos, no longer one's own.

These two manifestations of embodied immediacy—the repellent physicality of the body and the shameful physicality of the voice—converge in the third and final aspect of *Papa Hamlet* to be discussed: namely, the brief life and wretched death of the infant Fortinbras. From the beginning, Thienwiebel's child is animalized or objectified, described as "the little crab-red fellow" (der kleine Krebsrothe),[107] the "little wriggling worm" (kleinen, zappelnden Wurm),[108] "the little cherry-red philistine . . . ugly . . . as a little frog" (der kleine, kirschrothe Spiessbürger . . . hässlich . . . wie ein kleiner Frosch),[109] or simply "beast" (Bestie).[110] And sometimes worse: as Peter Sprengel has observed, Thienwiebel refers to his infant son at several points in *Papa Hamlet* with quotations that, in Shakespeare, actually designate the corpse of the murdered Polonius.[111] Sprengel reads this as a foreshadowing of baby Fortinbras's eventual death, and perhaps it is—but it is also an identification of the infant's passive body with the inhuman materiality of the corpse itself. *Already* in life, the allusion implies, *Papa Hamlet*'s heroically named baby is a mere dead weight, a milk-sucker and a diaper-shitter, a too, too, all too solid lump of flesh.

Indeed, throughout the piece, Fortinbras's physical and vocal presence is consistently offered as the converse to the delusional grandeur of his father's oratory. Here Holz and Schlaf's technique of anti-Shakespearean *détournement* once again comes into play. At the end of the second section of *Papa Hamlet*, for example, Hamlet's mocking description of the courtier Osric is made to do double duty as an indirect description of Thienwiebel's fussing offspring:

> Meanwhile, the little crab-red fellow was having a hard time of it in his corner. He had already cried himself to sleep a blessed many times. Now he was up again and could nowhere find his rubber pacifier. . . . He screamed as if someone had run a stake through him.
>
> Naturally, now more than ever the great Thienwiebel had no time for the scoundrel. He had just taken hold of little Ole Nissen . . . by his lapels and declaimed again:
>
> "'Tis a chuff, Horatio! A chuff! But, as I say, spacious in the possession of—dirt [mit weitläufigen Besitzungen von—Koth gesegnet]!"[112]

But the real punch line of this citational setup comes at the end of the next section. In the midst of a recitation of Hamlet's death scene, Thienwiebel suddenly notices that his son is watching him. Flattered in his fatherly pride and thespian ego alike, he concludes that Fortinbras has begun to understand the performance: "Amalie! There's no denying it: the child has truly exceptional abilities! Just now he gave me a smile. He's having a grand time with me! . . . I bet we could already start teaching him the basics of how to speak, Amalie!"[113] Such optimism comes to a quick end, however, as Thienwiebel, moved by the prospects of his son's talents, attempts to bestow a kiss on his young theater buff:

> It was really too kind of the great Thienwiebel! But now he had bent low over his sweet little Fortinbras, who was entitled to such high hopes, and wanted again—O, for the first time, for the first time in such a long, long while, Horatio!—to plant a kiss on his small, pale forehead.
>
> But it was not to be. He had staggered backwards before he could even bring the beautiful deed to fruition. . . .
>
> Being nature's livery or fortune's star, in short, the young Prince of Norway lay there once again pleased as punch in the midst of his spacious possessions [seelenvergnügt mitten in seinen weitläufigen Besitzungen da].[114]

Thus are the hopes for Fortinbras's precocious literacy cruelly dashed. But even before Fortinbras soils his diaper, he and his voice clearly function as the representatives of a desublimated materiality, one that gives the lie to his father's theatrical affectations—it is no coincidence that Thienwiebel's reaction to his son's stench is to recoil in silence—insofar as it is the vulgar counterpart to them. If the unemployed actor is the preeminent symbol of the exposure of theatrical fraudulence—the pathetic, incapacitated "man behind the curtain"—the infant can be said to be the anti-actor, unable to pose or seem, the possessor of a presemantic language of unadulterated natural expressivity.

It is thus all the more significant that what finally precipitates the story's tragic end is the colicky crying of baby Fortinbras himself. Having been woken up in the middle of the night by his quarrelling parents, Fortinbras begins once again to wail; drunk and annoyed, Thienwiebel shoves the pacifier roughly into his son's mouth, accidentally snapping his neck in the process:

> "Huh? You gonna be—quiet now? Huh?—You gonna be—quiet now? Huh? Huh?"
>
> "Oh God! Oh God, Niels, what—what're you doing? He, he's—not crying anymore! He's . . . Niels!"[115]

In other words, the climax of *Papa Hamlet* is the violent silencing of the natural voice, the voice that does not yet have logos, the shameful, obscene "excrement of the signifier." Despite Holz's professed scorn for Aristotelian theories of dramatic action, *Papa Hamlet* thus hides within it a plot that could hardly be more classical in structure, a well-nigh Sophoclean agon between two opposing forces, neither of whom will survive the encounter. Holz and Schlaf present baby Fortinbras's artless naturalism as the illusion-bursting negation of Thienwiebel's posturing—but his victory is almost as pyrrhic as his namesake's own. One can no doubt read this in a variety of ways, but one is surely as evidence of the fundamental ambivalence at the heart of Holz's naturalism itself. Baby Fortinbras should be the herald of the new theater, a theater of being over seeming, of a nature with no minus x in sight—yet he remains only an abject figure, a fat and filthy creature whose potential claim to authenticity is perpetually undermined by the sheer intolerability of his physical existence. In this way, Thienwiebel's feculent progeny does not subvert so much as reinforce the poetic idealization that Holz professes to disdain, as the ultimate in naturalist performance is portrayed as a debased and doomed existence in all ways "not to be endured" (nicht zum Aushalten).[116] Thienwiebel, who had earlier defended the naturalness of his son's crying, in analogy to breastfeeding, with the fateful words "I've read, there's nothing healthier!" (Ich habe gelesen, es ist nichts gesünder!),[117] in the end kills him for it. The rest is silence.

"Verily, I see a theater"

What the infant and its babble ultimately threaten is the principle of poetic "Verklärung" itself: the presence of an organizing consciousness, a sense of memory and time, self and other—and thus, of a discursive framework that would translate material immanence into transcendent human meaning.[118] The lack of such a framework has frequently been cited as a characteristic of Holz and Schlaf's style, often with moral and existential implications. John Osborne suggests that the absence of a subordinating logic in Holz and Schlaf's work "expresses . . . a sense of loss and anxiety in a fragmented world";[119] Fritz Martini speaks of the *Sekundenstil*'s "breakdown of language into instantaneity and incoherence";[120] and Adorno, less pathetically, writes, "The ruthless, effectively aconceptual presentation of empirical detail in [the naturalist novel] destroyed the familiar surface coherence of the novel in a fashion not unlike that of its later monadic-associative form."[121] In other words: naturalism replaces the metonymic continuity of classical realism with the parataxis of mere description, abandoning (albeit somewhat more inconsistently than Adorno's account would lead one to believe) realism's causal nexus for an atemporal tableau of disconnected objects and sensations. But one does not require the benefit of Adorno's post-modern hindsight to find "monadic-associative" elements in Holz's work. Already the contemporary critics of naturalism reproached its authors, not just with immorality and tastelessness, but also with considering, "in their quest for accuracy, only the juxtaposition of people and things, yet not discovering the true essence, the spirit of either."[122] This charge will achieve its most canonical form in Lukács's rebuke of the "leveling" quality of naturalist description, in which objects end up arranged, as it were, on a flat plane of seemingly equal validity.[123] But Lukács also notes a further consequence of this: "The method of observation and description developed as part of an attempt to make literature scientific. . . . But investigation of social phenomena through observation and their representation in description bring such paltry and schematic results that these modes of composition easily slip into their polar opposite—complete subjectivism."[124] Scientific impartiality devolves into a perspectivism more extreme than that of the most "poetic" of poetic realists: a literature that has as its aim the precise representation of the empirical world ends up as the record of the impressions of the one who represents it.[125]

Given Holz's own description of his late long poem *Phantasus* as the "autobiography of a soul"[126]—not to mention lines like ". . . Ich . . . Ich . . . // . . . Ich?!! . . ."[127]—Holz's eventual turn to subjectivism is not really in question. Indeed, what Lukács and others find so worthy of censure, Holz proclaims outright as the one possibility left to the poet in the modern age:

> For our new, so-called "scientific" ["naturwissenschaftliches"] age . . . It seemed to me that to try to fit a "world picture" into the frame of some kind of "fable" or "plot" would be but childish presumption! What today "belongs" to a world picture is in its individual components too widely dispersed, in its elements too multicoloredly kaleidoscopic [zu buntwimmelnd kaleidoskopisch] for even the most complicated, subtlest "legend" to create the necessary basis for such "content"![128]

Holz rejects the idea of a preexisting narrative in favor of a "scientific" assemblage of sensual impressions, unified only—but what an only!—by the mind that perceives them. Holz's pronouncement effectively turns Friedrich Spielhagen's early-realist denial that the "kaleidoscopically multicolored world" (kaleidoskopisch bunten Welt) could ever be captured by "the cumbersome method of objective representation"[129] completely on its head: for Holz, no transcendent idea (certainly not a Platonic one), but only the individual intake of facts and phenomena is up to the task of giving a halfway adequate picture of the modern world in all its complexity.

Though it is not certain if Holz ever read Husserl, his poetic efforts, like those of many of his contemporaries, thus have much in common, in their way, with the Husserlian project of making perception itself into an object of consciousness, in what Husserl himself calls the "marvelous correlation between the *phenomenon of cognition* and the *object of cognition*."[130] And yet, whatever the similarities, Holz's late poetics could in fact not be further from Husserl's notion of "pure 'seeing'"[131]—or at least, his poetics shows how such "pure 'seeing,'" with its explicitly anthropocentric presumptions, quickly runs into difficulties. If phenomenology maintains a basic epistemological humility in restricting the knowledge of the world to the apperception of its manifestations, Holz, in contrast, equates his apperceptions with knowledge of the world itself: "I design and shape the 'world,' I told myself, if I succeed in mirroring the reflection it has cast into my 'soul'! [wenn es mir gelingt, den Abglanz zu spiegeln, den sie mir in die 'Seele' geworfen!] And the more prolifically, the more variedly, the more vividly I do so, the truer, the deeper, the more powerful will be my work!"[132] Where once Holz had sought truth in the maximally precise recording of the outside world, now truth is sought in the maximally precise recording of the imprint of the outside world on the world within. What is at issue, in other words, is no longer the antiaesthetic reduction of artistic mediation—still less, the dynamic interaction between the object and its perception—but the aggrandizement of the "natural attitude" as lyric self-creation.[133]

In his late work, then, Holz's early goal of veristic description expands into a synoptic vision that goes far beyond slice-of-life sketches of the Berlin working poor to encompass no less than the entirety of the universe, from the poet's garret to the ends of time and space:

when everything is examined, when everything is considered,
when everything is
probed, dissected, summed up,

. . . .

a spiraling vortex, a spinning top, a
dancingwhirling
dervish
spins
on its axis
and precisely and exactly and
accurately,
intensively, positively, impulsively,
intuitively,
circumspectly, correctly, centrally, fundamentally,
most notoriously, energetically, categorically, habitually
gets to
the bottom
of things

wenn man alles prüft, wenn man alles erwägt, wenn man alles
sondiert, seziert, summiert,

. . . .

ein sich schraubender Wirbel, ein sich spulender Kreisel, ein
tanztaumelnder

Derwisch
um sich selber
dreht
und den Dingen präzis und den Dingen exakt und den Dingen
akkurat,
intensiv, positiv, impulsiv,
intuitiv,
zirkumspekt, korrekt, zentral, fundamental,
notorischst, energischst, kategorischst,
gewohnheitsgemäß
auf
den Grund
geht[134]

These lines, from the beginning of the section titled "Great Poetic Wednesday Afternoon in My Ever-Burning-Chair Den" ("Grosser Dichtermittwochnachmittag in meiner Feuerstuhlbude"), are part of an extended description of Holz's study (here, specifically, the floor), which eventually balloons into a lengthy daydream including imaginary conversations on literature and culture, a fantasy symphonic performance, and an ascension to a jewel-encrusted, hosanna-intoning paradise. Even before such Jugendstil effusion, however, the traditional representation of the lyrical *Schreibszene* is padded out to incorporate, not only the description of the poet's workspace and artistic ambitions, but also a reference to the form in which these ambitions are to be accomplished—the "dancingwhirling dervish" is surely a metaphor for Holz's device of the "invisible middle axis," or center justification, through which, he claims, he is able to achieve "the poem's audible image" (das Ohrbild [des] Gedichtes)[135]—and the proleptic assertion of these ambitions' fulfillment.

Here one can perhaps see the effects of the negative reviews of Holz's early work on his creative process: what was once a confident announcement of "a new form of art . . . that immerses itself in the life around us more instinctively, more germinally than the previous one [die sich triebsicherer senkt in das Leben um uns, keimtiefer als die bisherige]"[136] has now been transformed into a self-lacerating skepticism, in which Holz's characteristic bluster hardly suffices to hide the depths of his epistemological despair:

. . . the
so-called "reality" (If I may! Granted! "So-called"?)
so-called!! so-called!!
so-called
reality, reality,
in
quotation marks

. . . die
sogenannte "Realität" (Pardon! Gestatten! "Sogenannte"?)
sogenannte!! sogenannte!!
sogenannte
Realität, Realität,
in
Gänsefüßchen[137]

Such despair about the nature of "reality"—or, rather, the despair of the possibility of a reality *without* scare quotes—is nevertheless not a turn away from Holz's previous positivism so much as its direct consequence. Holz's former belief in his ability to describe things according to their—in Holz's unintentionally oxymoronic phrase—"innermost immanence" (innerste Immanenz)[138] ultimately leads him to the practice of an infinitely proliferating description of description itself, in a display of expository virtuosity that can only be reasserted, over and over, with increasingly manic insistence.

What Samuel Weber has described as "the tendency of the baroque theater toward ostentation, since the only saving grace it can envisage is the demonstration of its own theatricality,"[139] thus appears in Holz's "'baroque' / baroquebaroque / or / if you like, / . . . / even / Rennaisancebaroque" ("Barock," / Barockbarock / oder / meinethalb, / . . . / auch / Renaissance-barock)[140] late work as a growing tendency—a long way from the "language of life"!—not only to ostentation and self-referentiality, but also to redundancy, digression, neologism, purpleness, and plain old word count as a substitute for epistemological comprehensiveness.[141] In the thousand-some pages of *Phantasus*, nearly every adjective is a superlative or in some way expressive of superlativeness, while the adjectives themselves pile up to the point of proto-Seussian doggerel:

faustianest, enchantedest, alchemicalest, bizarrest, romanticest,
exorcisticest,
pandemoniacest, adventuresomest,
idolatrousest,
blackened, brownèd,
marbled, mottled, bronzèd, colored
pigmented,
benuanced, betinctured, bebarraged,
besmeared, bestained, besmoldered,
besmirched,
beschmooched, bemuddled, bemoodled,
besquallseminated,
berumpled,
becrumpled and bescrumpled

faustischst, verwunschenst, alchimistischst, bizarrst, romantischst,
exorzistischst,
pandämonischst, abenteuerlichst,
idolatristischst,
geschwärzten, gebräunten,
marmorierten, melierten, bronzierten, kolorierten,
pigmentierten,
benüanzierten, betinkturierten, bebombardierten,
beschmauchten, beschmorten, beschwelten,
beschmuddelten,
beschmudelten, bepruddelten, beprudelten,
beschwalschwängerten,
bepurkelten,
bemurkelten und beschmurkelten[142]

(Here Holz has moved on from the floor to describe the plaster ceiling of his study.) Meanwhile, in an earlier section, subtitled "Late-Autumn Sorrow" ("Spätherbsttrauer"), a sentimental lament for a bygone span of artistic labor—"Weeks, months / long / I sat, I / thought . . . and . . . wrote!"[143]—Holz brings the manic completism of his poem to its constative climax:

Things, that once, painfully, hurt me, things that once, joyfully, moved me, things
from thousands of years ago, things that never were,
. . . .
a
sea, a . . . desert . . . a mountain
of paper,
paper, paper
and
"things" . . . "things" . . . "things"
"things"!!

Dinge, die mich, qualvoll, einst geschmerzt, Dinge, die mich, freudig, einst bewegt, Dinge
von vor tausend Jahren, Dinge, die noch niemals waren,
. . . .
ein
Meer, ein . . . Wust . . . ein Berg
Papier,
Papier, Papier
und
"Dinge" . . . "Dinge" . . . "Dinge,"
"Dinge"!![144]

If in Zola, as Fredric Jameson has argued, a concern for scientific exactitude finally issues in an inventorial proliferation that "comes before us not as things or visible objects but [as] . . . the alien guts and insides of the words themselves,"[145] Holz's late lyric, converting the abundance of the empirical into a profusion of self-referentiality, raises this process to the *n*th power. Yet even if the referential concreteness of Holz's poetry often goes missing in its sheer accumulative prolixity, a *sensation* of material excess nevertheless remains. This sensation of material excess reaches perhaps its height in Holz's dramaturgical pendant to his manic verse autobiography, the elephantine theatrical pastiche *Die Blechschmiede*. With its 750-some pages—including a 3,118-person dramatis personae of "'active characters,' gods, voices, choruses, allegories, abstractions, phantasms, miasmas, pleonasms, protoplasms, sarcasms, etc." ("Handelnde Menschen," Götter, Stimmen, Chöre, Allegorien, Abstraktionen, Phantasmen, Miasmen, Pleonasmen, Protoplasmen, Sarkasmen etcetera)[146] containing such entries as "Small Pocket Natural Philosopher,"[147] "Autointoxication in Animals,"[148] and "A Pope Whose Name Has Slipped the Author's Mind"[149]—Holz's unperformable "monster-drama"[150] is, perhaps even more than *Phantasus*, an undeniable masterpiece of sensory overload, a polyphonic bombardment of words and images in which Faustian *Wißbegier* and bitter self-parody continually intersect with and feed off of one another. Indeed, if the ambition of *Phantasus* is the comparatively modest one of recounting the emergence (albeit through eons of time) of Holz himself, the ambition of *Die Blechschmiede* is no less than to produce, as Holz writes in a letter to Georg Hirth, a "gigantic mosaic"—"as documentary as possible"—of the natural history of the world, "whose thousand tiny individual multicolored stones [tausend bunte Einzelsteinchen] . . . should be wrought in such a way that each one of these particles, even when taken out of the whole, contains within itself the complete picture [seine Bildwirkung als Einzelnes behält]."[151]

It is particularly in the "Modern Walpurgis Night" act of *Die Blechschmiede*—Holz's contribution to the popular genre of the *Faust* parody—that it becomes clear just how literally Holz means to implement this task. The majority of the act is devoted to a Darwinian fantasia about the origins of life, enumerated in sections from "A" (the beginnings of organic life) to "M" (the appearance of the first humanoids).[152] Evolutionary biology also features in *Phantasus*, in which Holz, borrowing from Ernst Haeckel's morphological theories, narrates his own existence as a reverse chronological history of life on earth, from the "Stone Age man"[153] to the first "protoplasmic blob."[154] In *Die Blechschmiede*, however, a slightly different conceit is in play. In place of the universal-autobiographical perspective of the lyric I, Holz introduces the concept of a "diabolical eyepiece" (diabolischen Okular):[155] a literal zoetrope, "life-turning," that displays the history of the natural world in an unending series of flickering images. Janelle Blankenship has read this section as evidence of Holz's "unabashed enthusiasm for . . . media age knowledge," "a techno-world at a glance" inspired by "the sight-seeing aesthetic of early cinema."[156] Visual technology undeniably plays a role in Holz's epistemological spectacle (even if *Die Blechschmiede* probably owes as much to the magic lantern and the *Varieté* as it does to newer forms of media). Indeed, as Blankenship observes, Holz brings the fin de siècle's pet themes of media technology and Darwinist biology together in one huge evolutionary history, as in the following passage, where Holz compares the primitive "eyes" of mollusks, echinoderms, and the lower articulate animals to the very latest in optical technology:

on their eyerodsensitive, on their photoreceptorreceptive, on their
neuralbranching, neuralchaosing,
neuralmultilayeredastonishing,
retinal fundus,
through the "secretion," through the
"converging lens," through the "vitreous body,"
. . . .
already
ever so meticulously, ever so precisely,
chromophotographic, cameraobscuric, stimulustelegraphic,
de-, in-,
and
reflecting
the
"world" around them
redred
tiny ruby eyespots

auf ihrem sehstäbchenempfindlichen, auf ihrem sehzellenemfänglichen, auf ihrem
nervenästeligen, nervenwirrsaligen,
nervenvielschichtigverwunderlichen
Netzhauthintergrund,
quer durch "Sekret," quer durch
"Sammellinse," quer durch "Glaskörper,"
. . . .
die
"Welt" um sie
schon
peinlichst, genaust
buntphotographisch, kameraobskurahaft, reiztelegraphisch
zurück-, ab-
und
wiederspeigelnden,
rotroten
Rubinpunktäugelchen[157]

Fig. 1. Fritz Rumpf, title page of the first edition of Arno Holz, *Phantasus* (Berlin: Sassenbach, 1898). Courtesy Deutsches Textarchiv, Berlin-Brandenburgischen Akademie der Wissenschaften.

"If Holz is here parodying his own technologically inspired writing style," writes Blankenship, "his text is nonetheless . . . a utopic compendium of the hopes and dreams that nourish new media in the late nineteenth and early twentieth centuries."[158] However, a closer look at Holz's drama reveals it to be less a celebration of visual media than its nightmarish invocation. Where once in Stifter the diverging beams of the convex mirror organized disparate objects within the field of perception, now the irritated "Sammellinse" of the mollusk's primitive vision turns its gaze only on a chaotic flash of disordered images, and Holz's hallucinatory filmstrip itself eventually breaks off with the appearance of the first humans, descending into pages of bawdy couplets ridiculing the great men and women of history and then into an increasingly chaotic Witches' Sabbath, until the whole spectacle is finally dissolved by the Mephistophelean "Author" in a veil of sulfurous mist.

What the "diabolical eyepiece" of Holz's *Faust* parody thus gives to view is not the "source of all life / On which hang heaven and earth" but "only a show."[159] By the end of the act, the all-seeing, techno-demonic eye that opens the spectacle will be replaced with the "holecoal-black" (lochkohlschwarz) aperture of Satan's anus;[160] the "ruby eyespots"[161] with which the first arthropods gazed out at the world will reappear in the theater's "rubyred discs over the emergency exits" (rubinroten Scheiben über den Notausgängen),[162] which, after the end of the fantastic performance, blink out and go dark. Despite Holz's earlier paeans to the drama's "magnifying / telescope" (vergrößerndem / Perspektiv) as an "eruptivest, elementaryest, / . . . / . . . as if lust-gutted colossal . . . / . . . / firesparkflamefountain" (eruptivst, elementarst, / . . . / . . . wie geilwüst kolossale . . . / . . . / Feuerfunkenflammenfontaine),[163] the demonically visionary power of the "hocus-pocus-extralong-glass" (Hokuspokus-Überfernrohr)[164] is ultimately impotent to capture the form of things, much less, to penetrate their inner depths. (The priapic tenor of Holz's writing, meanwhile, seems to have been divined by his illustrators: while the Jugendstil arabesque of the cover of the first printing of *Phantasus* is undoubtedly a reference to the poem's "middle-axis" arrangement, its phallicness is hard to ignore.)

We are in many ways very far from the sentimental naturalism of *Papa Hamlet*, but in one aspect, at least, nothing has changed. From the standpoint of the transcendental subject—be it the "scientific" observer of Holz's early literary experiments, the cinematic phantasmagoria of *Die Blechschmiede*, or the transmorphic "soul" of *Phantasus*—the result of looking at things too closely, with too naked an eye, is *terror* and *disgust*:

in
impossible postures, in the most twisted figures,
more indecent
than breeding priests, more shameless than
whores,
with paunch-bellies and bulge-breasts, in all lecheries and lusts, with
fingers, limbs, tongues,
and
"devices,"
in all
rut-entanglements, in all
"art"-embroilments
and
obscenities

in
unmöglichen Posituren, in verrenktesten Figuren,
unzüchtiger
als Deckpriester, schamloser als
Huren,

mit Feistbäuchen und Prallbrüsten, in allen Lastern und Lüsten, mit
Fingern, Gliedern, Zungen
und
"Geräten,"
in allen Brunstverstricktheiten, in allen
"Kunst"verzwicktheiten
und
Obszönitäten[165]

There are a lot of words in *Phantasus*, and not all of them are carefully chosen. We would thus not make too much of the appearance of the word "Obszönitäten" in this passage, were it not for the fact that Holz's work continually evokes just that idea of the material world as an "unjustifiable facticity,"[166] as a senseless and unmediated physical presence, that later writers, working from the same intellectual tradition, will baptize with that name.[167] In Holz, the pseudoscientific wish to apprehend the world in all its immensity tips over almost immediately into a baroque hypertheatricality of ostensive objects; as Holz puts it in *Die Blechschmiede*: "the whole huge, varied, all oro-, hydro- and other topographical forms, norms, formations, possibilities, and magical stimuli of terrestrial, scenic, most eye-blindingly, spellbindingly sansarically thisworldly beauty" (das ganze, große, bunte, alle oro-, hydro- und sonstigen topographischen Formen, Normen, Bildungen, Möglichkeiten und Zauberreize irdischer, landschaftlicher, augenverblendendster, sinnberauschendster sansarischer Diesseitsschönheit),[168] a grotesque procession of profane and profaned phenomena "actually, / strictly speaking and by law / already / even just in a picture hardly / to / be borne" (eigentlich, / genau genommen und von Rechts wegen / auch schon / selbst im bloßen Bilde kaum noch / zu / duldenden).[169]

Holz's work thus necessitates a reassessment of Naomi Schor's assertion that "the ongoing valorization of the detail appears to be an essential aspect of that dismantling of idealist metaphysics which looms so large on the agenda of modernity."[170] That is: the detail confirms rather than dismantles idealist metaphysics, *to the extent that it is envisioned as "obscene."*[171] From the sticky hovels of ham actors to the ceaseless spool of biological life, to perceive things, for Holz, is to perceive them in their alien superabundance: a surfeit of "outrageous, salacious, / disgraceful, out of placeful" (widerlichen, liederlichen, / empörenden, sich nicht gehörenden) images that perpetually fails—again and again and again—to arrive at those things' "truth."[172] The problem with Holz's works, the reason they failed to become the harbingers of an art of the future that Holz imagined them to be, is thus not the problem that his contemporary critics divined in them, that they "debase the taste of the German public with that revolting mash of dung and rotgut that [their authors] call 'Nature.' "[173] Rather, the problem is that Holz's representation of "nature" as "dung and rotgut" is a sign of the persistence of the very aesthetics he claims to rebel against, such that this rebellion could only appear in the light, not just of the critics' scorn and disgust, but also, in the end, of Holz's own. Holz's fanatic empiricism glorifies presence only to run aground on the horror thereof. Despite his ambitions, Holz's work constitutes less idealism's death blow than its spectacular apotheosis, the culmination of the fear of materiality in the guise of its exaltation.

Chapter 5

✦

Dead Ends

Gottfried Benn

> The darkest of all things, indeed darkness itself according to some, is matter.
>
> —F. W. J. Schelling, *Ueber das Verhältniß des Realen und Idealen in der Natur*[1]

One of the leading metaphors of literary realism in its naturalist incarnations—second perhaps only to photography—was that of the doctor or medical scientist. "One senses," write Arno Holz and Johannes Schlaf in their "translator's preface" to *Papa Hamlet*, "how [the play's style] is the living product of an era of which it is said that its anatomists are poets, and its poets anatomists."[2] Such a metaphor was, of course, hardly unique to Holz and Schlaf. Büchner, Flaubert, Zola, Hauptmann, and many others made use of both specialized scientific knowledge and the popular medical imaginary to at once inform the contents of their works and justify their modes of representation. For writers and readers of the late nineteenth century, the author as doctor offered a model for a modern literature of cool precision and diagnostic insight, freed from the unreliability of speculation and the limitations of personal perspective into the unbiased search for truth.[3]

Needless to say, this "medical turn" was not universally beloved. A passage from Julian Schmidt provides a representative view of the dissenting camp:

> The young physician, in order to overcome his initial revulsion toward anatomy, is easily tempted to seek out the loathsome with a certain bravado and to become engrossed in it [das Widerliche mit einer gewissen Renommisterei aufzusuchen und sich darin zu vertiefen]. But only in recent times has one felt it incumbent on oneself to put such cynicism openly on display [offen zur Schau zu tragen]. If the spiritualists spoke of the infiniteness of the spirit and the finitude of matter, then the materialists emphasize in contrast the eternity of matter and the finiteness of the spirit, and from there draw the

> conclusion that matter is the main thing, and spirit only secondary; the latter is illusion [Schein], the former reality [Wirklichkeit].[4]

Such a passage is one that Gottfried Benn—a young doctor in point of fact—might well have taken for his motto. Though Schmidt's assessment of "materialism" is both oversimplified and ideologically laden, his hypothetical portrait is nevertheless a fitting description avant la lettre of Benn's early writing, which, filled with intentionally provocative images of the human body in states of corruption, disease, and death, pointedly puts a mordant "cynicism" about the relation of life to matter "openly on display." Certainly, there could be no better or more calculated illustration of the cavalier attitude toward human anatomy that Schmidt denounces than Benn's first major work, the short poem cycle *Morgue*, which, in brief, mostly unrhymed and apparently unadorned language, describes, with nonchalant swagger, a series of tableaus of autopsies such as those Benn himself presumably participated in during his medical training in the teaching hospitals of Berlin. A line from the cycle's concluding sonnet, "Requiem," offers the poems' succinct moral: "Each one three buckets full: from brain to balls" (Jeder drei Näpfe voll: von Hirn bis Hoden).[5] Here, the physician's "constant occupation with dead matter" (beständigen Beschäftigung mit der todten Materie)[6] leads indeed to a rejection of both the inherent dignity of human life and the aesthetic forms used to convey it. Little wonder that Benn's poems provoked ire and exasperation within the literary establishment from the very beginning. As one typically outraged critic writes of Benn's early efforts: "Incomprehensibility, sheer nonsense, perversity, and eroticism are presented as a guarantee of poetic talent. . . . What speaks in these verses is a repulsive delight in ugliness, filth, in shameless openness. Here a gaudy naturalism wants to serve only one purpose: *épater le bourgeois*."[7]

"The Romantic only *observes* the world, the Realist *dissects* it" (Der Romantiker *betrachtet* eben die Welt, der Realist *seziert* sie).[8] What then for the naturalists always remained, despite everything, essentially metaphor becomes in Benn aggressively, flamboyantly literalized. In his early poems and prose, Benn stages the image of an anatomized materiality as at once an intensified form of realism and a new antihumanist aesthetics, knowingly realizing precisely that which Schmidt, a few decades previous, warns against: "If one imagines that one can negate the spirit by returning it to its material basis, this is the same error as when, in aesthetics, one wants to abolish the idea of the sublime because the material object of this feeling can be broken down into gravel, earth, and dirt."[9] However, in spite of what most critics of the time seemed to assume, such a literalization of naturalist "dissection" is not the sign of Benn's intensified adherence to the naturalist program. Instead, it emerges out of a deeply conflicted *disillusionment* with naturalism's poetics as well as with the empirical spirit on which it claimed to be based.[10] For Benn not only presents both the human being and the natural world as mere material for examination; he also represents this examined human and nonhuman material in a way that is all too clearly intended to disturb and offend, amplifying the analytic coolness of what Michel Foucault terms the "medical gaze"[11] with the rhetoric of the *Schauerroman*, the torture chamber, and the pornographic tableau. Thus, in contrast to the other authors discussed so far, Benn practices a conscious poetics of obscenity: an intentionally antisentimental, antiaesthetic representation in which the scientific poses of naturalism are simultaneously exploited and turned against themselves, in which the naked sensuousness so feared by mid-nineteenth-century authors is now flaunted openly as horror, rebellion, and shock. Benn's scandalous modernism fulfills realism, in other words, by bringing to the surface precisely that which realism had sought to bury.

What Remains

Let us begin with one of Benn's best-known works, "Mann und Frau gehn durch die Krebsbaracke" ("Man and Woman Walk through the Cancer Ward") from his breakthrough 1912 chapbook, *Morgue und andere Gedichte* (*Morgue and Other Poems*):

> The man:
> In this row here are disintegrated wombs
> and this row are disintegrated breasts.
> Bed after bed stinks. The nurses change shifts hourly.
>
> Come, go ahead and lift up this blanket.
> See, these lumps of fat and foul sap
> were once some man's everything,
> and meant rapture and homeland.
>
> Come, take a look at the scar on this breast.
> Do you feel that rosary of tender knots?
> Go ahead and touch. The flesh is soft and feels no pain.
>
> This one here bleeds enough for thirty bodies.
> No one has so much blood.
> And from this one here, first they cut
> the child out of her cancered womb.
>
> They're kept asleep. Day and night.—To the new ones
> they say: Here you'll sleep yourselves well.—Only on Sundays
> for visits do they wake them up a bit.

Food is barely consumed. The backs
are covered in bedsores. You can see the flies. Sometimes
a nurse washes them. As one washes pews.

Here the soil is already rising up around each bed.
Flesh flattens out to land. Warmth dissipates.
Sap readies itself to flow. Earth calls.

Der Mann:
Hier diese Reihe sind zerfallene Schöße
und diese Reihe ist zerfallene Brust.
Bett stinkt bei Bett. Die Schwestern wechseln stündlich.

Komm, hebe ruhig diese Decke auf.
Sieh, dieser Klumpen Fett und faule Säfte,
das war einst irgendeinem Mann groß
und hieß auch Rausch und Heimat.

Komm, sieh auf diese Narbe an der Brust.
Fühlst du den Rosenkranz von weichen Knoten?
Fühl ruhig hin. Das Fleisch ist weich und schmerzt nicht.

Hier diese blutet wie aus dreißig Leibern.
Kein Mensch hat so viel Blut.
Hier dieser schnitt man
erst noch ein Kind aus dem verkrebsten Schoß.

Man läßt sie schlafen. Tag und Nacht.—Den Neuen
sagt man: Hier schläft man sich gesund.—Nur Sonntags
für den Besuch läßt man sie etwas wacher.

Nahrung wird wenig noch verzehrt. Die Rücken
sind wund. Du siehst die Fliegen. Manchmal
wäscht sie die Schwester. Wie man Bänke wäscht.

Hier schwillt der Acker schon um jedes Bett.
Fleisch ebnet sich zu Land. Glut gibt sich fort.
Saft schickt sich an zu rinnen. Erde ruft.[12]

What more can be said of this poem, or of the other works of Benn's early period, that has not been said already? Already the earliest commentators on Benn's succès de scandale condemned the poems' calm reduction of the human to its most grotesque physicality, deprived of all compassion, redemption, or, in most cases, even a proper lyric I to frame their parade of revolting images.[13] Such observations, substantiated not least by Benn's own pronouncements in various essays and talks, have continued to shape Benn criticism up to the present day—with the question most often being whether Benn's "juvenile shockers"[14] should be evaluated as a mark of radical Nietzschean honesty, latent theistic nostalgia, or protofascist nihilism presaging Benn's own wrong turn into Nazism as the false promise of a collective revaluation of all values.[15] What praise Benn's book did receive mainly focused on what was seen as the uncompromising realism of its representations in the context of what was, again, the era's leading metaphor: the scalpel-sharp gaze of a genuinely modern doctor-poet unsusceptible to Romantic euphemism. Positive reviews of the time describe the *Morgue* poems as a masterpiece of "reality, the power of fact [Tatsachenwucht],"[16] the "intensive and unmediated" reproduction of "what really went on in the hospital ward" (was damals im Krankensaal wirklich vor sich ging).[17]

Such a view is no longer current. At least since Joachim Dyck's commonsensical observation that the treatment of Benn's poems as documentary descriptions could be held only by readers who had never actually read a medical protocol or witnessed an autopsy,[18] attention has largely shifted to the rhetorical and symbolic strategies of Benn's writing, the ways in which it simulates naturalistic exactitude while being anything but.[19] Why, then, did so many of Benn's contemporaries fall into the naturalist trap? Helmut Lethen suggests that such impressions of verisimilitude were produced by the poems' "vague gestures," which "set off chains of associations, leading to a tabooed space that the reader only knows from hearsay."[20] However, this is only partly true: even if direct experience of the autopsy room would have been unknown to most readers, the autopsy room as literary and artistic topos was a far from uncommon phenomenon of the time. As Elisabeth Bronfen has shown, in the eighteenth and nineteenth centuries, the dead body—in particular, the beautiful, young, female dead body—functioned as an intensified site of imagination and knowledge production, at the intersection of several competing discourses.[21] At the same time as spiritualist teachings venerated the just-deceased person as a potential gateway to the beyond, the biological sciences elevated the fresh corpse to an exemplary object of study, a ready text from which to be able to read the secrets of organic life. In the contemplation of the dead yet not yet decomposed body, the observer could both safely objectify the human form and confirm his own agency in contradistinction. The autopsy room thus offered itself as the perfect mix of mystery and exhibition, a space of both metaphysical speculation and scientific inquiry in which objectivity, melancholy, and the prurience of the male gaze crossed and organically combined.

German literature was hardly insensitive to the appeal of such a combination. Friedrich Hebbel starts the trend in 1848 with his short poem "La Morgue"—which however largely eschews description of its two corpses in order to conjure up the respective scenes of their tragic, self-inflicted deaths.[22] In contrast to Hebbel's poem, the 1905 "In der Morgue" by the fin de siècle poet Julia Virginia Scheuermann turns its attention to the corpse itself, depicted in sentimental rhyming couplets "stretched out in youthful splendor," Snow White–style, under "bright, cold glass."[23] Similarly (though in literary quality a quantum leap from either of the first two poems), Rainer Maria Rilke's 1907 sonnet "Morgue" contemplates its row of corpses with a mixture of circumspect wonder and wry matter-of-factness, until the last stanza, in a typically Rilkean inversion, suddenly shifts to the perspective of the corpses themselves, whose "eyes have turned beneath their lids / and now look inward" (Die Augen haben hinter ihren Lidern / sich umgewandt und schauen jetzt hinein).[24] Finally, in 1912 (the same year as the appearance of Benn's own chapbook), Georg Heym's posthumously published "Die Morgue," in audible homage to François Villon's "Ballade des Pendus," uses the first-person plural to let the arrayed corpses speak collectively of their current fate, to express their hopes for salvation and their fears of eternal oblivion: "Over is our time. It is fulfilled. / We are below. Lo, now we are dead and done. / Already in our whitened eyes night dwells. / Ne'er more shall we behold another dawn" (Vorbei ist unsre Zeit. Es ist vollbracht. / Wir sind herunter. Seht, wir sind nun tot. / In weißen Augen wohnt uns schon die Nacht, / Wir schauen nimmermehr ein Morgenrot).[25]

It is in contrast to these poems that the provocation of Benn's work becomes clear.[26] Take the first poem from the title cycle of the *Morgue* volume, "Kleine Aster" ("Little Aster"):

> A drowned beer deliveryman was hauled onto the slab.
> Someone had jammed a dark pale lilac aster
> between his teeth.
> As I sliced into the chest
> under the skin
> with a long knife
> to cut out tongue and gums,
> I must have jarred it, because it slid
> into the adjacent brain.
> I packed it into the chest cavity
> among the wood shavings,
> as he was being sewn up.
> Drink up in your vase!
> Rest in peace,
> little aster!
>
> Ein ersoffener Bierfahrer wurde auf den Tisch gestemmt.
> Irgendeiner hatte ihm eine dunkelhellila Aster
> zwischen die Zähne geklemmt.

Als ich von der Brust aus
unter der Haut
mit einem langen Messer
Zunge und Gaumen herausschnitt,
muß ich sie angestoßen haben, denn sie glitt
in das nebenliegende Gehirn.
Ich packte sie ihm in die Brusthöhle
zwischen die Holzwolle,
als man zunähte.
Trinke dich satt in deiner Vase!
Ruhe sanft,
kleine Aster![27]

Gone is the elevated language of Hebbel's, Scheuermann's, Rilke's, and Heym's poems: the rhyme, meter, metaphors, inversions, and other devices that allow them to translate the grisliness of their settings into a familiar lyrical sublimity.[28] Gone, too, are those poems' sense of hushed awe in the house of death and the feeling of a mystery that transcends the poet's privileged but still infinitely limited knowledge. Gone above all, however, is the attempt to humanize the corpse itself, be it through sentimentalizing projection, prosopopoeic imagination, or prophetic insight. Or rather, what "humanization" there is in Benn's poem comes only in the form of a joke by some waggish colleague, who has stuck the titular flower in the dead man's mouth as if adding the final touches to the costume of some cabaret coquette. (Alternatively, one could read this gesture somewhat less anthropomorphically to mean that the dead man is already "pushing up daisies.")[29] Such a joke, however, only emphasizes what the poem already everywhere expresses: *this* corpse will be treated neither as the plaintive sign of its former humanity, nor as an oblique portal to the beyond, but simply as an object on which one operates: a material thing, severable and manipulatable, less deserving of eulogy even than the orphan flower buried within it. Here there is no need to wonder, as Heym's corpses tremblingly do, if the body "will . . . slowly disintegrate, / . . . / Crumble into nothing" (werden . . . langsam zerfallen, / . . . / Zerbröckeln in Nichts):[30] that which Heym's poem suggests as its speakers' last, tragic fate, Benn's poem opens by taking for granted.

Though "Kleine Aster" is almost unique among the poems in the volume in being spoken from a first-person perspective,[31] the sense of an observer is nevertheless minimal; the poem appears tossed-off, desultory,[32] certainly without the moralizing reflections and emotional commitments that, albeit in very different ways, suffuse the other writers' morgue-themed poems. Thus Martin Travers speaks, aptly, of Benn's "evacuation of the human as the centre of poetic focus": "Evocation has given way to demarcation, atmosphere to analysis. . . . This is . . . naturalism turned inside out, and forced to give itself up as material symbolism. It is a poem without poetry."[33] More accurate, however, would be to say that this is a poem without *Verklärung*. Benn's poem is no longer concerned with "the transfiguration of the mundane world through artistic sensibility":[34] the discursive contextualization and affective investment that allowed realist writers to reconcile empirical fact with human perception and experience. If there is an affective investment in the poem, it is only the affectless affect of what Helmut Lethen has called the "cool persona," whose gaze, "not without a hint of sadism," "*de*psychologizes the observed object, . . . assimilating it to the rules of natural scientific discourse."[35]

This is of course not to say that "Kleine Aster," any more than any of the other poems in Benn's collection, simply relates things "as they are." Rather, in their deliberate subversion of poetic conventions, Benn's poems *evoke* naturalism's descriptive objectivity while remaining themselves but the lyrical figurations thereof. Indeed, Benn's undercutting of the reader's expectations is virtually systematic in its inversions: in "Kleine Aster," the blue flowers of Romantic lyric are transformed into material for a bad practical joke; in "Schöne Jugend" ("Beautiful Youth"), what first appears to be an elegy for a drowned maiden ends up as an elegy for a nest of baby rats;[36] in "Kreislauf" ("Circulation"), the religious teaching of "dust to dust" is invoked to justify stealing the gold filling from a dead prostitute's tooth;[37] in "Negerbraut" ("Negro Bride"), the amatory ecstasies of the bridal bed turn into the promiscuous juxtapositions of the autopsy slab;[38] and finally, in "Requiem," most transparently, the Christian doctrine of the afterlife and the opening of the tombs in the Last Judgment is travestied as rows upon rows of disemboweled corpses and a slop bucket for the innards.[39]

Here, then, is one of the points where naturalism and the expressionism with which Benn maintained a close but conflicted relationship throughout his life,[40] despite all seeming unlikeness, touch: the unsentimental clinical exposure of quotidian horror as another form of expressionism's "ruthless getting-to-the-root-of-things" (rücksichtsloses An-die-Wurzel-der-Dinge-Gehen),[41] breaking down bourgeois pieties and conventional modes of representation for new and more authentic horizons of experience. On the one hand, then, Benn represents precisely that which the conservative critics of naturalism most feared: that the hidden rationale of naturalism's matter-of-fact descriptions is neither "knowledge" nor "science" but, rather, a sadistic pleasure in forcing people to look upon atrocity, a perverse joy in sensationalism for sensationalism's sake. Something of this, for example, is at work in "Mann und Frau gehn durch die Krebsbaracke," as the poem's narrator not only describes the insentient patients' wasted bodies, but also insists, with anaphoric imperative force, upon his companion seeing, touching, exposing them, reduplicating the poem's own deictic gesture on the level of its internal scene. On the other hand, however, this overbid of naturalist frankness is also the denaturalizing of naturalism itself. For Zola, at least according to his own account, there is no difference between the study of human biomechanics and the study of the human soul: "When it has been proved that the body of man is a machine, whose machinery can be taken apart and put together again at the will of the experimenter, then we can pass to the passionate and intellectual acts of man. . . . All things hang together; it is necessary to start from the determinism of inanimate bodies in order to arrive at the determinism of living beings."[42] At first, Benn's dissected corpses, scrutinized by the physician's cool gaze, would seem to be the culmination of such analytic confidence. But they are more properly its travesty: the "machinery" of the human body is indeed "taken apart and put together again," but there is no wisdom and no prognostic insight to be gained from this, unless it be the bleak wisdom of the inorganic basis of organic life itself and the ineluctable fact of what Bronfen calls "the obscenity of death."[43]

Thus, as Lethen affirms, "Benn uses the naturalist short circuits . . . as material for aesthetic play."[44] His naturalism is a naturalism *zweiten Grades*, a dark parody of its methods from the point of view of its inadequacy. Or as Giorgio Agamben has put it, in a synoptic description that does not fail to include Benn in its list: "Confronted with a world that glorifies man so much the more it reduces him to an object, modern poetry unmasks the humanitarian ideology by making rigorously its own the *boutade* that Balzac puts in George Brummell's mouth: 'Nothing less resembles man than man.' "[45] But even the fungible commodities and self-alienated poses of Balzac's dandy are radiant with humanistic warmth compared to Benn's cold catalogue of dismembered bodies and rotting organs, which not only objectify the human being as its physical body, but also reduce *this* body to its component parts, which are then further reduced to the undifferentiated slime of mingled innards, waste, excrement. Indeed, Benn even ups the ante by combining his images of disintegrated corpses with the favored expressionist tropes of poverty, crime, and urban decay. For these are not the mourned remains of beloved individuals in their last rest, but the bodies of whores, alcoholics, menials, murder victims: trash bodies already in life, whose clinical desecrations of their anonymous cadavers come merely as one more, final, violation.

What this means is that the *Morgue* poems are dependent on an aesthetics of *Verklärung* indeed—but it is a *Verklärung ex negativo*, in which the ostentatious subversion of Romantic tropes and the morbid fascination of the subject matter itself cause the things described to appear with all the shocking force of fact.[46] *This* is a "reality effect" of a quite different kind than either the calculated randomness of Barthesian detail-realism or the encyclopedic empiricism of Zola. However, this new, let us call it modernist reality effect is a war waged on two fronts. At the same time as it rejects realism's homey humanism (not to speak of more evidently sentimental forms of art), it repudiates the confident positivism of literary naturalism, which not only posits a basic correspondence between appearance and essence, but also always ultimately subordinates even the most unsparing descriptions of material phenomena to the higher goals of man's search for knowledge and the biopolitical betterment of the human race. If Zola, quoting the physiologist Claude Bernard, once compared his work to "a superb salon, flooded with light, which you can only reach by passing through a long and nauseating kitchen,"[47] Benn's *Morgue*, it would seem, is Bernard's kitchen without the illumination. Benn not only offers a vision of human being at its most material, but also of matter at its most *non*vital, mocking the idea that either living or inanimate bodies could ever be a source of anything beyond one's own nauseated contempt. Seventy years after Adalbert Stifter described the Vienna catacombs as "a region in which everything that we are used to contemplating in life with awe and reverence is violently destroyed" (ein Gebiet, wo alles gewaltsam zernichtet wird, was wir im Leben mit Scheu und Ehrfurcht zu betrachten gewohnt sind),[48] Benn takes a grim pleasure in figuratively mutilating his already decomposing corpses, as if to hasten Stifter's conclusion that, in the end, "the highest and holiest there is on this earth, the human form, turns into a worthless thing, tossed onto the dust heap to lie there like any other piece of trash [hingeworfen in das Kehricht, daß es liege, wie ein anderer Unrath]."[49]

The Veil of Flesh

Thus even the inflationary repurposing of naturalist aesthetics that Lethen and others have pointed out does not go far enough in registering the sheer horror of materiality that Benn's poems express: something that one might, in fact, expect *not* to find in a career doctor supposedly habituated to the practical reality of human physicality. A number of studies over the past decades have devoted themselves to the topic of Benn's medical training, in particular, his work under the tutelage of the neurologist Theodor Ziehen.[50] While these studies tend to differ widely in their assessment of how one should understand the connection between Benn's poetic and medical practices, all are in agreement that Benn's early writing reveals a profound dissatisfaction with the answers proposed by both literature and science to the fundamental problems of existence. For the young poet-doctor (and apostate pastor's son) Benn, neither psychology nor physiology finally succeed in accounting for what for him is the only question really worth asking: how human consciousness emerges out of the physical substance that constitutes it and what the mystery of the soul is in the context of the actual ineluctability of what Julian Schmidt once disparagingly called "the eternity of matter."

This was not always the case. An early fictional dialogue of Benn's that appeared in *Die Grenzboten* in 1910, simply titled "Gespräch" ("Conversation"), reveals Benn's initial enthusiasm for both naturalism's epistemological promises and the positivist science from which they drew their inspiration. In the dialogue, two friends, Gert and Thom, sit in a café discussing literature. Thom, revealing himself as a spokesperson for the new style, quickly takes the upper hand:

> Look here, nowadays if you say of someone that he composes poems or writes short stories, it's almost like saying he has a skin condition. . . . But if one can't leave it alone, then the only recourse is to restore things and events to their purely factual existence, to place them on a scientific basis [die Dinge und Geschehnisse auf ihren rein tatsächlichen Bestand zurückzuführen, sie auf eine wissenschaftliche Basis zu stellen].[51]

What follows from this (in fact, taking up most of the dialogue) is a plug for the Danish novelist, scientist, and Darwin-translator Jens Peter Jacobsen, whom Thom praises as a writer whose "entire style is absolutely scientific [absolut naturwissenschaftlich]. I mean, the way in which he sees things."[52] Significantly, while the dialogue itself is written in a mannered, fin de siècle style that belies its own models,[53] Thom's position in many ways goes even further than the naturalist orthodoxy of his day. For the art being advocated for here is no longer the mechanistic sociobiology of Zola, nor the reduplicative "Sekundenstil" of Holz and Schlaf's poetic endeavors. In contrast to both of these models, what Thom means by a literature "on a scientific basis" is a literature that (1) regards human actions and emotions as being entirely the result of biochemical processes, and (2) rejects standard narratives and fixed relations in favor of the thematic centrality of somatic experience itself.

In other words, we have moved from a literature that adopts scientific methods as *technique* to a literature that takes biological facts as *topic*:

> The whole chaos of events that results from people's relationships to one another, every dreamable dream and every experienceable desire, in the end all of it without exception can be traced back to a few particular functions, which are quite simply the functions of life itself and which silently play out in each individual cell. . . . I have to confess to you, a feeling of a very peculiar emotional tone always arises in me when I imagine Jacobsen at work, examining a cell with his microscope: how life, culminating in one of its most sophisticated specimens, in which the psychic, the cerebral has raveled out into its most refined and intense vibrations, bends over another life: dull, instinctual, moist, cramped [dumpf, triebhaft, feucht, alles eng beieinander], and how both lives nevertheless belong together and are traversed by *one* wave, and how both are physically related to each other, down to the chemical composition of their bodily fluids [leibsverwandt sind bis in die chemische Zusammensetzung ihrer Säfte].[54]

Such a biologism is one more radical than anything in Zola's (or, indeed, Jacobsen's) imaginings. In "Gespräch," the veracity of the natural sciences becomes, not just a means to a more advanced literature, but the primary truth of the world as a whole: human history is but a series of automatic cellular reactions, an aggregation of molecular and material activity wholly unconscious of its ultimate effects. A more Schopenhauerian form of élan vital could hardly be imagined: behind all life lies the blind, barely containable forces of a will with neither value nor sense. (Later, Thom will even apply this idea to the interpersonal relations in Jacobsen's novel, whose characters, in Thom's interpretation, come together and drift apart in obedience to a Heraclitan logic of perpetual change.) But Benn also goes several steps beyond Schopenhauer in resubstantializing this will as a literal physical substance, a hypostatization of all life and activity in the "dull, instinctual, moist" sludge of cellular matter itself.[55]

In "Gespräch," this conception is still positive, in both senses: the explanation of human activity as a result of chemical processes in organic matter is considered (at least by Thom) to be both necessary and sufficient, and the knowledge of the fact of these processes, together with its implementation in literature, is regarded as something clarifying and progressive. Benn repeats these opinions in his didactic essays of this period such as the 1911 "Zur Geschichte der Naturwissenschaften" ("On the History of the Natural Sciences"), where he praises contemporary medicine for having enabled "something until now unheard-of in the history of science: the psychological, the πνευμα, that which is above and outside of things, the intangible per se was made flesh and dwelt among us [das Über- und Außerhalb der Dinge, das Unfaßbare schlechthin ward Fleisch und wohnte unter uns]."[56] Two years later, everything will have changed. No trace of a belief in the materialist knowability of the soul—or rather, only an inverted and embittered trace—remains in *Morgue*'s postmortem parodies, which not only deny the material body either sentience or value, but also allow this lack of sentience and value to reflect back on the claims of spirit as a whole.[57] The naturalist faith in the possibility of knowledge of the material world is mocked by matter's very contingency and perishability, at the same time as this contingency and perishability is presented, in a fanatical exaggeration of naturalism's own principles, as the last word of knowledge itself. An opaque physicality and an absent spirituality face off on the contested field of the new poetic representation.

Benn dramatizes these conflicts in properly Oedipal terms in his early dramatic sketch *Ithaka*, set in a teaching hospital, as Benn's alter ego, the young assistant surgeon Rönne, spurs on a pair of medical students to the assault and murder of their professor. The play opens with Benn's Professor Albrecht sententiously lecturing his students on the coloration of rats' brains. When two of his students challenge him to draw conclusions from his data, he rebuffs them with a self-satisfied chuckle: "But, my dear fellow! Conclusions! We're not Thomas Aquinas here, ha ha ha!" (Aber, mein Lieber! Schlüsse! Wir sind doch nicht Thomas von Aquino, hi, hi, hi!).[58] But the last laugh will be on Professor Albrecht, as both Rönne and the students begin to back their mentor into a corner, berating him with increasing vehemence on the irrelevance of his research and its failure to pose questions of real consequence. *Ithaka* thus ends on a note of (vulgar-) Nietzschean irrationalism, with the play's three young protagonists strangling the pathetic Professor Albrecht to death in a collective frenzy as the student Lutz cries out triumphantly, "Soul! Soul! We want dream. We want ecstasy. We cry Dionysus and Ithaca!—" (Seele! Seele! Wir wollen den Traum. Wir wollen den Rausch. Wir rufen Dionysos und Ithaka!—).[59]

The primary target of the play's satire is obviously academic pedantry and the worthlessness of a science that contents itself with trivial facts and useless investigations—in Benn's comically hyperbolic example: "It would also be possible to distinguish the rats with a long black coat and dark eyes from those with a short rough coat and light eyes through these fine methods of coloration, on the condition that they are the same age, have been fed on rock sugar, have played every day for half an hour with a small puma, and have spontaneously defecated twice every evening at a temperature of 37.36°C"[60]—rather than tackling the essential problems of existence. Here Benn alludes to the popular critiques of science of the late nineteenth century, above all the 1872 lecture "Über die Grenzen des Naturerkennens" ("On the Limits of the Knowledge of Nature") by the physiologist Emil du Bois-Reymond. In his lecture, du Bois-Reymond draws a stark line between the capacities of natural science and the mysteries of human consciousness: "The astronomical [i.e., biomechanical] knowledge of the brain, the highest we can attain from it, reveals nothing therein but shifting matter. But there is no arrangement or movement of material particles we could imagine that would bridge the gap between it and the realm of consciousness."[61] Although great strides have been made in the understanding of the natural world and the constitution of biological life, says du Bois-Reymond, "faced with the riddle . . . of what matter and force are and how they become capable of thought, the natural scientist must cast his lot . . . with the motto: 'Ignorabimus!' ['We will never know!']."[62]

That of which one cannot speak, one must remain silent. Later in life, in a 1952 commentary on a new edition of his work, Benn will dismiss the early twentieth century's concern for such questions as a mark of the era's naïveté: "Those were the decades in which the opposition of instinct and soul, physical constitution and mental ability, spirit and life . . . weighed on us all . . . now all of it strangely far away and almost just a memory, a memory of something painful, of shackles and pressure [eine Erinnerung an Quälendes, an Fesseln und an einen Druck]."[63] In 1911, however, such questions are still experienced by Benn as a matter of paramount urgency. When Benn's Professor Albrecht, choking under the grip of his student Lutz, echoes du Bois-Reymond's cry, Lutz answers him with scorn and a harder throttling: "Ignorabimus! I'll give you ignorabimus! You haven't researched deep enough" (Ignorabimus! Das für Ignorabimus! Du hast nicht tief genug geforscht).[64] For the young Benn, du Bois-Reymond's untroubled abandonment of metaphysical speculation is an act of intellectual cowardice, albeit one for which Benn himself has no better answer at this point than the evocative metaphors (which will quickly acquire downright archetypical significance) of "blood," "ecstasy," "dream," and "the South."[65]

However, the drama staged in *Ithaka* is not just a drama of empirical science versus metaphysical passion; it is also a struggle over the form of literary representation itself. For while *Ithaka*'s main conflict may be epistemological in nature, the trigger for this conflict is a debate about language and description. "And now, gentlemen," expounds Benn's professor in the play's opening lines, "I have dyed the pyramidal cells from the hippocampus of the left cerebral hemisphere of a fourteen-day-old rat of the Catullus variety and, lo and behold, they aren't red, but rather pinkish-red with a light brown-violet tint shading into green."[66] The students leave; the professor's eventual murderers, Lutz and Kautski, approach the lectern: "Now, once one has looked closely at the preparation, Herr Professor, is there anything more to say than: well, well, so this isn't dyed red after all, but rather pinkish-red with a light brown-violet tint shading into green?"[67] Lutz's mockery of the professor's pedantic precision connects his accusation of the triviality of scientific research to the accusation of the triviality of descriptive (read: naturalist) poetics. (In this light, the oxymoronic descriptive specificity of the "dark pale lilac aster" in "Kleine Aster" takes on a new valence: Benn is mocking his own clinical precision in the poem that will announce its obsolescence.) Such accusations of descriptive triviality reappear in even more emphatic form in the monologue with which Rönne makes his entrance:

> Herr Professor, I hereby return to you the article on the peritoneal pouch in newborns. I haven't the slightest interest in describing the status of a dissected abdominal cavity to a particular group of specially trained people I've never met in such a way that they can now picture it for themselves [so zu schildern, daß sie sie sich nun vorstellen kann]. . . . Nor will I describe whether, in the prolapse of Frau Schmidt's fertile dell, the intestinal loops appeared in the fissure in question during the sixth or the eighth month, nor how elevated the diaphragm of a drowned body was toward morning. Gathering, systematizing knowledge—the most subaltern mental activities!—They've been gradually cretinizing these lands for a hundred years now, and they've succeeded in getting every sort of yahoo to stand slack-jawed in awe before the biggest bed-pisser, so long as he knows his way around an incubator, but haven't managed to produce even the atom of a thought that would stand outside the realm of banality![68]

"I was," cries Rönne a moment later, "so logical I could have puked shit" (logisch bis zum Koterbrechen).[69] This is over. The naturalist confidence in the inherent value of objective description, already tottering in Holz, has now completely collapsed. Mimesis has become "incest" (Blutschande)[70] and "thing-rape" (Notzucht gegen die Dinge),[71] a degenerate and shameful violence against what in the end will anyway always elude one's grasp. Yet Benn cannot go back to what he has already learned to reject, namely the "absurdity" (Lächerlichkeit)[72] of poetic abstraction he mocks in "Gespräch": "What does that actually mean: writing [Dichten], and what is it to want to describe something? One wants to get hold of finer, more fleeting, never before said things, and then preserve them in such a way that they don't lose the luster they had when they first came to us [Feiner, flüchtiger, noch nie gesagter Dinge will man doch habhaft werden und sie so aufbewahren, daß sie den Schmelz nicht verlieren, den sie trugen, als sie zu uns kamen]."[73] In Else Lasker-Schüler's praise of Benn's work: "He says: 'dead is dead' " (Er sagt: "tot ist tot").[74] But even this hard-boiled matter-of-factness of a career doctor no longer particularly satisfies, for it simply repeats the gestures of a previously professed naturalism now become otiose and commonplace. As the medical student Lutz mocks: "Every once and a while you dig up a so-called fact" (Hin und wieder buddeln Sie eine sogenannte Tatsache ans Licht).[75] Benn's formerly proud interpretation of life as matter backfires on him in the contempt for matter's basic unknowability.

One can only speculate on the reasons for Benn's turn from an almost unmitigated celebration of empirical materialism to a violent ambivalence, not to say disgust, in its regard. The continuing influence of expressionism (albeit an expressionism held at arm's length), the epochal mood of filial rebellion, the dismal medical apprenticeship of daily corpse dissection, the encounter with the spectrum of neurological disorders in the psychiatric clinic at Charité, the disappointment of the star student faced with the conceptual limits of his field and the blind spots of his teachers, the seductive pull of a late-Romantic primitivism as an antidote to the stultifying ceremoniousness of Wilhelmine Germany: any of these would be more than sufficient grounds to begin to question one's previously held beliefs in the inevitability of scientific progress and the empirical knowability of the human being.[76] But Benn's change of perspective is perhaps also the result of a more general and less biographically specific problematic: namely, a shift in the understanding of "reality" itself. Benn himself narrates this shift in the short prose piece from 1929 titled "Urgesicht" ("Primordial Vision"):

> Yes, this city, but, verily, not out of dew and birdsong, rather full of the jostling press of things [Gegenstandsgedränge]. . . . Bizarre epic of the instant: . . . rocket cars to the moon, projectile aviation into the stars, and the last hackney cab drives from Wannsee to Fontainebleau, the family trailing behind in the dog cart with kit and caboodle; two waiters walk in white tie from Brandenburg to Geneva to lay a wreath on their club's commemorative stone; three Hindus approach, they're cycling around the world—[77]

Benn's poem presents a typically Simmelian image of urban chaos, in which neither a romanticized nature nor a unifying cultural project can justify the random assortment of what Benn derisively calls "all truly noteworthy and reality-filled things" (alles wahrhaftig doch erwähnenswerte und wirklichkeitserfüllte Dinge).[78] But even this sensory chaos eventually recedes, replaced by the common denominator of "life" itself as undifferentiated and senseless striving:

> Ancient urges of ageless mass in the sound of the oceans and the spill of light. Life wants to live, but life also wants to die [Das Leben will sich erhalten, aber das Leben will auch untergehn], instinct and collapse—games of the night. Lost, the individual, the self, down . . . ; on science, banal method of veiling the facts, religion, the invective one,—dithyramb of youth, down, down![79]

What for Arno Holz was a repulsed panic in the face of the overwhelming multiplicity of things reappears transformed in Benn as an encounter with the basic substance of existence—but this substance is now merely abject and dumb, a "chthonic power"[80] that loses whatever sheen of healthy vitality it might have possessed to become an ooze of self-regulating protoplasm. This is the source of Benn's discontent with the "fact-veiling" methods of empirical science: not only does naturalist exactitude inevitably miss its mark; it also fails to comprehend that the *true* reality of the world resides in what *cannot* be thought, whether this be the absurd juxtapositions of the civilized world, the Dionysian depths of sensual intoxication, or the incomprehensible thereness of "ageless mass" itself.

In this way, a particular strategy of Benn's early poetics becomes clear: insofar as the resistance of the material is the criterion for the guarantee of reality, reality itself is experienced as an object of frustration and disgust (including, somewhat more complicatedly, self-disgust). This disgust is then expressed mimetically in aesthetically repellent images, which in turn become a form of cognitive resistance in their own right. Let us return to "Mann und Frau gehn durch die Krebsbaracke." Some critics have read into the last stanza a positive message, an affirmation of nature's fecundity and the eternal cycle of life even in the middle of disease and death.[81] But even if the last stanza of Benn's poem contains echoes of a Romantic vitalism (and/or Christian salvation), it is difficult to ignore the ways in which the previous stanzas already close off the possibility of a redemptive or transcendent nature. Or, more accurately, "Mann und Frau gehn durch die Krebsbaracke" flirts with the idea of a redemptive or transcendent nature, all the better to emphasize the bleakness of its eventual negation.[82] Indeed, the poem forecloses the idea of renewal early on, with the grotesque surgical birth from a tumor-ridden womb. (In reality, the co-occurrence of pregnancy and uterine cancer is vanishingly rare: Benn's image has more symbolic force than scientific truth.)[83]

Meanwhile, the subtle anthropomorphisms of the last stanza—the three quasi-anaphoric reflexive verbs and the concluding "Earth calls"—only serve to underscore the poem's previous depersonalization, in which the women's bodies are palpated like insentient beings, washed like planks of wood. In fact, it is almost incorrect to speak of anthropomorphism here, for the amorphous nature that rises up at the end is actually *more* alive than the poem's cancerous, rotting human bodies, more alive even than the robotic and interchangeable nurses or the nameless, voiceless woman to whom the poem is addressed. Long before the final stanza returns them to the primordial soup, Benn's women are already on their way to becoming matter.

It may be too much to compare the "zerfallene Schöße" of Benn's poem to the "zerfallendes Schloß"[84] of Stifter's *Nachsommer*, but it is at least certain that, where Stifter makes it his mission to halt decay through aesthetic reframing, Benn's poetics uses aesthetic framing to foreground the process of decay itself. In this anti-idyll, death is no longer merely a part of nature—*et in arcadia ego*—it is its essence. As Benn writes in the poem "Der Arzt" ("The Doctor"): "Sweet corporeality sticks to me / like a layer of plaque on the gums" (Mir klebt die süße Leiblichkeit / wie ein Belag am Gaumensaum).[85] That Benn was early on concerned with the organic basis of the human mind does not mitigate this anti-idyll, but exacerbates it as an enigma and as a scandal: the meaningless basis of the source of meaning as such. The dead and dissected bodies of Benn's early poems are thus but synecdoches for the perishable fleshliness of the material world in general, in which Benn's former vision of life as pure matter returns in the form of a horrified fascination with matter's simultaneous persistence and alterity: the immanent life force of a scientized *Naturphilosophie* transformed into the uncanny vitality of deadness itself.

"and also the saw was there with him"

It is a perhaps obvious but nevertheless crucial point that in Benn this alterity of matter is frequently, indeed overwhelmingly female gendered.[86] "I know," Benn writes in "Der Arzt," "how whores and madonnas smell / after a movement [nach einem Gang] and in the morning when they wake / and during the tides of their blood."[87] In "Mann und Frau gehn durch die Krebsbaracke," not only is the titular ward clearly marked as a women's ward; cancerousness *as such* is marked as female. Wombs, breasts: the sexual characteristics of the female body are presented from the very first lines as tainted objects, as if no other organs but these were capable of tumorous growth. Meanwhile, the hemorrhaging body of the fourth stanza, which "bleeds enough for thirty bodies" (blutet wie aus dreißig Leibern), not only evokes the process of menstruation—the rhyme "Leibern"/"Weibern," already used in "Requiem," easily suggests itself—but, thereby, also portrays menses itself as pathology and morbid symptom. In this sense, the poem's insistence on disease and death is almost superfluous, for the sexed body—read: the female body—is inherently a body of decay. (In this context, it is almost too fitting that one of Benn's areas of specialty as a physician was the treatment of sexually transmitted diseases.) Even if this decay can be temporally redeemed in moments of (male) sexual desire—"these lumps of fat and foul sap / were once some man's everything, / and meant rapture and homeland"—the withdrawal of desire, once such moments of ecstasy are past, gives the lie to such transfigurations. Insofar as it is necessarily material, beauty has its logical end in putrescence. The cancerous female body is at once the final truth of aesthetics and its betrayal; *Vénus*—Benn might say with a nod to Zola—*se sera toujours déjà décomposée.*[88]

It has become tiresome to point out the long history of associating the feminine with passive or abject matter, especially as a counterpoint to the "masculine" principles of form and/or spirit: not because this history is in any way subsidiary or trivial, but because there are so very many examples that one is never done with their enumeration. Still, even if the gendering of ontological categories is an evergreen practice, it must be admitted that Benn's work constitutes a high point in this regard—even *before* Benn has occasion to speak of the "phallus of the Spirit" (Phallus des Geistes).[89] In his earliest works, Benn dependably avails himself of the metaphors of unveiling, penetration, conquest, and coercion that dominate modern scientific discourse, for example in the essay "Beitrag zur Geschichte der Psychiatrie" ("Contribution to the History of Psychiatry"): "And now began, all down the line, a pledge to inductive research, to the causal analysis of experiments, a bearing down on nature 'with levers and screws' [ein Zu-Leiberücken der Natur 'mit Hebeln und mit Schrauben'], to force her to lift the veil that had hung for millennia over her features."[90] Marcus Hahn has suggested that the *Faust* quotation Benn semi-ironically inserts into his text here implies a certain skepticism about the prospects of success of such tactics: but this does not change the fact that it is *this* metaphor, and not another, with which Benn choses to represent scientific inquiry.[91] If Nature will not reveal her secrets under questioning, she will reveal them under torture; armed with the latest in scientific techniques, the modern experimenter transforms the epistemological melancholy of Goethe's scholar into an announcement of wry triumph.

What W. G. Sebald writes in regard to Stifter's empirical precision thus goes double for Benn's postnaturalist poetics: "The dividing lines, the golden ratio [der goldene Schnitt] that the fetishistic gaze draws on the female body . . . finally leads to the principle that only a segmented nature gives up its secret, in the dissecting room or in pornography."[92] And sometimes both at once. As both Maria Tatar and Arne Höcker have shown, the metaphorical identification of the artist, the surgeon, and the sex murderer was a common enough trope in the early twentieth century, ratcheting up naturalism's anatomical will to knowledge with the sublimity of abomination.[93] However, the particular centrality of rape and mutilation fantasies to Benn's work should not be underestimated. Paradigmatic is the fourth poem of the *Morgue* cycle, "Negerbraut" ("Negro Bride"), in which a virginal blonde corpse, epitome of eroticized vulnerability, is violated in stages of increasing grotesqueness: first, by the rays of sunlight playing over the autopsy table, then by the toes of a neighboring black man's cadaver, and finally—only partially concealed behind the impersonal pronoun "man"—by the attending pathologist himself. If in *Ithaka* Benn's stand-in, Dr. Rönne, had called Professor Albrecht's untroubled empiricism an act of "incest" and "thing-rape," it is then all the more surprising that this "Notzucht" and "Blutschande" (or, in this case, "Rassenschande") appears in "Negerbraut" radically intensified, made visual and all but literal, even to the point of the gash-like line break between the fourteenth and fifteenth lines.[94] And yet, despite the corpse's defilement by both gods and beasts—Benn amplifies the racist association of blackness and animality by making the man's cause of death a hoof to the head, perhaps also linking him to the mythological figure of the satyr—in the end the girl remains to the operating physician as chaste and closed off as mute nature itself.[95] Therefore he commits on her body a last act of force, opening it up in a way that, if it does not discover the corpse's secrets, at least prevents anyone else from doing so: "Until into her / white gorge the knife was sunk / and a crimson apron of dead blood / flung around her hips" (Bis man ihr / das Messer in die weiße Kehle senkte / und einen Purpurschurz aus totem Blut / ihr um die Hüften warf).[96] In this flamboyantly shocking image, it is perhaps the little preposition "bis" that does the most work, putting a rapid end to the mysteries of sexual pleasure of which the poem, like its imagined bride, had up to that point been on the "cusp" (Saume).[97] The poem's final act of violence, then, is the one it turns against itself: the physician's knife-plunge is not the consummation of the poem's fantasized epistemological rape but in fact its foreclosure, the end of all hopes for anatomization as knowledge in the petulant destruction of that which was to be anatomized.

The *Morgue* poems' affinity with the lyrical tradition of the baroque is a fact frequently referred to in Benn scholarship, if often only in passing.[98] It is in any case not hard to discern, in Benn's gallery of dead and dissected bodies, the echo of the *vanitas* and the Petrarchan *blason*, or to see in them the twentieth-century continuation of what the historian Jonathan Sawday calls the early modern era's "culture of dissection."[99] "An object's 'whole essence' "—Rudolf Drux summarizes a maxim from August Buchner's 1665 *Anleitung zur deutschen Poeterey* (*Manual for German Poetry*)—"consists in the sum of its 'inner qualities.' In order to understand these qualities, the work of dissection is necessary; the exposed components, translated into aggregations of concepts, metaphoric chains, or acoustic effects, 'approximate' the essential whole."[100] In other words, only when dissected into its component parts does the baroque body become a visible and legible object, knowable in the finitude of its materiality.[101] Indeed, in a certain sense, a whole body is not a visible body at all, for it always remains, so to speak, the evanescent expression of the soul that inhabits it. The characters of the *Trauerspiel* die," writes Walter Benjamin, "because it is only thus, as corpses, that they can enter into the homeland of allegory."[102] What Benjamin calls "the commandment which ordered the destruction of the organic so that the true meaning, as it was written and ordained, might be picked up from its fragments"[103] means in part that to gain access to things is first to dismantle them; dissection alone makes the human being available for both empirical investigation and symbolic investment, to being ascribed a signification that the living person is still too fleeting and fluid to bear.

On this view, anatomization is not merely an aid to visibility, but its *precondition.*[104] The consequence, however, is that the human body itself remains stuck uncomfortably between ineffability and materiality, the carrier of a meaning never quite adequate to either. This inadequacy of allegory was already a topic in the baroque, as poets wittily made use of literary conventions to lament those conventions' deficiency.[105] Benn, however, takes this strategy one step further, replacing the poetically dissected bodies of baroque lyric with actual body parts, transforming dead metaphors and allegorical anatomies into their real-life manifestations. Narcotized into a proleptic stupor, the cancer patients of "Mann und Frau gehn durch die Krebsbaracke" are emblems without anything to point to but themselves, zombie icons of their own decomposition. Such self-referentiality, however, does not bring nature and meaning closer together, say in a return to the synthetic self-evidence of the Romantic symbol. To the contrary: even where Benn's language is most allusively and affectively charged, the effect is rather to emphasize the *difference* between symbolic ideation and material fact and to ironize away any connection between the natural body and the ideas that have been projected onto it.

In this way, Benn's early poems are not just the overbid of naturalism; they are also the *mise en abyme* of allegory. For what they allegorize is no less than the failure of allegory itself: the failure of the symbolic order to redeem the "muteness" of an essentially fallen nature as a consequence of its dismemberment.[106] But this failure of allegory—its "frustration in the triumph of matter"[107]—is at the same time what calls out for the body's violation in the first place. Else Lasker-Schüler's designation of Benn as an "insatiable one" (Nimmersatt)[108] also refers to this: the final possession is always the next one, the attempt to seize the other by force always results in that other somehow slipping away from one's hold. Disappointment follows upon disappointment; a postcoital tristesse sets in, and a self-pitying shame in the face of one's own impotence against matter's semantic refusal.

The Rape of Belgium

"Earth bursts into crosses / riverbed and sea falls, / senseless phalluses snot / in the face of the world" (Erde birst sich zu Kreuzen / Flußbett und Meere fällt, / sinnlose Phallen schneuzen / sich ins Antlitz der Welt):[109] if Benn's early poems perform the contempt for a material nature that refuses to be transformed into meaning, this refusal then becomes the explicit theme of the so-called Rönne novellas, a series of short experimental prose pieces that Benn publishes in 1916 under the title *Gehirne* (*Brains*). In these novellas—which reprise Benn's alter ego Werff Rönne, now a young doctor stationed, as Benn himself was, at a hospital in German-occupied Belgium—the combination of disgust and frustration that Benn had once assigned to the human body is now generalized to the world at large. Benn portrays Rönne's environment as an antagonistic force, an accumulation of disparate elements that not only fail to bear a higher essential meaning, but, indeed, fail to bear any meaning at all:

> It was an unknown area [eine fremde Gegend] that he walked through . . . contemptuous stood the houses and trees; submissively he hurried past. House, he said to the next building, house to the one after that; tree to all of the lindens along the way. It was all only a question of mediation, the individual things remained in their untouched state; who would he have been, to seize or to ignore or, in revolt, to bring into being? [Nur um Vermittelung handelte es sich, in Unberührtheit blieben die Einzeldinge; wer wäre er gewesen, an sich zu nehmen oder zu übersehen oder, sich auflehnend, zu erschaffen?][110]

One reason for this failure of meaning is no doubt the novellas' setting: a Belgian village during the First World War, where Benn's protagonist is at once an official representative of a foreign hostile power and a passive (because noncombatant) bystander to the world-historical events taking place around and beyond him. But another and more pointed reason for this failure is the failure of poetic language itself. The insistence in the above passage on the necessity of a "mediation" (Vermittelung) between subject and object already betrays the fact that the linguistic bond between observer and observed, so confidently wielded in the *Morgue* poems, has now become something weak and nonobvious, subject to testing and doubt.[111] Rönne's obsessive repetition of the names for things is all too clearly an effort to will them into knowledge through classification, but this effort is no longer sufficient to break through these things' fundamental inviolability; they refuse to relinquish the resistance of their thereness, provoking the character Rönne to increasingly violent fantasies of conquest or to the rebellious indifference of self-enclosed creation.[112]

This newly uncertain status of language in Benn can be seen exemplarily in a scene from the novellas' concluding piece, "Der Geburtstag" ("The Birthday"), in which Rönne, on his way to work, suddenly becomes aware of a natural object before him:

> From the gardens the crocus threw itself against him [Da aus Gärten warf sich ihm der Krokus entgegen], matinal candle of the poet's mouth, and just that yellow kind that for the Greeks and Romans was the epitome of all things lovely, was it any wonder they transferred it to the realm of the heavens? In pools of crocus nectar bathed the god. A wreath of blossoms warded off intoxication. The saffron fields of the Mediterranean: the tripartite scar; flat lagoons; horsehair sieves over fires, light and open.
>
> He spurred himself on [Er trieb sich an]: Arabic Za-fara, Greek Kroké. A Corvinus appeared, King of the Hungarians, who knew how to avoid saffron stains while eating. Effortlessly the dye, the spice, the bed of blossoms and the Alpine valley came forward [Mühelos nahte sich der Färbestoff, das Gewürze, die Blütenmatte und das Alpental].[113]

At first glance, this passage—which also strikingly prefigures the climactic scene of Jean-Paul Sartre's debut novel[114]—seems to bespeak a Romantic intimacy with nature, a rare moment of happy communion between Rönne and his world. Rönne's sighting of the crocus, or rather, in a distinct echo of his own forename, its act of "throwing itself against him," calls up in him a whole complex of images and associations: the flower's symbolic connections and cultic significance, its culinary and aesthetic uses, the historical legends with which it is associated, its name in several languages and its geographic distribution. Such an allusive network would seem to be the solution to Rönne's alienation, transforming the world from the passivity of phenomenality into the activity of description and relation. In fact, however, the opposite is the case. Instead of an organic connection with nature, there is nature as projection screen; instead of experience, there is erudition; instead of a world saturated with meaning, there is a manic enumeration of concepts, cultural associations, and flat-out clichés, which moreover no longer even come naturally to Rönne, but to which he must, at least at first, "spur himself on."

Such free-associative techniques are what lead Friedrich Kittler to speak of Benn's prose as an example of "verbal transmission as neurosis, without any basis in a transcendental or creative Poet's ego; medial selection without reference to the real, to the incomprehensible background of all media."[115] It is no coincidence, certainly, that Rönne's primary associations with the crocus are taken either from Greek mythology, classical history, or botanical information, making the crocus less an object of phenomenal experience than a cultural conduit, an occasion for an improvisatory recitation from the storehouse of Western knowledge.[116] Indeed, for all its Romantic resonances, the above chain of images is little different than the one set off by Rönne's later encounter with the *second* nature of advertising posters, in which Rönne's thoughts move in similar fashion from the name of the cigarette brand being promoted to erotic fantasies of the Mediterranean seascape. And yet at first

Rönne's ego—and perhaps also the poet's—is bolstered by such associative play:

> Then he entered the clinic: an unyielding gaze, an unshakable will: to link the stimuli and sensations that he had encountered today to the previous stock of experiences, to leave nothing out, to connect everything [die heute ihm entgegentretenden Reize und Empfindungen anzuknüpfen an den bisherigen Bestand, keine auszulassen, jede zu verbinden]. A secret structure appeared to him, something of armoring and eagle flight, a kind of Napoleonic craving, like the conquest of a hedgerow behind which he lay, Werff Rönne, thirty, steadfast, a doctor [Werff Rönne, dreißigjährig, gefestigt, ein Arzt].[117]

In a move characteristic to the Rönne novellas, linguistic improvisation, orientalist escapism, and onanistic dreams of sensual intoxication temporarily shore up Rönne's sense of self, shielding him from the disaffection he otherwise feels in his Belgian backwater. But this shield will prove to be a flimsy one.[118] The extended fantasy set in motion by the encounter with the crocus ends, not merely with alienation and cultural noise, but with the brutal reentry of the real:

> In the grass lay a body [Leib]. A vapor swilled up from cellars; it was time for dinner, pipes and pork cracklings, the foul breath of a dying man.
>
> Looked up, the body: flesh, order, and preservation ripen. [Aufsah der Leib: Fleisch, Ordnung und Erhaltung reifen.] He smiled and drew back into himself; already vanishing he looked up at the house [sah er auf das Haus]: what had happened? What had been the path of humankind up to this point? It had wanted to establish order in something that should have remained a game. But in the end it had remained a game anyway, for nothing was real. Was he real? No; just everything possible, that was what he was.[119]

In an effective callback to the *Morgue* poems' grisly tableaus, the appearance of the corpse, or anyway body, in this passage breaks into the egotistic cohesiveness of Rönne's dream-world and destroys the epistemological confidence that he had, albeit briefly, been able to possess. The majority of "Der Geburtstag" follows this pattern, toggling between a euphoric *invitation au voyage* and tortured descriptions of the dreary here and now—that is to say, between a triumphant celebration of the seemingly infinite potentiality of Rönne's mind and a wounded recoiling from the objects against which it meets its limits. Later, in his infamous 1933 "Akademie-Rede," Benn will term such a meeting of limits "Realitätsverlust" (reality-loss) or "Realitätszerfall" (collapse of reality): "everywhere imaginary immensities, everywhere dynamic phantoms, even the most concrete forces such as state and society hardly able any more to be grasped substantially."[120] But even leaving aside the question of what this "substantial grasp" of "state and society" might be, it must be emphasized that such a "reality-loss" is so only from the point of view of a *particular* reality: a reality in which perception, concepts, and things still come together in one congruous experience of cognition, in which a clinical empiricism had not yet reduced the synthesizing force of the sovereign subject to a "pure functionalism . . . fully in dissolution" (reine Funktionalismus . . . , völlig in Auflösung),[121] in which, in the words of Michel Foucault, the "gaze of observation and the things it perceives [still] communicate through the same Logos."[122]

In this sense, it is fitting that despite all poetics of fragmentation, the Rönne novellas actually represent an emphatic *return* to the strategies of poetic realism, albeit in negative form. In stark contrast to the objectivity effects of Benn's early poems, *Gehirne* portrays its world exclusively through the thoughts and perceptions of Benn's autobiographical protagonist, who does not register that world in its objective presence so much as use it as a pretext for rumination and invention. Typical is the following passage, which slides from colonialist fantasies of a paradisiacal courtesan to Rönne's daily gynecological examinations of the local war prostitutes to an ecstatic vision of the creative self:

> And you, from the house of pleasure in Aden, brooding in the desert and at the Red Sea. Bluish water trickles constantly over the marble walls. From the floor grates rise clouds of aromatic smoke. . . . And you, in the brothel through which the war marched, between harness and leather daily burst hundredfold under unknown limbs or bales of hemorrhage and dung [zwischen Geschirr und Leder täglich hundertfach zerborsten unter unbekannten Gliedern oder auch unter Ballen aus Blutungen und Kot].
>
> He stood before himself, transfigured [Verklärt stand er vor sich selbst]. How he spun it out, what spun, rainbowed! greened! a May night utterly unnamable! Knew them all. He stood before them, unsullied and pristine. He had not been weak. Strong life bled through his head [Starkes Leben blutete durch sein Haupt].[123]

It is significant, for a reading of "Der Geburtstag," that the word "verklärt" appears here: in fact, the first of the word's three appearances in the piece's few pages. However, for Benn, this word—that watchword of poetic realism—has a somewhat different emphasis than it did for the novelists and critics of the nineteenth century. For the "transfiguration" represented here is no longer that of a happy correlation between subject and object, wherein the empirical world is restaged and intensified through the perceptions of the experiencing and feeling human subject. Rather—as Benn's metapoetical use of the term "verklärt" *within* the novella already indicates—this transfiguration is a forced and excruciatingly self-aware mediation, whose repeated failure "to link . . . stimuli and sensations . . . to the previous stock of experiences" is no less than the theme and plot of the Rönne novellas themselves.[124] Yet Benn's "Verklärung" has also become self-aware in another sense. For it is no longer the *world* that is transfigured through Rönne's perceptions, as in poetic realism, but Rönne *himself*.[125] Others remain bodies, abject under orgasming members and exploding bombs; Rönne, however, is "unsullied and pristine" (sauber und ursprünglich). More, he is "unsullied and pristine" as a result of those bodies: his cleanliness, such as it is, is the cleanliness of designating foulness *as* foreign.[126]

This dynamic will later take on even more sinister dimensions in such essays as the 1934 "Dorische Welt" ("Doric World"), in which Benn contrasts a decadent, feminized, orientalized Athens to the "victorious order and god-derived authority" of an imaginary Sparta.[127] But even before these explicitly political developments, Benn's "protest against the profanation of the world"[128] is already a nostalgic protest against the loss of those structures—including the structures of language itself—that had once seemed to be able to give meaning to the material world and without which that world reemerges in the mute, inhuman, shapeless form of "some sort of mass" (irgendeine Masse).[129] For as Benn's own title for the Rönne novellas already indicates, the "transfiguration" of the material world advocated by poetic realism was always only ever a metaphor for the cognizing activities of the human brain, the sole bearer, in realism's epistemology, of consistency, order, and meaning. But not only is the brain itself a material object, as Benn's own medical studies make plain, its continued inability to give adequate meaning to the things it perceives, to break through the blank self-containment of the world from which it, too, springs, is finally an inability of meaning to be properly meaningful at all, driving Benn ultimately to reactionary dreams of "the gray column without pedestal and the oracle favorable to the ruling class"[130] and keeping the poet who would "leave nothing out . . . connect everything" in a state of conflicted and querulous disgust. In this way, Benn's writing is at once the logical conclusion and the pessimistic inversion of poetic realism's "perspective of interiority,"[131] which posits the subjective mediation of the material world as the condition of that world's representability: a paradoxical aesthetics of *Verklärung* without *Verklärung* that leaves the untransfigured, unglorified material world more exposed than ever. "I live before the body: and in the middle / everywhere clings shame" (Ich lebe vor dem Leib: und in der Mitte / klebt überall die Scham):[132] in Benn, the shame of existence is matter all the way down.

Chapter 6

✦

Filth

Franz Kafka

> How we all took in the expression of transfiguration [Verklärung] from that martyred face, how we held up our cheeks in the glow of this at last attained and already vanishing righteousness! Those were the days, comrade!
>
> —Franz Kafka, *In der Strafkolonie*[1]

> One more step, and we would be in dirt.
>
> —Julian Schmidt, *Geschichte der deutschen Literatur seit Lessing's Tod*[2]

Kafka's Castle is built on the injury to shame. "Hadn't he witnessed the distribution of the files?" (Hat er nicht die Verteilung der Akten mitangesehn?), the Herrenhof's outraged proprietors berate K. after the latter accidentally stumbles across the forbidden bureaucratic apparatus in full swing:

> Something that no one was allowed to witness, except for those directly involved. . . . Well, since it has to be said: because of him, purely and exclusively because of him, the gentlemen weren't able to leave their rooms, since in the morning, right after they wake up, they are too bashful, too vulnerable to be able to subject themselves to the eyes of strangers [zu schamhaft, zu verletzlich . . . , um sich fremden Blicken aussetzen zu können]; however fully dressed they might be, they feel too exposed [zu sehr entblößt] to show themselves. Of course, it's difficult to say exactly why they're ashamed, maybe they're only ashamed, these eternal workers, because they've been sleeping. But perhaps, even more than being ashamed to show themselves, they are ashamed to see strangers; the very thing that they'd been happily able to overcome with the help of the nighttime interrogations, the sight of the individual parties, which for them is so unbearable, they hardly want to see bursting in on them now again

> in the morning, all of a sudden and unannounced, in all the truth of nature [plötzlich, unvermittelt, in aller Naturwahrheit]. . . . What kind of person must that be who doesn't respect such things![3]

The Castle's activity is ordinarily perceived only indirectly, cloaked by distance, rumor, and awe. But K.—the foreigner, the busybody, the bumbler who "ignores everything, not just the law but also the most ordinary human considerations" (sich über alles, über das Gesetz so wie über die allergewöhnlichste menschliche Rücksichtsnahmen . . . hinwegsetzt)[4]—ends up seeing what must never be seen, the immediate, unvarnished materiality of the mechanisms of power itself. And it is not just the modesty of the Castle functionaries that K.'s gaze violates. His presence in the novel, much like Amalia's scandalous act of ripping up Sortini's letter, continually forces the village to reveal the profanity of its anyway open secrets, in his very ignorance undermining the effects of sacralization that Castle and village alike seem to want to keep up. "Official decisions are as bashful as young girls" (Amtliche Entscheidungen sind scheu wie junge Mädchen),[5] says Olga, repeating the local saying to K. at the start of her family's long tale of woe. K.'s rejoinder—"Decisions may well have other traits in common with girls"[6]—has always been an obscure point in the interpretation of *Das Schloß*, easily elided with Olga's coy sidestep: "Perhaps. . . . Naturally I don't know what you mean by that" (Vielleicht. . . . Ich weiß freilich nicht, wie Du es meinst).[7] In the context of the novel's general atmosphere of defilement and scandal, however, one can also hear in Olga's evasiveness a sign that she has in fact understood K. perfectly well: official decisions, like young girls, can be deflowered.

The question this chapter pursues is a simple one: what happens to realism in the absence of "reality"? What happens to realism in the absence of the confidence that the representation of the material world gives access to the truth of that world, be it as direct evidence or mediated experiencing? For realism, as we have seen, is ultimately based on the principle that its representations always point beyond themselves, to a historical context, emotional depth, or scientific truth that transfigures the bare substance of the material world into a signifying constellation of experiences. What happens, then, when the access to that "beyond" is impeded, when the signifying constellation of experiences fails, somehow, to signify?

What is perhaps most striking about *Das Schloß*, for a contemporary reader, is not how much it deviates from the classical novel of bourgeois realism, but how much it *resembles* it. Part of this can be attributed to the interlocking histories of the Castle's world and the way its characters appear, in a way indeed new for Kafka, to have a complex independent existence outside the protagonist's individual experience. What Hans Blumenberg calls the "possibility of the novel"—the idea of reality as "an actualization, a progressive certainty which can never reach a total, final consistency"[8]—is exemplified in the world of *Das Schloß*, whose self-contained universe is nevertheless continually open to new developments, new plot twists that, like the realist novel in its heyday, grant it the saturated expansiveness of authentic lived life.[9] But it is not just its creation of a fully realized (albeit never finally realizable) microcosm that makes *Das Schloß* the most "realistic" of all of Kafka's works; it is also the vivid mise-en-scènes of Kafka's village and their evocation of a tangible, concrete world in which, however uncanny and opaque, real people could conceivably move and exist. From K.'s rude awakening in his makeshift bed on his first night in the village, to the desperate sex with Frieda in puddles of stale beer on the tavern floor, to the choreographed comedy of the officials' file distribution, to the grim desolation of the Barnabas household, *Das Schloß* is full of moments that impart a powerful feeling of life in the village, an example of that "atmospheric realism" in which, in the words of Erich Auerbach, "every milieu becomes a moral and physical atmosphere which impregnates the landscape, the dwelling, furniture, implements, clothing, physique, character, surroundings, ideas, activities, and fates of men."[10]

Kafka is not generally thought of as a particularly scenic writer. While attention has sometimes been paid to Kafka's striking imagery and mediatic fascinations,[11] more often his work is discussed in terms of a repudiation of sensory content: an austere, streamlined style that replaces the nineteenth century's descriptive and psychological fullness with a focus on performance, process, and modes of operation.[12] Certainly, in contrast to realist *Detailverliebtheit* or naturalist completism (not to speak of fin de siècle ornamentalism or expressionist bombast),[13] Kafka's writing indeed displays a conscious "poverty" and "sobriety" of style.[14] And yet, Kafka can borrow a page from the handbook of realism when he wants to. The opening sentences of *Das Schloß* are already a prime example:

> It was late evening when K. arrived. The village lay under deep snow. Of the Castle hill nothing was to be seen, fog and darkness surrounded it, not even the faintest glimmer of light gave a hint of the large castle. K. stood for a long time on the wooden bridge leading from the high road to the village and gazed up into the apparent emptiness.[15]

Most readers have interpreted this passage symbolically: in its misty concealment, the Castle announces itself from the very first as illusion and paradox, no more than the metaphorical projection of its never-to-be-fulfilled possibility.[16] However, the passage need not be read in such an antirealist fashion. Focalized through K.'s fog-bound, dusk-dimmed vision, the Castle's famous failure to appear is just as plausibly an instance of realist perspectivalism, at once a perfectly logical phenomenal description and a projection of K.'s own state of mind onto his environment.[17] Such focalizing techniques will come into play even more showily a few pages later, with K.'s entrance into the house of the tanner Lasemann:

> A large twilit room. One entering from outside saw nothing at first. K. stumbled against a washtub, a woman's hand held him back. From one corner came the cries of children. From another, smoke swirled up, turning the half-light into darkness, K. stood there as if in a cloudbank. "He's drunk," someone said. "Who are you?" cried a commanding voice. . . . "I am the Count's land surveyor," said K., trying in this way to explain himself to these still invisible people. . . .
>
> Finally the smoke dissipated a little and K. could get his bearings. It seemed to be a normal washday. Near the door, laundry was being washed. But the smoke had come from the left-hand corner, where in a wooden tub . . . two men were bathing in steaming water. But even more surprising . . . was the right-hand corner. Through a large roof hatch, the only opening in the back wall of the room, came a pale light of reflected snow, no doubt issuing from the courtyard and giving to the dress of a woman, sitting languidly almost prone in a tall armchair far back in the corner, a gleam as if of silk.[18]

This is textbook realism, and not just on account of the uncanny specificity of its atmospheric detail. K.'s lack of knowledge is figuratively converted into a lack of visibility; the dusk, smoke, steam, and reflected light that come together to block K.'s vision is the theater curtain that slowly opens upon the scene, gradually revealing to both K. and the reader the sensible contours of the interior of the tanner's home.[19] Indeed, the scene is even organized according to an ascending hierarchy of senses: first, touch, as half-seen objects reach out ominously from the general haze; then sound, discernable but from equally mysterious sources; and finally sight, as the smoke clears and K. begins to be able to see the room in all its particulars.[20] (The last step on this hierarchy would then be something like supersensible revelation, with the pale light suddenly falling on the *Madonna-lactans*-like "girl from the Castle" [Mädchen aus dem Schloß]).[21]

This staging of the process of perception as subjective experience is thematized to an almost farcical degree in the myriad "Gucklöcher" and "Guckfenster" (peepholes) of the Castle village. Such "Gucklöcher" are, most famously, what affords K. his first and only view of the desired Klamm. But they are also what lets K. contemplate in secret the "broad, aging" body of the Brückenhof's landlady Gardena;[22] what lets the crowd of murmuring villagers peer hungrily into the Brückenhof kitchen where K. has been holding up dinner;[23] what permits the Herrenhof innkeeper to look on surreptitiously as K. gets a talking-to from his wife;[24] what enables his wife, a moment previous, to determine that Klamm has finally exited the inn;[25] and what gives the spying chambermaids the bad habit, according to K., "to conclude, from some trivial detail that you actually see, a whole picture that is as grand as it is false" (von einer Kleinigkeit, die ihr wirklich seht, ebenso großartig wie falsch auf das Ganze zu schließen).[26] There will be more to say about these "Gucklöcher" below. For now, however, suffice it to say that this constant peephole-peeking is more than just what provides *Das Schloß* with its slightly louche air of casual voyeurism and general disciplinary surveillance. It is also the absurd epitome of realist literature's optical regime: the "visual inspection and inventory," in the words of Peter Brooks, that enables works of nineteenth-century realism to "give a sense of the thereness of the physical world, as in a still life painting."[27] Not unlike the literal and metaphorical frames that organize the objects of Stifter's *Nachsommer*, Kafka's gaps, chinks, apertures, and windows block out a discrete section of the world for examination, in a way that also always safely refers the examined object back to the gaze of the one doing the examining.

Indeed, at times the peephole even becomes a form of power in itself: "It grieved me to hear that Frieda had let you look through the peephole," laments the Herrenhof's landlady, in a particularly blatant Kafkan double entendre; "as soon as she did that, she was seduced" (schon als sie das tat, war sie von Ihnen verführt).[28] Perverse analog to the female genitals, the peephole grants its possessor both sexual and epistemological prerogatives, a total mastery over bodies and objects of a kind that the "experimental moralists"[29] of the late nineteenth century could only dream of.[30] And yet, in contrast to the confident epistemology of the naturalist novel, that which is given to be observed through the frame or peephole in *Das Schloß* is no longer quite so certain. The image of Klamm to which Frieda's surrender allows K. access proves to be an ultimately untrustworthy picture; as Olga relates: "[Klamm] is said to look completely different when he arrives in the village and different when he leaves it, different before he's had a beer, different after, different awake, different asleep, different alone, different in conversation, and, what after all that is easy to understand, almost totally different up in the Castle."[31] Meanwhile, the radical inconsistency of K.'s own statements in the novel—beginning with his claim to be a land surveyor in the first place—puts the traditional focalization of the realist novel on shaky, not to say eroded, ground. "'I cannot emigrate,'" says K. to Frieda after having thanked her for giving him a reason to stay in the village; "and in a contradiction he didn't even bother to explain, he added, as if to himself: 'What else could have lured me to this desolate country, other than the desire to stay.'"[32] And K. is not alone in his inconsistencies: the village foreman's explanation of K.'s hiring, for example, is an ode to bureaucratic casuistry and a veritable masterpiece of circular logic: "Are there supervisory bodies [Kontrollbehörden]? There's nothing but supervisory bodies. Of course, they aren't meant to find errors in the broad sense of the term, since naturally no errors occur, and even if an error does occur, as in your case, who can say in the end if it's actually an error."[33] K.'s observation upon receiving his first letter from the Castle can stand for the novel as a whole: "These were clearly contradictions, but they were so obvious they had to be intentional" (Das waren zweifellose Widersprüche, sie waren so sichtbar daß sie beabsichtigt sein mußten).[34]

How one is actually to interpret such inconsistencies is a matter of some debate.[35] What is certain, however, is that this lack of stable perspective or narrative logic radically undermines the potential verisimilitude of the novel's representations.[36] Thus, at the same time as *Das Schloß*'s peephole-peeping pushes realism's representational techniques from the background to the comically blatant fore, the novel's self-contradictions and -cancellations place the truth-value of these representations themselves into question.[37] What Walter Benjamin writes of Kafka's portrayal of movement—"He divests human gesture of its traditional supports, and then has a subject for reflection without end"[38]—can also be applied to his poetics: where realism stressed the real-life meaningfulness that exculpates the material image, Kafka amplifies the image, but strikes its truth out.

In short: *Das Schloß* approaches the conventions of nineteenth-century realism, but fails to keep realism's referential pact. Georg Lukács was one of the first to notice that "formally, [Kafka's] treatment of detail is not dissimilar to that of a realist."[39] However, Kafka's selective deployment of realist detail is more than just what Lukács calls "a precondition for the communication of a sense of absurdity";[40] nor is it merely a way to highlight the "intolerable idling [Leerlauf] of the descriptions,"[41] in which—much in the manner of the painter Titorelli's infamous "heathscapes" in *Der Prozeß* (*The Trial*)[42]—the detail always results in nothing more than the need for more detail, the image for more images. It is also an interrogation of the ontological status of those details and images themselves, in the context of a tradition that both equates sensual representation with reality and locates the meaningfulness of that reality in something outside of—or indeed, opposed to—sensual representation. A diary entry from around the time of the composition of *Das Schloß* makes Kafka's quarrel with this tradition, if not yet its consequences, clear:

> the leap out of the murderous sequence act–observation, act–observation [das Hinausspringen aus der Totschlägerreihe Tat–Beobachtung, Tat–Beobachtung] in the creation of a higher form of observation, a higher, not a more precise [eine höhere, keine schärfere], and the higher it is, the more it cannot be reached from such a "sequence," the more independent it becomes, the more it follows its own laws of motion, the more unpredictable, the more joyful, the more elevated its path.[43]

The art of extracting meaning from materiality is a dead end: not, however, because of materiality's deceptiveness or debasement, but because such an extraction mechanism is what first produces the falseness and debasement of materiality as meaning's residue. *Shame* is the remainder of an aesthetics that demands both the real and its sublimation. "Besides, it's not at all certain that a secretary to whom such a thing has happened would ever admit it," concedes the Castle Secretary Bürgel about the prospect of an official being caught unawares by a petitioner. "It's after all a very personal affair, and one as it were touching closely on matters of ministerial shame" (eine sehr persönliche und gewissermaßen die amtliche Scham eng berührende Angelegenheit).[44] "The most shameless of all of them you call modest" (die schamloseste von allen nennst Du zurückhaltend),[45] cries an outraged Frieda at K.'s equivocating description of her rival Olga. "'How should I know [the Count],'" whispers the teacher in response to K.'s attempt at information-gathering, "adding loudly in French: 'Have some consideration for the presence of innocent children.'"[46]

Readers of *Das Schloß* have always tended to assume that Kafka occupies the position of K.: but what if he occupies the position of the Castle? What if he occupies the position, not of the perpetually frustrated seeker of truth, grace, meaning, insight, or purpose, but of the untrustworthy and ironic determiner of what could count as truth, grace, meaning, insight, or purpose in the first place? With *Das Schloß*, Kafka surveys both realism's problematic relationship to the material world and the metaphysical principles that underlie it. As Kafka writes several years earlier, in one of the so-called Zürau Aphorisms: "It is not the sensible world that is semblance [Schein], but the evil of it, which is nevertheless for our eyes that which makes up the sensible world."[47] Kafka's provocation in *Das Schloß* is to refuse the implicit transcendence of the sensible world of realist mimesis while cultivating the appearance of a mimetic poetics taken to its limit, in which squalor and trash appear as the universal substrate of a reality that consistently fails to become more than what it is, muddying even the potentially allegorical value of its aggressively profane images. In this way, *Das Schloß* imitates not reality, but realism, not nature, but naturalism: a parodic naturalism through which the nineteenth-century anxiety regarding sensual representation is exposed as the scattered debris of so many crumbling edifices and bureaucratic apparatuses. In an aesthetics without grace, nothing is obscene.

Expletive Deleted

What is left, then, in the ruins of the never actually accessed Castle? What is left in the ruins of a naturalism without nature, a representation without reference, a reality that fails to realize? The answer this chapter proposes is as basic as it is in need of explanation: *words* and *matter*.

This answer is in need of explanation, first of all, because the question of matter is already a question about language. On the one hand, language is the original means by which material presence is transformed into meaning, by which the naked contingency of the phenomenal world is reclothed in transcendent significance. On the other hand, language is itself matter, at least of a kind: a lingual and auditory phenomenon with no necessary connection to the things it designates. In the late nineteenth and early twentieth centuries, this perpetual tension between language's semantic and material aspects gains new life in what would later come to be known as the doctrine of *Sprachskepsis*. In the work of Nietzsche, Hofmannsthal, Fritz Mauthner, and others, language's inherent arbitrariness is seen to make it a dubious or indeed a wholly unsuitable medium for the conveyance of factual truth, whose unproblematized use is no less than, in Mauthner's words, an "idolatry with names" (Götzendienst mit Namen).[48] In his multivolume manifesto *Beiträge zu einer Kritik der Sprache* (*Contribution to a Critique of Language*), Mauthner particularly singles out literary naturalism for derision, on account of its misguided attempt to achieve something like scientific objectivity through what is, for him, the quintessentially *un*scientific medium. However, naturalism may have more in common with Mauthner's theories than he himself realizes.[49] Thus Arno Holz declares, for example, in *Evolution der Lyrik*, in regard to his decision to increase the amount of line breaks in his poems: "Only now . . . does each word appear in its whole, original resonance, in the purest crystal clarity, and as a result completely emerges the innermost meaning, the convincing manifestness [überzeugenden Sinnfälligkeit] of that which I had, through these words, wanted to 'express'!"[50] In other words, a literature that demands accuracy of representation eventually demands accuracy from the vehicle of that representation itself—whereby, it goes almost without saying, Holz's use of scare quotes in the above passage already belies his claim to linguistic equivalence. *Sprachskepsis* is the cul-de-sac in which the veristic ambitions of naturalism end up: the inevitable failure of the signifier to *be* the signified results in a bitter disappointment with signifiers as such.[51] Once again, the images are of impurity, corporeality, and death: "Language . . . begets nothing and at best performs midwife duties. And if its fingers are dirty, then the mother dies in childbed" (Die Sprache . . . zeugt nicht und leistet höchstens Hebammendienst. Und hat sie unreine Finger, so bringt sie die Wöchnerin um).[52]

Kafka did not remain untouched by the discourse of *Sprachskepsis*, though his opinion of it appears to have been an ambivalent one.[53] Certainly, there is no shortage of statements by Kafka about the repulsiveness of words, particularly his own: "In the afternoon couldn't restrain myself from reading yesterday's 'previous day's dirt'" (Konnte mich Nachmittag nicht abhalten, das gestern geschriebene "den Schmutz des vorigen Tages" zu lesen),[54] goes one diary entry; another boasts, "the story came out of me like a proper birth, covered in dirt and slime" (die Geschichte ist wie eine regelrechte Geburt mit Schmutz und Schleim bedeckt aus mir herausgekommen).[55] Winfried Menninghaus has described such statements as evidence of a separation in Kafka's thought between an unreachable language of perfect expression and an abject one of mannerisms and untruths to which Kafka felt himself bound.[56] However, Kafka's abjection of language involves something more than just a tortured idealism or act of perverse self-critique. In a diary entry from December 1915, Kafka relates a comment of his acquaintance, the writer and recent convert to Orthodox Judaism Jiří Langer:

> He can only read Max's book 13 days from now. He could have read it over Christmas, since according to an old custom one can't read Torah on Christmas day (one rabbi always cut enough toilet paper on Christmas Eve for the whole year), but this year Christmas fell on a Saturday. But in 13 days it's Orthodox Christmas, then he can read it. According to a medieval tradition, one should only engage with fine literature or other forms of secular knowledge after one's 70th year, according to a milder view after one's 40th. . . . It's not permitted to think about the Torah when you're on the toilet, so reading secular books [weltliche Bücher] is allowed. A very devout Prague man, a certain Kornfeld, knew a lot about worldly things [wußte viel Weltliches], he studied everything on the toilet.[57]

With fine irony, Kafka retells Langer's account as a by-product of two separate but related profanations: the holidays of the Christian calendar, and the exercise of the excretory functions. Such profane or quasi-profane phenomena must be kept rigorously separate from sacred study; indeed, the only acceptable purpose of secular literature, according to the tradition Kafka cites, is to serve as a *distraction* from holy thoughts at particular unholy moments. Humorous though Kafka's account is, it will find a serious echo a year later in the essay by his friend Jizchak Löwy that Kafka transcribes and revises under the title "Vom jüdischen Theater" ("On the Jewish Theater"). In that essay—a fragmentary autobiographical sketch of Löwy's childhood and entry into acting—Löwy emphasizes that, for his pious Hasidic family, the theater was something "trefe" (*treyf*, unclean, unkosher) and "chaser" (pig-like).[58] "Only on Purim was there a play, because then cousin Chaskel would glue a big black beard over his small blond one, put his caftan on backwards and play a comical Jewish peddler";[59] outside of Purim's carnivalesque impunity, however, "a Jewish child should know nothing about the theater; that is not permitted; the theater is only there for the goys and the sinners."[60] For devout Jews like the Löwys, sacred texts are to be revered; secular literature, on the other hand—not just the bad translations of American dime novels that Löwy and his school friends secretly devour, but also the "enlightened books" (aufgeklärten Bücher)[61] of the European classics—is fit to be read only on the pot.

Mauthner (like Langer and Kafka, an assimilated German-speaking Bohemian Jew)[62] gives special attention to Judaism's attitude toward language in the *Beiträge*, where, unsurprisingly, he reveals himself to be no great fan of the people of the book: "The 'true' words of the Bible took the place [of the old fetishes], and Talmudic logic converted the rule, for example, that one must not cook the baby goat in the milk of its mother into a whole system of dietary laws. The sacrifice of the intellect is brought to the new word-fetish, but there is no one left to digest it."[63] The facile wit of Mauthner's metaphor nevertheless underscores a crucial point: in the eyes of the radical empiricist, cultic practices and linguistic signs are alike fetishes, the indigestible material residue of a truth that cannot actually be materially manifested. In this, Mauthner shows himself to be an apt, if idiosyncratic, pupil of the Paul of Second Corinthians, for whom, in his infinitely consequential formulation, "the letter killeth, but the spirit giveth life."[64] For Paul, the Jewish prohibition against the graven image does not go far enough: even the supposedly sacred language of the law profanes the God it claims to exalt, attempting to represent through the sensual concreteness of words and deeds a divinity infinitely beyond either. But what follows this is just as important:

> If the ministration of death, written and engraven in stones, was glorious [So aber das Amt, das durch die Buchstaben tötet und in die Steine gebildet war, Klarheit hatte] . . .
>
> How shall not the ministration of the spirit be rather glorious? . . .
>
> For even that which was made glorious had no glory in this respect, by reason of the glory that excelleth [Denn auch jenes Teil, das verklärt war, ist nicht für Klarheit zu achten gegen die überschwengliche Klarheit].[65]

"Made glorious," "verklärt": the same word that Paul uses to describe the transformation from profane law to divine presence—and thus, from the codified religiosity of Judaic practice to the spiritual transcendence of Christian faith—is the word that Theodor Fontane and others will later use to describe the literary transformation of the phenomenal world through the representation of its experiencing. Here we see the Protestant core of German realism indeed: realism is a kind of secular typology, illuminating the profane objects of earthly existence in their true humanistic glory. In the same way that Christian teaching is said to disclose the essence of the laws it has superseded, realism discloses the essence of the material world formerly hidden by the concreteness of its actuality.

At first glance, Kafka's association between that least hallowed of all physical activities and the necessity of abstaining from reading scripture would appear to countenance the divide between sacred and profane contained in both Jewish law and, differently, its Pauline revision. In fact, however, Kafka flips the script. For what Kafka emphasizes is not the conflict between sacred study and physical impurity, much less the transcendence of both scripture and body through the incorporeal power of spirit, but rather—in a way that might also be interpreted as a subtle dig at Max Brod's novel *Tycho Brahes Weg zu Gott* (*Tycho Brahe's Path to God*), the "book" here in question[66]— the *affinity* between physical impurity and *secular* forms of writing. In Kafka's anecdote, the Jewish taboo also entails a permission: worldly literature may be consumed, even in large amounts, when doubled by the sign of its uncleanness, in an ironically willed identity between language and contamination that is moreover not to be separated—"for the first time Shakespeare, Schiller, Lord Byron"[67]—from the monuments of modern high culture. What *Sprachskepsis* realizes with pain and disappointment—the fallen nature of worldly language—Jewish tradition accepts with the equanimity proper to self-evidence. Only two little vowels, Kafka reminds us, make the difference between *Deifikation* and *Defäkation*.[68]

The conversation with Langer takes place in 1915, several years before Kafka begins work on *Das Schloß*. But *Das Schloß* is also filled with examples where Kafka parodies the idea of a spiritualized or "verklärte" language, in particular, by emphasizing precisely that which Mauthner et al. disdain: language's mediatic and material underside. In the nineteenth chapter of the novel, K.'s inadvertent witnessing of the distribution of the files in the corridor of the Herrenhof is presented as an extraordinary violation, a veritable glimpse of the forbidden face of God Himself. Yet earlier, in the scene at the home of the village foreman, these same files whose delivery must be so rigorously protected from the sight of the uninitiated are stacked up and tossed around as the most desultory of *Papierkram*:

> "Mizzi," [the foreman] said, suddenly interrupting his narrative, . . . "please have a look in the cabinet, perhaps you can find the order." . . . The woman opened the cabinet, K. and the foreman looked on. The cabinet was stuffed full with papers; as soon as it was opened, two large sheaves of files tumbled out, tied together like bundles of firewood, the woman jumped aside in fright. "At the bottom, it should be at the bottom," said the foreman, directing from his bed. Obediently, the woman, gathering the files in both arms, threw everything in the cabinet aside to get at the bottommost papers. The papers already covered half the room. "A lot of work has already been done," said the foreman, nodding, "and that's only a small part of it. I've stored the greater part in the barn, but most of it has gone missing. Who could keep all that together! But in the barn there's still quite a lot."[69]

If the Word is the essence of the divine Law, the file is its material instance. However, the alignment of the two is entirely circumstantial. As Cornelia Vismann has argued, "only as long as they are in use are files in conformity with the registry's symbolic order. As soon as they are no longer in use, they fall back into a disorder without limit."[70] Only a temporary transubstantiation, a tentative and always revocable framing, transforms the file from material remnant to active bearer of meaning; "once removed from their ordering furniture," however, "they fall outside the chancery's system of reuse. . . . The classification of a piece of writing as file or document determines its fate as trash or treasure [Trash oder Thesaurus]."[71]

In this light, it is telling that K.'s file is the one file that fails to appear. In *Das Schloß*'s comic pendant to *Der Prozeß*'s sadistic "junk room of the law" (Rumpelkammer des Rechts),[72] the only files that turn up are the ones that have ceased to signify: spilling out of file cabinets, piled high in barns, able neither to be sorted nor stuffed back into oblivion, they stick out; they overflow; they extrude; they are, in short, text as the "by- or waste product of the chancery,"[73] the conspicuously *un*glorious "ministration" of its excremental presence.[74] Lest one conclude from this, however, that Kafka returns in the end to a Mauthnerian revulsion for the uncleanliness of the word, we should remember that Kafka holds at a distance the very question of whether there is a pure experience or pure understanding that the untrustworthy materiality of language could be unclean *against*. The "intractable materiality of [the Castle's] operations" is thus not, as has been claimed, a satire of its "ultra-rational organization"—for there can in fact be nothing less rational than the Castle's bureaucracy—but instead the exposure of the false premises of such satire itself.[75] Kafka's representation of the word as a form of "trash" that becomes "treasure" without ceasing to be trash[76] mocks the disappointed metaphysics of *Sprachskepsis*, establishing in its place a ubiquity of empty signifiers as the lingua franca of a new profane poetics, in which the long-standing dispute between idolatry and revelation, pure expression and impure sign, "law" and "spirit" is closed and (at least temporarily) filed away.

Material Culture

From the contingent materiality of the word to the contingent materiality of its referents is but a small step. K.'s dubious calling as surveyor is the almost all too obvious analogue to the dubious realism of the novel in which he appears: K. *would* describe the land, record its dimensions, map out its contours,[77] but not only is he consistently prevented from doing so, fails to gain access to his instruments, is shunted ever further from the lofty vantage point of the sovereign gaze into the cramped recesses of the village's interiors, even when he does get the opportunity to look he is unable to make things out properly, focuses on the wrong things, misconstrues the evidence, is dependent on others' unreliable accounts for the interpretation of sensory information.[78] And yet, one can hardly say that K. doesn't get an impression of the village; it presses in on him at every turn, shoving him into corners, rolling him in muck, sinking him in pillows, flaunting its shabby voluptuousness like the buxom and beribboned Pepi, before whose plump body K., despite all disinclination, "had to . . . cover his eyes for a moment, so greedily was he looking at her."[79]

So much attention has been paid to the various evocations of invisibility and indiscernibility in *Das Schloß* that one easily forgets just how strongly sensual (visual, but also tactile, aural, olfactory, and even gustatory) the novel actually is. One particularly striking example of the novel's saturated detail is found at the beginning of the twelfth chapter, in the description of K.'s first morning with Frieda and the assistants in the schoolhouse where he has just been employed as janitor:

> The next morning they awakened only as the first schoolchildren had already arrived and were inquisitively gathering around their bed. That was unpleasant, for, because of the heat, which had in any case given way to a bitter chill toward morning, they had all undressed down to their undershirts, and just as they were beginning to put their clothes on appeared in the doorway the schoolmistress Gisa, a tall blond good-looking though rather stiff girl. She was clearly informed about the new janitor and had probably also received instructions from the teacher, since, before she even crossed the threshold, she declared: "This I cannot abide. A fine mess that would be [Das wären schöne Verhältnisse]. You have permission to sleep in the schoolroom, but I'm not obliged to teach in your bedroom. A janitor's family that lolls about in bed all morning. Fie!" Well, some of that could be disputed, especially about the family and the beds, thought K., while he and Frieda—here the assistants were of no use, lying on the floor staring in amazement at the schoolmistress and the children—hurriedly pushed the parallel bars and the pommel horse to one side and threw the blankets over them, creating a little room where one could at least get dressed away from the children's stares. Even so, there wasn't a moment's peace, the schoolmistress was already complaining that there was no fresh water in the washbasin—K. had just been thinking of bringing over the washbasin for Frieda and himself, but he abandoned the thought for now, so as not to further provoke the schoolmistress, but the sacrifice was in vain, for just then there was a loud crash, they had unfortunately forgotten to clear the remnants of their evening meal from the teacher's desk, the schoolmistress shoved it all aside with her ruler, everything was sent flying to the floor; and anyhow the spilled sardine oil and the dribbling coffee dregs and the smashed coffee pot was nothing the schoolmistress had to trouble herself about, the janitor would of course tidy everything up right away. Still not fully clothed, K. and Frieda watched the destruction of their few possessions, leaning on the parallel bars; the assistants, who clearly had no thought of getting dressed, were peeping out through the blankets below, to the children's great delight. Frieda was naturally most upset by the loss of the coffee pot; only when K., in an effort to console her, assured her that he would go to the foreman at

> once to demand and obtain compensation did she compose herself enough to run out of the enclosure, dressed only in camisole and slip, to fetch the tablecloth and protect at least that from further soiling.[80]

Though the descriptive thickness of this passage is partly obscured by the theatrical rapidity of the narration and the free indirect discourse of K.'s own thoughts, it is nonetheless the case that the passage is as overstuffed with objects and sensations as K. and Frieda's schoolhouse-cum-bedroom itself. In the exaggerated disorder of K. and Frieda's *ménage*—stale water in the sink, gym equipment doubling as room partitions, ceramic shards mixed with food waste, the assistants playing peekaboo with the schoolchildren as K. and Frieda hurry to cover up their dishabille—Kafka's description reads almost as a grotesque parody of a realist interior, with its signifying assemblages of lived-in bric-a-brac, or, even more, as a slapstick reprise of naturalist scenography, in which the seediness of the milieu and the lowness of the objects described act as a guarantee that the author has made no concessions to either aesthetic convention or bourgeois prudery.

To be sure, the representation of an unpleasant or squalid materiality in Kafka is not exclusive to *Das Schloß*. From the suppurating, worm-filled wound of *Ein Landarzt* (*A Country Doctor*), to the sweaty crevices of Brunelda's bosom in *Der Verschollene* (*Amerika*), to the rancid victuals of Gregor Samsa in *Die Verwandlung* (*The Metamorphosis*), to the pulverized corpse of the officer of *In der Strafkolonie* (*In the Penal Colony*), a foul yet vividly present *physis* makes itself felt in nearly all of Kafka's works.[81] But it is in *Das Schloß*, more than anywhere, that such imagery becomes, so to speak, part of the landscape. Even the infamously elusive Castle eventually presents itself to view, and indeed as the most prosaic object possible: "It was only a rather wretched little town, cobbled together out of village houses, distinguished only by the fact that everything might have been made of stone, but the paint had long since worn off, and the stone seemed to be crumbling."[82] Those ruined castles which Stifter's characters once took such pains to restore now lie around in a state of abject neglect, a mess of chipping paint, stones, and architectural jetsam whose appearance is barely worth describing and whose proprietor's existence is actively shameful to mention.

More even than this, however, there is an undeniable heaviness, a kind of terrible gravitational pull to *Das Schloß* hardly to be found to the same extent in any of Kafka's other writings. This pull can be felt in the general snow- and rule-bound torpor of village life, in the overpowering drowsiness that constantly befalls both K. and the Castle officials, in the inexorable magnetic force of the Castle itself. But it can also be felt in the enervated inertia of the novel's plot and in the bureaucratically sluggish, comma-laden syntax of the novel's sentences, in which every undertaking and every assertion is held in suspension by a nested sequence of qualifications, revisions, conditionals, and counterclaims.[83] This pull is even present, inconspicuously but nevertheless insistently, in the novel's vocabulary, which contains over one hundred instances of the words *schwer* (heavy, weighty, difficult) or *schwierig* (difficult, arduous), not to mention semantically similar words such as *Last* (burden, load), *Gewicht* (weight, importance), *Fülle* (glut, abundance), *dick* (fat, thick, bulky), *stark* (strong, powerful, massive), *groß* (big, massive, great), *drücken* (to press, push down), *hängen* (to hang, cling, droop), and *senken* (to sink, sag). Most often, these words are used figuratively: "He can't prevent it, but he can unfortunately delay it, make it more difficult" (Er kann es nicht verhindern, aber verzögern, erschweren kann er es leider),[84] comments the Herrenhof innkeeper on K.'s thoughtless loitering in the corridors of bureaucratic power; "I don't know why you give it so much weight" (Ich weiß nicht warum Du so übermäßig großes Gewicht gerade darauf legst),[85] says K. to Olga in regard to Sortini's letter; "From what I hear, he takes everything very seriously" (Wie man mir berichtet nimmt er alles sehr schwer),[86] Jeremias informs K. on the reports circulating about him. But the words are also sometimes used in their literal sense: the novel's sole vision of the fateful Klamm presents him as "a gentleman of medium height, fat, ponderous. His face was still smooth, but his jowls sagged a little under the weight of age" (ein mittelgroßer dicker schwerfälliger Herr. Das Gesicht war noch glatt, aber die Wangen senkten sich doch schon mit dem Gewicht des Alters ein wenig hinab);[87] on K.'s first walk through the village, he "finally tore himself away from the clinging street, . . . even deeper snow, it was hard work to pull out his sinking feet, he broke into a sweat, suddenly stood still and could go no further" (endlich riß er sich los von dieser festhaltenden Straße, . . . noch tieferer Schnee, das Herausziehen der einsinkenden Füße war eine schwere Arbeit, Schweiß brach ihm aus, plötzlich stand er still und konnte nicht mehr weiter).[88] The Castle officials are "mostly older gentlemen, sluggish [schwerfällig] in their habits,"[89] and their servants, similarly, are "generally quiet people, made spoiled and sluggish [schwerfällig] through easy service."[90] Meanwhile, upon his return Jeremias's cheeks appear "flushed, but as if out of too loose flesh [wie aus allzu lockerem Fleisch],"[91] and even the schoolteacher Gisa's cat is described as a "huge old fleshy [fleischige]" creature, "sprawled out lethargically" (träg ausgebreitet) on the schoolhouse desk.[92] Even the tendency of *Das Schloß*'s characters to conduct business from their bedrooms, often read in terms of its psychosexual aspect,[93] can be interpreted in this light. "The foreman, a friendly fat clean-shaven man, was sick, had a severe attack of gout [einen schweren Gichtanfall] and received K. in bed":[94] the novel's boudoir sociality is not just a confusion of public and private and an ominous sexualization of bureaucratic relations; it is also the result of a generalized obesity epidemic.

Evidently, if obscurity and indistinctness are leitmotifs in *Das Schloß*, so is materiality, tangibility, corporeality. Such a poetics of materiality once again recalls (here in particularly literal fashion) the naturalist logic by which, in the words of Fredric Jameson, description "sheds its allegorical meanings and approaches the state of a more purely physical and bodily registering of external contingency."[95] But though Kafka's novel presents its objects in all their massiveness, filth, and randomness, the descriptions nevertheless withdraw from making truth claims; they present the illusion of an illusion even when the images themselves could not be clearer or more concrete. Such a withdrawal, however, is more than simply a predilection for the fantastical or a retreat into the certain uncertainties of apophaticism. It is also Kafka's cut through the Gordian knot of realist aesthetics, in which the material world, whether it is avoided or run toward, always emerges as something foreign and opaque, the abject other of spirit and meaning. "The nature art shows to us," writes Karl Rosenkranz, "is real nature and yet not ordinary empirical nature. It is nature as it could be if its finitude permitted it such perfection."[96] In the ponderous physicality of the Castle village, Kafka takes this logic to its farcically opposite extreme: abstracted from reference, cut off from purpose, a chaos of common matter proliferates.

Das Schloß thus ends in the same place that both the erudite Kornfeld and the discarded file end up: in the closet. Just as K. is on the point of taking up Pepi's offer to move in with her and the other maids at the Herrenhof, the landlady enters and starts up a quarrel with K., lambasting him for some offhand remarks he had previously made about her dress. K. apologizes, protesting his ignorance in sartorial matters, but the landlady continues to press the issue and demands he accompany her to her office. Once there, however, K. suddenly appears to know something about fashion after all, telling the landlady that her expensive clothes are "made of good material, quite expensive, but they are outdated, fussy, altered too many times, worn out [veraltet, überladen, oft überarbeitet, abgenützt], suited neither to your age, nor your figure, nor your position."[97] Yet the reader who expects the landlady to be further enraged by K.'s sudden outspokenness will be mistaken:

> "So you can see that without even thinking about it. You don't have to ask around and still immediately know what fashion demands. There you'll be indispensable to me, because I admittedly have a weakness for nice clothes. And what will you say to the fact that this closet here is full of dresses." She pushed the sliding doors aside, one could see the dresses pressed tightly against one another throughout the whole breadth and depth of the closet, mostly dark-colored, gray, brown, black dresses, all of them carefully hung up and spread out. "These are my dresses, all of them outdated and fussy, according to you. But these are only the dresses I have no space for up in my room, there I have two more whole closets full, two closets, each almost as large as this one. Are you surprised?"[98]

The scene (and almost the novel) then breaks off with the landlady's abrupt dismissal of K., in an offer that sounds more like a threat: "I'm getting a new dress tomorrow, perhaps I'll have you sent for."[99]

Thus K., who began as a land surveyor, appears to be headed for a position as ladies' maid and fashion consultant. The novel ends with one more step down the career ladder, a further degradation (also in the form of an emasculation), leaving K. further than ever from his apparent goal of recognition by the Castle, in a way that distinctly echoes both Karl Roßmann's riches-to-rags tale and Josef K.'s slow slide from innocent to condemned man. Still, in its non sequitur–ness and apparent triviality, the scene is strange, even for Kafka. Some have read in it an implication that the landlady is a kind of prostitute or would-be prostitute, and the oddly prominent motif of clothing in *Das Schloß* correspondingly as Kafka's critique of social conventions, striving, and worldly dissimulation.[100] This interpretation is admittedly consistent with the Castle's seemingly limitless prerogative over women's bodies, as well as with K.'s own voiced suspicion, in the same scene, that the landlady must have ulterior motives for her unsuitable attire. However, this age-old linkage of fashion and artifice fails to exhaust the full weirdness of the interest in clothing in Kafka's novel, which reappears, so to speak as a red thread, constantly and at the most incongruous moments. "Look, isn't it a beautiful shawl?" Gardena asks K. about the blanket he has just handed her (later revealed to be a gift from Klamm), "to K. it seemed to be an ordinary woolen shawl, he felt it out of courtesy, but said nothing. 'Yes, it's a beautiful shawl,' said Gardena and wrapped herself up in it."[101] The mysterious "girl from the Castle" wears "a diaphanous silk headscarf" (ein seidenes durchsichtiges Kopftuch),[102] and her dress has "a gleam as if of silk" (einen Schein wie von Seide);[103] Barnabas's coat is described as being "probably not silk, it was a winter coat like all the others, but it had the delicacy and elegance of a silk coat [die Zartheit und Feierlichkeit eines Seidenkleides]";[104] Klamm's carriage is equipped with piles of "blankets, cushions, and furs; one could turn and stretch out in every direction and always sink down soft and warm";[105] amid the many inconsistencies in the accounts of Klamm's appearance, "only concerning his clothes do the reports happily agree, he always wears the same coat, a black morning coat [Jackettkleid] with long tails";[106] and the fate of Amalia, "who knew how to sew very beautiful clothes,"[107] is sealed at least in part by the dress she wears to the firemen's festival, its white blouse "puffed out in front with row upon row of lace" (vorn hoch aufgebauscht, eine Spitzenreihe über der andern).[108] Meanwhile, a good part of Pepi's long monologue toward the end of the novel is occupied with the story of the outfit she hastily assembles on taking over Frieda's position, previously described through K.'s eyes as "a poorly fitting, flat-hanging dress of shiny gray fabric [aus grauglänzendem Stoff], . . . gathered at the bottom with childish clumsiness by a silk band tied into a bow."[109] As Pepi herself relates:

> One of the girls had long had some expensive fabric lying around, it was her treasure, she had often let the others admire it and no doubt dreamt of putting it to great use for herself at some point, but . . . now since Pepi needed it, she offered it to her. . . . And isn't the dress in fact

> beautiful? Of course, it's already crushed and a little dirty, . . . but you can still see how beautiful it is, not even that accursed Barnabas woman could have come up with anything better.[110]

In this change of costume, Pepi's only regrets are her boots and her "coarse underwear" (grobe Wäsche),[111] which she compares enviously to Frieda's "silk slip" (seidener Unterrock), "the only thing she spends money on."[112]

Again, where such scenes have been paid attention to, they have usually been read as the symbol of worldly superficiality and inauthenticity in contrast to the rarefied, all-signifying yet immaterial world of the Castle. In the context of the current inquiry, however, the odd motif of clothing and textiles in *Das Schloß* may be considered from a slightly different angle. Here an early short prose text of Kafka's, "Kleider" ("Clothes"), from his first published story collection, *Betrachtung* (*Contemplation*), provides a useful point of comparison. In this text—a strikingly derivative, Jugendstil piece of writing—Kafka avails himself of the rather hoary metaphor of worn-out finery to describe the aging faces of once-beautiful women. No one, writes Kafka, would think of wearing their fancy dress all the time,

> and yet I see girls that are beautiful and display charming muscles and delicate ankles [Knöchelchen] and taut skin and masses of fine hair, and still appear, day in and day out, in this same natural mask-garment [in diesem einen natürlichen Maskenanzug], always laying the same face in the same hands and letting it reappear in their mirror.
>
> Only sometimes, in the evening, when they come home late from a party, does it seem to them in the mirror worn out, bloated, dusty, already seen by everyone and barely any longer wearable.[113]

As Mark Anderson comments: "Metamorphosed into clothes, the faces of these girls appear grotesque, alien, opaque. . . . The body is only its 'clothing,' only a dirty, ornamental surface; and the feminine psyche is vacant."[114] We have, naturally, encountered this idea before. This is the "inversion of the face in femininity," the "presence of non-signifyingness in the signifyingness of the face" that Levinas, a few decades after Kafka, names the "primordial event of feminine beauty":[115] the sudden efflorescence of thingly materiality that turns the ordinarily signifying, expressive human countenance into an object of repulsion, violence, and desire. In Kafka's text, of course, the emphasis is less on the sexual allure of the objectified face than on the pathos of its future disrepair. However, in the well-formed bone structure and taut skin of the not-yet-tattered girls' appearances, reified into a "natural mask-garment," they are just as much "at the limit of the obscene yet repelled but already close at hand and promising,"[116] hovering between the soliciting face of the ethical individual and the "dead face [of] form," "a mortuary mask" of pure surface, which "is shown instead of letting see."[117]

In this context, Kafka's clothes/face comparison must be read as more than just a metaphor for the "guilt" of terrestrial being or the shame of public pretense vis-à-vis the authentic private self.[118] These aspects are perhaps present in Kafka's description, but one can go further: insofar as Kafka uses clothing as a symbol for the perishable flesh of the female body—itself the stereotypically misogynist emblem for fleshly perishability—clothing comes to stand in for finite matter in general, the inexpressive, resistant "Stoff" of the phenomenal world itself. However, if in *Betrachtung* Kafka still retains a conventional idea of earthly perfidy, by the time of *Das Schloß*, his thinking will have deepened. While it would no doubt be wishful thinking to claim that the late Kafka was entirely free of antimaterialist prejudices—much less, of gynophobic ideations[119]—the idea of a shameful fall into temporal materiality no longer has the axiomatic status to which "Kleider" still seems to subscribe. The landlady's opulent, outmoded dresses are the pendant to the foreman's inactive files: packed tightly in closets or heaped up in barns, they are, like K. himself, things taken out of commission, objects that appear only as the material insistence of their henceforth useless presence. But these things are no longer *opposed* to the meaning-making force of comital sanction; now, they are its *substance*. "Filth," Walter Benjamin writes, "is the element of the officials" (Schmutz ist das Lebenselement der Beamten).[120] If dirt, according to the famous phrase of Mary Douglas, is "matter out of place,"[121] the village of *Das Schloß* is dirt writ large, the dislocated location where the material ground of facticity, emptied of all content, bodies itself forth as infinite formless dross, in which even the air one breathes causes torpor and illness, in which the Brückenhof chambermaids trail their unwashed bundles of "familiar dirty rags" (wohlbekannten schmutzigen Fetzen),[122] in which K.'s "extra-official, thoroughly impenetrable, opaque, alien life" (außeramtliche, völlig unübersichtliche, trübe, fremdartige Leben), where the authorities could appear any moment "to clear him out of the way,"[123] makes him more suited to his surroundings than he knows. But this universality of dirt also announces a further change. For dirt, continues Douglas, "implies two conditions: a set of ordered relations and a contravention of that order."[124] "Dirt is the by-product of a systematic ordering and classification of matter"[125] by which things are deemed proper or improper, sacred or profane. When this ordering itself is disordered, however, another set of values may enter in.

According to Max Brod, Kafka drew part of his inspiration for *Das Schloß* from Božena Němcová's 1855 novel *Babička* (*Grandmother*),[126] an idealized, semiautobiographical portrait of multigenerational life in a Bohemian village and one of the milestones of the Czech national revival.[127] While Brod's account of Němcová's novel is seriously misleading,[128] it is clear that at least a few details in *Das Schloß* are taken from Němcová's provincial idyll, albeit submitted to Kafka's usual combinatory and anamorphic operations.[129] The most significant of these is the subplot in *Babička* in which the pretty barmaid Kristla (Christl in Anton Smital's 1885 German translation) is harassed by a foppish Italian courtier, the comic precursor to Amalia's bitter tragedy in *Das Schloß*. (However, the proof that Brod offers for this connection, namely that Němcová's courtier bears the same name as Amalia's tormenter, Sortini, is a baffling fiction: in both the Czech original and the German translation, the character in question is called Piccolo.)[130] From this farcical subplot of the lovesick Italian—who is first chased away from Kristla's window and publicly humiliated by a gang of local boys, and eventually dealt with at the grandmother's behest by no less than the princess of the realm herself[131]—Kafka distills a story of omnipresent droit du seigneur, where refusal to submit to the master's desire means scandal and social death.[132]

It is with reference to such distillations that Elizabeth Boa reads Kafka's work as a "crossing-over of naturalistic techniques into symbolic representation," in which "naturalist detail . . . immediately becomes loaded with obscene meaning."[133] In grafting realist description onto allegorical significance, Kafka reveals the "sacred phallus" as the profane penis, turns the symbolic law, "unveiled in naturalist description, . . . into that which it forbids or taboos."[134] Certainly, of *Babička*'s nostalgic portrait of village life, nothing remains in *Das Schloß* but the ubiquity of male desire and a seemingly inexhaustible supply of fungible female flesh to fulfill it.[135] However, Kafka's obscenification of *Babička* is more than just an example of a "subterranean humour [that] makes the scandal of patriarchy ludicrous,"[136] an exposure of the "naked truth" of political and paternal hegemony through its crudely material instantiation. Far more, it is the parodic overbid of all claims to expose the "naked truth" through material instantiation—or, rather, of all claims for crude materiality and/or physical desire as the bedrock realness of reality itself. Such claims are based on the selfsame logic of opposition between the sensual and the symbolic that ground the realist and the naturalist novel's ontology alike: the logic of obscenity itself, which posits matter as at once the essence of the real and the disgraceful outside of signification, such that immanence as such appears as something inherently inexpressive and abject.[137] As Joseph Vogl has written (in regard to Sade, but in direct analogy to Kafka), "In these obscene demonstrations . . . a hidden existence of the body comes into view that exposes, not the body itself, but the discourse of the body, the dimensions of a cultural compact."[138] If there is to be a way out of this compact—a Sorti(e)(ni), perhaps—it cannot be one that replicates its logic, be it through allegory, psychology, or the ever bolder, ever *sachlicher* incursion on the phenomenon. Rather, an art that wants to move away from the aporias of realism must universalize the violation, wallow in filth, strew the world's trash without hope of transfiguration.

It is in this transition from the reframings of realism to the grubby leftovers of an exhausted naturalism—too random and sordid even for naturalism itself—that the peephole once again comes into play. For the peephole in fact performs a double function. On the one hand, it serves to frame and organize a part of the world for viewing—just as one might do through surveying instruments—transforming the chaos of the material world into a rational digestible image. On the other hand, as a device that allows one to bring something into view without being viewed oneself, it serves to objectify the thing seen, replacing a potential intersubjective encounter with the commanding violence of the gaze. Voyeurism is the sadism of the eye: even—especially—if the "thing" seen is a human being, it *becomes* an object by being forced to expose itself, to be laid bare for the viewer without knowledge, consent, or control. (In this sense, the tendency of the assistants to enter rooms through the windows is doubly disturbing, insofar as it disrupts the passivity of the frame and allows the viewed object—"this not very appetizing assistant, this flesh, which sometimes gave the impression of not even being entirely alive" [dieser nicht sehr appetitliche Gehilfe, dieses Fleisch, das manchmal den Eindruck machte, als sei es nicht recht lebendig][139]—to suddenly accost the subject doing the viewing.)

This sadism of the eye is particularly notable in the lengthiest and most important of all the glimpses through the peephole, the aforementioned view of Klamm in his room at the Herrenhof:

> Through the small hole, which had clearly been drilled for the purposes of observation, [K.] could see almost the entire room. At a desk in the middle, in a comfortable round armchair sat Mr. Klamm, harshly illuminated by a lightbulb hanging down low in front of him [grell von einer vor ihm niederhängenden Glühlampe beleuchtet]. A gentleman of medium height, fat, ponderous. His face was still smooth, but his jowls sagged a little under the weight of age. . . . Had Mr. Klamm been sitting facing the desk, K. would have seen only his profile, but since Klamm was turned directly toward him, he had a view of his whole face. Klamm had lain his left elbow on the desk, his right hand, in which he held a Virginia cigar, rested on his knee.[140]

Later, of course, this picture will be qualified, not to say put radically into question, and Klamm himself will increasingly recede into a protean composite image: half rumor, half *Bildverbot*. But in this first and only view, Klamm appears to K. as nothing so much as a blank mass of inertial flesh on display, full frontal, with the phallic cigar—just to cap the image—held erect at waist height. Nothing could be less transfigured, less chaste; filling up the peephole's eye with his sagging, hulking body, Klamm is at this moment incarnation incarnate.[141]

In his final conversation with Frieda, K. chides his former fiancée for letting herself be taken in by the assistants, such that "even in their dirt and their unchastity [in ihrem Schmutz und ihrer Unzucht] you thought you could find traces of Klamm, like someone who thinks he sees in a dung heap a long-lost jewel, whereas in fact he wouldn't be able to find it even if it were there."[142] But K. is perhaps just as guilty of imagining that the way to the

Castle lies through its muck: his infinitely thwarted quest can be read as a veritable parody of poetic realism's "transfer of everything material into the spiritual realm" (Uebertragung alles Materiellen ins Seelische)[143] that allows it to continue to represent the phenomenal world while denying meaning to the phenomenal world as such. However, it is not even necessary to read the hyperbolic materiality of *Das Schloß* as an allegory for the sticky appeal of the sensual and the quixoticness of its spiritualization. For this materiality is anyway what remains once realism is stripped of its humanist framings and justificatory logic. Such a logic was one with which Kafka was eminently familiar:

> Psychology is the description of the reflection [Spiegelung] of the earthly world on the heavenly plane, or rather: the description of a reflection, as we, saturated with the world, imagine it to be [wie wir, Vollgesogene der Erde, sie uns denken], for no reflection actually takes place, we see only earth, wherever we turn.[144]

This is the hope of nineteenth-century aesthetics, to effect the representation of the material world on a higher plane than that world itself, in what is a not merely metaphorical secularization of the Christian idea of transcendence. But not only is this hope in many ways a deceptive one—Kafka cannily speaks, not of a "reflection of the earthly world," but of a "description of a reflection"—it also results in the propagation of exactly that which it wanted to avoid: the transformation of the earthly world into the "dirty rags" (schmutzigen Fetzen) of an unjustifiable materiality, something that should be hidden from the sight of innocents, though in truth that is all there is to see.

The fight at the dawn of Western philosophy over the concept of mimesis is so well known as to have the character of a fable: Plato condemns mimesis as the copy of a copy; Aristotle counters his teacher's criticism by shifting the idea of mimesis from the reproduction of physical objects in space to the imitation of character and action in time. This fight continues all the way through into the nineteenth and twentieth centuries, from the Platonesque disdain for "photographic" representation, to the Aristotelian compromises of perspectival transfiguration, to the replicative rigors of naturalist description (in which, we recall, Plato's mimesis-critique is turned on its head and made into a positive recommendation). This is the aesthetic tradition that not just Kafka, but all representational writers have had in some way to grapple with. Some choose the Platonic way, some the Aristotelian. Kafka chooses neither.

"Thou shalt not unto thee any image—" (Ihr sollt Euch kein Bild—).[145] As Werner Hamacher has observed, Kafka's interruption of the commandment in his diary both suspends it and performatively confirms its force: "The prohibition that the sentence is about to express intervenes into this very sentence and makes it into the fragment of a language that would correspond to the prohibition. By adhering to the prohibition, however, the only sentence in which it could present itself as law is interrupted."[146] This is no doubt true; but Kafka's interruption also has the further effect of transforming the prohibition itself, shifting its object from a "Bildnis"—an effigy or portraiture of the human figure—to a "Bild," any picture, image, metaphor, or representation, all the way to the extended Wittgensteinian sense of a mental image or concept. If that is indeed the commandment (even if a fragmented or interrupted one), then what is left to the writer of realist fiction? What, if anything, would be a nonidolatrous form of mimesis, a form of narration or description that avoids the twin traps of obscenity or idealism? One option might be to deflect the idolatrous gaze, to blur it, to make it fail to satisfy the observer's curiosity.[147] Another way, however, might be to go through the commandment right out to the other side, to the materiality that underlies all image-making, in comparison to which even the fetish and the idol, perpetually pointing away from themselves to the significations that they promise, are already a kind of sublimation. This option puts us on the dangerous ground of another Aristotle, the Aristotle of *De Anima* and the *Physics*, who posits matter, *hyle*, as the formless substrate of everything that exists: "what first underlies each thing, out of which something comes into being."[148]

It takes a long history, of course, to move from the vitalized matter of Aristotle's *hyle* to the grimy inertia of Kafka's village: to move, so to speak, from an idea of matter as "potentiality" to matter as "dirt."[149] This history is the history of obscenity, of the "set of violations"[150] that turns matter into something irredeemably prior to signification—and its display, correspondingly, into a sin and a scandal. If Kafka could not entirely avoid being influenced by this history, *Das Schloß*'s ironically flaunted waste products of realism at least represent an attempt to look at it from the outside in—through the peephole, as it were—to find no more than "an earthly building—what else can we build?" (ein irdisches Gebäude—was können wir anders bauen?).[151]

Coda

"As if she were saying something shameless"

> Dead matter, the pure idea, and God in fact answer a question in the same way (in other words perfectly, and as flatly as the docile student in a classroom)—a question that can only be posed by philosophers, the question of the essence of things, precisely of the *idea* by which things become intelligible.
>
> — Georges Bataille, "Materialism"[1]

In a commentary essay appended to the first edition of *Das Schloß*, Max Brod writes: "Without excluding more specific interpretations, which might be completely correct, but are contained within this overarching interpretation like the inner containers of a Chinese box are contained by its outermost one,—this 'Castle' to which K. is never granted entry, which, inexplicably, he can never even really approach, is precisely that which the theologians call 'grace' [genau das, was die Theologen 'Gnade' nennen]."[2] Brod's idea is familiar from almost a century of reading Kafka as a prophet of existential despair (a reading, naturally, for which Brod himself is largely responsible). However, the argument of the present book has suggested another way of understanding Brod's statement, if only as etymological pun. For what the theologians call *Gnade*, according to Brod, is only one of the possible translations of the Greek *charis* or the Latin *gratia*, which—in another register and according to another tradition—may also be rendered as *Anmut*. The linguistic distinction between the two translations also makes their conceptual difference clear: *Anmut* is the profane form of *Gnade*, the pagan, sensual, "chthonic-matriarchal" counterpart to "the patriarchal-monotheistic transcendence" of celestial bliss.[3] The German language codifies the split by which Pauline Christianity converts classical aesthetics into divine beatitude, lexically separating physical harmony from that spiritual wholeness for which the former is now, henceforth, only the semblance.

But the profaneness of *Anmut* goes even beyond this. For the original signification of the term is in fact not physical elegance or beauty of movement, but rather sensual desire, inclination, physical appetite itself (analogous to

Unmut, "displeasure"). Thus it appears, for example, in a *Spruchgedicht* of the baroque *Meistersinger* Hans Sachs:

> You are unthinking beasts
> And live controlled by your needs
> By your lust and affect
> In which you shamelessly are kept.
>
> Ir seyt unvernünfftige Thier
> Und lebet nach ewer begier
> Nach ewrem anmut und affect,
> Darinn ir unverschemet steckt.[4]

Anmut, in other words, is already obscenity, the shamelessness of *un*graceful corporeal display and uncontrolled physical drives that the term would later be mobilized to counteract. If one cannot exactly claim this etymology (which also entails an interesting gender shift from masculine to feminine) as the reason for the suspicion of sensuousness in German thought, it may at least be counted as a symptomatic manifestation, as well as perhaps a latent rhetorical influence.[5] The semantic drift between base physicality and its aesthetic sublimation—from sensual desire to the desirability of desensualization—haunts the idea of *Anmut* as the "expression of the soul in volitional movements,"[6] in which, precisely, the "dead forces of nature"[7] represented by the earlier meaning of the word are conquered and neutralized. The shift from lust to grace—from "*der* anmut" to "*die* Anmut"—circumvents the shame of the body by making the body a sign for the soul: a semantic turn, as it were, that leaves a remnant of meaninglessness in its wake.

In this sense, Brod's remark on Kafka's *Schloß* can be affirmed, but with a twist: the grace that both the character K. and the novel that contains him fail to achieve is not Brod's "divine guidance of human destiny"—much less, the bourgeois happiness of "career choice and marriage" that Brod cites (with reference to Flaubert of all people!) as its modern secular interpretation.[8] Rather, the absent grace of Kafka's novel may be read as the nonexistent transfiguration of "mere matter" into the *Verklärtheit* of a spiritualized mimesis, which would once and for all clothe the nakedly material world of the Castle village in the garments of transcendent meaning.[9] In this, too, the villagers seem to know something K. doesn't—or doesn't always: "[The maids] didn't answer and only awkwardly [verlegen] turned over their bundles, from which K. saw sticking out the familiar dirty rags. 'You've never actually even washed your things' ["Ihr habt wohl Euere Sachen noch niemals gewaschen"], said K., not angrily but rather with a certain fondness [Zuneigung]. They noticed, opened both at once their hard mouth, bared their beautiful strong animal-like teeth, and laughed silently."[10] The perverse attraction K. expresses in this moment toward the maids' filthy laundry and animal mouths points to the perverse attraction of Kafka's narrative toward its own sensual representations, in which the humanistic ends of the realist novel are constantly undercut by the brazen foregrounding of its material means. The abandonment of "the description of the reflection of the earthly world on the heavenly plane"[11] leads, not to a renunciation of the earthly world, but to the ever deeper, ever grubbier immersion within it. In the village, everyone is always washing up—but nothing ever seems to get clean.[12]

As Paul North comments in a comparison between the "atheologies" of Kafka and Georges Bataille: "Once God withdraws, once the nothing or the impossible is exposed as the basis of all things, faith shifts its attention to sex, shit, and dirt, the imperfect, the low, the fallen—to God's residue, if you will."[13] Yet unlike Bataille (whose militant indecencies always maintain the force of their prohibition), Kafka does not merely affirm this residue as a new positivity, for instance as "the beautiful blustering eruptions that alone are capable of answering the needs that torment the bowels of most men."[14] Rather, Kafka disempowers the prohibition by making its violation ubiquitous. The fact that there is no outside to the village, no idyllic counterpart to the filth—as there still was, for example, in the chaste rooms of the secretary Therese in *Der Verschollene* or the healthy nubility of Gregor's sister at the end of *Die Verwandlung*—means that there is not even the possibility of regarding dirt as either tragedy or transgression. Nor is there the possibility of fixing or eliminating it, as (in very different ways) in the novels of Stifter and Freytag, or of approaching it from the position of a superior authorial irony, as in Holz's satirical squalor or the supercilious mutilations of Gottfried Benn. In this way, *Das Schloß* could indeed be said to be the fulfillment of Schlegel's dictum that "every perfect novel should be obscene" (Jeder vollkommne Roman muß obscön sein).[15] In the very omnipresence and banality of its dirt, Kafka's famously *unvollkommen* novel delivers "the absolute in voluptuousness and sensuality" that Schlegel had once demanded—but now also with the consciousness of the efforts that have been made to suppress it and the side effects that these entail. "And everybody thinks about us more than is necessary," Olga relates to K., "but nobody will tell you anything about it, because they're ashamed to let such things cross their lips" (aber geradezu erzählen wird es niemand, diese Dinge in den Mund zu nehmen scheuen sie sich)."[16] Or, as Gardena responds to K.'s request for a meeting with Klamm: "'Fine,' said the landlady, and pressed her face into the pillows, as if she were saying something shameless" ("Gut," sagte die Wirtin, und drückte ihr Gesicht in die Kissen, als sage sie etwas Schamloses).[17]

German realism has a problem with matter. Time and again, authors and critics distance themselves from what Theodor Fontane once called the "naked reproduction of everyday life,"[18] promoting in its stead a *mediated* sensuality of experiential and narrative context, a semanticization of the material world that literature, as an essentially verbal medium, can anyway never actually not be. In this sense, German realism is anything but the stolid and pragmatic, antiphilosophical form of literature that many readers have assumed, and indeed as many of its own practitioners would have had their readers believe.[19] To the contrary, German realism is a *profoundly* philosophical form of literature—albeit one that goes to great lengths to hide its theoretical labors behind a screen of comprehensiveness, fellow feeling, and practical common sense. Through practices of ordering and separation, through the strategic distribution of value judgments, through implicit and explicit forms of emotional investment, the fictions of German realism establish a mimetic framework that—though certainly not without tension, change, or nuance—consistently establishes the priority of spirit over matter as the indispensible precondition of matter's representation. If the apparently random details of realist literature famously say, "We are the real,"[20] the not-at-all-random portrayal of these details through the lives of its characters and the forms of their perception says to its readers, "But *you* are the true."

This mimetic framework, historically situated though it is, has implications that go well beyond the particulars of a handful of German poems, plays, and novels. For what is left behind in this process of mediation is *matter itself*: the more realism represents the sensual as something necessarily intellectualized, the more it relegates the sensual per se to a presence without purpose, a literal incarnation of asemanticity that can be neither managed nor got around. Thus works of realist literature are not simply examples of "obscenity"; they are agents in the history of its creation, stages in a conceptual evolution every bit as consequential as the shift from *anmut* to *Anmut* or from *Anmut* to *Gnade*. It is perhaps no accident that when Jean-Paul Sartre first presents his idea of "the obscene," it is in the form of a novel, since the question posed by Sartre's existential phenomenology—how to understand the material world in the truth of its appearing—is already the question posed by literary realism, which "brackets" the world in its own way as an object of sustained aesthetic attention. Roquentin's climactic realization of "the meaning of 'existence' "[21] is first of all a dramatization—or, depending on one's point of view, a travesty—of the Husserlian phenomenological reduction, right down to the exemplary object of the tree in nature;[22] Husserl's encounter with "the things themselves"[23] is transformed into a nightmare vision in which "the words had vanished and with them the significance of things, their methods of use, and the feeble points of reference which men have traced on their surface."[24] But Roquentin's epiphany is also, and precisely thereby, the culmination of the perspectival logic of realist *Verklärung* itself. What for Husserl (in what might be described as the methodological refinement of poetic realism's sentimental humanism) was the first provision of a science of consciousness, is for Sartre the catastrophe that exposes the world in the shamelessness of its thereness. The disappearance of those categories, forms, and emotional investments that had once been able to clothe the material world in human meaning results in the return of the material world as crisis: "The diversity of things, their individuality, were only an appearance, a veneer. This veneer had melted, leaving soft, monstrous masses, all in disorder—naked, in a frightful, obscene nakedness."[25]

Sartre's notion of the obscene will be taken up and developed by later thinkers such as Emmanuel Levinas, Jacques Lacan, Slavoj Žižek, and Jean Baudrillard, where it functions, respectively, as an "existence 'without ceremonies,' . . . a 'non-signifying' and raw density,"[26] as the "gap opened up in the imaginary by any and every rejection of the commandments of speech,"[27] as the "nauseous inert presence" of a perversely self-enjoying God,[28] or, most extravagantly, as "the absolute proximity of the thing seen, the gaze stuck in the screen of vision . . . pure objects, transparent to each other, which would shatter against each other like pure kernels of truth."[29] But its roots lie in the nineteenth century's turn to the profane, everyday world and the corresponding rewriting of the classical dyad of matter and form, "sensuousness" and "soul,"[30] as a dichotomy between phenomenal existence and its human apprehension—in which, moreover, the idea of an existence *outside* human apprehension emerges in the form of a danger and a scandal, an insult to the shame of materiality from the point of view of its transcendence. Obscenity, in other words, is the appearance of matter as a by-product of its transfiguration. German realism is one of the stages of this appearance, and a place where its boundaries are drawn.

NOTES

Unless otherwise indicated, all translations are my own. Quoted existing English translations have occasionally been silently modified with reference to the original.

Introduction

1. Alain Robbe-Grillet, "Nature, Humanism and Tragedy," *New Left Review* 31 (May/June 1965): 67.

2. While Coetzee's scenario is fictional, both the novel in question and its author are in fact quite real: Paul West, *The Very Rich Hours of Count von Stauffenberg* (New York: Harper & Row, 1980).

3. J. M. Coetzee, *Elizabeth Costello* (New York: Penguin, 2004), 158–59.

4. Coetzee, *Elizabeth Costello*, 168–69.

5. The famous derivation of the word "obscene" from "off-stage," to which Elizabeth Costello here alludes, is not only etymologically spurious, but hermeneutically double-edged: while the common understanding is in the sense of what must *not* be shown, the interpretation by Varro—the likely propagator of the pseudo-etymology—has precisely the opposite implication: "Wherefore anything shameful is called *obscaenum*, because it ought not to be said openly except on the *scaena* 'stage.'" [Marcus Terentius] Varro, *On the Latin Language, Books V–VII*, trans. Roland G. Kent (Cambridge, Mass.: Harvard University Press, 1993), 351.

6. Coetzee, *Elizabeth Costello*, 177, 180.

7. J. M. Coetzee, "The Harms of Pornography: Catharine MacKinnon," in *Giving Offense: Essays on Censorship* (Chicago: University of Chicago Press, 1996), 75.

8. Lynn Hunt, introduction to *The Invention of Pornography: Obscenity and the Origins of Modernity, 1500–1800*, ed. Lynn Hunt (New York: Zone Books, 1996), 37.

9. Linda Williams, *Hard Core: Power, Pleasure, and the "Frenzy of the Visible"* (Berkeley: University of California Press, 1989), 46, 41.

10. See René Wellek, "The Concept of Realism in Literary Scholarship," *Neophilologus* 45, no. 1 (January 1961): 3–4.

11. On the history of the idea of truth as unveiling, see Pierre Hadot, *The Veil of Isis: An Essay on the History of the Idea of Nature*, trans. Michael Chase (Cambridge, Mass.: Harvard University Press, 2006). On pornography's "rhetoric of rhetoriclessness," see also Barbara Vinken, "Cover up—Die nackte Wahrheit der Pornographie," in *Die nackte Wahrheit: Zur Pornographie und zur Rolle des Obszönen in der Gegenwart*, ed. Barbara Vinken (Munich: dtv, 1997), 10.

12. That is, the idea that pre-twentieth-century society established a conspiracy of silence around sexuality that later generations would successfully break. Michel Foucault, *The History of Sexuality*, vol. 1: *An Introduction*, trans. Robert Hurley (New York: Vintage, 1990), esp. 3–12. Notable engagements with the theme of obscenity along these lines include D. H. Lawrence, *Pornography and Obscenity* (London: Faber & Faber, 1929); Henry Miller, *Obscenity and the Law of Reflection* (Yonkers, N.Y.: Alicat, 1944); Ludwig Marcuse, *Obszön: Geschichte einer Entrüstung* (Munich: List, 1962); Peter Gorsen, *Das Prinzip Obszön: Kunst, Pornographie und Gesellschaft* (Reinbek bei Hamburg: Rowohlt, 1969); Edgar Mertner and Herbert Mainusch, *Pornotopia: Das Obszöne und die Pornographie in der literarischen Landschaft* (Frankfurt am Main: Athenäum, 1970); Steven Marcus, *The Other Victorians: A Study of Sexuality and Pornography in Mid-Nineteenth-Century England* (New York: Basic Books, 1966); Walter Kendrick, *The Secret Museum: Pornography in Modern Culture* (Berkeley: University of California Press, 1987); Lynn Hunt, ed., *The Invention of Pornography: Obscenity and the Origins of Modernity, 1500–1800* (New York: Zone Books, 1996); Jan M. Ziolkowski, ed., *Obscenity: Social Control and Artistic Creation in the European Middle Ages* (Leiden: Brill, 1998); Allison Pease, *Modernism, Mass Culture, and the Aesthetics of Obscenity* (Cambridge: Cambridge University Press, 2000); Joan DeJean, *The Reinvention of Obscenity: Sex, Lies, and Tabloids in Early Modern France* (Chicago: University of Chicago Press, 2002); Florence Dore, *The Novel and the Obscene: Sexual Subjects in American Modernism* (Stanford, Calif.: Stanford University Press, 2005); Elisabeth Ladenson, *Dirt for Art's Sake: Books on Trial from "Madame Bovary" to "Lolita"* (Ithaca, N.Y.: Cornell University Press, 2007); and Chris Forster, *Filthy Material: Modernism and the Media of Obscenity* (New York: Oxford University Press, 2019).

13. *Jacobellis v. Ohio*, 378 U.S. 184 (1964), 198.

14. This term is most often associated with Barthes's assessment of the *nouveau roman*: "The indiscreet object remains *there*; it has the same freedom of exposition as one of Balzac's portraits, though not the same psychological necessity." Roland Barthes, "Objective Literature," in *Critical Essays*, trans. Richard Howard (Evanston, Ill.: Northwestern University Press, 1972), 14.

15. E.g., "Simply imagine Laocoön's mouth forced wide open, and then judge! . . . The wide-open mouth . . . becomes in a painting a mere spot and in sculpture a cavity, with most repulsive effect." Gotthold Ephraim Lessing, *Laocoön: An Essay on the Limits of Painting and Poetry*, trans. Edward Allen McCormick (Baltimore: Johns Hopkins University Press, 1984), 17. Compare Jean-Paul Sartre on the female sex as representative of "the obscenity of . . . that of everything which 'gapes open' [celle de toute chose *béante*]." Jean-Paul Sartre, *Being and Nothingness: A Phenomenological Essay on Ontology*, trans. Hazel E. Barnes (New York: Washington Square Press, 1992), 782; *L'être et le néant: Essai d'ontologie phénoménologique* (Paris: Gallimard: 2016), 802.

16. "Agreeable is what everyone calls that which gratifies him. . . . Agreeableness is also valid for nonrational animals; beauty is valid only for human beings, i.e., animal but also rational beings." Immanuel Kant, *Critique of the Power of Judgment*, trans. Paul Guyer and Eric Matthews (New York: Cambridge University Press, 2000), 95. While Kant does not use the word "obscene" here, his

separation of judgment and sensual gratification is decisive for all subsequent discussions of obscenity.

17. "Only works dealing with that specific and sharpest inflection of the themes of lust, 'the obscene,' [speak of death]. It's toward the gratifications of death, succeeding and surpassing those of eros, that every truly obscene quest tends." Susan Sontag, "The Pornographic Imagination," in *Styles of Radical Will* (New York: Anchor, 1991), 60.

18. "If I understand rightly: not the denuding of the foot, for example, but the denuding of the shoes that have become naked things again, without usefulness, stripped of their use-value? Presenting the shoes as things . . . would involve exhibiting a certain nudity, or even an obscenity." Jacques Derrida, "Restitutions of the Truth in Pointing," in *The Truth in Painting*, trans. Geoff Bennington and Ian McLeod (Chicago: University of Chicago Press, 1987), 300.

19. "Never, until these last few days, had I understood the meaning of 'existence.' . . . And then all of a sudden, there it was, clear as day: existence had suddenly unveiled itself . . . the diversity of things, their individuality, were only an appearance, a veneer. This veneer had melted, leaving soft, monstrous masses, all in disorder—naked, in a frightful, obscene nakedness." Jean-Paul Sartre, *Nausea*, trans. Lloyd Alexander (New York: New Directions, 2007), 126–27. Sartre's notion of obscenity will be taken up in greater detail below; see this chapter, 14–15, and coda, 182–83.

20. "We are living, in effect, amongst pure forms, in a radical obscenity, that is to say, in the visible, undifferentiated obscenity of figures that were once secret and discrete." Jean Baudrillard, *Seduction*, trans. Brian Singer (New York: St. Martin's, 1990), 179. What follows this is a cursory discussion of Walter Benjamin's "The Work of Art in the Age of Mechanical Reproduction."

21. "An irruption of excremental forces (the excessive violation of modesty, positive algolagnia, the violent excretion of the sexual object coinciding with a powerful or tortured ejaculation, the libidinal interest in cadavers, vomiting, defecation . . .)." Georges Bataille, "The Use Value of D. A. F. de Sade (An Open Letter to My Current Comrades)," in *Visions of Excess: Selected Writings, 1927–1939*, ed. and trans. Allan Stoekl (Minneapolis: University of Minnesota Press, 1985), 92–93. Ellipsis in original. To be fair, Bataille sometimes argues against the designation of such "excremental forces" as "obscene," but still often uses the term when it is convenient.

22. "The *obscene*, where the object-gaze is presented *as if there were no scene to stage it, no frame of representation to contain it, no screen*." Hal Foster, *The Return of the Real: The Avant-Garde at the End of the Twentieth Century* (Cambridge, Mass.: MIT Press, 1996), 149.

23. In current U.S. law, this distinction is known colloquially as the "Miller Test," after the 1973 U.S. Supreme Court case *Miller v. California*, in which the lack of "serious literary, artistic, political, or scientific value" is cited as the last of the three criteria that constitute "obscene material." *Miller v. California*, 413 U.S. 15 (1973).

24. Kant, *Critique of the Power of Judgment*, 95.

25. Robert Musil, "The Obscene and the Pathological in Art," in *Precision and Soul*, ed. and trans. Burton Pike and David S. Luft (Chicago: University of Chicago Press, 1990), 7; "Das Unanständige und Kranke in der Kunst," in

Gesammelte Werke, vol. 2: *Prosa und Stücke: Kleine Prosa, Aphorismen, Autobiographisches, Essays und Reden, Kritik*, ed. Adolf Frisé (Reinbek bei Hamburg: Rowohlt, 1978), 980.

26. Musil, "The Obscene and the Pathological," 8; "Das Unanständige und Kranke," 982.

27. G. W. F. Hegel, *Aesthetics: Lectures on Fine Art*, trans. T. M. Knox (Oxford: Oxford University Press, 1998), 162–63; *Vorlesungen über die Ästhetik I*, in *Werke*, vol. 13, ed. Eva Moldenhauer and Karl Markus Michel (Frankfurt am Main: Suhrkamp, 1970), 214–15.

28. Jean-Luc Marion, *The Erotic Phenomenon*, trans. Stephen E. Lewis (Chicago: University of Chicago Press, 2007), 121–22.

29. Jean-Luc Nancy, "On Painting and Presence," trans. Emily McVarish, in *The Birth to Presence* (Stanford, Calif.: Stanford University Press, 1993), 354.

30. Jean Baudrillard, *Passwords*, trans. Chris Turner (London: Verso, 2003), 29.

31. See also Freud's attribution of the origins of the obscene joke to "the desire to see what is sexual," as well as Sándor Ferenczi's claim that the obscenity of obscene words comes from their "power of compelling the hearer to imagine the [designated] object . . . *in substantial actuality*." Sigmund Freud, *Jokes and Their Relation to the Unconscious*, trans. James Strachey (New York: W. W. Norton, 1960), 116; Sándor Ferenczi, "On Obscene Words," in *Sex in Psychoanalysis* (New York: Brunner, 1950), 137.

32. See, for example, Peter Brooks, *Realist Vision* (New Haven, Conn.: Yale University Press, 2005); Fredric Jameson, *The Antinomies of Realism* (London: Verso, 2013); and Anna Kornbluh, *The Order of Forms: Realism, Formalism, and Social Space* (Chicago: University of Chicago Press, 2019), the latter of which unfortunately appeared too late for me to take into account.

33. For example, Richard Brinkmann, *Wirklichkeit und Illusion: Studien über Gehalt und Grenzen des Begriffs Realismus für die erzählende Dichtung des neunzehnten Jahrhunderts* (Tübingen: Niemeyer, 1957); Wolfgang Preisendanz, *Wege des Realismus* (Munich: Fink, 1977); Robert Holub, *Reflections of Realism: Paradox, Norm, and Ideology in Nineteenth-Century German Prose* (Detroit: Wayne State University Press, 1991); Eva Geulen, *Worthörig wider Willen: Darstellungsproblematik und Sprachreflexion in der Prosa Adalbert Stifters* (Munich: iudicum, 1992); Christian Begemann, *Die Welt der Zeichen: Stifter-Lektüren* (Stuttgart: Metzler, 1995); Eric Downing, *Double Exposures: Repetition and Realism in Nineteenth-Century German Fiction* (Stanford, Calif.: Stanford University Press, 2000); Christiane Arndt, *Abschied von der Wirklichkeit: Probleme bei der Darstellung von Realität im deutschsprachigen literarischen Realismus* (Freiburg im Breisgau: Rombach, 2009).

34. See Brinkmann, *Wirklichkeit und Illusion*, 215–16; Downing, *Double Exposures*, esp. 21–22.

35. See Eric Downing, *The Chain of Things: Divinatory Magic and the Practice of Reading in German Literature and Thought, 1850–1940* (Ithaca, N.Y.: Cornell University Press, 2018).

36. Downing, *The Chain of Things*, 113.

37. Jane Bennett, *Vibrant Matter: A Political Ecology of Things* (Durham, N.C.: Duke University Press, 2010), 65. Bennett's reference is to Kant, *Critique of*

the Power of Judgment, §81, 292; Guyer and Matthews translate Kant's phrase, closer to the original, as "raw matter" (rohe Materie).

38. E.g., "In Germany life itself was much more provincial, much more old-fashioned, much less 'contemporary.' . . . It yielded no subject matter for a realism so generally national, so materially modern, so intent upon an analysis of the emerging destiny of European society, as the realism of France." Erich Auerbach, *Mimesis: The Representation of Reality in Western Literature*, trans. Willard R. Trask (Princeton, N.J.: Princeton University Press, 1953), 516.

39. Paul Fleming, *Exemplarity and Mediocrity: The Art of the Average from Bourgeois Tragedy to Realism* (Stanford, Calif.: Stanford University Press; 2009), 127.

40. Fleming, *Exemplarity and Mediocrity*, 131.

41. Hegel, *Lectures on Aesthetics*, 596; *Vorlesungen über die Ästhetik II*, in *Werke*, vol. 14, ed. Eva Moldenhauer and Karl Markus Michel (Frankfurt am Main: Suhrkamp, 1970), 223.

42. A number of new works in German literary studies have begun to investigate this knot of materiality and representation. See, for example, Sabine Schneider and Barbara Hunfeld, eds., *Die Dinge und die Zeichen: Dimensionen des Realistischen in der Erzählliteratur des 19. Jahrhunderts* (Würzburg: Königshausen & Neumann, 2008); Christiane Arndt and Silke Brodersen, eds., *Organismus und Gesellschaft: Der Körper in der deutschsprachigen Literatur des Realismus (1830–1930)* (Bielefeld: Transcript, 2011); Elisabeth Strowick, ed., *Wirklichkeit und Wahrnehmung: Neue Perspektiven auf Theodor Storm* (Bern: Lang, 2013); Catriona MacLeod, *Fugitive Objects: Sculpture and Literature in the German Nineteenth Century* (Evanston, Ill.: Northwestern University Press, 2014); John Hamilton, *Philology of the Flesh* (Chicago: University of Chicago Press, 2018); and Elisabeth Strowick, *Gespenster des Realismus: Zur literarischen Wahrnehmung von Wirklichkeit* (Munich: Fink, 2019).

43. Hegel, *Aesthetics*, 607; *Ästhetik II*, 237–38. Compare Hegel, *Aesthetics*, 607; *Ästhetik II*, 238: "For art does not need any longer to represent only what is absolutely at home at one of its specific stages, but everything in which man as such is capable of being at home" (da die Kunst nicht mehr das nur darzustellen braucht, was auf einer ihrer bestimmten Stufen absolut zu Hause ist, sondern alles, worin der Mensch überhaupt heimisch zu sein die Befähigung hat).

44. Williams, *Hard Core*, 48.

45. Judith Butler, *Bodies That Matter: On the Discursive Limits of Sex* (London: Routledge, 1993), 4.

46. Forster also notes the idea of obscenity "as a sort of mere, or even pathological, materiality," but bypasses the broader dimensions of this idea to focus on the media-historical materiality of the *text* and a reversion to an idea of obscenity as sexuality. Forster, *Filthy Material*, 26.

47. Friedrich Schlegel, Fragment 579, *Kritische Friedrich-Schlegel-Ausgabe*, ed. Ernst Behler, vol. 16: *Schriften aus dem Nachlaß: Fragmente zur Poesie und Literatur, Erster Teil*, ed. Hans Eichner (Paderborn: Schöningh, 1981), 133. I have normalized Schlegel's notebook abbreviations.

48. Schlegel's aphorism is in part a swipe at Goethe, continuing, "In *Meister* there is neither sensuality nor Christianity enough for a novel" (Im Meister ist weder Wollust noch Christentum genug für einen Roman). For an analysis

of Schlegel's "obscenity" in terms of the performativity of gender—and the performative gendering of philosophy—in his scandal novel *Lucinde*, see Marc Redfield, "*Lucinde*'s Obscenity," in *Rereading Romanticism*, ed. Martha B. Helfer (Amsterdam: Rodopi, 2000).

49. Julian Schmidt, *Geschichte der deutschen Literatur seit Lessing's Tod*, vol. 3 (Leipzig: Herbig, 1858), 146. Schmidt's book is one of several encyclopedic histories of German literature he would write in his lifetime, often recycling passages from one work to the next. Where passages appear in more than one place, I have generally made an effort to quote from this work.

50. Schmidt, *Geschichte der deutschen Literatur seit Lessing's Tod*, vol. 3, 146.

51. Schmidt, *Geschichte der deutschen Literatur seit Lessing's Tod*, vol. 3, 308.

52. Julian Schmidt, *Geschichte der deutschen Literatur von Leibniz bis auf unsere Zeit*, vol. 5: *1814–1866* (Berlin: Hertz, 1896), 510. For Schmidt, not unproblematically, this "intimation of the whole" is found above all in the idea of a national language and, by extension, national-racial belonging.

53. Theodor Fontane, "Unsere lyrische und epische Poesie seit 1848," in *Sämtliche Werke*, ed. Edgar Groß, Kurt Schreinert et al., 24 vols. (Munich: Nymphenburger Verlagshandlung, 1959–75), 21.1:12.

54. Schmidt, *Geschichte der deutschen Literatur seit Lessing's Tod*, vol. 3, 146.

55. Hegel, *Aesthetics*, 9; *Ästhetik I*, 23.

56. Schmidt, *Geschichte der deutschen Literatur seit Lessing's Tod*, vol. 3, 417.

57. Though Schmidt himself has few kind words for Hegel, he seems to have only a superficial understanding of Hegel's philosophy, interpreting it mostly as a kind of speculative nihilism.

58. Schmidt, *Geschichte der deutschen Literatur von Leibniz bis auf unsere Zeit*, vol. 5, 573.

59. Schmidt, *Geschichte der deutschen Literatur von Leibniz bis auf unsere Zeit*, vol. 5, 510.

60. Schmidt, *Geschichte der deutschen Literatur von Leibniz bis auf unsere Zeit*, vol. 5, 508: "Now the age has become very serious, it no longer derives the idea of art, like Schiller, from the play drive, but demands truth from it as it does from science."

61. Downing, *Double Exposures*, 37.

62. Baudrillard, *Passwords*, 28. Or, as Baudrillard proclaims a page later, even more peremptorily: "Objective truth is obscene." *Passwords*, 29.

63. Sarah L. Leonard, *Fragile Minds and Vulnerable Souls: The Matter of Obscenity in Nineteenth-Century Germany* (Philadelphia: University of Pennsylvania Press, 2015), 23.

64. *Königliches sächsisches Kriminalgesetzbuch* (May 30, 1838), §309. Quoted in H. Josef Haubach, *Der strafrechtliche Schutz des Schamgefühls* (Würzburg: Memminger, 1917), 36.

65. *Strafgesetzbuch für das Grossherzogthum Hessen, nebst den damit zusammenhängenden Gesetzen* (Darmstadt: Verlag der Invaliden-Anstalt, 1841), 107, www.mdz-nbn-resolving.de/urn/resolver.pl?urn=urn:nbn:de:bvb:12-bsb10395527-6. See also Leonard, *Fragile Minds*, 129.

66. Such imprecision reaches its peak in 1893, in the infamous §184 of the controversial "Lex Heinze" bill, according to which the disseminators of texts and images which are "apt to cause offense through gross injury to modesty

and morality" (durch gröbliche Verletzung des Scham- und Sittlichkeitsgefühls Ärgernis zu erregen geeignet) may be subject to punishment even "*without* being indecent" (*ohne* unzüchtig zu sein). Quoted in Haubach, *Der strafrechtliche Schutz des Schamgefühls*, 25. My emphasis. It should be noted that this version of the Lex Heinze ultimately failed to pass, not least due to its potential overreach.

67. Karl Rosenkranz, *The Aesthetics of Ugliness: A Critical Edition*, trans. Andrei Pop and Mechtild Widrich (London: Bloomsbury, 2015), 150; *Ästhetik des Häßlichen*, ed. Dieter Kliche (Stuttgart: Reclam, 1990), 222–23. See also Erica Weitzman, "'An Injury to Shame': Obscenity and Affect in Nineteenth-Century German Aesthetics," *Orbis Litterarum* 74, no. 1 (February 2019): 2–7.

68. Rosenkranz, *Aesthetics of Ugliness*, 150; *Ästhetik des Häßlichen*, 222.

69. Rosenkranz, *Aesthetics of Ugliness*, 152; *Ästhetik des Häßlichen*, 226. These and other erotic artworks from the Pompeii and Herculaneum excavations were collected in the "secret cabinet" of the Royal Museum in Naples. Rosenkranz's source for these paintings appears to be the *catalogue raisonné* of H. Roux aîné and Louis Barré, *Herculanum et Pompéi: Recueil général des peintures, bronzes, mosaïques, etc., découverts jusqu'à ce jour, et reproduits d'après le Antichita di Ercolano, il Museo Borbonico, et tous les ouvrages analogues, augmenté de sujets inédits*, vol. 8: *Musée secret* (Paris: Didot, 1877).

70. Rosenkranz, *Aesthetics of Ugliness*, 152; *Ästhetik des Häßlichen*, 226.

71. On the "softening" of obscenity, see Rosenkranz, *Aesthetics of Ugliness*, 152; *Ästhetik des Häßlichen*, 226.

72. Rosenkranz, *Aesthetics of Ugliness, 152; Ästhetik des Häßlichen*, 226.

73. Rosenkranz, *Aesthetics of Ugliness*, 150–51; *Ästhetik des Häßlichen*, 223.

74. Antonio Varone suggests that the presence of the servant in many of the Pompeian images—not to mention during the sex acts themselves—functioned as a form of exhibitionism meant to increase sexual arousal. See Antonio Varone, *Eroticism in Pompeii*, trans. Maureen Fant (Los Angeles: J. Paul Getty Museum, 2001), 74–78.

75. The reference is to Michael Fried, *Absorption and Theatricality: Painting and Beholder in the Age of Diderot* (Chicago: University of Chicago Press, 1980); see esp. 96–97, 178, on the staging of the spectator as voyeur.

76. See Julie Stone Peters: "If theater was troubling because it always verged on the obscene, obscenity was troubling in part because it always verged on the theatrical." Julie Stone Peters, "Performing Obscene Modernism: Theatrical Censorship and the Making of Modern Drama," in *Against Theater: Creative Destructions on the Modernist Stage*, ed. Alan Ackerman and Martin Puchner (New York: Palgrave, 2006), 214.

77. Gen. 2:25 (KJV).

78. Gen. 3:7 (KJV).

79. Augustine, "On Marriage and Concupiscence," in *A Select Library of the Nicene and Post-Nicene Fathers of the Christian Church*, vol. 5: *Saint Augustin: Anti-Pelagian Writings*, ed. Philip Schaff (Grand Rapids: Eerdmans, 1956), 266.

80. Giorgio Agamben, "Nudity," in *Nudities*, trans. David Kishik and Stefan Pedatella (Stanford, Calif.: Stanford University Press, 2015), 64. Agamben's essay is ultimately an attempt to "defuse the theological apparatus" and create an alternative way of thinking in which we can "see, beyond the prestige of grace and

the chimeras of corrupt nature, a simple, inapparent human body." Agamben, "Nudity," 90.

81. Rosenkranz, *Aesthetics of Ugliness*, 150; *Ästhetik des Häßlichen*, 222.

82. Agamben, "Nudity," 69–70. Compare Jean-Luc Nancy and Federico Ferrari: "Of all human nudity—and there's no other kind of nudity—the penis is the only part that reveals more than, or something other than, nudity. . . . Nudity here lacks any reserve of modesty. The skin is not the luminous transparence of the body: it is only an organ and an additional limb. In truth, the body is left behind: we are before another presence that is singular, independent—and hanging out." Jean-Luc Nancy and Federico Ferrari, *Being Nude: The Skin of Images*, trans. Anne O'Byrne and Carlie Anglemire (New York: Fordham University Press, 2014), 51–53.

83. See Agamben, "Nudity," 69.

84. The biblical scholar Michaela Bauks suggests that Adam and Eve's shame is not self-reflexive so much as intersubjective. Michaela Bauks, "Nacktheit und Scham in Genesis 2–3," in *Zur Kulturgeschichte der Scham*, ed. Michaela Bauks and Martin F. Meyer (Hamburg: Meiner, 2011), esp. 17–18. See also Erica Weitzman, "Scham, oder die Metaphysik," in *Rücksendungen zu Jacques Derridas "Die Postkarte": Ein essayistisches Glossar*, ed. Matthias Schmidt (Vienna: Turia + Kant, 2015), 333–35.

85. Friedrich Schiller, "On Grace and Dignity," in *Schiller's "On Grace and Dignity" in Its Cultural Context: Essays and a New Translation*, ed. Jane V. Curran and Christopher Fricker (Rochester, N.Y.: Camden House, 2005), 134; "Über Anmut und Würde," in *Werke und Briefe in zwölf Bänden*, vol. 8: *Theoretische Schriften*, ed. Rolf-Peter Janz (Frankfurt am Main: Deutscher Klassiker Verlag, 1992), 344.

86. Schiller, "On Grace and Dignity," 127; "Über Anmut und Würde," 334.

87. Schiller, "On Grace and Dignity," 126; "Über Anmut und Würde," 333–34.

88. Schiller, "On Grace and Dignity," 147; "Über Anmut und Würde," 363–64.

89. On the political subtexts of Schiller's concept, see Kenneth S. Calhoon, *Affecting Grace: Theater, Subject, and the Shakespearean Paradox in German Literature from Lessing to Kleist* (Toronto: University of Toronto Press, 2013), esp. 4–5.

90. Schiller, "On Grace and Dignity," 148; "Über Anmut und Würde," 364.

91. Schiller, "On Grace and Dignity," 143; "Über Anmut und Würde," 357. Emphases in original.

92. Compare Georges Bataille's notion of formlessness as "a term that serves to bring things down in the world, generally requiring that each thing have its form . . . affirming that the universe resembles nothing and is only *formless* amounts to saying that the universe is something like a spider or spit." Georges Bataille, "Formless," in *Visions of Excess*, 31.

93. Schiller, "On Grace and Dignity," 148; "Über Anmut und Würde," 364.

94. Schiller, "On Grace and Dignity," 143; "Über Anmut und Würde," 357.

95. While Sartre credits his conception of grace to Bergson, Bergson himself clearly has Schiller in mind: "In every human form [our imagination] sees the effort of a soul which is shaping matter, a soul which is infinitely supple and perpetually in motion, subject to no law of gravitation, for it is not the earth that attracts it. This soul imparts a portion of its winged lightness to the body it

animates: the immateriality which thus passes into matter is what is called gracefulness. Matter, however, is obstinate and resists." Henri Bergson, *Laughter: An Essay on the Meaning of the Comic*, trans. Cloudesely Brereton and Fred Rothwell (Rockville, Md.: Arc Manor, 2008), 20–21.

96. Agamben traces Sartre's idea of grace to Augustine, but overlooks the Schiller-Bergson connection; see "Nudity," esp. 73.

97. Sartre, *Being and Nothingness*, 519–20.

98. Sartre, *Being and Nothingness*, 471, passim.

99. Sartre, *Being and Nothingness*, 520; *L'être et le néant*, 535.

100. Sartre, *Being and Nothingness*, 520.

101. Sartre, *Being and Nothingness*, 518.

102. Sartre, *Being and Nothingness*, 519.

103. Sartre, *Being and Nothingness*, 520–21.

104. Schiller, "On Grace and Dignity," 143; "Über Anmut und Würde," 357.

105. Sartre, *Being and Nothingness*, 521.

106. Compare Heinrich Wölfflin's description of baroque art as the product of an unresolved tension between an idea of matter as inert substance and an idea of matter as vital force: "This emotion of wild, ecstatic delight cannot be expressed uniformly by the whole body: emotion breaks out with violence in certain organs, while the rest of the body remains subject only to gravity. But this enormous expenditure of effort is not a sign of greater strength. On the contrary: the movement of voluntary organs is deficient; the mental impulses are far from completely controlling the movements of the body. The two elements, mind and body, have, as it were, parted company. It is as if these men no longer have full power over their own bodies, no longer permeate them with their own will." Heinrich Wölfflin, *Renaissance and Baroque*, trans. Kathrin Simon (Ithaca, N.Y.: Cornell University Press, 1964), 81.

107. Sartre, *Nausea*, 134. Tilottama Rajan has argued that Sartre's account of "obscene" existence effects a "double defacement of being and the human" anticipating the deconstructive critique of presence. Tilottama Rajan, *Deconstruction and the Remainders of Phenomenology: Sartre, Derrida, Foucault, Baudrillard* (Stanford, Calif.: Stanford University Press, 2002), 75. Be that as it may, for Sartre himself, the "obscenity" of being is still something strongly negative, redeemable by the freedom of the sovereign subject alone.

108. Schiller, "On Grace and Dignity," 126; "Über Anmut und Würde," 334. Emphasis in original.

109. James I. Porter, "The Disgrace of Matter in Ancient Aesthetics," in *KAKOS: Badness and Anti-value in Classical Antiquity*, ed. Ineke Sluiter and Ralph M. Rosen (Leiden: Brill, 2008), 288–89; see also James I. Porter, *The Origins of Aesthetic Thought in Ancient Greece: Matter, Sensation, and Experience* (Cambridge: Cambridge University Press, 2010). Porter moreover demonstrates that the emergence of the form/matter divide in Plato and Aristotle is a specific *change* in aesthetic thought and a conscious repression of earlier traditions.

110. Schiller, "On Grace and Dignity," 126; "Über Anmut und Würde," 334.

111. For Silvan Tomkins, such projective self-regard means that within shame, "the phenomenological distinction between the subject and object of shame is lost." Silvan Tomkins, *Shame and Its Sisters: A Silvan Tomkins Reader*, ed. Eve Kosofsky Sedgwick and Adam Frank (Durham, N.C.: Duke University Press,

1995), 136. However, this is not quite correct: the specific peculiarity of shame is that it depends on a simultaneous *dis*identification (the self is an other) and identification (the other is the self).

112. Max Scheler, "Shame and Feelings of Modesty," in *Person and Self-Value: Three Essays*, trans. M. S. Frings (Dordrecht: Martinus Nijhoff, 1987), 73; "Über Scham und Schamgefühl," in *Schriften aus dem Nachlass*, vol. 1: *Zur Ethik und Erkenntnislehre* (Berlin: Neue Geist, 1933), 134. Emphasis in original.

113. Scheler, "Shame and Feelings of Modesty," 23; "Über Scham und Schamgefühl," 77–78. Here one thinks inevitably of the young man in Kleist's "Über das Marionettentheater" ("On the Marionette Theater")—surprisingly unmentioned in Scheler—whose glimpse of himself in the mirror leads him to a permanent loss of innocence in the separation of his body from the "soul (vis motrix)" that animates it. Heinrich von Kleist, "Über das Marionettentheater," in *Sämtliche Werke und Briefe*, vol. 2, ed. Helmut Sembdner (Frankfurt am Main: Deutscher Taschenbuch Verlag, 2008), 344.

114. Eric Santner, *On Creaturely Life: Rilke, Benjamin, Sebald* (Chicago: University of Chicago Press, 2006), 23.

115. Giorgio Agamben, "In Praise of Profanation," in *Profanations*, trans. Jeff Fort (New York: Zone Books, 2007), 90. As Agamben's title indicates, his essay is in fact an argument *against* the shamefulness of exhibition and for a rethinking of such pure showing as liberatory gesture.

116. See Michael Fried, "Art and Objecthood," in *Art and Objecthood: Essays and Reviews* (Chicago: University of Chicago Press, 1998), 168.

117. Georg Lukács, "Narrate or Describe?," in *Writer and Critic, and Other Essays*, ed. and trans. Arthur D. Kahn (New York: Grosset & Dunlap, 1971), 133; "Erzählen oder beschreiben?," in *Werke*, vol. 4: *Probleme des Realismus* (Neuwied: Luchterhand, 1971), 219.

118. See, e.g., Emily Apter, *Feminizing the Fetish: Psychoanalysis and Narrative Obsession in Turn-of-the-Century France* (Ithaca, N.Y.: Cornell University Press, 1991); Emily Apter and William Pietz, eds., *Fetishism as Cultural Discourse* (Ithaca, N.Y.: Cornell University Press, 1993); Martin Jay, *Downcast Eyes: The Denigration of Vision in Twentieth-Century French Thought* (Berkeley: University of California Press, 1993), esp. 171–75; Barbara Vinken, "Zola—alles sehen, alles wissen, alles heilen: Der Fetischismus im Naturalismus," in *Historische Anthropologie und Literatur: Romanistische Beiträge zu einem neuen Paradigma der Literaturwissenschaft*, ed. Rudolf Behrens and Roland Galle (Würzburg: Königshausen & Neumann, 1995); Barbara Vinken, "Pygmalion à rebours: Fetischismus in Zolas Œuvre," in *Pygmalion: Die Geschichte des Mythos in der abendländischen Kultur*, ed. Matthias Meyer and Gerhard Neumann (Freiburg im Breisgau: Rombach, 1997); Hartmut Böhme, *Fetischismus und Kultur: Eine andere Geschichte der Moderne* (Reinbek bei Hamburg: Rowohlt, 2006); Naomi Schor, *Reading in Detail: Aesthetics and the Feminine* (London: Routledge, 2007); Neil Hertz, "Medusa's Head: Male Hysteria under Political Pressure," in *The End of the Line* (Aurora, Colo.: Davies, 2009); and Doerte Bischoff, *Poetischer Fetischismus: Der Kult der Dinge im 19. Jahrhundert* (Munich: Fink, 2013).

119. On the fetish as an "embodiment of knowledge," see Bischoff, *Poetischer Fetischismus*, 32.

120. Schor, *Reading in Detail*, 15.

121. Schor, *Reading in Detail*, 9.

122. Lukács, "Narrate or Describe?," 139; "Erzählen oder beschreiben?," 225.

123. Friedrich Spielhagen, "Ueber Objectivetät im Roman," in *Vermischte Schriften*, vol. 1 (Berlin: Janke, 1864), 186–87.

124. Spielhagen, "Ueber Objectivetät im Roman," 174–75. Compare Schmidt, *Geschichte der deutschen Literatur seit Lessing's Tod*, vol. 3, 181: "True realism goes hand in hand with true idealism" (Der echte Realismus geht mit dem echten Idealismus Hand in Hand).

125. Schmidt, *Geschichte der deutschen Literatur von Leibniz bis auf unsere Zeit*, vol. 5, 569.

126. Schmidt, *Geschichte der deutschen Literatur von Leibniz bis auf unsere Zeit*, vol. 5, 570.

127. Schmidt, *Geschichte der deutschen Literatur von Leibniz bis auf unsere Zeit*, vol. 5, 570.

128. Schmidt, *Geschichte der deutschen Literatur von Leibniz bis auf unsere Zeit*, vol. 5, 570.

129. Theodor Fontane, review of Paul Lindau, *Zug nach dem Westen* (1886), in *Schriften zur Literatur* (Berlin: Aufbau, 1960), 108.

130. See, e.g., Hugo Aust, *Theodor Fontane: "Verklärung." Eine Untersuchung zum Ideengehalt seiner Werke* (Bonn: Bouvier, 1974).

131. Thus Wolfgang Preisendanz: "*Verklärung* means a way of writing that does not efface but upholds the difference between the life-given image and the poetic one, a way of writing in which representation is more than reproduction or inventory, but rather basis and origin of a reality." Wolfgang Preisendanz, *Wege des Realismus* (Munich: Fink, 1977), 83. On the biblical provenance of *Verklärung*, see page 164 above and 216n67 below.

132. The term "poetic realism" was first used by Schelling in his 1803 *Vorlesungen über die Methode des akademischen Studiums*, albeit not in an emphatic manner. See F. W. J. Schelling, "Über die Wissenschaft der Kunst, in bezug auf das akademische Studium," in *Werke: Auswahl in Drei Bänden*, vol. 2: *Schriften zur Identitätsphilosophie*, ed. Otto Weiß (Leipzig: Eckart, 1907), 676.

133. Otto Ludwig, "Der poetische Realismus," in *Nachlaßschriften*, vol. 2: *Shakespeare-Studien*, ed. Moritz Heydrich (Leipzig: Cnoblauch, 1872), 264. On Ludwig's idea of poetic totality, see Preisendanz, *Wege des Realismus*, esp. 69–70.

134. Hegel, *Aesthetics*, 9; *Ästhetik I*, 23.

135. Rosenkranz, *Aesthetics of Ugliness*, 151; *Ästhetik des Häßlichen*, 225.

136. Rosenkranz, *Aesthetics of Ugliness*, 151; *Ästhetik des Häßlichen*, 225.

137. I borrow this phrase from Adrian Daub's definition of the obscene (in reference, as in Rosenkranz, to the spectacle of dance): "Features that are just meaninglessly 'out there,' exposed without any hope of being interpretively recuperated." Adrian Daub, "The Ob-scene of the Total Work of Art: Frank Wedekind, Richard Strauss, and the Spectacle of Dance," *19th-Century Music* 39, no. 3 (Spring 2016): 286.

138. Slavoj Žižek, *Looking Awry: An Introduction to Jacques Lacan through Popular Culture* (Cambridge, Mass.: MIT Press, 1991), 142–43.

139. See also Eric Santner, *On Creaturely Life*, xv: "The opacity and recalcitrance that we associate with the materiality of nature—the mute 'thingness' of nature—is, paradoxically, most palpable where we encounter it as a piece

of human history that has become an enigmatic ruin beyond our capacity to endow it with meaning, to integrate it into our symbolic universe." Speaking in psychoanalytic terms, one might consider Santner's concept of the "creaturely" as the melancholy, narcissistic complement (history becoming obsolete ruin) to the obscene's phobic and outward-facing (object failing to become history) configuration.

140. Downing, *The Chain of Things*, 292n170. Downing's comment specifically regards Heinrich's thingification of the dead Anna in Gottfried Keller's *Der grüne Heinrich*.

141. Emmanuel Levinas, *Totality and Infinity: An Essay on Exteriority*, trans. Alphonso Lingis (Pittsburgh: Duquesne University Press, 1969), 256–66; *Totalité et infini: Essai sur l'extériorité* (Paris: Le Livre de Poche, 1990), 286–99.

142. See also Levinas's earlier, more rudimentary version of this analysis in Emmanuel Levinas, *Time and the Other, and Additional Essays*, trans. Richard A. Cohen (Pittsburgh: Duquesne University Press, 1987), 84–90, where Levinas is even more explicit about his quarrel with Sartre.

143. Levinas, *Totality and Infinity*, 262; *Totalité et infini*, 294–95.

144. Levinas, *Totality and Infinity*, 262.

145. Levinas, *Totality and Infinity*, 256.

146. Levinas, *Totality and Infinity*, 262–63. My emphasis.

147. "The feminine: essentially other." Levinas, *Totality and Infinity*, 86.

148. Levinas, *Totality and Infinity*, 79.

149. "The artist will have to convert this beauty into 'weightless grace' by carving in the cold matter of color or stone, where beauty will become calm presence, sovereignty in flight, existence unfounded for without foundations. The beautiful of art *inverts* the beauty of the feminine face." Levinas, *Totality and Infinity*, 263. On this process of the reinversion of the face in Levinas in relationship to mimetic taboo, see also Philippe Crignon, "Figuration: Emmanuel Levinas and the Image," trans. Nicole Simek and Zahi Zalloua, *Yale French Studies* 104 (2004).

150. Levinas, *Totality and Infinity*, 263.

151. Levinas, *Totality and Infinity*, 263.

152. Fritz Martini, *Deutsche Literatur im bürgerlichen Realismus 1848–1898* (Stuttgart: J. B. Metzlersche Verlagsbuchhandlung, 1981), 15.

153. Martini, *Deutsche Literatur im bürgerlichen Realismus*, 15.

154. Thus Susan Sontag, in her defense of pornography against the "demand that literature stick with the 'human,' " nevertheless overlooks the degree to which "the human" was, for nineteenth-century writers, *already* a means of countering "the pornographic." Sontag, "The Pornographic Imagination," 41.

155. Coetzee, *Elizabeth Costello*, 177.

156. Fontane, "Unsere lyrische und epische Poesie seit 1848," 21.1:8.

157. Coetzee, *Elizabeth Costello*, 177.

Chapter 1

1. William Gilpin, *Observations on the River Wye, and Several Parts of South Wales, &c, Relative Chiefly to Picturesque Beauty: Made in the Summer of the Year 1770* (London: Blamire, 1782), 13.

2. "Ich habe diese Gattung Scham so gern." Adalbert Stifter, *Feldblumen (Buchfassung)*, ed. Helmut Bergner and Ulrich Dittman, in *Werke und Briefe:*

Historisch-Kritische Gesamtausgabe, ed. Alfred Doppler and Wolfgang Frühwald, 11 vols. (Stuttgart: Kohlhammer, 1978–2020), 1.4:48.

3. Adalbert Stifter, *Der Nachsommer*, ed. Wolfgang Frühwald and Walter Hettche, in *Historisch-Kritische Gesamtausgabe*, 4.2:34.

4. Stifter, *Der Nachsommer*, 4.2:34.

5. Stifter, *Der Nachsommer*, 4.2:34.

6. Friedrich Hebbel, "Das Komma im Frack," in *Werke*, vol. 3, ed. Gerhard Fricke, Werner Keller, and Karl Pörnbacher (Munich: Hanser, 1965), 685–86. See also Arno Schmidt's similar (though comparatively sophomoric) lampoon of Stifter in *Der sanfte Unmensch: Unverbindliche Betrachtungen eines Überflüssigen* (Frankfurt am Main: Ullstein: 1958), 75–100.

7. Hebbel, "Das Komma im Frack," 687.

8. Hebbel, "Das Komma im Frack," 686.

9. See A. Stillmark, "Stifter Contra Hebbel—An Examination of the Sources of Their Disagreement," *German Life and Letters* 21, no. 2 (January 1968); and Alfred Doppler, "Hebbel und Stifter—Gegensätze und Gemeinsamkeiten," *Vierteljahresschrift des Adalbert-Stifter-Instituts des Landes Österreich* 34, nos. 1–2 (1985).

10. Stifter, preface to *Bunte Steine*, in *Historisch-Kritische Gesamtausgabe*, 2.2:9.

11. Stifter, preface to *Bunte Steine*, 2.2:12. On the "gentle law," see Eric Downing, *Double Exposures: Repetition and Realism in Nineteenth-Century German Fiction* (Stanford, Calif.: Stanford University Press, 2000), esp. 28–40; Christian Begemann, *Die Welt der Zeichen: Stifter-Lektüren* (Stuttgart: Metzler, 1995), esp. 332–34, 371–94; and Paul Fleming, *Exemplarity and Mediocrity: The Art of the Average from Bourgeois Tragedy to Realism* (Stanford, Calif.: Stanford University Press, 2009), esp. 139–62.

12. Downing, *Double Exposures*, 30.

13. Downing, *Double Exposures*, 31. For Downing, Stifter finds this common reality primarily in the idea of a transcendent, law-giving God.

14. Hebbel, "Das Komma im Frack," 687.

15. Julian Schmidt, *Geschichte der deutschen Literatur seit Lessing's Tod*, vol. 3 (Leipzig: Herbig, 1858), 372.

16. On Stifter's thematization of optical instruments in his writing, see Sylvain Guarda, "Stifters *Abdias*: Kindheit in ästhetischer Spiegelung," *German Life and Letters* 61, no. 3 (July 2008); Downing, *Double Exposures*, 77–90; Elisabeth Strowick, "Poetological-Technical Operations: Representation of Motion in Adalbert Stifter," *Configurations* 18, no. 3 (Fall 2010); and Elisabeth Strowick, *Gespenster des Realismus: Zur literarischen Wahrnehmung von Wirklichkeit* (Munich: Fink, 2019), esp. 63–73, 82–89. See also below, 27.

17. Schmidt, *Geschichte der deutschen Literatur seit Lessing's Tod*, vol. 3, 372.

18. Schmidt, *Geschichte der deutschen Literatur seit Lessing's Tod*, vol. 3, 372.

19. Schmidt, *Geschichte der deutschen Literatur seit Lessing's Tod*, vol. 3, 370.

20. Schmidt, *Geschichte der deutschen Literatur seit Lessing's Tod*, vol. 3, 378.

21. Schmidt, *Geschichte der deutschen Literatur seit Lessing's Tod*, vol. 3, 377.

22. Georg Lukács, "Narrate or Describe?," in *Writer and Critic, and Other Essays*, ed. and trans. Arthur D. Kahn (New York: Grosset & Dunlap, 1971), 136. Lukács references Hebbel's critique of Stifter on 131–32.

23. Eva Geulen, *Worthörig wider Willen: Darstellungsproblematik und Sprachreflexion in der Prosa Adalbert Stifters* (Munich: iudicum, 1992), 33, 35.

24. Strowick, *Gespenster des Realismus*, 61.

25. Strowick, *Gespenster des Realismus*, 138. Emphasis in original.

26. Russell A. Berman, *The Rise of the Modern German Novel: Crisis and Charisma* (Cambridge, Mass.: Harvard University Press, 1986), 120.

27. Stifter, *Der Nachsommer*, 4.2:34.

28. Stifter, *Der Nachsommer*, 4.2:30.

29. On the later point, see Berman, *The Rise of the Modern German Novel*, 107.

30. See, among others, Thomas Macho, "Stifters Dinge," *Merkur: Deutsche Zeitschrift für europäisches Denken* 676 (2005); Peter M. McIsaac, *Museums of the Mind: German Modernity and the Dynamics of Collecting* (University Park: Pennsylvania State University Press, 2007), 89–125; Silke Arnold-De Simine, "Musealisierungsphänomene im Werk Adalbert Stifters," in *Ordnung—Raum—Ritual: Adalbert Stifters artifizieller Realismus*, ed. Sabina Becker and Katharina Grätz (Heidelberg: Winter, 2007); Dominik Finkelde, "Tautologien der Ordnung: Zu einer Poetologie des Sammelns bei Adalbert Stifter," *German Quarterly* 80, no. 1 (Winter 2007); Doerte Bischoff, *Poetischer Fetischismus: Der Kult der Dinge im 19. Jahrhundert* (Munich: Fink, 2013), 232–54; and Catriona MacLeod, *Fugitive Objects: Sculpture and Literature in the German Nineteenth Century* (Evanston, Ill.: Northwestern University Press, 2014), esp. 129–42.

31. Some exceptions are found in Martin and Erika Swales, *Adalbert Stifter: A Critical Study* (Cambridge: Cambridge University Press, 1984), esp. 38–41; Bischoff, *Poetischer Fetischismus*, esp. 240–46; and Barbara Hunfeld, "Zeichen als Dinge bei Stifter, Keller und Raabe: Ironisierung von Repräsentation als Selbstkritik des Realismus," in *Die Dinge und die Zeichen: Dimensionen des Realistischen in der Erzählliteratur des 19. Jahrhunderts*, ed. Sabine Schneider and Barbara Hunfeld (Würzburg: Königshausen & Neumann, 2008), 124–28.

32. Stifter, "Der Tandelmarkt," in *Wien und die Wiener, in Bildern aus dem Leben*, ed. Johann Lachinger, in *Historisch-Kritische Gesamtausgabe*, 9.1:227.

33. Stifter, "Der Tandelmarkt," 9.1:227.

34. Stifter, "Der Tandelmarkt," 9.1:227.

35. See Markus Fauser, "Die Kulturbedeutung des Alten in Adalbert Stifters *Studien*," in *Ordnung—Raum—Ritual: Adalbert Stifters artifizieller Realismus*, ed. Sabina Becker and Katharina Grätz (Heidelberg: Winter, 2007), 38–39.

36. Carl E. Schorske, *Fin de Siècle Vienna: Politics and Culture* (New York: Vintage, 1981), 292; see also Bischoff, *Poetischer Fetischismus*, esp. 238–46, 272–74.

37. Tove Holmes, "'. . . was ich in diesem Hause geworden bin': Adalbert Stifter's Visual Curriculum," *Zeitschrift für deutsche Philologie* 129, no. 4 (2010).

38. See Eva Geulen, "Tales of a Collector," in *A New History of German Literature*, ed. David E. Wellbery, Judith Ryan, and Hans Ulrich Gumbrecht (Cambridge, Mass.: Harvard University Press, 2004), 588.

39. Stifter, *Der Nachsommer*, 4.1:96.

40. I am grateful to Harris Feinsod for this insight.

41. Sean Ireton, "Between Dirty and Disruptive Nature: Adalbert Stifter in the Context of Nineteenth-Century American Environmental Literature," *Colloquia*

Germanica 44, no. 2 (2011): 161. However, Ireton's corresponding claim that, unlike natural catastrophes, "deep organic processes such as decomposition are noticeably absent from Stifter's oeuvre" is, as the present chapter shows, incorrect. Ireton, "Between Dirty and Disruptive Nature," 161.

42. Michael Thompson, *Rubbish Theory: The Creation and Destruction of Value* (Oxford: Oxford University Press, 1979), 9, passim.

43. See Thompson, *Rubbish Theory*, 44–45.

44. "The third and missing element between cultural and social order: control." Thompson, *Rubbish Theory*, 45.

45. Swales and Swales, *Stifter*, 33–34.

46. Swales and Swales, *Stifter*, 40.

47. Stifter, *Der Nachsommer*, 4.2:143.

48. Stifter, *Der Nachsommer*, 4.2:146.

49. Stifter, *Der Nachsommer*, 4.2:146.

50. Compare Sabina Becker, "Nachsommerliche Sublimationsrituale: Inszenierte Ordnung in Adalbert Stifters *Nachsommer*," in *Ordnung—Raum—Ritual: Adalbert Stifters artifizieller Realismus*, ed. Sabina Becker and Katharina Grätz (Heidelberg: Winter, 2007), 338; and Berman, *Rise of the Modern German Novel*, 107–8.

51. Stifter, "Ein Gang durch die Katakomben," in *Wien und die Wiener, in Bildern aus dem Leben*, ed. Johann Lachinger, in *Historisch-Kritische Gesamtausgabe*, 9.1:59.

52. Stifter, "Ein Gang durch die Katakomben," 9.1:62.

53. Stifter, "Ein Gang durch die Katakomben," 9.1:60.

54. Walter Benjamin, *The Origin of German Tragic Drama*, trans. John Osborne (London: Verso, 1998), 217–18. See also Bischoff, *Poetischer Fetischismus*, 236–37, on the relation between Benjamin's allegorist and Stifter's collector.

55. See also Joseph Metz, "'Es ist ein seltsam, furchtbar erhabenes Ding, der Mensch': Verdinglichung, absoluter Mehrwert und das perverse Erhabene in Adalbert Stifters proto-benjaminischen Stadtbildern," in *Organismus und Gesellschaft: Der Körper in der deutschsprachigen Literatur des Realismus (1830–1930)*, ed. Christiane Arndt and Silke Brodersen (Bielefeld: Transcript, 2011), 55–56.

56. Stifter, "Ein Gang durch die Katakomben," 9.1:59.

57. Compare Strowick on "motionlessness" (Bewegungslosigkeit) as the "precarious dowry/flipside of Stifter's dynamically composed reality" (die prekäre Mitgift/Kehrseite von Stifters dynamisch verfasster Wirklichkeit). *Gespenster des Realismus*, 123.

58. Joseph Vogl, "Der Text als Schleier: Zu Stifters *Der Nachsommer*," *Jahrbuch der deutschen Schillergesellschaft* 37 (1993): 309. My thoughts here are greatly indebted to Vogl's analysis of this dialectic as a dialectic of beautiful body and corpse, humanist and the inhuman.

59. Here I differ with Christian Begemann's claim that "Stifter's world is legible, because it consists of signs, because it is continuously semiotically structured." Begemann, *Welt der Zeichen*, 25. While this is certainly true on one level (though it could also be argued that such a statement applies to all literature), for Stifter, there is always also the fear of an illegible materiality that resists such structuring and which lies behind Stifter's sign-world in the first place.

60. MacLeod, *Fugitive Objects*, 141.

61. On the challenges that such visual desire nevertheless poses for realism (on the example of Theodor Storm's novella *Psyche*), see also Catriona MacLeod, "The Indecent Body of Sculpture: Theodor Storm's Realist *Psyche*," in *Sculpture, Sexuality, and History*, ed. Jana Funke and Jen Grove (Cham: Palgrave, 2019).

62. MacLeod, *Fugitive Objects*, 122. On "petrification as literature's emblem of itself and its relation to life" in relation to Stifter's descriptive practice, see Eva Geulen, "Depicting Description: Lukács and Stifter," *Germanic Review* 73, no. 3 (Summer 1998): 276.

63. If Lukács is to be believed, between a "tedious academic classicism" and "the decadence of the future." Georg Lukács, *The Historical Novel*, trans. Hannah and Stanley Mitchell (Lincoln: University of Nebraska Press, 1983), 249.

64. Arnold Maillet, *The Claude Glass: Use and Meaning of the Black Mirror in Western Art*, trans. Jeff Fort (New York: Zone Books, 2004), 152. On "the picturesque's appreciation of the landscape [as] in part a compliment to a newly revalued portion of the real," see also Kim Ian Michasiw, "Nine Revisionist Theses on the Picturesque," *Representations* 38 (Spring 1992): 78. On the use of the term "picturesque" in contrast to the "plastic" (i.e., classical/sculptural), see MacLeod, *Fugitive Objects*, 29–35.

65. William Gilpin, "On Picturesque Beauty," in *Three Essays: On Picturesque Beauty; On Picturesque Travel; and On Sketching Landscape: To Which Is Added a Poem, On Landscape Painting* (London: Blamire, 1792), 6–7.

66. Gilpin, "On Picturesque Beauty," 17,

67. Gilpin, "On Picturesque Beauty," 19.

68. See, e.g., Helena Ragg-Kirkby, *Adalbert Stifter's Late Prose: The Mania for Moderation* (Rochester, N.Y.: Camden House, 2000), esp. 65–75, 94–111; and Claudia Nitschke, "Chaos und Form, Raum und Ethos in Stifters *Bunte Steine*," *German Life and Letters* 68, no. 4 (October 2015).

69. For a historical contextualization of Stifter's painting and ideas about visual art, see Karl Mösender, "Stimmung und Erdleben: Adalbert Stifters Ikonologie der Landschaftsmalerei," in *Adalbert Stifter: Dichter und Maler, Denkmalpfleger und Schulmann. Neue Zugänge zu seinem Werk*, ed. Hartmut Laufhütte and Karl Mösender (Tübingen: Niemeyer, 1996). Mösender only brings up the picturesque in the context of Stifter's minor divergence from it (see 32, 33); however, both this denegation and Mösender's tracing of Stifter's ideas to aesthetic trends from England, especially in garden design (see 21), speak strongly for the picturesque as an influence on Stifter.

70. Stifter, *Der Nachsommer*, 4.2:140.

71. See Stifter, *Der Nachsommer*, 4.2:36–37.

72. Gilpin, "On Picturesque Beauty," 27.

73. Stifter, *Der Nachsommer*, 4.1:94.

74. See Stifter, *Der Nachsommer*, 4.1:48.

75. Stifter, *Der Nachsommer*, 4.2:13. On the eccentricity of Roland's position within Stifter's novel, see Uwe Japp, "Die Signifikation des Ästhetischen im Raum des Realen bei Adalbert Stifter," in *Die Dinge und die Zeichen: Dimensionen des Realistischen in der Erzählliteratur des 19. Jahrhunderts*, ed. Sabine Schneider and Barbara Hunfeld (Würzburg: Königshausen & Neumann, 2008), 104.

76. Stifter, *Der Nachsommer*, 4.2:12.

77. Gilpin, "On Picturesque Beauty," 3.

78. Susan Sontag names photography "the art where 'the interesting' first triumphed"; however, such a "way of seeing [that] proposed everything as a potential subject" is already implicit in the picturesque's aestheticization of ruin and randomness. Susan Sontag, "An Argument about Beauty," *Daedalus* 131, no. 4 (Fall 2002): 24. On the "overlap" between the interesting and the picturesque, "another anticlassical, nonbeautiful aesthetic category invented to embrace aesthetic irregularity," see Sianne Ngai, *Our Aesthetic Categories: Zany, Cute, Interesting* (Cambridge, Mass.: Harvard University Press, 2012), 138.

79. On the antiaesthetics of trash and the "anxious dream of a world without a residue," see Maurizia Boscagli, *Stuff Theory: Everyday Objects, Radical Materialism* (New York: Bloomsbury, 2014), 233.

80. Stifter, *Der Nachsommer*, 4.2:148.

81. Stifter, *Der Nachsommer*, 4.3:282.

82. Fleming, *Exemplarity and Mediocrity*, 149.

83. David Martyn, "The Picturesque as Art of the Average: Stifter's Statistical Poetics of Observation," *Monatshefte* 105, no. 3 (Fall 2013): 435.

84. Stifter, "Ausstellung des oberösterreichischen Kunstvereins (1860)," in *Historisch-Kritische Gesamtausgabe*, 8.4:283.

85. Stifter, "Ausstellung," 8.4:284.

86. Fleming, *Exemplarity and Mediocrity*, 147.

87. Gilpin, "On Picturesque Beauty," 26.

88. In this sense, the picturesque also diverges from that which it seems most to resemble, namely, dialectical *Aufhebung*. In *Aufhebung*, things are preserved insofar as they are transformed and reintegrated into a new whole, whose inevitable waste products are then forgotten. In the picturesque, on the other hand, things are preserved insofar as they are waste products, balanced precariously between their fascination and their inessentiality.

89. Stifter, *Der Nachsommer*, 4.2:30.

90. W. G. Sebald, "Bis an den Rand der Natur: Versuch über Stifter," in *Die Beschreibung des Unglücks. Zur österreichischen Literatur von Stifter bis Handke* (Frankfurt am Main: Fischer, 1994), 26–27.

91. Thus Mösender, in reference to the naturalist Friedrich Simony and the aesthetician Carl Gustav Carus, speaks of Stifter's landscape paintings an attempt to represent not just the natural object, but the natural object in and through geological time. See Mösender, "Stimmung und Erdleben," 38–39.

92. On the picturesque as antiaesthetic, see Michasiw, "Nine Revisionist Theses on the Picturesque," 87. See also Karl Rosenkranz's comments on ruins in the concluding paragraphs of the section "The Aesthetically Ugly" ("Das Kunsthäßliche") in Karl Rosenkranz, *The Aesthetics of Ugliness: A Critical Edition*, trans. Andrei Pop and Mechtild Widrich (London: Bloomsbury, 2015), 52; Karl Rosenkranz, *Ästhetik des Häßlichen*, ed. Dieter Kliche (Stuttgart: Reclam, 1990), 50–51.

93. Maillet, *The Claude Glass*, 180.

94. "Stifter has a dual nature, two faces. The impulse toward purity sometimes becomes divorced from the yearning for justice. It then loses itself in minutiae only to re-emerge like a phantom, exaggerated (this is quite possible!) in large-scale events as a mixture in which purity and impurity can no longer be distinguished." Walter Benjamin, "Stifter," in *Selected Writings*, vol. 1: *1913–1926*, ed. Marcus Bullock and Michael W. Jennings (Cambridge, Mass.: Harvard University Press, 1996), 112.

95. Stifter, *Der Nachsommer*, 4.3:118–19.

96. William Gilpin, "On Landscape Painting," in *Three Essays: On Picturesque Beauty; On Picturesque Travel; and On Sketching Landscape: To Which Is Added a Poem, On Landscape Painting* (London: Blamire, 1792), 2, lines 39–42.

97. Stifter, *Der Nachsommer*, 4.3:119.

98. Robert Holub also sees the fact of Roland's painting from imagination as his primary failure, insofar as Roland thereby "[breaks] the sacred aesthetic commandment of verisimilitude." Robert C. Holub, *Reflections of Realism: Paradox, Norm, and Ideology in Nineteenth-Century German Prose* (Detroit: Wayne State University Press, 1991), 75. However, there is nothing in Stifter's description that would indicate that Roland's painting is not *realistic* enough; to the contrary, the problem is rather that it emphasizes the realistic details of raw materiality over their aesthetic recomposition.

99. Stifter, *Der Nachsommer*, 4.3:278.

100. Stifter, *Der Nachsommer*, 4.3:120.

101. Toward the end of the novel, Roland's stormy temperament and taste for aesthetic bombast is revealed to be a symptom of his frustrated erotic desires; as Heinrich's jeweler friend informs him, Roland is pining for the daughter of a local verderer, and uses his art—as well as a proxy desire for Natalie, who coincidentally happens to resemble her (see 4.3:278)—as a sublimating substitute.

102. Gilpin, "On Picturesque Beauty," 7–8.

103. MacLeod thus calls Roland's artwork a "deviant painting" in contrast to what she sees as *Der Nachsommer*'s dominant neoclassicism. MacLeod, *Fugitive Objects*, 116. I would suggest, however, that Roland's painting is deviant precisely because it comes so close to, but swerves fatally away from, the formal recuperation of material nature that Stifter everywhere tries to achieve.

104. Stifter, *Der Nachsommer*, 4.2:214.

105. Stifter, *Der Nachsommer*, 4.2:216.

106. Stifter, *Der Nachsommer*, 4.3:64.

107. Stifter, *Der Nachsommer*, 4.2:107.

108. Immanuel Kant, *Critique of the Power of Judgment*, trans. Paul Guyer and Eric Matthews (Cambridge: Cambridge University Press, 2000), 112.

109. Kant, *Critique of the Power of Judgment*, 113.

110. Mary Douglas, *Purity and Danger: An Analysis of Concepts of Pollution and Taboo* (London: Routledge, 2002), 45.

111. Stifter, *Der Nachsommer*, 4.2:103–4.

112. Stifter, *Der Nachsommer*, 4.2:110, 4.2:106.

113. Douglas, *Purity and Danger*, 45.

114. See Thompson, *Rubbish Theory*, 2, passim.

115. Thompson takes Douglas's argument one step further, arguing that even the process of classificatory rejection by which dirt is characterized is invisible to thought: "Rubbish is a consequence of the impossibility of ever fully specifying the relationship between a process and its cognition from a position which must always be contained by such a relationship." Thompson, *Rubbish Theory*, 88.

116. William Gilpin, "On Picturesque Travel," in *Three Essays: On Picturesque Beauty, On Picturesque Travel, and On Sketching Landscape: To Which Is Added a Poem, On Landscape Painting* (London: Blamire, 1792), 45.

117. Maillet, *The Claude Glass*, 137.

118. However, Maillet disputes the idea that the Claude glass was ever used by Lorrain himself; see *The Claude Glass*, 34–35.

119. Maillet, *The Claude Glass*, 138–39; see also E. H. Gombrich, *Art and Illusion: A Study in the Psychology of Pictorial Representation* (Princeton, N.J.: Princeton University Press, 1960), 46–49, 315.

120. See Stifter, *Der Nachsommer*, 4.2:154–55. On Stifter's early artistic influences (including Lorrain), see Moriz Enzinger, *Adalbert Stifters Studienjahre (1818–1830)* (Innsbruck: Österreichische Verlagsanstalt, 1950), 110–27.

121. Stifter, *Feldblumen*, 1.4:63–64.

122. Stifter, *Feldblumen*, 1.4:65.

123. Stifter, *Feldblumen*, 1.4:65.

124. Stifter, *Feldblumen*, 1.4:61.

125. Peter Fenves, "Die Scham der Schönheit: Einige Bemerkungen zu Stifter," in *"geteilte Aufmerksamkeit": Zur Frage des Lesens*, ed. Thomas Schestag (Frankfurt am Main: Lang, 1997), 94.

126. See Maillet, *The Claude Glass*, 180–83.

127. Compare Begemann's observation of the frequency with which the characters of *Der Nachsommer* look out from an interior space through the organizing frame of a window, as well as Juliane Vogel's examination of the grid or lattice as ordering construction in Stifter. Begemann, *Welt der Zeichen*, 328; Juliane Vogel, "Stifters Gitter: Poetologische Dimensionen einer Grenzfigur," in *Die Dinge und die Zeichen: Dimensionen des Realistischen in der Erzählliteratur des 19. Jahrhunderts*, ed. Sabine Schneider and Barbara Hunfeld (Würzburg: Königshausen & Neumann, 2008).

128. "It needed to be rolled up on account of its size, had a gold frame that needed to be dismantled, and then was displayed on an easel in the marble hall. . . . The picture was observed and discussed many times over. Roland was in an elevated floating mood; for the opinion of those around him . . . corresponded to his internal sense of things that one day he would be able to achieve something even higher than this, indeed, something truly great." Stifter, *Der Nachsommer*, 4.3:281.

129. Stifter, *Der Nachsommer*, 4.2:108–9.

130. Stifter, *Der Nachsommer*, 4.2:109–10. A prototype of this story appears already in "Der Tandelmarkt," which differs from the *Nachsommer* episode mainly in the fact that it is not one but several paintings, and that, of them, the two valuable ones are not Renaissance Madonnas but "two of the loveliest, barely visibly damaged Teniers." Stifter, "Der Tandelmarkt," 9.1.239.

131. Stifter, *Der Nachsommer*, 4.2:31.

132. Stifter, *Der Nachsommer*, 4.2:31.

133. Hal Foster, *The Return of the Real: The Avant-Garde at the End of the Twentieth Century* (Cambridge, Mass.: MIT Press, 1996), 149. See also Hal Foster, "Obscene, Abject, Traumatic," *October* 78 (Autumn 1996).

134. Foster, *The Return of the Real*, 149. Foster also rightly raises doubts about whether such experiences can ever really be represented, given that representation already implies a form of symbolic order: "In a sense this is the other part of the question: can there be an evocation of the obscene that is *not* pornographic?" Foster, *The Return of the Real*, 156.

135. Foster, *The Return of the Real*, 146.

136. See Michael Minden, "Stifter and the Postmodern Sublime," in *History, Text, Value: Essays on Adalbert Stifter*, ed. Michael Minden, Martin Swales, and Godela Weiss-Sussex (Linz: Stifter-Haus, 2006).

137. See Quentin Meillassoux's notion of "ancestrality" as "an event anterior to terrestrial life and hence anterior to givenness itself." Quentin Meillassoux, *After Finitude: An Essay on the Necessity of Contingency*, trans. Ray Brassier (London: Bloomsbury, 2008), 20.

138. Stifter, *Der Nachsommer*, 4.2:32–33.

139. Stifter, *Der Nachsommer*, 4.2:33.

140. Stifter, *Der Nachsommer*, 4.2:33.

141. Stifter, *Der Nachsommer*, 4.2:33.

142. Compare Jean-Luc Marion: "To look—in other words, to be protected from the excess of the visible—requires centering it in a frame." Jean-Luc Marion, *In Excess: Studies of Saturated Phenomena*, trans. Robyn Horner and Vincent Berrand (New York: Fordham University Press, 2002), 62.

143. Stifter, *Der Nachsommer*, 4.3:268.

144. On the "conversion of woman to artwork" by means of the frame, see Catriona MacLeod, *Embodying Ambiguity: Androgyny and Aesthetics from Winckelmann to Keller* (Detroit: Wayne State University Press, 1998), 200.

145. Jacques Derrida, "Parergon," in *The Truth in Painting*, trans. Geoff Bennington and Ian McLeod (Chicago: University of Chicago Press, 1987), 64.

146. Foster, *The Return of the Real*, 146.

147. As Vogl comments: "The surface exists solely to efface itself, and for precisely this reason there is nothing but surface." Vogl, "Der Text als Schleier," 307.

148. See also Metz, "'Es ist ein seltsam, furchtbar erhabenes Ding,'" 65, on the "obscene surplus" of Stifter's corpse descriptions.

Chapter 2

1. Rainer Maria Rilke, "Die zehnte Elegie," in *Duineser Elegien*, in *Werke*, vol. 2: *Gedichte 1910 bis 1926*, ed. Manfred Engel and Ulrich Fülleborn (Frankfurt am Main: Insel, 1996), 230–31, lines 29–33. Translation adapted from Rainer Maria Rilke, *"The Duino Elegies" and "The Sonnets to Orpheus": A Dual Language Edition*, trans. Stephen Mitchell (New York: Vintage International, 2009), 61–63.

2. Karl Gutzkow, *Wally, die Zweiflerin*, ed. Günter Heintz (Stuttgart: Reclam, 1979), 120.

3. Gutzkow, *Wally*, 120.

4. Gutzkow, *Wally*, 126.

5. Gutzkow, *Wally*, 121.

6. Otto Ludwig, "Der poetische Realismus," in *Nachlaßschriften*, vol. 2: *Shakespeare-Studien*, ed. Moritz Heydrich (Leipzig: Cnoblauch, 1872), 265.

7. Otto Ludwig, "Die Ideale der Gegenwart," in *Nachlaßschriften*, vol. 2: *Shakespeare-Studien*, 351–52.

8. Gustav Freytag, *Soll und Haben: Roman in sechs Büchern* (Bochum: Manuscriptum, 2007).

9. Russell A. Berman, *The Rise of the Modern German Novel: Crisis and Charisma* (Cambridge, Mass.: Harvard University Press, 1986), 104.

10. Berman, *Rise of the Modern German Novel*, 76.

11. See Julian Schmidt, *Geschichte der deutschen Literatur seit Lessing's Tod*, vol. 3 (Leipzig: Herbig, 1858), 377.

12. Schmidt, *Geschichte der deutschen Literatur seit Lessing's Tod*, vol. 3, 417.

13. "Moderne Charaktermasken," *Die Grenzboten: Zeitschrift für Politik und Literatur* 8, no. 2.1 (1849): 251.

14. Berman, *Rise of the Modern German Novel*, 78.

15. Eric Downing, *The Chain of Things: Divinatory Magic and the Practice of Reading in German Literature and Thought, 1850–1940* (Ithaca, N.Y.: Cornell University Press, 2018), 21.

16. Jane Bennett, *Vibrant Matter: A Political Ecology of Things* (Durham, N.C.: Duke University Press, 2010), xvi.

17. Thus Berman: "The realist text is . . . defined less by an absence of normality than by a perpetual reenactment of the punishment of deviant behavior in order to reassert the unquestionability of the normative law." Berman, *Rise of the Modern German Novel*, 77.

18. Julian Schmidt and Gustav Freytag, "Den Lesern der Grenzboten," *Die Grenzboten: Zeitschrift für Politik und Literatur* 7, no. 2.3 (1848): 2.

19. Schmidt and Freytag, "Den Lesern der Grenzboten," 2.

20. See Michael Thormann, "Der programmatische Realismus der *Grenzboten* im Kontext von liberaler Politik, Philosophie und Geschichtsschreibung," *Internationales Archiv für Sozialgeschichte der deutschen Literatur* 18, no. 1 (1993): 58–62; and Ulla Schirmeyer-Klein, "Realismus-Literaturprogramm für einen bürgerlichen Staat: Der programmatische Realismus in den 'Grenzboten' 1848–1860" (Ph.D. diss., Ludwig-Maximilian-Universität [Munich], 1974), esp. 20.

21. John Ruskin, *Modern Painters*, ed. David Barrie (New York: Knopf, 1987), 362.

22. Ruskin, *Modern Painters*, 365.

23. F. C. Delius, *Der Held und sein Wetter: Ein Kunstmittel und sein ideologischer Gebrauch im Roman des bürgerlichen Realismus* (Munich: Hanser, 1971), 59.

24. Paul de Man, "Anthropomorphism and Trope in the Lyric," in *The Rhetoric of Romanticism* (New York: Columbia University Press, 1984), 247.

25. See Jonathan Culler, *The Pursuit of Signs: Semiotics, Literature, Deconstruction* (Ithaca, N.Y.: Cornell University Press, 1981), 143.

26. In *Vibrant Matter*, Bennett advocates for the *reintroduction* of anthropomorphization as a potential "[tactic] for cultivating an ability to discern the vitality of matter" in which "a chord is struck between person and thing." Bennett, *Vibrant Matter*, 119–120. Whatever the viability of such a strategy, the differences between Bennett's aims for anthropomorphism and those of programmatic realism should be clear.

27. Georg Lukács, "Narrate or Describe?," in *Writer and Critic, and Other Essays*, ed. and trans. Arthur D. Kahn (New York: Grosset & Dunlap, 1971), 137.

28. Wolfgang Preisendanz, *Humor als dichterische Einbildungskraft: Studien zur Erzählkunst des poetischen Realismus* (Munich: Eidos, 1963), 28.

29. On the "metaphor of the lyrical voice as subject" see de Man, "Anthropomorphism and Trope," 256. See also Barbara Johnson, *Persons and Things* (Cambridge, Mass.: Harvard University Press, 2008), esp. 206–7.

30. See Delius, *Der Held und sein Wetter*, 77: "That which Romanticism still took seriously as content appears to live on [in realism] only in certain techniques of correlation."

31. See J. Hillis Miller, "Catachresis, Prosopopoeia, and the Pathetic Fallacy: The Rhetoric of Ruskin," in *Poetry and Epistemology: Turning Points in the History of Poetic Knowledge*, ed. Roland Hagenbüchle and Laura Skandera (Regensburg: Pustet, 1986), 401.

32. Lukács, "Narrate or Describe?," 137.

33. See Lothar Schneider, "Die Diätetik der Dinge: Dimensionen des Gegenständlichen in Gustav Freytags *Soll und Haben*," in *150 Jahre "Soll und Haben": Studien zu Gustav Freytags kontroversem Roman*, ed. Florian Krobb (Würzburg: Königshausen & Neumann, 2005).

34. Quoted in Freytag, *Soll und Haben*, 4. Compare Schmidt's initial formulation of this phrase (in an attack on the contemporary "social novel") in Julian Schmidt, *Geschichte der deutschen Literatur im neunzehnten Jahrhundert*, vol. 3 (Leipzig: Herbig, 1855), 318.

35. On the commodity fetish in Freytag as a "sacralization of the profane," see Irmtraud Hnilica, *Im Zauberkreis der großen Waage: Die Romantisierung des bürgerlichen Kaufmanns in Gustav Freytags "Soll und Haben"* (Heidelberg: Synchron, 2012), 118.

36. Kristin Kopp, *Germany's Wild East: Constructing Poland as Colonial Space* (Ann Arbor: University of Michigan Press, 2012), esp. 36–37.

37. Freytag, *Soll und Haben*, 61.

38. Freytag, *Soll und Haben*, 61.

39. Freytag, *Soll und Haben*, 61.

40. Schmidt, *Geschichte der deutschen Literatur seit Lessing's Tod*, vol. 3, 416.

41. Roland Barthes, "The Reality Effect," in *The Rustle of Language*, trans. Richard Howard (Berkeley: University of California Press, 1989), 146–47.

42. It is worth repeating, however, that for Barthes, the useless detail as a sign of the real ultimately tips over into the pure signification of "the real" as such—and thus is also motivated or allegorical, if only on a metatextual level.

43. Freytag, *Soll und Haben*, 5.

44. Freytag, *Soll und Haben*, 204.

45. Freytag, *Soll und Haben*, 400.

46. See Thomas Eicher, "Poesie, Poetisierung und Poetizität in Gustav Freytags *Soll und Haben*," *Wirkendes Wort* 45, no. 1 (1995): 72–75. See also Mark Grunert, "Lenore oder die Versuchung des Bürgers: Romantischer 'Zauber' und realistische Ideologie in Gustav Freytags *Soll und Haben*," *Monatshefte* 85, no. 2 (1993). Grunert, however, focuses less on the novel's rhetoric than on its "romantic conceptions of 'nature' and 'freedom'" as incarnated in the characters of Lenore and Fink, respectively. Grunert, "Lenore," 148.

47. Ruskin, *Modern Painters*, 366.

48. Ruskin, *Modern Painters*, 365. Fredric Jameson similarly suggests that "what is poetically inauthentic in traditional 'pathetic fallacy' is not so much its illicit use of nature as its presupposition of named emotions as such, which reacts back on the former to endow it with . . . 'meanings.'" Fredric Jameson, *The Antinomies of Realism* (London: Verso, 2013), 50.

49. Christine Achinger, *Gespaltene Moderne: Gustav Freytags "Soll und Haben." Nation, Geschlecht und Judenbild* (Würzburg: Königshausen & Neumann, 2007), 300.

50. Achinger, *Gespaltene Moderne*, 300.

51. Freytag, *Soll und Haben*, 327. On Freytag's models for this idea, especially the character Werner in Goethe's *Wilhelm Meister*, see Philipp Böttcher, *Gustav Freytag—Konstellationen des Realismus* (Berlin: De Gruyter, 2018), esp. 379–83.

52. See Alyssa A. Lonner, *Mediating the Past: Gustav Freytag, Progress, and German Historical Identity, 1848–1871* (Bern: Lang, 2005), 120–31. Lonner, for her part, reads these moments of anthropomorphization primarily as forms of intentional archaism intended to evoke a German historical rootedness.

53. Freytag, *Soll und Haben*, 142.

54. See Bernd Bräutigam, "Candide im Comptoir: Zur Bedeutung der Poesie in Gustav Freytags 'Soll und Haben,'" *Germanistisch-Romanische Monatsschrift* 35, no. 4 (1985): 402–3.

55. Hnilica, *Im Zauberkreis der großen Waage*, 119.

56. Johnson, *Persons and Things*, 18.

57. Gustav Freytag, "Ein Dank für Charles Dickens," *Die Grenzboten: Zeitschrift für Politik und Literatur* 26, no. 1.2 (1870): 484.

58. See Robert C. Holub, *Reflections of Realism: Paradox, Norm, and Ideology in Nineteenth-Century German Prose* (Detroit: Wayne State University Press, 1991), 198: "Anton's worldview is that of the romantic idealist; Itzig's that of the crude realist." Similar interpretations appear in Berman, *Rise of the Modern German Novel*, 98–100; Achinger, *Gespaltene Moderne*, 334–38; Ulrich Kittstein, "Vom Zwang poetischer Ordnung: Die Rolle der jüdischen Figuren in Gustav Freytags *Soll und Haben* und Wilhelm Raabes *Der Hungerpastor*," in *Poetische Ordnungen. Zur Erzählprosa des deutschen Realismus,* ed. Ulrich Kittstein and Stefani Kugler (Würzburg: Königshausen & Neumann, 2007); and Marcus Twellmann, "Das deutsche Bürgerhaus: Zum oikonomisch Imaginären in Gustav Freytags *Soll und Haben*," *Deutsche Vierteljahrsschrift für Literatur und Geistesgeschichte* 87, no. 3 (2013).

59. Freytag's portrayal of his Jewish characters in *Soll und Haben* is more nuanced than is often acknowledged; nevertheless, each one still fails, in their own way, to meet the criteria for admissibility into Freytag's bourgeois utopia. The accusation of antisemitic representation in *Soll und Haben* begins already with Theodor Fontane's review of the novel: "Gustav Freytag," in Theodor Fontane, *Sämtliche Werke*, ed. Edgar Groß, Kurt Schreinert et al., 24 vols. (Munich: Nymphenburger Verlagshandlung, 1959–75), esp. 21.1:227–28. For contemporary discussions, see, among others, Mark H. Gelber, "An Alternate Reading of the Role of the Jewish Scholar in Gustav Freytag's *Soll und Haben*," *Germanic Review* 58, no. 2 (1983); Martin Gubser, *Literarischer Antisemitismus: Untersuchungen zu Gustav Freytag und anderen bürgerlichen Schriftstellern des 19. Jahrhunderts* (Göttingen: Wallstein, 1998), 187–238; and Kittstein, "Vom Zwang poetischer Ordnung," 61–80.

60. Alain Finkielkraut, *The Imaginary Jew*, trans. Kevin O'Neill and David Suchoff (Lincoln: University of Nebraska Press, 1994), 66.

61. See Eric Santner, *On Creaturely Life: Rilke, Benjamin, Sebald* (Chicago: University of Chicago Press, 2006), xv.

62. See Anna H. Helm, *The Intersection of Material and Poetic Economy: Gustav Freytag's "Soll und Haben" and Adalbert Stifter's "Der Nachsommer"* (Oxford: Lang, 2009), 62.

63. Freytag, *Soll und Haben*, 103.

64. Santner also stresses the political and biopolitical (rather than natural) basis of "creaturely life," whereby the creatureliness of the human being is "an excess that is produced in the space of the political . . . that, paradoxically, accounts for their 'humanity.' " Santner, *On Creaturely Life*, 26.

65. Freytag, *Soll und Haben*, 18.

66. "The system of abominations sets in motion the persecuting machine in which I assume the place of the victim in order to justify the purification that will separate me from that place as it will from any other, from all others." Julia Kristeva, *Powers of Horror*, trans. Leon S. Roudiez (New York: Columbia University Press, 1982), 112. Significantly for the present context, Kristeva implies that it is the very rigidity of Levitical prohibition that leads to this reflexive structure.

67. In the context of the novel's antisemitic messaging, it may be observed that this passage also allows Freytag to have it both ways: Anton is not merely no antisemite, but a defender of his Jewish peer against antisemitic provocation; if Veitel turns out to be unworthy of such kindnesses, it is then not because of any preconceptions on Anton's (or Freytag's) part, but because he is truly, essentially vile. It should also be noted that this is the only moment in the novel in which Veitel's religious practice is mentioned at all: otherwise, his Jewishness is relevant only as racial and sociocultural identity.

68. J. Hillis Miller, "*Praeteria* and the Pathetic Fallacy," in *Victorian Connections*, ed. Jerome McGann (Charlottesville: University of Virginia Press, 1989), 177; see also Miller, "Catachresis, Prosopopoeia, and the Pathetic Fallacy," 404–7.

69. Miller, "*Praeteria* and the Pathetic Fallacy," 177.

70. Christine Achinger, "'Prosa der Verhältnisse' und Poesie der Ware: Versöhnte Moderne und Realismus in *Soll und Haben*," in *150 Jahre "Soll und Haben": Studien zu Gustav Freytags kontroversem Roman*, ed. Florian Krobb (Würzburg: Königshausen & Neumann, 2005), 69.

71. On the historical association between Jews and occultism, see Carol Margaret Davison, *Anti-Semitism and British Gothic Literature* (Basingstoke: Palgrave, 2004), e.g., 191n20.

72. Freytag, *Soll und Haben*, 20.

73. Freytag, *Soll und Haben*, 20.

74. Kittstein, "Vom Zwang poetischer Ordnung," 72.

75. Marcus Twellmann evokes this affinity, as it were in passing, with his mention of the "imaginary vouchers" (unwirkliche Wertzeichen) that "haunt . . . the houses of the money brokers." Twellmann, "Das deutsche Bürgerhaus," 384. Lonner, meanwhile, addresses the topic of the uncanny in Freytag directly, but only in relation to Freytag's 1864 novel *Die verlorene Handschrift*; see Lonner, *Mediating the Past*, 134–36.

76. Karl Marx, *A Contribution to the Critique of Political Economy*, ed. Maurice Dobb, trans. S. W. Ryanskaya (New York: International Publishers, 1970), 134; *Zur Kritik der politischen Ökonomie: Erstes Heft*, in *Marx-Engels-Gesamtausgabe*, 2.2: *Ökonomische Manuskripte und Schriften, 1858–1861*, ed. Larissa Miskewitsch et al. (Berlin: Dietz, 1980), 196.

77. Karl Marx, *Capital: A Critique of Political Economy*, vol. 1, trans. Ben Fowkes (New York: Vintage, 1977), 229. The Latin phrase translates to "sacred things, outside human commerce."

78. Marx, *Capital*, 231.

79. Freytag, *Soll und Haben*, 850.

80. Marx, *A Contribution to the Critique of Political Economy*, 37; *Zur Kritik der politischen Ökonomie*, 116.

81. Marx, *A Contribution to the Critique of Political Economy*, 134; *Zur Kritik der politischen Ökonomie*, 196.

82. Freytag, *Soll und Haben*, 102.

83. Freytag, *Soll und Haben*, 282.

84. Walter Benjamin, "Stifter," in *Selected Writings*, vol. 1: *1913–1926*, ed. Marcus Bullock and Michael W. Jennings (Cambridge, Mass.: Harvard University Press, 1996), 112; "Stifter," in *Gesammelte Schriften*, 2.2: *Aufsätze, Essays, Vorträge*, ed. Rolf Tiedemann and Hermann Schweppenhäuser (Frankfurt am Main: Suhrkamp, 1977), 608.

85. Benjamin, "Stifter," in *Selected Writings*, 112; "Stifter," in *Gesammelte Schriften*, 608.

86. For an extended (if critically naive) typological comparison of Dickens's and Freytag's villains, see Roland Freymond, *Der Einfluß von Charles Dickens auf Gustav Freytag: Mit besonderer Berücksichtigung der Romane "David Copperfield" und "Soll und Haben"* (Hildesheim: Gerstenberg, 1973), 39–46.

87. Steven Marcus sees in Uriah Heep an incarnation of the Victorian era's image of the compulsive masturbator. Steven Marcus, *The Other Victorians: A Study of Sexuality and Pornography in Mid-Nineteenth Century England* (New York: Basic Books, 1966), 19. While it seems doubtful that Freytag was thinking precisely along these lines, his villain does evince a similar sort of clammy physicality and barely sublimated sexual ugliness.

88. For a summary of Jews' figuration as weird, spectral, preternatural, etc., see Susan E. Shapiro, "The Uncanny Jew: A Brief History of an Image," *Judaism: A Quarterly Journal of Jewish Life and Thought* 46, no. 1 (Winter 1997).

89. Freytag, "Ein Dank für Charles Dickens," 484.

90. The pun of the above subhead appears in act 2, scene 2, of the Second Quarto edition of *The Merchant of Venice*, as a malapropism of Shylock's servant Launcelot Gobbo: "Certainly the Iew is the very deuill incarnall; and, in my conscience, my conscience is but a kinde of hard conscience, to offer to counsell me to stay with the Iew." William Shakespeare, *The Excellent History of the Merchant of Venice* ([London]: J. Roberts, 1600), 2.2.7–9. *Folger Shakespeare Library, Luna Digital Image Collection*, https://luna.folger.edu/luna/servlet/s/241ms1.

91. Erich Auerbach, *Mimesis: The Representation of Reality in Western Literature*, trans. Willard R. Trask (Princeton, N.J.: Princeton University Press, 1953), 473.

92. Auerbach, *Mimesis*, 472.

93. See Jörg Kreienbrock, *Malicious Objects, Anger Management, and the Question of Modern Literature* (New York: Fordham University Press, 2013), 5–6, passim. Kreienbrock further suggests that the anthropomorphic attribution of malevolence (or, milder, "malice") to inanimate objects may in fact be a coping mechanism against the even more threatening possibility that accidents with

objects could occur *without* motivation or reason. See Kreienbrock, *Malicious Objects,* 235–39.

94. Auerbach, *Mimesis*, 472.

95. Auerbach, *Mimesis*, 473.

96. Freytag, *Soll und Haben*, 34.

97. Freytag, *Soll und Haben*, 41.

98. Freytag, *Soll und Haben*, 49.

99. Freytag, *Soll und Haben*, 112.

100. Tzvetan Todorov, *The Fantastic: A Structural Approach to a Literary Genre*, trans. Richard Howard (Ithaca, N.Y.: Cornell University Press, 1975), 120.

101. Freytag, *Soll und Haben*, 12–13.

102. As Jean Baudrillard declaims, eminently in Freytag's sense of things: "This is also the principle of Evil, as expressed in the 'evil genie' of the object, in the ecstatic form of the pure object and in its strategy, victorious over that of the subject." Jean Baudrillard, *Fatal Strategies*, trans. Philippe Beitchman and W. G. J. Niesluchowski (Los Angeles: Semiotext(e), 2008), 25.

103. Freytag, *Soll und Haben*, 834–35.

104. Richards defines "projectile adjectives" as "words [such as "beautiful," "ugly," etc.] which really indicate not so much the nature of the object as the character of our feeling towards it." I. A. Richards, *Practical Criticism: A Study of Literary Judgment* (New York: Harcourt, Brace & Co., 1946), 220.

105. Ruskin, *Modern Painters*, 365.

106. Freytag, *Soll und Haben*, 20. Compare Marx and Engels: "Modern bourgeois society with its relations of production, of exchange and of property, a society that has conjured up such gigantic means of production and of exchange, is like the sorcerer, who is no longer able to control the powers of the nether world whom he has called up by his spells." Karl Marx and Friedrich Engels, "The Communist Manifesto," in Karl Marx, *Selected Writings*, ed. Lawrence H. Simon (Indianapolis: Hackett, 1994), 163.

107. On the term *Judenblick* for "evil eye," see Davison, *Anti-Semitism and British Gothic Literature*, 24.

108. Freytag, *Soll und Haben*, 851.

109. In his review of *Soll und Haben*, Theodor Fontane praises the tidiness of the novel's plot thus: "[Freytag] nowhere has superfluous characters [überflüssige Personen] and thus has no need for any of them to die." Fontane, "Gustav Freytag," 21.1:218. Fontane's bizarre claim nevertheless highlights the extent to which Veitel's death—in which he becomes, precisely, not *über-* but *unter*flüssig—merely confirms his alienness within Freytag's social and tropological system.

Chapter 3

1. John Calvin, *Institutes of the Christian Religion*, vol. 1, trans. John Allen (New Haven, Conn.: Howe, 1816), 113.

2. "Die schönen Epitaphia / Zerfallen sind und nicht mehr da; / Und was sonst an Geschmuck und Zier / Man sehen konte mit Begier, / Ist alles kommen in den Brand, / Und meiner Kirchen abgewand." Caspar Helmrich, *Annales Tangermundenses*, in *Antiquitates Tangermundenses*, ed. Georg Gottfried Küster (Berlin: Auctor, 1729), 57.

3. "Detail-Blödsinn schadet nichts, wenn nur das Ganze richtig gefüllt und gedacht ist." Theodor Fontane, *Briefe*, vol. 2: *1860–1878*, ed. Walter Keitel and Helmuth Nürnberger (Munich: Hanser, 1979), 432.

4. Theodor Fontane, *Grete Minde*, in *Sämtliche Werke*, ed. Edgar Groß, Kurt Schreinert et al. 24 vols. (Munich: Nymphenburger Verlagshandlung, 1959–75), 3:5.

5. See, e.g., Gunter H. Hertling, "Kleists *Michael Kohlhaas* und Fontanes *Grete Minde*: Freiheit und Fügung," *German Quarterly* 40, no. 1 (January 1967); Klaus Globig, "Theodor Fontanes 'Grete Minde': Psychologische Studie, Ausdruck des Historismus oder soziopolitischer Apell?," *Fontane Blätter* 32 (1981); Bernhard Losch, "Widerstandsrecht bei Fontane: Grete Minde gegen Unterdrückung und Rechtsverweigerung," *Fontane Blätter* 67 (1999); Hang-Kyun Jeong, *Dialogische Offenheit: Eine Studie zum Erzählwerk Theodor Fontanes* (Würzburg: Königshausen & Neumann, 2001), 156–68; and Dania Hückmann, *Rache im Realismus: Recht und Rechtsgefühl bei Droste-Hülshoff, Gotthelf, Fontane und Heyse* (Bielefeld: Transcript, 2018), 89–116.

6. See, e.g., Sylvain Guarda, *Theodor Fontanes "Neben"-werke: "Grete Minde," "Ellernkipp," "Unterm Birnbaum," "Quitt." Ritualisierter Raubmord im Spiegelkreuz* (Würzburg: Königshausen & Neumann, 2004).

7. See Eckart Pastor, "Das Hänflingsnest: Zu Theodor Fontanes *Grete Minde*," *Tijdschrift voor levende talen / Revue des langues vivantes* 44, no. 2 (1978); Volker Giel, "*Grete Minde*: Versuch einer Interpretation," *Fontane Blätter* 33 (1982); and Sabine Cramer, "*Grete Minde*: Structures of Social Disturbance," in *New Approaches to Theodor Fontane: Cultural Codes in Flux*, ed. Marion Doebeling (Rochester, N.Y.: Camden House, 2000).

8. See Helen Elizabeth Chambers, *Supernatural and Irrational Elements in the Works of Theodor Fontane* (Stuttgart: Akademischer Verlag Hans-Dieter Heinz, 1980), 77–98, esp. 86–87.

9. From a May 6, 1878, letter of inquiry to Paul Lindau. Fontane, *Briefe*, vol. 2, 568.

10. Fontane, "Unsere lyrische und epische Poesie seit 1848," in *Sämtliche Werke*, 21.1:13.

11. See John Osborne, *Theodor Fontane: Vor den Romanen. Krieg und Kunst* (Göttingen: Vandenhoeck & Ruprecht, 1999), esp. 171–93. On Fontane's relationship to visual art, see also Nora Hoffmann, *Photographie, Malerei und visuelle Wahrnehmung bei Theodor Fontane* (Berlin: De Gruyter, 2011), esp. 59–66, and Carmen Aus der Au, *Theodor Fontane als Kunstkritiker* (Berlin: De Gruyter, 2017).

12. Fontane, "Unsere lyrische und epische Poesie seit 1848," 21.1:12.

13. On the discursivization of the empirical in Fontane, see Hubert Ohl, "Bilder, die die Kunst stellt: Die Landschaftsdarstellung in den Romanen Theodor Fontanes," in *Theodor Fontane*, ed. Wolfgang Preisendanz (Darmstadt: Wissenschaftliche Buchgesellschaft, 1973); Thomas Pfau, "Metasprache und Bilderfahrung in *Der Stechlin*," *German Quarterly* 86, no. 4 (Fall 2013); and Eric Downing, *The Chain of Things: Divinatory Magic and the Practice of Reading in German Literature and Thought, 1850–1940* (Ithaca, N.Y.: Cornell University Press, 2018), esp. 142–61.

14. Gerhart von Graevenitz, *Theodor Fontane: Ängstliche Moderne. Über das Imaginäre* (Konstanz: Konstanz University Press, 2014), 311.

15. Downing, *The Chain of Things*, 151.

16. Osborne, *Theodor Fontane*, 198.

17. Fontane himself was fairly ecumenical as far as generic categories were concerned. Typical is the following remark from a short newspaper essay: "What in art currently goes around everywhere under all sorts of names: 'realism,' 'naturalism,' 'impressionism,' etc. etc. is *au fond* nothing more than a protest against the *production of indifference* [*Gleichgültigkeitsproduktion*], against that which has settled into being conventional and everyday and has thereby become boring. . . . Despite their seeming differences, the left and right flanks have something in common." Fontane, "Über das Gemeinsame im Realismus und Idealismus der modernen Kunstbestrebung," in *Sämtliche Werke*, 23.2:171.

18. Although in the mid-nineteenth century, the historical novel was still a more established genre than the "realist" one: see, e.g., Georg Lukács, *The Historical Novel*, trans. Hannah and Stanley Mitchell (Lincoln: University of Nebraska Press, 1983), 260–61. Fontane's first novel, *Vor dem Sturm*, can also be counted as a work of historical fiction, albeit set in the much more recent past of (hence the novel's subtitle) "dem Winter 1812 auf 13." On the "balladesque" aspect of Fontane's early work, see Conrad Wandrey, *Theodor Fontane* (Munich: Beck'sche Verlagsbuchhandlung, 1919), esp. 137–45 (part of the chapter "Die balladesken Novellen"); and Alan Bance, *Theodor Fontane: The Major Novels* (Cambridge: Cambridge University Press, 1982), 38–77.

19. Accounts differ in detail, but the basic story runs more or less as follows. After the death of one Peter von Minden, a Tangermünde patrician gone into exile to evade manslaughter charges, a woman claiming to be his widow arrives in the town and demands his inheritance for herself and her daughter, Margarete. After some hesitation, the dead man's family agrees to grant Margarete a small pension upon her reaching marriageable age. Margarete eventually marries an outlaw named Tonnies Meilahn, with whom she quickly squanders her inheritance, keeping the rough company of itinerant beggars and thieves. On September 13, 1617, a fire destroys Tangermünde. In 1619, Tonnies is arrested for robbery. Questioned, he admits not only to the robbery but also to the arson, furthermore implicating his wife in the bargain. Later, under torture, Margarete also admits to the arson, whereupon she is administered a gruesome public execution in the town square by dismemberment and burning at the stake. See Helmrich, *Annales Tangermundenses*, esp. 52–57; Andreas Rittner, *Alt-Märckisches Geschichtbuch*, in *Antiquitates Tangermundenses*, esp. 16–21. For later reconstructions of the story, see August Wilhelm Pohlmann, *Geschichte der Stadt Tangermünde seit Gründung derselben bis zu dem laufenden Jahre 1829, aus Urkunden und glaubwürdigen Nachrichten* (Stendal: Franzen und Große, 1829), esp. 300–304; W. Däther, *Der Prozeß gegen Margarete Minden und Genossen: Ein dunkles Kapitel Tangermünder Stadtgeschichte* (Tangermünde: Friedrich Becker und Sohn, 1927); and Heiner Lück, "Leben und Sterben am Abgrund: Das Schicksal der Grete Minde zwischen Patriziat und Bandenkriminalität," in *Tangermünde: 1000 Jahre Geschichte* (Dössel: Janos Stekovics, 2008).

20. Fritz Martini, *Deutsche Literatur im bürgerlichen Realismus 1848–1898* (Stuttgart: J. B. Metzlersche Verlagsbuchhandlung, 1962), 756.

21. Petra Spies [McGillen], "A Creative Machine: The Media History of Theodor Fontane's Library Network and Reading Practices," *Germanic Review* 87, no. 1 (March 2012): 73.

22. Graevenitz, *Theodor Fontane*, 337.

23. Perhaps the earliest and most extensive commentator on *Grete Minde*'s anachronicity is Otto Pniower, "Grete Minde," in *Dichtungen und Dichter: Essays und Studien* (Berlin: Fischer, 1912), 295–331; see also Peter Demetz, *Formen des Realismus: Theodor Fontane. Kritische Untersuchungen* (Munich: Hanser, 1964), esp. 94–95; and Walter Müller-Seidel, *Theodor Fontane: Soziale Romankunst in Deutschland* (Stuttgart: Metzler, 1975), esp. 72.

24. Fontane, *Grete Minde*, 3:46.

25. Indeed, the passage is a rather literal example of Peter Demetz's claim that "the novel characters of the nineteenth century are the first ones (naively put) who wear clothes and live in visible rooms." Peter Demetz, "Zur Definition des Realismus," in *Bürgerlicher Realismus: Grundlagen und Interpretationen*, ed. Klaus-Detlef Müller (Königstein: Athenäum, 1981), 34.

26. See Ingrid Leitner, *Sprachliche Archaisierung: Historisch-typologische Untersuchung zur deutschen Literatur des 19. Jahrhunderts* (Frankfurt am Main: Lang, 1978), esp. 215–21.

27. Birgit A. Jensen argues that the novella's plot acts out a conflict between a premodern Christian ethos of force and mercy and an early modern protocapitalist ethos of rational action, while Bernhard Losch similarly stresses the contrast between a feudal and extrajudicial retributive justice and modern democratic channels of legal dissent. See Birgit A. Jensen, *Auf der morschen Gartenschaukel: Kindheit als Problem bei Theodor Fontane* (Amsterdam: Rodopi, 1998), 46–55; Losch, "Widerstandsrecht bei Fontane," esp. 69–71.

28. Friedrich Schiller, *Geschichte des Dreißigjährigen Kriegs*, in *Werke und Briefe*, vol. 7: *Historische Schriften und Erzählungen II*, ed. Otto Dann (Frankfurt am Main: Deutscher Klassiker Verlag, 2002), 12.

29. Schiller, *Geschichte des Dreißigjährigen Kriegs*, 14.

30. In this sense, *Grete Minde* constitutes a paradigmatic example of the becoming-idyll of the epic as described by Hegel: "For the whole state of the world today has assumed a form diametrically opposed in its prosaic organization to the requirements which we found irremissible for genuine epic [welche in ihrer prosaischen Ordnung sich schnurstracks den Anforderungen entgegenstellt, welche wir für das echte Epos unerläßlich fanden], and the revolutions to which the recent circumstances of states and peoples have been subject are still too fixed in our memory as actual experiences to be compatible with the epic form of art. Consequently epic poetry has fled from great national events into the restrictedness of private domestic situations in the countryside or a small town in order to find there situations which might be fit for presentation in epic. Therefore, especially in Germany, epic has become idyllic." G. W. F. Hegel, *Aesthetics: Lectures on Fine Art*, trans. T. M. Knox (Oxford: Oxford University Press, 1998), 1109; *Vorlesungen über die Ästhetik III*, in *Werke*, vol. 15, ed. Eva Moldenhauer and Karl Markus Michel (Frankfurt am Main: Suhrkamp, 1970), 414. Fontane himself thematizes this process of becoming-idyll in Valtin's teasing commentary to Grete after her recounting of a local anecdote: "But Grete, how do you know all that? You don't know anything about the history of the great battle of Tanger or the Tangermünde treasures, but the pastor in Fischbeck, about *that* you know everything!" Fontane, *Grete Minde*, 3:50.

31. Fontane, *Grete Minde*, 3:73.

32. Fontane, *Grete Minde*, 3:66.

33. Fontane, *Grete Minde*, 3:45. Fontane's pastor is based on (or at least named after) Georg Gigas, the actual pastor of Tangermünde from 1602 or 1603 to his death in 1626. See Georg Gottfried Küster, *Tangermündische Denkwürdigkeiten*, in *Antiquitates Tangermundenses*, 71–72; and Pohlmann, *Geschichte der Stadt Tangermünde*, 226–27.

34. There exists an abundance of scholarship (much of it theologically informed) on the question of Fontane's personal religiosity. See, e.g., Eckart Beutel, *Fontane und die Religion: Neuzeitliches Christentum in Beziehungsfeld von Tradition und Individuation* (Gütersloh: Kaiser/Gütersloher Verlagshaus, 2003); Wilhelm Hüffmeier, "'Alles ist Gnade': Beobachtungen zu Kirche und Theologie bei Theodor Fontane," *Zeitschrift für Theologie und Kirche* 95, no. 2 (June 1998); Wilhelm Hüffmeier, "'Was ist, ist durch Vorherbestimmen': Spuren Calvins bei Theodor Fontane," *Zeitschrift für Theologie und Kirche* 107, no. 2 (June 2010); Richard Faber, *". . . der hebe den ersten Stein auf sie": Humanität, Politik und Religion bei Theodor Fontane* (Würzburg: Königshausen & Neumann, 2012); and several of the essays in *Religion als Relikt? Christliche Traditionen im Werk Fontanes*, ed. Hanna Delf von Wolzogen and Hubertus Fischer (Würzburg: Königshausen & Neumann, 2006).

35. For an exhaustive collection of Fontane's remarks on the topic of religion—without *Grete Minde*—see Anett Lütteken, "'Ich sehe viele, die nicht da sind.'—Theodor Fontane und die Krise des Protestantismus," *Euphorion* 100 (2006).

36. Hans-Jürgen Schrader is one of the few to have emphasized the background of religious conflict in *Grete Minde*, though he reads this merely as an allegory for the religious politics of the *Kaiserreich*. Hans-Jürgen Schrader, "Frühneuzeitliche Munizipien in religiös-sozialen Hassausbrüchen: Raabes 'Höxter und Corvey' (1874) und Fontanes 'Grete Minde' (1879)," in *Metropole, Provinz und Welt: Raum und Mobilität in der Literatur des Realismus*, ed. Roland Berbig and Dirk Göttsche (Berlin: De Gruyter, 2013). See also Friedmar Coppoletta, *"Und er bückte sich wieder und schrieb auf die Erde": Theodor Fontanes zunehmende Differenzierung der Bibel in seinem Romanwerk* (Potsdam: Universitätsverlag Potsdam, 2017), esp. 205–48.

37. Fontane, *Grete Minde*, 3:9.

38. Fontane, *Grete Minde*, 3:27.

39. As Richard Brinkman has pointed out, Fontane likely borrows Trud's phrase from Friedrich Schleiermacher, in a passage that could hardly be more relevant for the present context: "Nothing should be a dead mass that is moved only by dead impact and resists only by unconscious friction. . . . Blind instinct, unthinking habit, dead obedience [toter Gehorsam], everything indolent and passive—all these sad symptoms of the asphyxia of freedom and humanity are to be annihilated." Friedrich Schleiermacher, *On Religion: Speeches to Its Cultured Despisers*, trans. Richard Crouter (Cambridge: Cambridge University Press, 1996), 43; *Über die Religion: Reden an die Gebildeten unter ihren Verächtern*, ed. Andreas Arndt (Hamburg: Meiner, 2004), 58. On Fontane's relation to Schleiermacher, see Richard Brinkmann, *Theodor Fontane: Über die Verbindlichkeit des Unverbindlichen* (Tübingen: Niemeyer, 1977), 53–55.

40. See, e.g., Horst Bredekamp, *Kunst als Medium sozialer Konflikte: Bilderkämpfe von der Spätantike bis zur Hussitenrevolution* (Frankfurt am Main: Suhrkamp, 1975); Carlos M. N. Eire, *War against the Idols: The Reformation of Worship from Erasmus to Calvin* (Cambridge: Cambridge University Press, 1986); Sergiusz Michalski, *The Reformation and the Visual Arts: The Protestant Image Question in Western and Eastern Europe* (London: Routledge, 1993); Norbert Schnitzler, *Ikonoklasmus—Bildersturm: Theologischer Bilderstreit und ikonoklastisches Handeln während des 15. und 16. Jahrhunderts* (Munich: Fink, 1996); Alain Besançon, *The Forbidden Image: An Intellectual History of Iconoclasm*, trans. Jane Marie Todd (Chicago: University of Chicago Press, 2000); Hans Belting, "Macht und Ohnmacht der Bilder," in *Macht und Ohnmacht der Bilder: Reformatorischer Bildersturm im Kontext der europäischen Geschichte*, ed. Peter Blickle, Andre Holenstein, Heinrich Richard Schmidt, and Franz-Josef Sladeczek (Munich: Oldenbourg, 2002).

41. Andreas Karlstadt, "On the Removal of Images," in *A Reformation Debate: Karlstadt, Emser, and Eck on Sacred Images. Three Treatises in Translation*, trans. Bryan D. Mangrum and Giuseppe Scavizzi (Ottawa: Dovehouse, 1991), 25; "Von Abtuhung der Bilder," in *Kleine Texte für theologische und philologische Vorlesungen und Übungen*, vol. 74, ed. Hans Lietzmann (Bonn: Marcus und Weber, 1911), 9. On Gregory I's claim, see, e.g., Besançon, *The Forbidden Image*, 149–51.

42. Karlstadt, "On the Removal of Images," 26; "Von Abtuhung der Bilder," 10. Compare Habakkuk 2:19.

43. Karlstadt, "On the Removal of Images," 34; "Von Abtuhung der Bilder," 17.

44. Karlstadt, "On the Removal of Images," 34; "Von Abtuhung der Bilder," 17–18.

45. Fontane, *Jenseits des Tweed*, in *Sämtliche Werke*, 17:210.

46. "Let the sick and those in need / Rouse my pity with their pleas; / What I here on earth afford, / Is in heaven my reward" (Laß der Kranken und der Armen / Mich in ihrer Not erbarmen; / Was ich irdisch gebe hin, / Ist mir himmlischer Gewinn). Fontane, *Grete Minde*, 3:25.

47. Fontane, *Grete Minde*, 3:25–26. First two ellipses in original.

48. Karlstadt, "On the Removal of Images," 29; "Von Abtuhung der Bilder," 12.

49. Isaiah 44:18 (KJV/LUT1545).

50. Isaiah 44:19 (KJV).

51. Karlstadt, "On the Removal of Images," 35–36; "Von Abtuhung der Bilder," 19.

52. John 1:14 (KJV/LUT1545).

53. Calvin, *Institutes of the Christian Religion*, 116.

54. Jennifer Waldron, *Reformations of the Body: Idolatry, Sacrifice, and Early Modern Theater* (New York: Palgrave, 2013), 34. On the living human body as "motivated sign," see 46.

55. Waldron, *Reformations of the Body*, 14.

56. Besançon, *The Forbidden Image*, 187. Besançon's remark is a comment on the passage from Calvin quoted in the epigraph to this chapter.

57. Sabina Becker, *Bürgerlicher Realismus: Literatur und Kultur im bürgerlichen Zeitalter 1848–1900* (Tübingen: Francke, 2003), 19.

58. J[ulian] S[chmidt], "Die Märzpoeten," *Die Grenzboten: Zeitschrift für Politik und Literatur* 9, no. 1.1 (1850): 7.

59. W. J. T. Mitchell, *Iconology: Image, Text, Ideology* (Chicago: University of Chicago Press, 1986), 106. Compare Gotthold Ephraim Lessing, *Laocoön: An Essay on the Limits of Painting and Poetry*, trans. Edward Allen McCormick (Baltimore: Johns Hopkins University Press, 1984), 55–56.

60. S[chmidt], "Die Märzpoeten," 8.

61. On the qualifications, see Peter James Bowman, "Fontane and the Programmatic Realists: Contrasting Theories of the Novel," *Modern Language Review* 103, no. 1 (January 2008).

62. Julian Schmidt, *Geschichte der deutschen Literatur im neunzehnten Jahrhundert*, vol. 1: *Weimar und Jena in den Jahren 1794 bis 1806* (Leipzig: Herbig, 1855), 520–21. Compare Hegel's praise of Dutch genre painting: "In religion the Dutch were Protestants, an important matter, and to Protestantism alone the important thing is to get a sure footing in the prose of life [dem Protestantismus allein kommt es zu, sich auch ganz in die Prosa des Lebens einzunisten], to make it absolutely valid in itself independently of religious associations, and to let it develop in unrestricted freedom." Hegel, *Aesthetics*, 598; *Vorlesungen über die Ästhetik II*, in *Werke*, vol. 14, ed. Eva Moldenhauer and Karl Markus Michel (Frankfurt am Main: Suhrkamp, 1970), 226.

63. Compare Jean-Luc Marion on the idol as an appearance "that sight cannot pierce and abandon, because it saturates it for the first time and hoards up all admiration in it." Jean-Luc Marion, *In Excess: Studies of Saturated Phenomena*, trans. Robyn Horner and Vincent Berraud (New York: Fordham University Press, 2002), 60–61. For Marion, this saturation is the essence of aesthetic experience—an opinion that the programmatic realists, needless to say, would not have shared.

64. Wandrey, *Theodor Fontane*, 144.

65. Friedrich Schlegel, Fragment 579, *Kritische Friedrich-Schlegel-Ausgabe*, ed. Ernst Behler, vol. 16: *Schriften aus dem Nachlaß: Fragmente zur Poesie und Literatur, Erster Teil*, ed. Hans Eichner (Paderborn: Schöningh, 1981), 133.

66. Fontane, "Unsere lyrische und epische Poesie seit 1848," 21.1:12.

67. See, e.g., Matthew 17:1–2: "And after six days Jesus taketh Peter, James, and John his brother, and bringeth them up into an high mountain apart, And was transfigured before them: and his face did shine as the sun, and his raiment was white as the light [Und er ward verklärt vor ihnen, und sein Angesicht leuchtete wie die Sonne, und seine Kleider wurden weiß wie ein Licht]" (KJV/LUT1545).

68. See Wolfgang Preisendanz, *Wege des Realismus* (Munich: Fink, 1977), esp. 82–83; and Wolfgang Preisendanz, *Humor als dichterische Einbildungskraft: Studien zur Erzählkunst des poetischen Realismus* (Munich: Eidos, 1963), esp. 214–41. For a discussion of Hegel's concept in relation to its alternatives, see Erica Weitzman, *Irony's Antics: Walser, Kafka, Roth, and the German Comic Tradition* (Evanston, Ill.: Northwestern University Press, 2015), 42–49.

69. For Downing, this mediation is especially one of language: "the medium or, better, the 'life-form' (*Lebensform*) that envelops or encompasses the world of man and man's relation to the world." Downing, *The Chain of Things*, 150.

70. Pfau, "Metasprache und Bilderfahrung," 431.

71. F. W. J. Schelling, *Über das Verhältnis der bildenden Kunst zu der Natur*, ed. Lucia Sziborsky (Hamburg: Meiner, 1983), 24.

72. Fontane, “Die diesjährige Kunstausstellung,” in *Sämtliche Werke*, 23.1:226.

73. Fontane, “Unsere lyrische und epische Poesie seit 1848,” 21.1:13.

74. Theodor Fontane, *Briefe*, vol. 1: *1833–1866*, ed. Walter Keitel and Helmuth Nürnberger (Munich: Hanser, 1976), 376.

75. Fontane, *Briefe*, vol. 1, 376.

76. Fontane, *Grete Minde*, 3:26.

77. On the pervasive gendering of ekphrasis, see W. J. T. Mitchell, “Ekphrasis and the Other,” in *Picture Theory* (Chicago: University of Chicago Press, 1994), 168–71.

78. Fontane, *Grete Minde*, 3:26.

79. See Bernhard Böschenstein, “Religiosität in Fontanes Verhältnis zur bildenden Kunst?,” in *Religion als Relikt? Christliche Traditionen im Werk Fontanes*, ed. Hanna Delf von Wolzogen and Hubertus Fischer (Würzburg: Königshausen & Neumann, 2006).

80. Fontane, *Grete Minde*, 3:49.

81. Fontane makes a similar point in having the boulder’s “absonderliche Form” echo the “absonderlich reich” costumes of Trud and Emrenz just a few pages earlier. Fontane, *Grete Minde*, 3:46. Vanity of vanities: ruffs, like runes, go out of style.

82. Fontane, *Grete Minde*, 3:8.

83. Sigmund Freud, “Fetishism,” in *The Standard Edition of the Complete Psychological Works of Sigmund Freud*, vol. 21: *1927–1931*, trans. James Strachey (London: Hogarth, 1964), 155.

84. Jacques Lacan, “The Signification of the Phallus,” in *Écrits*, trans. Bruce Fink (New York: W. W. Norton, 2006), 579.

85. Thus Werner Hamacher glosses Kant’s *Religion within the Limits of Reason Alone*: “The sacrilegious perversion of the maker of fetishes lies in his belief that he has stopped up the yawning abyss of the unknowable, that he has grasped the thing which he has in fact erected there himself. . . . The fetishist closes the argument badly, because he *closes* it.” Werner Hamacher, *Pleroma*, trans. Nicholas Walker and Simon Jarvis (Stanford, Calif.: Stanford University Press, 1998), 28.

86. Karlstadt, “On the Removal of Images,” 36; “Von Abtuhung der Bilder,” 19.

87. Compare Emmanuel Levinas, *Totality and Infinity: An Essay on Exteriority*, trans. Alphonso Lingis (Pittsburgh: Duquesne University Press, 1969), 262.

88. This concern for the failure of the sign in the absence of a shared interpretive context is carried through well into Fontane’s late work; see Downing, *The Chain of Things*, esp. 200.

89. Fontane, *Grete Minde*, 3:15.

90. Gaby Pailer suggests that the acting troupe in *Grete Minde* was inspired by the “gypsy” clan in Cervantes’s novella *La gitanilla*, with Fontane complicating Cervantes’s broader racial stereotypes. Gaby Pailer, “Schwarzäugige Mordbrennerin: Fontanes *Grete Minde*, eine Tochter von Cervantes’ *La gitanilla*,” in *rebellisch. verzweifelt. infame. Das böse Mädchen als ästhetische Figur*, ed. Renate Möhrmann (Bielefeld: Aisthesis, 2012).

91. Fontane, *Grete Minde*, 3:16.

92. Fontane, *Grete Minde*, 3:16.

93. Fontane, *Grete Minde*, 3:15.

94. Mikhail Bakhtin, *Rabelais and His World*, trans. Hélène Iswolsky (Bloomington: Indiana University Press, 1984), 19.

95. On the relationship between medieval parodic practices and *Bildersturm* ideology, see Michalski, *The Reformation and the Visual Arts*, 93–96; Schnitzler, *Ikonoklasmus*, 213–16.

96. Fontane, *Grete Minde*, 3:19. Trud's words, and indeed the whole episode, are taken from Küster's account of a 1646 fire in the Tangermünde town hall, also during a performance of the Last Judgment. Küster quotes the valedictory sermon of a certain Pastor Seidels: "That is to say: GOd does not allow Himself to be mocked [Das heißt: GOtt läßt sich nicht spotten]. And that such solemn laws of GOd have been presented as child's-play / thereby are *Atheistic* and *Epicurian* thoughts unknowingly induced or increased / as if all that / which is said of GOd and godly things / were but a puppet-show." Küster, *Tangermündische Denkwürdigkeiten*, 11.

97. Jonas A. Barish, *The Antitheatrical Prejudice* (Berkeley: University of California Press, 1981).

98. Fontane, *Grete Minde*, 3:21.

99. Fontane introduces this dialogue with an image of Jakob Minde savoring a handful of raspberries "that had been plucked with the little stem still on, like he liked them." Fontane, *Grete Minde*, 3:18.

100. Fontane, *Grete Minde*, 3:18–19.

101. Christopher J. Wild, *Theater der Keuschheit, Keuschheit des Theaters: Zu einer Geschichte der (Anti-) Theatralität von Gryphius bis Kleist* (Freiburg im Bresgau: Rombach, 2003), 184, 201.

102. See Barish, *The Antitheatrical Prejudice*, 42–43.

103. Wild, *Theater der Keuschheit*, 190.

104. See Barish, *The Antitheatrical Prejudice*, 70–71.

105. See Wild, *Theater der Keuschheit*, 14.

106. Fontane, *Grete Minde*, 3:64. Ellipsis in original.

107. Fontane, *Grete Minde*, 3:64.

108. Fontane, *Grete Minde*, 3:65.

109. Fontane, *Grete Minde*, 3:91.

110. See Waldron, *Reformations of the Body*, 46.

111. Compare Wild, *Theater der Keuschheit*, 39–44.

112. Fontane, *Grete Minde*, 3:69–70.

113. Fontane, *Grete Minde*, 3:65.

114. Fontane, *Grete Minde*, 3:86.

115. Fontane, *Grete Minde*, 3:77.

116. Fontane, *Grete Minde*, 3:78. One might also see an ironic connection between original sin (*Erbsünde*) and Grete's withheld inheritance (*Erbe*), particularly in light of her final words to her half-brother: "So be it, Gerdt. But one more word. . . . I've come here as a petitioner, not a beggar. For I am no beggar. I am the daughter of the wealthy Jacob Minde. And I want my *inheritance*. [Und so will ich denn mein *Erbe*.] Do you hear, Gerdt, my inheritance." Fontane, *Grete Minde*, 3:81. On the theme of inheritance in *Grete Minde* (though without mention of its theological implications), see Ulrike Vedder, "Münzen, Bilder, Frauen, Romane: Fontanes Erbstucke," in *Realien des Realismus: Wissenschaft—Technik—Medien*

in Theodor Fontanes Erzählprosa, ed. Stephan Braese and Anne-Kathrin Reulecke (Berlin: Vorwerk 8, 2010), 82–83.

117. Compare Wild, *Theater der Keuschheit*, 107.

118. Jean-Luc Nancy and Federico Ferrari, *Being Nude: The Skin of Images*, trans. Anne O'Byrne and Carlie Anglemire (New York: Fordham University Press, 2014), 42.

119. From the official March 13, 1619, verdict on Margarete Minden: "Thereupon the prisoner shall formally repeat her confession before the court; so may she thus, before she is put to death, *be carried on a cart to the place of judgment, her five fingers on the right hand be pulled off one after another with glowing tongs, and thereupon her body be seized by four glowing tongs, namely in her breast and arm, . . . thence shall she be bound to a high post by iron chains, burned alive and in this manner conducted from life to death, as the law decrees*" (Da nun gefangene solches bekendniß vor dem peinlichen halßgericht nochmalen bestendig wiederholen wirdt; *So mag Sie deswegen vor endlicher Tötung uff einem wagen biß zu der Richtstädte umbgeführet, ihre fünff finger an der Rechten Hand einer nach dem andern mit glühenden Zangen abgezwacket, Nachmalen ihr leib mitt vier glühenden Zangen, nemlich in der brust und arm gegriffen, . . . Folglich mitt eisernen Ketten uff einem erhabenen Pfahll angeschmiedet, lebendig geschmochet und allso vom leben zum tode verrichtett werden, von Rechtts wegen*). Quoted in Däther, *Der Prozeß gegen Margarete Minden und Genossen*, 80–81.

120. Fontane's interest in burning women precedes the writing of *Grete Minde*: see for example the end of the "Spukhäuser" chapter in *Jenseit des Tweed*, where he writes of a certain local legend, "A particular appeal of this tale and its characteristic distinguishing feature lies in the *appearance of the female figure in flames*." Fontane, *Jenseit des Tweed*, 17:256. Emphasis in original.

121. Fontane, *Grete Minde*, 3:65–66.

122. Indeed, the actor's words are repeated almost verbatim by the servant girl that Grete first encounters outside the cloister, who, to Grete's inquiry if the resident is "one of the nuns," replies bemusedly, "One of the nuns? There aren't any nuns here anymore." Fontane, *Grete Minde*, 3:71.

123. To the actor's comments, the innkeeper responds provocatively that there *are* still nuns in the country, who, as he claims, continue to be tolerated "because they've got the blueblood connection" (Weil sie den adligen Anhang haben). Fontane, *Grete Minde*, 3:66.

124. Fontane, *Grete Minde*, 3:66.

125. Georg Lukács, "Der alte Fontane," in *Deutsche Realisten des 19. Jahrhunderts* (Berlin: Aufbau-Verlag, 1956), 272.

126. Calvin, *Institutes of the Christian Religion*, 119. My emphasis.

127. Hegel, *Aesthetics*, 527; *Ästhetik II*, 140.

128. Gerhard Neumann, "Speisesaal und Gemäldegalerie: Die Geburt des Erzählens aus der bildenden Kunst. Fontanes Roman *L'Adultera*," in *Theodor Fontane: Romankunst als Gespräch* (Freiburg am Breisgau: Rombach, 2011), 98.

129. Walter Benjamin, *The Origin of German Tragic Drama*, trans. John Osborne (London: Verso, 1998), 66.

130. Benjamin, *Origin*, 185.

131. Giorgio Agamben, "In Praise of Profanation," trans. Kevin Attell, in *Profanations* (New York: Zone Books, 2007), 77.

132. Agamben, "In Praise of Profanation," 87.

133. Samuel Weber, *Theatricality as Medium* (New York: Fordham University Press, 2004), 179–80.

134. Fontane, *Grete Minde*, 3:15.

135. Fontane, *Grete Minde*, 3:49.

Chapter 4

1. Jean Baudrillard, *Passwords*, trans. Chris Turner (London: Verso, 2003), 5.

2. William Shakespeare, *Hamlet*, in *The Arden Shakespeare Complete Works*, ed. Richard Proudfoot, Ann Thompson, and David Scott Kastan (London: Methuen, 2011), 3.2.247–49, 313.

3. Julian Schmidt, *Geschichte der deutschen Literatur seit Lessing's Tod*, vol. 3 (Leipzig: Herbig, 1858), 66.

4. Friedrich Schiller, "On Grace and Dignity," in *Schiller's "On Grace and Dignity" in Its Cultural Context: Essays and a New Translation*, ed. Jane V. Curran and Christopher Fricker (Rochester, N.Y.: Camden House, 2005), 126; "Über Anmut und Würde," in *Werke und Briefe in zwölf Bänden*, vol. 8: *Theoretische Schriften*, ed. Rolf-Peter Janz (Frankfurt am Main: Deutscher Klassiker Verlag, 1992), 334. See also introduction, 13–15.

5. F. Brunetière, "La banqueroute du naturalisme," *Revue des deux mondes* 57, no. 83 (September 1, 1887), 214–15.

6. "Zur Ästhetik des Häßlichen," *Die Grenzboten: Zeitschrift für Politik, Litteratur und Kunst* 47, no. 2 (1888): 534.

7. Adolf Bartels, "Die Ziele der gegenwärtigen Litteraturbewegung in Deutschland," *Die Grenzboten: Zeitschrift für Politik, Litteratur und Kunst* 52, no. 4 (1893): 134.

8. Heine's term is adapted from the Saint-Simonian reformer Barthélemy Prosper Enfantin's idea of a "rehabilitation of the flesh." See Michael Bittner, *Die Emanzipation des Fleisches und ihre Gegner* (Dresden: Thelem, 2016), esp. 11, 280–81.

9. "Die naturalistische Schule in Deutschland," *Die Grenzboten: Zeitschrift für Politik, Literatur und Kunst* 45, no. 2 (1886): 73.

10. Émile Zola, "The Experimental Novel," in *The Experimental Novel and Other Essays*, trans. Belle M. Sherman (New York: Haskell House, 1964), 27.

11. Wilhelm Bölsche, *Die naturwissenschaftlichen Grundlagen der Poesie: Prolegomena einer realistischen Ästhetik*, ed. Johannes J. Braakenburg (Tübingen: Niemeyer, 1976), 50. Bölsche however emphasizes that, for a *truly* scientific literature, the focus should ultimately be on "the normal, the natural, the consciously regular." Bölsche, *Die naturwissenschaftlichen Grundlagen der Poesie*, 46.

12. Bölsche, *Die naturwissenschaftlichen Grundlagen der Poesie*, 50.

13. Elisabeth Ladenson, *Dirt for Art's Sake: Books on Trial from "Madame Bovary" to "Lolita"* (Ithaca, N.Y.: Cornell University Press, 2007), 190.

14. Karl Rosenkranz, *The Aesthetics of Ugliness: A Critical Edition*, trans. Andrei Pop and Mechtild Widrich (London: Bloomsbury, 2015), 193; *Ästhetik des Häßlichen*, ed. Dieter Kliche (Stuttgart: Reclam, 1990), 298–99. My emphasis.

15. Max Nordau, *Degeneration* (Lincoln: University of Nebraska Press, 1993), 498; *Entartung* (Berlin: Duncker, 1896), 442.

16. Hans Blumenberg, "The Concept of Reality and the Possibility of the Novel," in *New Perspectives in German Literary Criticism*, ed. Richard E. Amacher and Victor Lange (Princeton, N.J.: Princeton University Press, 1979), 34. For Blumenberg, however, the paradigm for this "reality concept" is less the cognitive resistance of matter than the logical resistance of the paradox.

17. On naturalism's inner class conflicts, see Fredric Jameson, *The Antinomies of Realism* (London: Verso, 2013), 149–50.

18. Nordau, *Degeneration*, 499; *Entartung*, 444.

19. Nordau, *Degeneration*, 500; *Entartung*, 447.

20. Nordau, *Degeneration*, 502; *Entartung*, 450.

21. Nordau, *Degeneration*, 506; *Entartung*, 457.

22. Émile Zola, *Nana*, ed. Henri Mitterand (Paris: Gallimard, 2002), 23.

23. Georg Lukács, "Narrate or Describe?," in *Writer and Critic, and Other Essays*, ed. and trans. Arthur D. Kahn (New York: Grosset & Dunlap, 1971), 136.

24. Zola, *Nana*, 47.

25. Jameson, *Antinomies of Realism*, 55. I have chosen the obvious example to illustrate the sensual pleasure of spectacle, but the dynamic is no less apparent in the descriptive passages that Jameson analyzes of household linens and cheese.

26. Zola, "The Experimental Novel," 25–26.

27. Peter Brooks, *Realist Vision* (New Haven, Conn.: Yale University Press, 2005), 118.

28. For all his frankness, Zola is too discreet to mention pubic hair, though "the golden hairs of her underarms," revealed by Nana's raised arm during her first nude appearance, may be taken as a kind of euphemistic metonymy. Zola, *Nana*, 47.

29. Brooks, *Realist Vision*, 125.

30. Brooks, *Realist Vision*, 128.

31. On the end of the naturalist drive for knowledge in gynocidal fantasy, see Barbara Vinken, "Zola—alles sehen, alles wissen, alles heilen: Der Fetischismus im Naturalismus," in *Historische Anthropologie und Literatur: Romanistische Beiträge zu einem neuen Paradigma der Literaturwissenschaft*, ed. Rudolf Behrens and Roland Galle (Würzburg: Königshausen & Neumann, 1995), esp. 223–24.

32. Zola, *Nana*, 49.

33. Zola, *Nana*, 474.

34. Brooks, *Realist Vision*, 115.

35. Brooks, *Realist Vision*, 120.

36. That is, for Jameson, the liberation of affect in Zola's works nevertheless eventually returns to discursive conceptualization and bourgeois discipline, insofar as it becomes a *topic*. See Jameson, *Antinomies of Realism*, 73–76.

37. Hauptmann's epithet (actually given to "Bjarne P. Holmsen," a pseudonym of Holz and his then collaborator Johannes Schlaf) is likely taken from Hegel, e.g., "Consistent realism [Der konsequente Realismus] denies consciousness as spontaneous self-positing activity altogether. But even when the object, which the realist takes to be the real ground of consciousness, is expressed as non-Ego = non-Ego, when he exhibits the reality of his object in consciousness, and is therefore validly challenged by the identity of consciousness as something absolute over and against his objective serialization of finites running on and on; then

he must certainly abandon the form of his principle of pure objectivity." G. W. F. Hegel, *The Difference between Fichte's and Schelling's System of Philosophy*, trans. H. S. Harris and Walter Cerf (Albany: State University of New York Press, 1977), 127; *Differenz des Fichteschen und Schellingschen Systems der Philosophie*, in *Werke*, vol. 2: *Jenaer Schriften 1801–1807*, ed. Eva Moldenhauer and Karl Markus Michel (Frankfurt am Main: Suhrkamp, 1970), 62.

38. Holz explicitly claims Nietzsche's mantle in his early manifesto *Die Kunst: Ihr Wesen und ihre Gesetze*: "His 'hammer' may have already fallen from his tired hands, but its work is not yet therefore done. It would be high time to use it to knock also on the old idolatrous mystery that calls itself 'the philosophy of art' [das alte Götzenmysterium . . . das sich 'Kunstphilosophie' nennt]. It might be that one will then make thc discovery that nothing sounds as hollow!" Arno Holz, *Die Kunst: Ihr Wesen und ihre Gesetze*, in *Das Werk von Arno Holz: Monumental-Ausgabe in zwölf Bänden*, vol. 10: *Die Neue Wortkunst: Eine Zusammenfassung ihrer ersten grundlegenden Dokumente*, ed. Hans W. Fischer (Berlin: Dietz, 1925), 60–61.

39. See, e.g., Klaus R. Scherpe, "Der Fall Arno Holz: Zur sozialen und ideologischen Motivationen der naturalistischen Literaturrevolution," in *Positionen der literarischen Intelligenz zwischen bürgerlicher Reaktion und Imperialismus*, ed. Gert Mattenklott and Klaus R. Scherpe (Kronberg: Scriptor, 1973); and Onno Frels, "Zum Verhältnis von Wirklichkeit und künstlerischer Form bei Arno Holz," in *Naturalismus/Ästhetizismus*, ed. Christa Bürger, Peter Bürger, and Jochen Schulte-Sasse (Frankfurt am Main: Suhrkamp, 1979).

40. This is, at least, how Holz saw himself. From *Phantasus*: "They blessed me, they / cursed me, / they shouted hosannas, they / scorned me / they spit at me, they / knelt before me, / they kissed adoringly, they kissed devoutly, they / kissed / most humbly / enrapturedly, ecstatically / my anointed, my holy, my / exalted / feet, / waved, / rejoicing, fluttering palms, / betrayed me / and / then crucified me!" (Man segnete mich, man / fluchte mir, / man jubelte Hosianna, man / höhnte mich, / man spie mich an, man / kniete vor mir, / man küßte anbetend, man küßte inbrünstig, man / küßte / demütigst, / entrückt, verzückt / meine gesalbten, meine heiligen, meine / gebenedeiten / Füße, / schwenkte, / jauchzend, wehende Palmen, / verriet mich / und / kreuzigte mich dann!). Arno Holz, *Phantasus*, in *Werke*, ed. Wilhelm Emrich and Anita Holz, 7 vols. (Neuwied am Rhein: Luchterhand, 1961–64), 3:523.

41. See, exemplarily, Wilhelm Emrich's afterword to his edition (with Holz's widow, Anita) of Holz's complete works, "Arno Holz und die moderne Kunst," in Holz, *Werke*, 7:453–71; first printed in *Protest und Verheißung: Studien zur klassischen und modernen Dichtung* (Frankfurt am Main: Athenäum, 1960); and, somewhat more equivocally, Alfred Döblin, introduction to *Verschollene und Vergessene: Arno Holz, Die Revolution der Lyrik. Eine Einführung in sein Werk und eine Auswahl* (Wiesbaden: Steiner, 1951).

42. On Holz's appropriations of *vormärzlich* revolutionary rhetoric, see Scherpe, "Der Fall Arno Holz," esp. 129–36; and Eva Axer, "'Zwischen Alt und Neu': Arno Holz's *Buch der Zeit* and his Concept of 'soziale Lyrik,'" in *Protest and Reform in the German Literature and Art of Modernity, 1871–1918*, ed. Godela Weiss-Sussex and Charlotte Woodford (Munich: iudicium, 2014).

43. Winfried Menninghaus, *Disgust: Theory and History of a Strong Sensation*, trans. Howard Eiland and Joel Golb (Albany: State University of New York Press, 2003), 42.

44. Zola ends the first essay in his collection *Le Naturalisme au théâtre* with the rallying cry: "The domain of the novel is overcrowded [encombré]; the domain of the theater is free"—though one wonders if the thing that has taken up all the space in the naturalist novel is not Zola himself. Émile Zola, "Le Naturalisme," in *Œuvres complètes*, vol. 11: *Œuvres critiques II*, ed. Henri Mitterand (Paris: Cercle du Livre Précieux, 1968), 291.

45. See John Osborne, *The Naturalist Drama in Germany* (Manchester: Manchester University Press, 1971), 42–43; Kirk Williams, "Anti-Theatricality and the Limits of Naturalism," in *Against Theater: Creative Destructions on the Modernist Stage*, ed. Alan Ackerman and Martin Puchner (New York: Palgrave, 2006). For an exhaustive account of Holz's personal involvement in the theater of his day, see Thorsten Fricke, *Arno Holz und das Theater: Biografie—Werkgeschichte—Interpretation* (Bielefeld: Aisthesis, 2010).

46. See, e.g., Hermann Grom-Rottmayer, "Bühne und Naturalismus," *Merker: Österreichische Zeitschrift für Musik und Theater* 11, nos. 19–20 (October 1, 1920): 475.

47. Holz and Schlaf's disagreement about the exact nature of their collaboration eventually turned into a bitter public battle, waged in an increasingly vitriolic series of open letters, articles, and pamphlets. See, exemplarily, Johannes Schlaf, *Noch einmal "Arno Holz und ich"* (Berlin: Messer & Cie, 1902). For a late defense of Holz's side of things, see Peter Sprengel, "Holz & Co. Die Zusammenarbeit von Arno Holz mit Johannes Schlaf und Oskar Jerschke—oder: Die Grenzen der Freiheit," *Text + Kritik* 121 (January 1994).

48. Holz, *Evolution des Dramas*, in *Das Werk*, vol. 10: *Die Neue Wortkunst*, 214.

49. August Strindberg, "On Realism: Some Views," in *Strindberg on Drama and Theater: A Source Book*, ed. and trans. Egil Törnqvist and Birgitta Steene (Amsterdam: Amsterdam University Press, 2007), 33. Strindberg would however later come to criticize what he termed "the misconceived naturalism which believes that art simply consists in copying a piece of nature in a natural way." August Strindberg, "On Modern Drama and the Modern Theater," in *Strindberg on Drama and Theater*, 81.

50. Shakespeare, *Hamlet*, 3.2.23–25, 311; compare Strindberg, "On Realism," 34.

51. Holz, *Evolution des Dramas*, 222.

52. Wolfgang Rothe, introduction to *Deutsches Theater des Naturalismus* (Munich: Langen/Müller, 1972), 17.

53. Holz, *Evolution des Dramas*, 222.

54. Holz, *Evolution des Dramas*, 215.

55. See Jonas A. Barish, *The Antitheatrical Prejudice* (Berkeley: University of California Press, 1981), 343.

56. Gesine Lenore Schiewer reads the elaborate stage directions of Holz's *Sonnenfinsternis* and *Ignorabimus* as applications of then-recent studies of physiological expression by Darwin, Mill, and others. Gesine Lenore Schiewer,

"Verbales Verhalten im Horizont von Ethnologie und Psychologie: Zur 'Sprache des Lebens' in dem dramatischen Spätwerk von Arno Holz," in *Dialogue Analysis IX: Dialogue in Literature and the Media (Selected Papers from the 9th IADA Conference, Salzburg 2003)*, part 1: *Literature* (Tübingen: Niemeyer, 2005).

57. Holz, *Die Kunst*, 80.

58. See Clement Greenberg, "Modernist Painting," in *The Collected Essays and Criticism*, vol. 4: *Modernism with a Vengeance, 1957–1969*, ed. John O'Brian (Chicago: University of Chicago Press, 1993), 88–89.

59. Holz, *Die Kunst*, 83.

60. Holz, *Die Kunst*, 84.

61. Holz, *Die Kunst*, 84.

62. In a later supplement to *Die Kunst*—essentially an extended rebuttal to a negative review by Carl Erdmann—Holz denies that he ever meant to imply that art and nature should match up perfectly, mainly on the grounds that (1) obviously this could never really happen, and (2) by "nature" he actually meant "truth." See *Die Kunst*, 120–73.

63. Rob Burns sees in Holz's obsession with authenticity the precursor to modern documentary and nonfiction. This is true enough, although there is also a fundamental difference between Holz's formal concern to reproduce sensual surfaces and documentary art's primarily thematic interest in events and situations. See Rob Burns, *The Quest for Modernity: The Place of Arno Holz in Modern German Literature* (Frankfurt am Main: Lang, 1981), esp. 71–72.

64. Arno Holz and Johannes Schlaf, *Papa Hamlet*, in *Neue Gleise* (Berlin: Fontane & Co., 1892), 111–60.

65. Adalbert von Hanstein, *Das jüngste Deutschland: Zwei Jahrzehnte miterlebter Litteraturgeschichte* (Leipzig: Voigtländer, 1901), 157.

66. Holz and Schlaf, *Papa Hamlet*, 159. Holz and Schlaf's ellipses modified.

67. See Holz and Schlaf, *Papa Hamlet*, 150–55. In *Evolution des Dramas*, Holz describes how, during the writing of *Papa Hamlet*, he and Schlaf procured and examined a real oil lamp in order to be able to reproduce in their text "the desired night effects" (die gewünschten Nachteffekte). Holz, *Evolution des Dramas*, 253.

68. Holz and Schlaf, *Papa Hamlet*, 112.

69. Holz and Schlaf, *Papa Hamlet*, 115. Ellipsis in original.

70. Holz and Schlaf, *Papa Hamlet*, 114. Ellipsis in original.

71. The most striking example of this comes at the beginning of the third section, where the excerpting from Hamlet's "What a piece of work is man?" monologue eventually dissolves into a discombobulated pastiche of wounded self-love: "Man delighted not he—and woman neither. The time was out of joint! It was unbelievable! But—er—they still hadn't written to him. They were ungrateful in Christiania. Poor Yorick!" Holz and Schlaf, *Papa Hamlet*, 121.

72. Johann Wolfgang von Goethe, "Zum Schäkespears Tag," in *Sämtliche Werke*, vol. 1.2: *Der junge Goethe 1757–1775*, ed. Gerhard Sauder (Munich: Hanser, 1987), 413; see also Johann Wolfgang von Goethe, "Shakespear und kein Ende!," in *Sämtliche Werke*, vol. 11.2: *Divan-Jahre 1814–1819*, ed. Johannes John et al. (Munich: Hanser, 1994). In an irony of which they do not seem to be aware, Holz and Schlaf's attack on Shakespeare effectively repeats Goethe's critique of French drama as a theater of simulation and artifice, to which Shakespeare was to offer an alternative.

73. Goethe, "Shakespear und keine Ende!," 181.

74. Shakespeare, *Hamlet*, 3.2.35–36, 311.

75. Thus it is clear that the real target of Holz and Schlaf's satire, whether they realize it or not, is not Shakespeare so much as his nineteenth-century bourgeois reception. On the similar use of the figure of Goethe in *Die Familie Selicke*, see Dieter Martin, "'Ein Buch für Schwächlinge': 'Werther'-Allusionen in Dramen des Naturalismus," *Zeitschrift für deutsche Philologie* 122, no. 2 (2003).

76. Holz, *Die Kunst*, 52.

77. J. M. R. Lenz already proposes a similar idea in his *Anmerkungen übers Theater*, although, in contrast to Holz, Lenz sees this as a continuation of Aristotelian poetics rather than its overturning. See J. M. R. Lenz, *Anmerkungen übers Theater*, in *Werke und Schriften*, vol. 1, ed. Britta Titel and Hellmut Haug (Darmstadt: Wissenschaftliche Buchgesellschaft, 1966), 339–41.

78. Holz, *Evolution des Dramas*, 225.

79. Holz, *Evolution des Dramas*, 225–26.

80. Holz and Schlaf, *Papa Hamlet*, 112–13. Ellipses in original.

81. Holz and Schlaf, *Papa Hamlet*, 116–17. Second ellipsis in original.

82. Johannes Schlaf, *Ein Dachstubenidyll*, in Arno Holz and Johannes Schlaf, *Papa Hamlet. Ein Tod* (Stuttgart: Reclam 1963), 91–92.

83. Holz and Schlaf, *Papa Hamlet*, 117.

84. Holz, *Evolution der Lyrik*, in *Das Werk*, vol. 10: *Die Neue Wortkunst*, 489.

85. Holz and Schlaf, *Papa Hamlet*, 116. Emphasis in original.

86. Holz and Schlaf, *Papa Hamlet*, 117.

87. Franz Servaes, "Arno Holz," in *Praeludien: Ein Essaybuch* (Berlin: Schuster & Loeffler, 1899), 85. For a historical contextualization of paralingual elements in Holz, see Gesine Lenore Schiewer, *Poetische Gestaltkonzepte und Automatentheorie: Arno Holz—Robert Musil—Oswald Wiener* (Würzburg: Königshausen & Neumann, 2004), esp. 160–67.

88. Holz and Schlaf, *Papa Hamlet*, 112.

89. Holz and Schlaf, *Papa Hamlet*, 140. Ellipses in original.

90. Holz and Schlaf, *Papa Hamlet*, 127. Ellipsis in original.

91. Holz and Schlaf, *Papa Hamlet*, 135. Ellipses in original.

92. Holz and Schlaf, *Papa Hamlet*, 156. Ellipses in original.

93. As Adorno notes in his brief but incisive passage on German naturalism in *Aesthetic Theory*: "Carrying out intentions contradicts [naturalism's] principle. Yet naturalist plays abound in passages whose intention is plain: People are to speak plainly, yet in following the author's stage directions they speak as no one would ever speak. . . . Perhaps it would be impossible to organize a realistic play according to its conception without its becoming, á contre coeur, dadaistic; through its unavoidable minimum of stylization, however, realism admits its impossibility and virtually abolishes itself." Theodor W. Adorno, *Aesthetic Theory*, trans. Robert Hullot-Kentor (Minneapolis: University of Minnesota Press, 1997), 249. On the paradoxes of antimimesis in Artaud's work, see Jacques Derrida, "The Theater of Cruelty and the Closure of Representation," in *Writing and Difference*, trans. Alan Bass (Chicago: University of Chicago Press, 1978).

94. Fritz Martini, *Das Wagnis der Sprache* (Stuttgart: Klett, 1954), 125–26.

95. Mladen Dolar, *A Voice and Nothing More* (Cambridge, Mass.: MIT Press, 2006), 15.

96. Servaes, "Arno Holz," 85.
97. Dolar, *Voice*, 20.
98. See Servaes, "Arno Holz," 71.
99. See Holz and Schlaf, *Papa Hamlet*, 113.
100. See Holz and Schlaf, *Papa Hamlet*, 149.
101. See Holz and Schlaf, *Papa Hamlet*, 116.
102. Holz, *Evolution des Dramas*, 227.
103. Martini, *Wagnis*, 120.
104. Hugo von Hofmannsthal, "Ein Brief," in *Sämtliche Werke*, vol. 31: *Erfundene Gespräche und Briefe*, ed. Ellen Ritter (Frankfurt am Main: Fischer, 1991), 48–49. On Holz's poetry in the context of late nineteenth-century language critique, see Helmut Henne, *Sprachliche Spur der Moderne in Gedichten um 1900: Nietzsche, Holz, George, Rilke, Morgenstern* (Berlin: De Gruyter, 2010).
105. Holz, *Evolution der Lyrik*, 658. See also *Evolution der Lyrik*, 662, on Holz's "numerical architectonics" (Zahlenarchitektonik), by which, so he contends, the number of words in a line, lines in a section, etc., are intrinsically bound to the poem's theme.
106. Thus to claim, as Ingrid Strohschneider-Kohrs does, that Holz's use of language in *Papa Hamlet* merely poses a "question about the accuracy and immediacy of linguistic representation" is to overlook the profound *nostalgia* for immediacy that runs through Holz's work and that makes even this questioning a source of revulsion. Ingrid Strohschneider-Kohrs, "Sprache und Wirklichkeit bei Arno Holz," in *Poesie und Reflexion: Aufsätze zur Literatur* (Tübingen: Niemeyer, 1999), 311.
107. Holz and Schlaf, *Papa Hamlet*, 114, 115.
108. Holz and Schlaf, *Papa Hamlet*, 117.
109. Holz and Schlaf, *Papa Hamlet*, 113.
110. Holz and Schlaf, *Papa Hamlet*, 154, 158.
111. Peter Sprengel, "'Hamlet' in 'Papa Hamlet': Zur Funktion des Zitats im Naturalismus," *Literatur für Leser* 84, no. 1 (March 1984): 38–39.
112. Holz and Schlaf, *Papa Hamlet*, 120–21. Compare Shakespeare, *Hamlet*, 5.2.89–90, 328.
113. Holz and Schlaf, *Papa Hamlet*, 126.
114. Holz and Schlaf, *Papa Hamlet*, 128.
115. Holz and Schlaf, *Papa Hamlet*, 158. Ellipsis in original.
116. Holz and Schlaf, *Papa Hamlet*, 112. The same structure appears in *Die Familie Selicke*, as the Selickes' boarder, the seminarian Gustav Wendt, finds himself forced to repudiate his idealism faced with the ugly reality of the Selickes' life: "Yes, that opened my eyes! . . . People aren't what I thought they were! They're selfish! Brutally selfish! They're no better than animals, sophisticated beasts, walking appetites doing battle with one another." Arno Holz and Johannes Schlaf, *Die Familie Selicke*, in *Neue Gleise*, 258–59.
117. Holz and Schlaf, *Papa Hamlet*, 117.
118. The quotation in the above subhead is from Johann Wolfgang von Goethe, *Faust: Eine Tragödie*, ed. Albrecht Schöne, in *Sämtliche Werke*, vol. 7.1, ed. Friedmar Apel et al. (Frankfurt am Main: Deutscher Klassiker Verlag, 1994), 180, line 4212.
119. Osborne, *The Naturalist Drama in Germany*, 47.

120. Martini, *Wagnis*, 117.
121. Adorno, *Aesthetic Theory*, 249.
122. Bartels, "Die Ziele der gegenwärtigen Litteraturbewegung," 136.
123. Lukács, "Narrate or Describe?," 127.
124. Lukács, "Narrate or Describe?," 140.
125. See Frels, "Wirklichkeit," esp. 115.
126. Holz, *Evolution der Lyrik*, 653.
127. Holz, *Phantasus*, 1:69. Ellipses in original.
128. Holz, *Evolution der Lyrik*, 650–51.
129. Friedrich Spielhagen, "Ueber Objectivetät im Roman," in *Vermischte Schriften*, vol. 1 (Berlin: Janke, 1864), 186–87. See also introduction, 17.
130. Edmund Husserl, *The Idea of Phenomenology*, trans. William P. Alston and George Nakhnikian (The Hague: Martinus Nijhoff, 1964), 10.
131. Husserl, *The Idea of Phenomenology*, 6, passim.
132. Holz, *Evolution der Lyrik*, 651.
133. Compare Benjamin Specht, "'Empirisierte Transzendentalpoesie': Wirklichkeits- und Subjektbegriff in Poetik und Lyrik von Arno Holz," *KulturPoetik* 17, no. 1 (2017). On the "natural attitude," see Husserl, *The Idea of Phenomenology*, 13–15.
134. Holz, *Phantasus*, 3:9–10.
135. Holz, *Evolution der Lyrik*, 659.
136. Holz, *Evolution des Dramas*, 251–52.
137. Holz, *Phantasus*, 3:8.
138. Holz, *Evolution der Lyrik*, 649.
139. Samuel Weber, *Theatricality as Medium* (New York: Fordham University Press, 2004), 191. Holz himself draws on the German baroque tradition in his parodic book of "Gobble-Guzzle-and-Venus-Songs" (Fres-Sauff-und-Venus-Lieder), *Dafnis*, though the poems in that collection—mostly ribald pastiches of baroque *Minnesang*—are arguably less "baroque" than the poems discussed here. See also Conrad Wiedemann, "Schwierigkeiten mit 'Dafnis': Gedanken zu den Barocknachdichtungen von Arno Holz," *Text + Kritik* 121 (January 1994).
140. Holz, *Die Blechschmiede*, in *Werke*, 7:109.
141. Holz's tendency to adjectival excess can be seen as early as the prose vignette *Ein Tod* (*A Death*), e.g.: "the small, blue bit of carpet," "the white, low door," "the large, damp towel," "the old, wobbly sofa," "the dirty, yellow spot of light above on the old, cracked ceiling." Arno Holz and Johannes Schlaf, *Ein Tod*, in *Neue Gleise*, 199.
142. Holz, *Phantasus*, 3:19.
143. Holz, *Phantasus*, 1:373. Ellipses in original.
144. Holz, *Phantasus*, 1:373–74. Short ellipses in original.
145. Jameson, *Antinomies of Realism*, 61.
146. Holz, *Die Blechschmiede*, 7:405.
147. Holz, *Die Blechschmiede*, 7:432.
148. Holz, *Die Blechschmiede*, 7:409.
149. Holz, *Die Blechschmiede*, 7:420.
150. Karl Riha, "Blechschmied Arno Holz: Zur Struktur des satirischen Monstredramas 'Die Blechschmiede,'" *Text + Kritik* 121 (January 1994); see also Karl Riha, "Veränderung des Dramas in der Satire: Arno Holz, *Die Blechschmiede*,

Karl Kraus, *Die letzten Tage der Menschheit*," in *Kritik, Satire, Parodie: Gesammelte Aufsätze* (Opladen: Westdeutscher Verlag, 1992).

151. Arno Holz, *Briefe: Eine Auswahl*, ed. Anita Holz and Max Wagner (Munich: Piper & Co., 1948), 113.

152. On Holz's use of contemporary scientific ideas in his work, see Peter Sprengel, *Darwin in der Poesie. Spuren der Evolutionslehre in der deutschsprachigen Literatur des 19. und 20. Jahrhunderts* (Würzburg: Königshausen & Neumann, 1998), esp. 25–30 and 72–75; and Alexander Nebrig, "Entbindung von der Disziplin: Arno Holz' Begründung des Lebenswissens in *Phantasus*," in *Das Wissen der Poesie: Lyrik, Versepik und die Wissenschaften im 19. Jahrhundert*, ed. Henning Hufnagel and Olav Krämer (Berlin: De Gruyter, 2015).

153. Holz, *Phantasus*, 1:167.

154. Holz, *Phantasus*, 1:179.

155. Holz, *Die Blechschmiede*, 6:219.

156. Janelle Blankenship, "Arno Holz vs. Thomas Mann: Modernist Media Fantasies," *Modernist Cultures* 1, no. 2 (Winter 2005): 84.

157. Holz, *Die Blechschmiede*, 6:245–46.

158. Blankenship, "Modernist Media Fantasies," 84.

159. Goethe, *Faust*, 36, lines 454–57.

160. Holz, *Die Blechschmiede*, 6:344.

161. Holz, *Die Blechschmiede*, 6:246.

162. Holz, *Die Blechschmiede*, 6:348.

163. Holz, *Die Blechschmiede*, 6:222.

164. Holz, *Die Blechschmiede*, 6:223.

165. Holz, *Phantasus*, 1:19.

166. Jean-Paul Sartre, *Being and Nothingness: A Phenomenological Essay on Ontology*, trans. Hazel E. Barnes (New York: Washington Square Press, 1992), 521.

167. The word *obszön* pops up a few more times in Holz's work, often in similar word-constellations, e.g.: "a magical instrument ending in an obscene-looking, turgid, tongue-flickering serpent's head" (einen wie obszön wirkenden, geschwollenen, züngelnden Schlangenkopf mündenden Wunderinstrument), *Die Blechschmiede,* 7:244; "with / a / wanton-salaciously pleasing joke-word, with a cheeky-indecently obscene word-joke" (mit / einem / lose-schlüpfrig amönen Witzwort, mit einem frech-anrüchig obszönen Wortwitz), *Die Blechschmiede,* 7:89; "obscene, lovely, charming, gallant" (obszön, amön, scharmant, galant), *Phantasus*, 3:35; or simply "Massiver! Lovelier! / Lewder! Obscener!" (Massiver! Amöner! / Lasziver! Obszöner!), *Die Blechschmiede,* 6:352.

168. Holz, *Die Blechschmiede*, 7:143.

169. Holz, *Die Blechschmiede*, 7:144. On this "Kippmoment" of literary naturalism, see also Ingo Stöckmann, "Über Fülle/Überfülle: Textverfahren der Copia um 1890," in *Entsagung und Routines: Aporien des Spätrealismus und Verfahren der frühen Moderne*, ed. Moritz Baßler (Berlin: De Gruyter, 2013), 320–21.

170. Naomi Schor, *Reading in Detail: Aesthetics and the Feminine* (London: Routledge, 2007), xlii.

171. Thus Martini's judgment that Holz's disillusioned naturalism "supplants the pathos and idealism of great tragedy" is precisely false, insofar as this naturalism is explicitly presented *as* disillusionment. Martini, *Wagnis*, 131.

172. Holz, *Die Blechschmiede*, 7:144. Unsurprisingly, this idea of the perfidious unreachability of phenomena has a gendered aspect, for example: "The curved line of beauty, objectified in the shape of woman!" that eventually turns into a description of woman as "genital- and breeding-animal" (Genital- und Zeugungstier) whose beautiful appearance is only a cover for the ugly truth that she withholds. *Die Blechschmiede*, 7:224, 7:251.

173. "Das Evangelium des Naturalismus," *Die Grenzboten: Zeitschrift für Politik, Litteratur und Kunst* 50, no. 3 (1891): 35.

Chapter 5

1. "Das Dunkelste aller Dinge, ja das Dunkel selbst nach einigen, ist die Materie." F. W. J. Schelling, *Ueber das Verhältniß des Realen und Idealen in der Natur, oder Entwickelung der ersten Grundsätze der Naturphilosophie an den Principien der Schwere und des Lichts* (Hamburg: Perthes, 1806), 3.

2. Arno Holz and Johannes Schlaf [Dr. Bruno Franzius, pseud.], "Einleitung des Uebersetzers," in *Neue Gleise* (Berlin: Fontane & Co., 1892), 108.

3. Lawrence Rothfeld, *Vital Signs: Medical Realism in Nineteenth-Century Fiction* (Princeton, N.J.: Princeton University Press, 1992); Martin von Koppenfels, *Immune Erzähler: Flaubert und die Affektpolitik des modernen Romans* (Munich: Fink, 2007).

4. Julian Schmidt, *Geschichte der deutschen Literatur seit Lessing's Tod*, vol. 3 (Leipzig: Herbig, 1858), 306.

5. Gottfried Benn, "Requiem," in *Sämtliche Werke*, ed. Gerhard Schuster, 7 vols. (Stuttgart: Klett-Cotta, 1986–2003), 1:13, line 5.

6. Schmidt, *Geschichte der deutschen Literatur seit Lessing's Tod*, vol. 3, 306.

7. Hanns Wegener, "Gottfried Benn: 'Morgue und andere Gedichte,'" in *Benn—Wirkung wider Willen: Dokumente zur Wirkungsgeschichte Benns*, ed. Peter Uwe Hohendahl (Frankfurt am Main: Athenäum, 1971).

8. Heinrich Hart, "Die realistische Bewegung: Ihr Ursprung, ihr Wesen, ihr Ziel," *Kritisches Jahrbuch: Beiträge zur Charakteristik der zeitgenössischen Literatur sowie zur Verständigung über den modernen Realismus* 1, no. 1 (1889): 49.

9. Schmidt, *Geschichte der deutschen Literatur seit Lessing's Tod*, vol. 3, 307.

10. Compare Schmidt, *Geschichte der deutschen Literatur seit Lessing's Tod*, vol. 3, 305–6: "The cynic analyses by virtue of his 'healthy common sense' the concrete appearances of life, and believes, when he finds everywhere the same basic substances, to have abrogated every difference in the dignity of same."

11. Michel Foucault, *The Birth of the Clinic: An Archeology of Medical Perception*, trans. A. M. Sheridan Smith (New York: Pantheon, 1973), 14, passim.

12. Benn, "Mann und Frau gehn durch die Krebsbaracke," in *Sämtliche Werke*, 1:16.

13. See Peter Uwe Hohendahl, introduction to Hohendahl, *Wirkung wider Willen*, 25–30; Augustinus P. Dierick, *Gottfried Benn and His Critics: Major Interpretations, 1912–1922* (Columbia, S.C.: Camden House, 1992); Christian M. Hanna and Friederike Reents, eds., *Benn-Handbuch: Leben—Werk—Wirkung* (Stuttgart: Metzler, 2016), 362–63.

14. E. B. Ashton, introduction to Gottfried Benn, *Primal Vision: Selected Writings*, ed. E. B. Ashton (New York: New Directions, 1971), xii.

15. This last question is what has come to be known as the "expressionism debate"; see especially Georg Lukács, "Expressionism: Its Significance and Decline," in *Essays on Realism*, ed. Rodney Livingstone, trans. David Fernbach (London: Lawrence and Wishart, 1980), 110–13.

16. Ernst Stadler, "Lyrische Flugblätter (Sammelrezension)," in Hohendahl, *Wirkung wider Willen*, 96.

17. Wolfgang Martens, "Klinische Lyrik," in Hohendahl, *Wirkung wider Willen*, 90.

18. Joachim Dyck, "Requiem—Es gibt keine Hoffnung jenseits des Nichts," in *Gedichte von Gottfried Benn*, ed. Harald Steinhagen (Stuttgart: Reclam, 1997); see also Christoph Hoffmann, "In der Prosektur: Zwischen B. und Benn," in *". . . im Trunk der Augen": Gottfried Benn—Arzt und Dichter in der Pathologie Westend*, ed. Anne Marie Freybourg and Ernst Kraas (Göttingen: Wallstein, 2008).

19. However, Mark Roche's claim that Benn's poems (and, by extension, expressionist poetry as a whole) are thereby "nonmimetic, nonrepresentional [in] character" takes things too far in the other direction. Mark W. Roche, "Provocation and Parataxis," in *A New History of German Literature*, ed. David E. Wellbery, Judith Ryan, and Hans Ulrich Gumbrecht (Cambridge, Mass.: Harvard University Press, 2004), 682.

20. Helmut Lethen, *Der Sound der Väter: Gottfried Benn und seine Zeit* (Berlin: Rowohlt, 2006), 80.

21. Elisabeth Bronfen, *Over Her Dead Body: Death, Femininity and the Aesthetic* (Manchester: Manchester University Press, 1992), esp. 3–4, 11–13.

22. Friedrich Hebbel, *Neue Gedichte* (Leipzig: Weber, 1848), 153–54.

23. Julia Virginia [Scheuermann], "In der Morgue," in *Sturm und Stern* (Berlin: Schuster & Loeffler, 1905), 102, lines 1–2.

24. Rainer Maria Rilke, "Morgue," in *Werke*, vol. 1: *Gedichte 1895 bis 1910*, ed. Manfred Engel and Ulrich Fülleborn (Frankfurt am Main: Insel, 1996), 468, lines 13–14. See also the slightly later "Leichen-Wäsche" ("Washing the Body"), in *Werke*, vol. 1, 540.

25. Georg Heym, "Die Morgue (Letzte Fassung)," in *Dichtungen und Schriften: Gesamtausgabe*, vol. 1: *Lyrik*, ed. Karl Ludwig Schneider (Hamburg: Ellermann, 1964), 474, lines 9–12.

26. For a comparison of Scheuermann's and Benn's poems, see also Achim Aurnhammer, "Inszenierung der Moderne im Traditionsbruch: Die lyrischen Anfänge von Benn und Brecht," in *Gottfried Benn, Bertold Brecht: Das Janusgesicht der Moderne*, ed. Achim Aurnhammer (Würzburg: Ergon-Verlag, 2009), 51–54.

27. Benn, "Kleine Aster," in *Sämtliche Werke*, 1:11.

28. Benn's poems are not without their own poetic devices (for example, the slant rhymes in "Kleine Aster" "gestemmt/geklemmt," "aus/Haut," "herausschnitt/glitt," and "Brusthöhle/Holzwolle"), but they are far less regular or apparent than in the other poems discussed here.

29. Or, in German, "looking up at the radishes" (die Radieschen von unten betrachten).

30. Heym, "Die Morgue," 478, lines 106–9.

31. "Morgue II" and "Café des Westens" also contain lines in the first person, but the effect is more of an observed scene than an internal lyric I.

32. Benn claimed to have written the poems of the *Morgue* cycle in one night, while working as a mortuary assistant in a Berlin-Moabit hospital. See Martin Travers, *The Hour That Breaks: Gottfried Benn. A Biography* (Bern: Lang, 2015), 39.

33. Martin Travers, *The Poetry of Gottfried Benn: Text and Selfhood* (Bern: Lang, 2007), 21.

34. Travers, *The Poetry of Gottfried Benn*, 20–21.

35. Helmut Lethen, *Cool Conduct: The Culture of Distance in Weimar Germany*, trans. Don Renau (Berkeley: University of California Press, 2002), 147. *Pace* Lethen, the example of Benn's *Morgue* poems shows that this attitude, as well as its corresponding aesthetic of "conceptual realism," well predates the Weimar era.

36. Benn, "Schöne Jugend," in *Sämtliche Werke*, 1:11. "Schöne Jugend" is in fact an all but outright parody of Georg Heym's 1919 poem "Ophelia," which begins, "In the hair, a nest of young river rats." In *Dichtungen und Schriften*, vol. 1, 160, line 1.

37. Benn, "Kreislauf," in *Sämtliche Werke*, 1:12.

38. Benn, "Negerbraut," in *Sämtliche Werke*, 1:12.

39. Benn, "Requiem," in *Sämtliche Werke*, 1:13.

40. Most problematically, in his 1933 essay "Bekenntnis zum Expressionismus" ("Confession of Faith in Expressionism"), in which he both apologizes for the now stigmatized movement and attempts to paint it as a proper forerunner to National Socialism.

41. Benn, "Bekenntnis zum Expressionismus," in *Sämtliche Werke*, 4:79.

42. Émile Zola, "The Experimental Novel," in *The Experimental Novel and Other Essays*, trans. Belle M. Sherman (New York: Haskell House, 1964), 16–17.

43. Bronfen, *Over Her Dead Body*, 45.

44. Lethen, *Der Sound der Väter*, 81.

45. Giorgio Agamben, *Stanzas: Word and Phantasm in Western Culture*, trans. Ronald L. Martinez (Minneapolis: University of Minnesota Press, 1993), 50.

46. For Travers, the reaction to the *Morgue* poems thus "takes place almost entirely through the readerly mechanics of compensation: the moral-humanistic occupancy of an absence that is necessary (as Benn well knew) if shock is to be registered." Travers, *The Poetry of Gottfried Benn*, 33.

47. Zola, "The Experimental Novel," 27.

48. Adalbert Stifter, "Ein Gang durch die Katakomben," in *Wien und die Wiener, in Bildern aus dem Leben*, ed. Johann Lachinger, in *Werke und Briefe: Historisch-Kritische Gesamtausgabe*, ed. Alfred Doppler and Wolfgang Frühwald, 11 vols. (Stuttgart: Kohlhammer, 1978–2020), 9.1:57.

49. Stifter, "Ein Gang durch die Katakomben," 9.1:57.

50. Most exhaustively, Marcus Hahn, *Gottfried Benn und das Wissen der Moderne: 1905–1932*, 2 vols. (Göttingen: Wallstein, 2011). See also Marion Adams, *Gottfried Benn's Critique of Substance* (Assen: Van Gorcum & Co., 1969); Gerlinde F. Miller, *Die Bedeutung des Entwicklungsbegriffs für Menschenbild und Dichtungstheorie bei Gottfried Benn* (New York: Lang, 1990); Ursula Kirchdörfer-Boßmann, *"Eine Pranke in den Nacken der Erkenntnis": Zur Beziehung von Dichtung und Naturwissenschaft im Frühwerk Gottfried Benns* (St. Ingbert: Röhrig, 2003); Thomas Gann, *Gehirn und Züchtung: Gottfried*

Benns psychiatrische Poetik 1910–1933/34 (Bielefeld: Transcript, 2007); Monika Fick, "'Komm, Schöpfer Tod': Zum Verhältnis von Biologie und Dichtung bei Gottfried Benn," *Deutsche Vierteljahrsschrift für Literaturwissenschaft und Geistesgeschichte* 81, no. 2 (June 2007); and Andreas Gailus, "Brains: Forms of Life in Gottfried Benn's Rönne Novellas," *New German Critique* 45, no. 2 (August 2018).

51. Benn, "Gespräch," in *Sämtliche Werke*, 7.1:164–65.

52. Benn, "Gespräch," 7.1:169.

53. E.g., "The forest moved further away; a thin skin of fog laid itself down over the lake; the light became gentler and more transparent and lost some of its fullness" (Die Wälder wurden uns ferner; von Nebeln eine dünne Haut legte sich über den See; das Licht wurde zarter und durchsichtiger und nahm an Fülle ab). Benn, "Gespräch," 7.1:164. By my count, this example of "absolutely scientific" writing contains at least five metaphors and four anthropomorphisms.

54. Benn, "Gespräch," 7.1:168.

55. Indeed, Schopenhauer himself explicitly rejects such a materialist view: "True physiology . . . shows the spiritual in humans (cognition) to be the product of the physical in humans. . . . But true metaphysics teaches us that the physical is itself merely a product, or rather an appearance, of something spiritual (of the will), indeed, that matter itself is conditioned through representation, in which it alone exists. . . . For, properly considered, an objective world is something absolutely inconceivable without a subject in the consciousness of which it exists." Arthur Schopenhauer, *On Will in Nature*, in *On the Fourfold Root of the Principle of Sufficient Reason; On Vision and Colours; On Will in Nature*, trans. and ed. David E. Cartwright, Edward E. Erdmann, and Christopher Janaway (Cambridge: Cambridge University Press, 2012), 340.

56. Benn, "Zur Geschichte der Naturwissenschaften," in *Sämtliche Werke*, 3:9.

57. Benn's choice of title for his first book, *Morgue und andere Gedichte*, may also be a kind of parody of the title of Jens Peter Jacobsen's short story collection, *Mogens og andre Noveller*, albeit without semantic connection (Mogens is a proper name).

58. Benn, *Ithaka*, in *Sämtliche Werke*, 7.1:8.

59. Benn, *Ithaka*, 7.1:16.

60. Benn, *Ithaka*, 7.1:7–8.

61. Emil du Bois-Reymond, *Über die Grenzen des Naturerkennens: Ein Vortrag in der zweiten öffentlichen Sitzung der 45. Versammlung deutscher Naturforscher und Ärzte zu Leipzig am 14. August 1872* (Leipzig: Veit & Co., 1876), 28.

62. Du Bois-Reymond, *Über die Grenzen des Naturerkennens*, 39. Du Bois-Reymond's maxim also serves Arno Holz for the title of his 1913 drama *Ignorabimus*.

63. Benn, "Frühe Lyrik und Dramen. Vorbemerkung," in *Sämtliche Werke*, 6:70.

64. Benn, *Ithaka*, 7.1:16.

65. Benn, *Ithaka*, 7.1:16.

66. Benn, *Ithaka*, 7.1:7.

67. Benn, *Ithaka*, 7.1:8.

68. Benn, *Ithaka*, 7.1:9–10.

69. Benn, *Ithaka*, 7.1:12.

70. Benn, *Ithaka*, 7.1:12.
71. Benn, *Ithaka*, 7.1:12.
72. Benn, "Gespräch," 7.1:164.
73. Benn, "Gespräch," 7.1:166.
74. Else Lasker-Schüler, "Doktor Benn," in Hohendahl, *Benn—Wirkung wider Willen*, 98.
75. Benn, *Ithaka*, 7.1:10.
76. Benn gives a hint of his growing skepticism toward biological positivism in the 1911 essay "Medizinische Psychologie" ("Medicinal Psychology"), where he refers to phrenology as psychobiology's corrupted offshoot. See Benn, "Medizinische Psychologie," in *Sämtliche Werke*, 3:18–22.
77. Benn, "Urgesicht," in *Sämtliche Werke*, 3:203.
78. Benn, "Urgesicht," 3:203.
79. Benn, "Urgesicht," 3:211.
80. Benn, "Urgesicht," 3:206.
81. See, e.g., Michael Winkler, "Benn's Cancer Ward and George's Autumnal Park: A Case of Lyrical *Kontrafaktur*," *Colloquia Germanica* 13, no. 3 (1980): 263.
82. Compare the reading of Benn's poem "Pappel" ("Poplar") in Larson Powell, *The Technological Unconscious in German Modernist Literature* (Rochester, N.Y.: Camden House, 2008), 118–23.
83. See Sean Kehoe, "Cervical and Endometrial Cancer during Pregnancy," in *Cancer and Pregnancy: Recent Results in Cancer Research*, vol. 178, ed. A. Surbone, F. Peccatori, and N. Pavlidis (Berlin and Heidelberg: Springer, 2008), 72–73.
84. Adalbert Stifter, *Der Nachsommer*, in *Historisch-Kritische Gesamtausgabe*, 4.2:216.
85. Benn, "Der Arzt," in *Sämtliche Werke*, 1:14, lines 1–2.
86. The quotation in the above subhead is from Benn, "Diesterweg," in *Sämtliche Werke*, 3:72.
87. Benn, "Der Arzt," 1:14, lines 6–8.
88. Compare Winfried Menninghaus on the figure of the *vetula*, or old woman, as "the embodiment of everything tabooed . . . an obscene, decaying corpse in her own lifetime." Winfried Menninghaus, *Disgust: Theory and History of a Strong Sensation*, trans. Howard Eiland and Joel Golb (Albany: State University of New York Press, 2003), 7.
89. Specifically: "The Word is the phallus of the Spirit, centrally rooted" (Das Wort ist der Phallus des Geistes, zentral verwurzelt). From Benn, "Probleme der Lyrik" ("Problems of Lyric Poetry"), in *Sämtliche Werke*, 6:24. On Benn's representation of the male-female relation (esp. in his correspondence with Else Lasker-Schüler) as one between creative potency and receptive instance, see Dorothee Ostmeier, *Poetische Dialoge zu Liebe, Gender und Sex im frühen zwanzigsten Jahrhundert* (Bielefeld: Aisthesis, 2014), 97–146.
90. Benn, "Beitrag zur Geschichte der Psychiatrie," in *Sämtliche Werke*, 3:8.
91. See Hahn, *Gottfried Benn und das Wissen der Moderne*, 57. On unveiling as scientific metaphor, see Ludmilla Jordanova, *Sexual Visions: Images of Gender in Science and Medicine between the Eighteenth and Twentieth Centuries* (Madison: University of Wisconsin Press, 1989), esp. 87–110.

92. W. G. Sebald, "Bis an den Rand der Natur: Versuch über Stifter," in *Die Beschreibung des Unglücks: Zur österreichischen Literatur von Stifter bis Handke* (Frankfurt am Main: Fischer, 1994), 34–35.

93. Maria Tatar, *Lustmord: Sexual Murder in Weimar Germany* (Princeton, N.J.: Princeton University Press, 1995); Arne Höcker, *Epistemologie des Extremen: Lustmord in Kriminologie und Literatur um 1900* (Munich: Fink, 2012).

94. See Kirchdörfer-Boßmann, "*Eine Pranke in den Nacken der Erkenntnis*," 115; and Jan Mieszkowski, "Who's Afraid of Anacoluthon?," *MLN* 124, no. 3 (April 2009): 660.

95. All the more so if one takes Anette and Peter Horn's suggestion that the girl is presented as a willing partner in her desecration. Anette and Peter Horn, *Was aber neu ist, ist die Frage nach dem Satzbau: Die Gedichte Gottfried Benns* (Oberhausen: Athena, 2017), 81.

96. Benn, "Negerbraut," 1:12, lines 15–18.

97. Benn, "Negerbraut," 1:12, line 12.

98. See Dyck, "Requiem"; Aurnhammer, "Inszenierung der Moderne," esp. 57–58; Horn and Horn, *Was aber neu ist*, 72.

99. See Jonathan Sawday, *The Body Emblazoned: Dissection and the Human Body in Renaissance Culture* (London: Routledge, 1995); Hartmut Böhme, "Erotische Anatomie: Körperfragmentierung als ästhetisches Verfahren in Renaissance und Barock," in *Körperteile: Eine kulturelle Anatomie*, ed. Claudia Benthien and Christoph Wulf (Reinbek bei Hamburg: Rowohlt, 2001); and Peter-André Alt, *Von der Schönheit zerbrechender Ordnungen: Körper, Politik und Geschlecht in der Literatur des 17. Jahrhunderts* (Göttingen: Wallstein, 2007), esp. 45–49.

100. Rudolf Drux, "Über das anatomische Verfahren der Körperdarstellung in barocken 'Sprachgemälden': Am Beispiel der dekonstruierten Geliebten," *Deutsche Vierteljahrsschrift für Literaturwissenschaft und Geistesgeschichte* 83, no. 1 (March 2009): 93.

101. This idea of making-visible is also latently present in Benn's title for his breakthrough poem, derived from the Middle French *morguer*, "to treat with arrogance, to regard haughtily."

102. Walter Benjamin, *The Origin of German Tragic Drama*, trans. John Osborne (London: Verso, 1998), 217.

103. Benjamin, *Origin*, 216–17.

104. See also Claudia Benthien on decapitation as a "transformational process of image-production." Claudia Benthien, *Barockes Schweigen: Rhetorik und Performativität des Sprachlosen im 17. Jahrhundert* (Munich: Fink, 2006), 125.

105. See Peter J. Burgard, "Dead Metaphor Society? From Opitz to Hoffmannswaldau," *Neophilologus* 93, no. 2 (April 2009).

106. See Benjamin, *Origin*, 224.

107. Benjamin, *Origin*, 227.

108. Lasker-Schüler, "Doktor Benn," 98.

109. Benn, "Banane," in *Sämtliche Werke*, 1.83, lines 37–40.

110. Benn, "Die Reise," in *Sämtliche Werke*, 3:46.

111. On Benn's "clinical" approach to his own language, see Arne Höcker, "Brainless: Scientific Observation and Literary Writing in Gottfried Benn," *Monatshefte* 105, no. 3 (Fall 2013); Hoffmann, "In der Prosektur"; and Gailus, "Brains," esp. 16.

112. Compare Blumenberg on the "awareness of reality that is determined by resistance, and . . . a corresponding and confirmatory art form that is made up of means of expression that annihilate themselves, and use their own inconsistencies to demonstrate their own lack of meaning." Hans Blumenberg, "The Concept of Reality and the Possibility of the Novel," in *New Perspectives in German Literary Criticism*, ed. Richard E. Amacher and Victor Lange (Princeton, N.J.: Princeton University Press, 1979), 43. As Blumenberg continues in a footnote, such a form of self-cancellation, while fatal for the realist novel, is fundamental to lyric poetry.

113. Benn, "Der Geburtstag," in *Sämtliche Werke*, 3:51–52.

114. Benn himself alludes, somewhat petulantly, to the similarity between his work and that of his younger contemporary in his introductory comments to a reissued edition of his early work: "After I started to be spoken about again in 1945, the *Weltwoche* in Zurich wrote that the *Static Poems* (1947) were weak compared to the earlier ones from 1912–20. The critic added: what's all this talk about Sartre's existential nausea [Lebensekel]—thirty years after Benn? So a piece of historical evidence [Also ein historischer Hinweis]." Benn, "Frühe Lyrik und Dramen. Vorbemerkung," 6:69.

115. Friedrich Kittler, *Discourse Networks 1800/1900*, trans. Michael Metteer (Stanford, Calif.: Stanford University Press, 1900), 243.

116. As Gailus comments on this passage: "Who would *know* these [associations], if not a subject thoroughly shaped by a late nineteenth-century humanistic education, perhaps at a Wilhelminian Gymnasium?" Gailus, "Brains," 27.

117. Benn, "Der Geburtstag," 3:52.

118. Thus Andreas Huyssen: "Here the physiology of association is not in the service of some new perception of a world in flux but functions as a pseudoscientific strategy to reassert the armored self." Andreas Huyssen, "Benn in Occupied Brussels: The Rönne Novellas," in *Miniature Metropolis: Literature in an Age of Photography and Film* (Cambridge, Mass.: Harvard University Press, 2015), 110.

119. Benn, "Der Geburtstag," 3:56–57.

120. Benn, "Akademie-Rede," in *Sämtliche Werke*, 3:388.

121. Benn, "Akademie-Rede," 3:390.

122. Foucault, *Birth of the Clinic*, 109.

123. Benn, "Der Geburtstag," 3:53–54.

124. See Moritz Baßler, *Deutsche Erzählprosa 1850–1950: Eine Geschichte literarischer Verfahren* (Berlin: Schmidt, 2015), 227.

125. This is also effectively the case in the term's second and third appearances in the piece: "Edmée stretched herself out. Her shoulders flattened, two warm pools. Now she closed her hand, slowly, around a shaft, ripe in its fullness, scythed off brownish at the fingers, under great sheaves of transfigured pleasure——" (Nun schloß sie die Hand, langsam, um einen Schaft, die Reife in ihrer Fülle, bräunlich abgemäht, an den Fingern, unter großen Garben verklärter Lust——), and "Rönne looked around: transfigured [verklärt], and yet nothing had changed. But for him: happiness up to the lips." Benn, "Der Geburtstag," 3:56, 3:59.

126. Thus I disagree with Gailus that Benn's representations of misogynist and colonialist violence can be read as deconstructive critiques. See Gailus, "Brains," 29. Rather, as in much expressionist work, Benn's representations of violence oscillate between self-conscious provocation, real aversion, and the acting out of that aversion in the form of even more self-conscious provocation.

127. Benn, "Dorische Welt," in *Sämtliche Werke*, 4:140.

128. Dieter Wellershoff, *Gottfried Benn: Phänotyp dieser Stunde* (Munich: dtv, 1958), 22.

129. Benn, "Urgesicht," 3:210. On the paradoxical conservatism of Benn's avant-garde, see Peter Uwe Hohendahl, "The Loss of Reality: Gottfried Benn's Early Prose," in *Modernity and the Text: Revisions of German Modernism*, ed. Andreas Huyssen and David Bathrick (New York: Columbia University Press, 1989).

130. Benn, "Dorische Welt," 4:139.

131. Fritz Martini, *Deutsche Literatur im bürgerlichen Realismus 1848–1898* (Stuttgart: J. B. Metzlersche Verlagsbuchhandlung, 1962), 15.

132. Benn, "Der Arzt," 1:14, lines 16–17.

Chapter 6

1. "Wie nahmen wir alle den Ausdruck der Verklärung von dem gemarterten Gesicht, wie hielten wir unsere Wangen in den Schein dieser endlich erreichten und schon vergehenden Gerechtigkeit! Was für Zeiten, mein Kamerad!" Franz Kafka, *In der Strafkolonie*, in *Drucke zu Lebzeiten*, ed. Wolf Kittler, Hans-Gerd Koch, and Gerhard Neumann, in *Schriften—Tagebücher: Kritische Ausgabe*, ed. Jürgen Born, Gerhard Neumann, Malcolm Pasley, and Jost Schillemeit, 15 vols. (Frankfurt am Main: Fischer, 2002), 226.

2. "Einen Schritt weiter, und wir wären im Schmutz." Julian Schmidt, *Geschichte der deutschen Literatur seit Lessing's Tod*, vol. 1 (Leipzig: Herbig, 1858), 213. Schmidt's comment is specifically in regard to Goethe's *Wilhelm Meisters Lehrjahre*.

3. Kafka, *Das Schloß*, ed. Malcolm Pasley, in *Kritische Ausgabe*, 444–45.

4. Kafka, *Das Schloß*, 446.

5. Kafka, *Das Schloß*, 273.

6. Kafka, *Das Schloß*, 273.

7. Kafka, *Das Schloß*, 273.

8. Hans Blumenberg, "The Concept of Reality and the Possibility of the Novel," in *New Perspectives in German Literary Criticism*, ed. Richard E. Amacher and Victor Lange (Princeton, N.J.: Princeton University Press, 1979), 33.

9. In the words of Walter Sokel, "Castle and village constitute a society, a social universe, that is closer to Dickens's London, Balzac's Paris, Flaubert's French provinces and Tolstoy's Russia than anything else Kafka ever wrote." Walter H. Sokel, *Franz Kafka—Tragik und Ironie: Zur Struktur seiner Kunst* (Munich: Albert Langen Georg Müller Verlag, 1963), 397.

10. Erich Auerbach, *Mimesis: The Representation of Reality in Western Literature*, trans. Willard R. Trask. (Princeton, N.J.: Princeton University Press, 1953), 473. Meanwhile, Nacim Ghanbari places *Das Schloß* at the end of the history of the nineteenth-century bourgeois novel in a different sense: as the undermining of the narrative model of dynastic continuity inaugurated by *Soll und Haben*. Nacim Ghanbari, *Das Haus: Eine deutsche Literaturgeschichte 1850–1926* (Berlin: De Gruyter, 2011), esp. 67–72.

11. See, e.g., Hanns Zischler, *Kafka Goes to the Movies*, trans. Susan H. Gillespie (Chicago: University of Chicago Press, 2003); Carolin Duttlinger, *Kafka and Photography* (Oxford: Oxford University Press, 2007); and Gesa Schneider,

Das Andere schreiben: Kafkas fotographische Poetik (Würzburg: Königshausen & Neumann, 2008).

12. See Klaus R. Scherpe, "Kafkas Poetik der Beschreibung," in *Kontinent Kafka: Mosse-Lektures an der Humboldt-Universität zu Berlin*, ed. Klaus R. Scherpe and Elisabeth Wagner (Berlin: Vorwerk 8, 2006), 96.

13. On Kafka's "ascetic purge of ornament," see Mark M. Anderson, *Kafka's Clothes: Ornament and Aestheticism in the Habsburg Fin de Siècle* (Oxford: Clarendon Press, 1992), 14.

14. Gilles Deleuze and Félix Guattari, *Kafka: Toward a Minor Literature*, trans. Dana Polan (Minneapolis: University of Minneapolis Press, 1986), 19. Deleuze and Guattari take their notion of Prague German as a "poor" language from Klaus Wagenbach, *Franz Kafka: Eine Biographie seiner Jugend, 1883–1912* (Bern: Francke, 1958), 81–89, who for his part takes it from Fritz Mauthner, *Erinnerungen*, vol. 1: *Prager Jugendjahre* (Munich: Müller, 1918), 51. See also John Zilcosky's instructive comparison between *Das Schloß* and the nineteenth-century adventure novels of Schaffstein's *Grüne Bändchen*; John Zilcosky, *Kafka's Travels: Exoticism, Colonialism, and the Traffic of Writing* (New York: Palgrave, 2003), esp. 142–45.

15. Kafka, *Das Schloß*, 7.

16. See, e.g., Henry Sussman, *Franz Kafka: Geometrician of Metaphor* (Madison: Coda Press, 1979), esp. 114–19.

17. As Manfred Engel comments on a similar passage: "He observes here the object of his desire and in doing so articulates his desire itself." Manfred Engel, "Franz Kafka: *Das Schloss*," in *Klassiker: Neu-Lektüren*, ed. Ralf Georg Bogner and Manfred Leber (Saarbrücken: Universaar, 2013), 188. See also the analysis by Peter Benson, "Entering *The Castle*," *Journal of Narrative Technique* 23, no. 3 (Spring 1993), which however overlooks the potential irony of Kafka's narrative traditionalism.

18. Kafka, *Das Schloß*, 22–23.

19. Such techniques are not exclusive to *Das Schloß*. Compare for example Karl Roßmann's first glimpse of New York from the deck of the ship in *Der Verschollene*, Georg Bendemann's gradually clearing view of his father's room in "Das Urteil," or Gregor Samsa's initial scan of his bedroom in his newly transformed state in *Die Verwandlung*.

20. Kafka makes this point explicit in the (altogether similar) description of K.'s entrance into the Brückenhof landlady's room: "Only once one had entered and one's eyes had adjusted could one make out details." Kafka, *Das Schloß*, 122.

21. Kafka, *Das Schloß*, 22–23.

22. Kafka, *Das Schloß*, 15.

23. Kafka, *Das Schloß*, 139–40.

24. Kafka, *Das Schloß*, 184.

25. Kafka, *Das Schloß*, 172.

26. Kafka, *Das Schloß*, 480.

27. "For realism is almost by definition highly visual, concerned with registering what the world looks like. We tend to believe—and centuries of philosophical tradition stand behind the belief—that sight is the most objective and impartial of our senses. Thus any honest accounting for the real, in the sense of the appearances of the world, needs to call upon visual inspection and inventory. It needs to

give a sense of the thereness of the physical world, as in a still-life painting." Peter Brooks, *Realist Vision* (New Haven, Conn.: Yale University Press, 2005), 16. On Kafka's awareness—and complication—of this paradigm, see Gerhard Neumann, "Chinesische Mauer und Schacht von Babel: Franz Kafkas Architekturen," in *Kafka-Lektüren* (Berlin: De Gruyter, 2013).

28. Kafka, *Das Schloß*, 80.

29. Émile Zola, "The Experimental Novel," in *The Experimental Novel and Other Essays*, trans. Belle M. Sherman (New York: Haskell House, 1964), 25.

30. On "the peephole effect" in *Das Schloß* as something productive of the "phantasm of power," see Paul North, "Castle Logic: Hints in Kafka's Novel," in *1922: Literature, Culture, Politics*, ed. Jean-Michel Rabaté (New York: Cambridge University Press, 2015), 67.

31. Kafka, *Das Schloß*, 278.

32. Kafka, *Das Schloß*, 215.

33. Kafka, *Das Schloß*, 104.

34. Kafka, *Das Schloß*, 41. K.'s comment is also decisive for the development of the novel's plot, insofar as K. (mis)interprets the Castle's contradictions as possible *options*.

35. While Charles Bernheimer credits K.'s words, blaming the Castle for "refus[ing] to confront [K.] on his own terms," others stress the on-the-fly quality of K.'s utterances and the inconstancy of his desires and opinions. See Charles Bernheimer, *Flaubert and Kafka: Studies in Psychopoetic Structure* (New Haven, Conn.: Yale University Press, 1982), 208–9; and, in contrast, Erwin R. Steinberg, "K. of the Castle: Ostensible Land-Surveyor," *College English* 27, no. 3 (December 1965); Sokel, *Kafka*, 403–7; Karen J. Campbell, "Kafka's *Schloß* and the Subversion of Plot," *Journal of English and Germanic Philology* 85, no. 3 (July 1986); and Ludo Verbeek, "Auswandern—Unnütze Prolegomena zu Kafkas *Schloß*," in *"Schloß"-Geschichten: Zu Kafkas drittem Romanplan—Eine Diskussion* (Eggingen: Isele, 2007), esp. 19–22. Meanwhile, Avital Ronell offers a third possibility: that K.'s statements should be evaluated not according to their credibility or noncredibility, but as a performative act aimed at suspending categories of credibility altogether. Avital Ronell, "Doing Kafka in *The Castle*," in *Finitude's Score* (Lincoln: University of Nebraska Press, 1994), esp. 186.

36. On the novel's dissolving of a biographical narrative logic, see Gerhard Neumann, "Kafkas *Schloß*-Roman: Das parasitäre Spiel der Zeichen," in *Franz Kafka, Experte der Macht* (Munich: Hanser, 2012), esp. 144–45; Joseph Vogl, "Lebende Anstalt," in *Für alle und keinen: Lektüre, Schrift und Leben bei Nietzsche und Kafka*, ed. Friedrich Balke, Joseph Vogl, and Benno Wagner (Zurich: Diaphanes, 2008); and J. Hillis Miller, "The Sense of an Un-ending: The Resistance to Narrative Closure in Kafka's *Das Schloss*," in *Franz Kafka: Narration, Rhetoric, and Reading*, ed. Jakob Lothe, Beatrice Sandberg, and Ronald Speirs (Columbus: Ohio State University Press, 2011).

37. Stanley Corngold specifies "three orders of delay and distraction from the reader's expectation of a narrative *telos* found . . . in the nineteenth century, *dit* Realist, novels of Kafka's declared masters": (1) the lack of a clear or convincing motivation for K.'s actions, (2) the creation of suspense out the hope that K.'s motivation *will* eventually become clear, and (3) the various counterfactuals and subjunctive statements in the novel which demand to be, but never actually

are, resolved. Stanley Corngold, "Ritardando in *Das Schloß*," in *From Kafka to Sebald: Modernism and Narrative Form*, ed. Sabine Wilke (New York: Continuum, 2012), 21.

38. Walter Benjamin, "Franz Kafka: On the Tenth Anniversary of his Death," in *Selected Writings*, vol. 2: *1927–1934*, trans. Rodney Livingston et al., ed. Michael W. Jennings, Howard Eiland, and Gary Smith (Cambridge, Mass.: Harvard University Press, 1999), 802; "Franz Kafka: Zur zehnten Wiederkehr seines Todestages," in *Gesammelte Schriften*, vol. 2.2: *Aufsätze, Essays, Vorträge*, ed. Rolf Tiedemann and Hermann Schweppenhäuser (Frankfurt am Main: Suhrkamp, 1977), 420.

39. Georg Lukács, "Franz Kafka or Thomas Mann?," in *The Meaning of Contemporary Realism*, trans. John and Necke Mander (London: Merlin, 1962), 52.

40. Lukács, "Franz Kafka or Thomas Mann?," 48.

41. Scherpe, "Kafkas Poetik der Beschreibung," 101.

42. Franz Kafka, *Der Proceß*, ed. Malcolm Pasley, in *Kritische Ausgabe*, 221. On the resemblance between Titorelli's landscapes and *Das Schloß*'s descriptive practices, see Stanley Corngold, *Lambent Traces: Franz Kafka* (Princeton, N.J.: Princeton University Press, 2004), 5–6.

43. Franz Kafka, *Tagebücher*, ed. Hans-Gerd Koch, Michael Müller, and Malcolm Pasley, in *Kritische Ausgabe*, 892.

44. Kafka, *Das Schloß*, 421.

45. Kafka, *Das Schloß*, 387.

46. Kafka, *Das Schloß*, 20. On K.'s lack of consideration for the presence of innocent children as a parodic answer to Stifter's *Kalkstein*, see Claudia Nitschke, "Chaos und Form, Raum und Ethos in Stifters *Bunte Steine*," *German Life and Letters* 68, no. 4 (October 2015): 558.

47. Franz Kafka, *Nachgelassene Schriften und Fragmente II*, ed. Jost Schillemeit, in *Kritische Ausgabe*, 132. As Paul North comments: "The division of experience into the sensible and the true is what, for Kafka, makes knowledge into a quest and the sensual world into sin. We must understand, however, that the world is not sinful because it is not yet knowledge; Kafka's turn on this screw is to argue that the world is sinful because it feigns to lead out of itself." Or, more succinctly (and directly on this aphorism): "This evil is seduction toward a reality beyond semblance." Paul North, *The Yield: Kafka's Atheological Reformation* (Stanford, Calif.: Stanford University Press, 2015), 209, 187.

48. Fritz Mauthner, *Beiträge zu einer Kritik der Sprache*, vol. 1: *Sprache und Psychologie* (Stuttgart: Cotta, 1901), 146.

49. In his memoirs, Mauthner himself traces the development of his ideas to Otto Ludwig's critique of Schiller's poetic language; or, as he puts it more drastically in *Beiträge zu einer Kritik der Sprache*, the "opposition to Schillerian artificiality [Unnatur]." See Mauthner, *Erinnerungen*, 213–18; Mauthner, *Beiträge*, 100.

50. Arno Holz, *Evolution der Lyrik*, in *Das Werk von Arno Holz: Monumental-Ausgabe in zwölf Bänden*, vol. 10: *Die Neue Wortkunst: Eine Zusammenfassung ihrer ersten grundlegenden Dokumente*, ed. Hans W. Fischer (Berlin: Dietz, 1925), 568. On Stifter's similar (if less confident) "sought-after convertability of word and thing" see Eva Geulen, *Worthörig wider Willen: Darstellungsproblematik und Sprachreflexion in der Prosa Adalbert Stifters* (Munich: iudicum, 1992), 154.

51. See Walter Eschenbacher, *Fritz Mauthner und die deutsche Literatur um 1900: Eine Untersuchung zur Sprachkrise der Jahrhundertwende* (Frankfurt am Main: Lang, 1977), esp. 43.

52. Mauthner, *Beiträge*, 28.

53. See Peter-André Alt, "Doppelte Schrift, Unterbrechung und Grenze: Franz Kafkas Poetik des Unsagbaren im Kontext der Sprachskepsis um 1900," *Jahrbuch der deutschen Schillergesellschaft* 29 (1985); and Winfried Menninghaus, *Disgust: Theory and History of a Strong Sensation*, trans. Howard Eiland and Joel Golb (Albany: State University of New York Press, 2003), 337–41.

54. Kafka, *Tagebücher*, 756.

55. Kafka, *Tagebücher*, 491.

56. See Menninghaus, *Disgust*, 340–41.

57. Kafka, *Tagebücher*, 776–77.

58. Isaak [Jizchak] Löwy, "Vom jüdischen Theater," in Franz Kafka, *Nachgelassene Schriften und Fragmente I*, ed. Jost Schillemeit, in *Kritische Ausgabe*, 430.

59. Löwy, "Vom jüdischen Theater," 430.

60. Löwy, "Vom jüdischen Theater," 432.

61. Löwy, "Vom jüdischen Theater," 434.

62. On the role played by Mauthner's upbringing in the development of his ideas, see Jacques le Rider, *Fritz Mauthner: Scepticisme linguistique et modernité* (Paris: Bartillat, 2012), esp. 32–35.

63. Mauthner, *Beiträge*, 158.

64. 2 Cor. 3:6 (KJV).

65. 2 Cor. 3:7–10 (KJV/LUT1545).

66. See Franz Kafka, *Tagebücher: Kommentarband*, ed. Hans-Gerd Koch, Michael Müller, and Malcolm Pasley, in *Kritische Ausgabe*, 193. On Kafka's ambivalent feelings toward Brod at the time of the writing of this entry, see Peter Fenves, "The Kafka-Werfel-Einstein Effect," in Max Brod, *Tycho Brahe's Path to God*, trans. Felix Warren Crosse (Evanston, Ill.: Northwestern University Press, 2007), xxi.

67. Löwy, "Vom jüdischen Theater," 434.

68. Thus Menninghaus's reading of Kafka's relation to his writing as one "not of simple excretion but of pleasurable rumination" does not go far enough: Kafka's emphasis on the materiality of writing is not just a form of guilty coprophiliac *jouissance*, but a questioning of the guilt attached to such enjoyment in the first place. Menninghaus, *Disgust*, 341.

69. Kafka, *Das Schloß*, 96–97.

70. Cornelia Vismann, *Files: Law and Media Technology*, trans. Geoffrey Winthrop-Young (Stanford, Calif.: Stanford University Press, 2008), 98; *Akten: Medientechnik und Recht* (Frankfurt am Main: Fischer, 2000), 176–77.

71. Vismann, *Files*, 98; *Akten*, 176–77. Vismann is alluding to the original meaning of "thesaurus" as "storehouse, treasure, treasury": see *Files*, 77–78; *Akten*, 135.

72. Vismann, *Files*, 28; *Akten*, 47.

73. Vismann, *Files*, 99; *Akten*, 177.

74. See also Kafka's description of Mizzi and the assistants' futile attempt to clean up the mess left by their search: "They . . . tried to lock everything back

into the cabinet, but the disordered abundance of the files made it impossible. That must have been what gave the assistants the idea they were now carrying out. They had placed the cabinet on the floor, stuffed all the files in, and were now sitting with Mizzi on the cabinet doors to try to slowly force them closed." Kafka, *Das Schloß*, 112–13.

75. See Ritchie Robertson, "Myth vs. Enlightenment in Kafka's *Das Schloß*," *Monatshefte* 103, no. 3 (January 2011): 390. On the myriad connections in Kafka between bureaucratic and literary writing, see Stanley Corngold and Benno Wagner, "The Ministry of Writing (*The Castle*)," in *Franz Kafka: The Ghosts in the Machine* (Evanston, Ill.: Northwestern University Press, 2011).

76. The reference is to Michael Thompson, *Rubbish Theory: The Creation and Destruction of Value* (Oxford: Oxford University Press, 1979), esp. 9. See also chapter 1, 31.

77. On land surveying and the panoptic gaze, see Zilcosky, *Kafka's Travels*, 132–38; Schneider, *Das Andere schreiben*, 116–21.

78. See Duttlinger, *Kafka and Photography*, 225–49. However, Duttlinger's emphasis on the "all-pervading sense of ambiguity, opacity, and isolation" in *Das Schloß* problematically implies that what is at stake is merely a hope for a more *accurate* form of representation, rather than a reevaluation of representation entirely. Duttlinger, *Kafka and Photography*, 246.

79. Kafka, *Das Schloß*, 160.

80. Kafka, *Das Schloß*, 202–3.

81. See Eric Santner, "Kafka's *Metamorphosis* and the Writing of Abjection," in Franz Kafka, *The Metamorphosis*, trans. and ed. Stanley Corngold (New York: W. W. Norton, 1996); Rainer Nägele, "Schloß ohne Schluß: Kafka, Benjamin und kein Ende," in *Lesarten der Moderne: Essays* (Eggingen: Isele, 1998); Menninghaus, *Disgust*, 227–341; John Hamilton, *Philology of the Flesh* (Chicago: University of Chicago Press, 2018), 169–80; and Ian Fleishman, *An Aesthetics of Injury: The Narrative Wound from Baudelaire to Tarantino* (Evanston, Ill.: Northwestern University Press, 2018), 50–73.

82. Kafka, *Das Schloß*, 17.

83. On suspension as principle in Kafka's prose, see Michael G. Levine, "'A Place So Insanely Enchanting': Kafka and the Poetics of Suspension," *MLN* 123, no. 5 (December 2008); Malte Kleinwort, *Der späte Kafka: Spätstil als Stilsuspension* (Munich: Fink, 2013), esp. 35–49.

84. Kafka, *Das Schloß*, 444.

85. Kafka, *Das Schloß*, 304.

86. Kafka, *Das Schloß*, 367–68.

87. Kafka, *Das Schloß*, 60–61.

88. Kafka, *Das Schloß*, 21.

89. Kafka, *Das Schloß*, 472.

90. Kafka, *Das Schloß*, 348.

91. Kafka, *Das Schloß*, 399.

92. Kafka, *Das Schloß*, 205.

93. See, e.g., Detlef Kremer, *Kafka: Die Erotik des Schreibens* (Mainz: Philo, 1998), 163–65.

94. Kafka, *Das Schloß*, 94.

95. Fredric Jameson, *The Antinomies of Realism* (London: Verso, 2013), 51–52.

96. Karl Rosenkranz, *The Aesthetics of Ugliness: A Critical Edition*, trans. Andrei Pop and Mechtild Widrich (London: Bloomsbury, 2015), 50; *Ästhetik des Häßlichen*, ed. Dieter Kliche (Stuttgart: Reclam, 1990), 47.
97. Kafka, *Das Schloß*, 493.
98. Kafka, *Das Schloß*, 493.
99. Kafka, *Das Schloß*, 494.
100. See in particular Anderson, *Kafka's Clothes*, 53–54; Linda C. Hsu, "*Klamotten*: Reading Nietzsche Reading Kafka," *German Quarterly* 67, no. 2 (Spring 1994); and Kleinwort, *Der späte Kafka*, 209–15.
101. Kafka, *Das Schloß*, 123.
102. Kafka, *Das Schloß*, 25.
103. Kafka, *Das Schloß*, 23.
104. Kafka, *Das Schloß*, 38.
105. Kafka, *Das Schloß*, 163.
106. Kafka, *Das Schloß*, 278.
107. Kafka, *Das Schloß*, 327.
108. Kafka, *Das Schloß*, 296.
109. Kafka, *Das Schloß*, 158.
110. Kafka, *Das Schloß*, 467–68.
111. Kafka, *Das Schloß*, 469.
112. Kafka, *Das Schloß*, 474.
113. Franz Kafka, "Kleider," in *Drucke zu Lebzeiten*, in *Kritische Ausgabe*, 28–29.
114. Anderson, *Kafka's Clothes*, 31–32.
115. Emmanuel Levinas, *Totality and Infinity: An Essay on Exteriority*, trans. Alphonso Lingis (Pittsburgh: Duquesne University Press, 1969), 263.
116. Levinas, *Totality and Infinity*, 263.
117. Levinas, *Totality and Infinity*, 262.
118. See Anderson, *Kafka's Clothes*, 4.
119. On Kafka's frequent associations between women, sexuality, and uncleanness, see, e.g., Ritchie Robertson, *Kafka: Judaism, Politics, and Literature* (Oxford: Clarendon Press, 1985), 257–58; Elizabeth Boa, *Kafka: Gender, Class, and Race in the Letters and Fictions* (Oxford: Clarendon Press, 1996), esp. 59–60, 129; and Menninghaus, *Disgust*, 261–81.
120. Benjamin, "Franz Kafka: On the Tenth Anniversary of his Death," 796; "Franz Kafka: Zur zehnten Wiederkehr seines Todestages," 411.
121. Mary Douglas, *Purity and Danger: An Analysis of Concepts of Pollution and Taboo* (London: Routledge, 2002), 35.
122. Kafka, *Das Schloß*, 154.
123. Kafka, *Das Schloß*, 93.
124. Douglas, *Purity and Danger*, 35.
125. Douglas, *Purity and Danger*, 35.
126. See Max Brod, "Eine Bemerkung zu Kafkas 'Schloß,'" in *Über Franz Kafka* (Frankfurt am Main: Fischer, 1966).
127. Božena Němcová, *Babička* (Toronto: Sixty-Eight, 1982), translated into German as *Großmutter: Bilder aus dem böhmischen Landleben*, trans. Anton Smital (Leipzig: Reclam, 1885).

128. Maurice Blanchot regrettably takes Brod's account at face value, including the unquestioning repetition of a passage from Němcová's novel that Brod himself quotes out of context and from an entirely different episode. See Maurice Blanchot, *The Infinite Conversation*, trans. Susan Hanson (Minneapolis: University of Minnesota Press, 1993), 463, note 3. For a more careful assessment of Němcová's novel in relation to Kafka's literary milieu, see Rajendra A. Chitnis, "Putting Granny in a Home: Czech Writers and the Village in Kafka's Lifetime," in *Kafka, Prag und der Erste Weltkrieg / Kafka, Prague and the First World War*, ed. Manfred Engel and Ritchie Robertson (Würzburg: Königshausen & Neumann, 2012), 111–15.

129. On Kafka's intertextual practices, see Andreas Kilcher and Detlef Kremer, "Die Genealogie der Schrift. Eine transtextuelle Lektüre von Kafkas *Bericht für eine Akademie*," in *Textverkehr: Franz Kafka und die Tradition*, ed. Claudia Liebrand and Franziska Schößler (Würzburg: Königshausen & Neumann, 2004); and Erica Weitzman, "'Ich, von dem du ausgingst?': Inheritance and Anamorphosis between Freytag and Kafka," *Monatshefte* 111, no. 1 (2019).

130. See Brod, "Bemerkung," 374.

131. "And there Grandmother related what Kristla had told her that morning. '. . . But now the girl is afraid that the man will take revenge.' 'She has nothing to be afraid of, I shall take care of it,' said the princess; thereupon she signaled to the countess, both climbed onto their horses and, amiably waving farewell to the assembled company, set off in a gallop toward the castle. 'That's the truth, not everyone would dare to talk to the princess like Grandmother does,' said Mrs. Prošek." Němcová, *Großmutter*, 153. Needless to say, this is hardly the "dark hordes of valets, castle officials, self-seeking, pompous, deceitful bureaucrats" of Brod's imagination. Brod, "Bemerkung," 373.

132. In *Babička*, more conventionally, disgrace comes from succumbing (or appearing to succumb) to sexual demands, as the grandmother explains to the princess: "If anyone had seen that popinjay at night in front of the girl's window, the news'd spread like it'd been heralded with trumpets, and've ruined the girl's reputation and her happiness; for then people'd say, 'Oh that one! She's the one the gentlemen went to, she's none of ours.'" Němcová, *Großmutter*, 153.

133. Boa, *Kafka*, 183.

134. Boa, *Kafka*, 183.

135. A smaller point of connection between the two novels can be found in the wedding present of "beautiful garnets" given to Kristla for her wedding, converted by Kafka into the "necklace of Bohemian garnets" that Olga fatefully lends to Amalia on the day of the festival. Němcová, *Großmutter*, 287; Kafka, *Das Schloß*, 296.

136. Boa, *Kafka*, 286. Curiously, Boa does *not* mention Němcová's novel in this context.

137. Thus Nägele's description of Kafka's two conceptions of the body—the (Greek and Christian) "divinely transfigured body" (der im Göttlichen verklärte Leib) versus the (Jewish) "idea of the body as yet unredeemed creatureliness" (Vorstellung vom Körper als noch unerlöste Kreatürlichkeit)—fails to take the extra step of asking how Kafka might put this very division, as *historical* division, into question. Nägele, "Schloß ohne Schluß," 172–73.

138. Joseph Vogl, *Ort der Gewalt: Kafkas literarische Ethik* (Zurich: diaphanes, 2010), 69.

139. Kafka, *Das Schloß*, 371.

140. Kafka, *Das Schloß*, 60–61.

141. Thus Susanne Hochreiter: "In its obscenity, the scene is reminiscent of peepshows, where normally women are the ones on display." Susanne Hochreiter, *Franz Kafka: Raum und Geschlecht* (Würzburg: Königshausen & Neumann, 2007), 158–59.

142. Kafka, *Das Schloß*, 398.

143. Julian Schmidt, *Geschichte der deutschen Literatur von Leibniz bis auf unsere Zeit*, vol. 5 (Berlin: Hertz, 1896), 510.

144. Kafka, *Nachgelassene Schriften und Fragmente II*, 32.

145. Kafka, *Nachgelassene Schriften und Fragmente II*, 360.

146. Werner Hamacher, "The Gesture in the Name: On Benjamin and Kafka," in *Premises: Essays on Philosophy from Kant to Celan*, trans. Peter Fenves (Cambridge, Mass.: Harvard University Press, 1997), 336.

147. On Kafka's dimming of the mimetic image, see North, *Yield*, esp. 198–209, 214–17.

148. Aristotle, *Physics: A Guided Study*, trans. Joe Sachs (New Brunswick, N.J.: Rutgers University Press, 1995), 1.9:46.

149. Although, as James I. Porter reminds us, Aristotle's aesthetics (and perhaps also his metaphysics) already entails a devaluation of the sensual as a consequence of the separation of form and matter in the first place. See James I. Porter, "The Disgrace of Matter in Ancient Aesthetics," in *KAKOS: Badness and Anti-value in Classical Antiquity*, ed. Ineke Sluiter and Ralph M. Rosen (Leiden: Brill, 2008), 292–96.

150. See Judith Butler, *Bodies That Matter: On the Discursive Limits of Sex* (London: Routledge, 1993), 5.

151. Kafka, *Das Schloß*, 18.

Coda

1. Georges Bataille, "Materialism," in *Visions of Excess: Selected Writings, 1927–1939*, ed. and trans. Allan Stoekl (Minneapolis: University of Minnesota Press, 1985), 15.

2. Max Brod, "Nachwort," in Franz Kafka, *Das Schloß* (Munich: Wolff, 1926), 495.

3. Gerd Kleiner, "Anmut/Grazie," in *Ästhetische Grundbegriffe: Historisches Wörterbuch*, vol. 1, ed. Karlheinz Barck et al. (Stuttgart: Metzler, 2010), 196.

4. Hans Sachs, "Ein straffred Diogenis Philosophi, uber das viehische verkerte leben menschliches geschlechts" (Nürnberg: Neuber, 1555), Staatsbibliothek zu Berlin, http://resolver.staatsbibliothek-berlin.de/SBB0001B15400000000. Also cited in "Anmut (m.)," *Deutsches Wörterbuch von Jacob und Wilhelm Grimm (DWB)*, http://www.woerterbuchnetz.de/DWB?lemma=anmut.

5. The Grimms' dictionary also notes that "even in the sixteenth and seventeenth centuries, the feminine word still displays the meaning of the masculine, desire and lust" (auch das weibliche wort zeigt im 16. 17 jh. noch jene bedeutung des männlichen, begierde und lust). "Anmut (f.)," *DWB*, http://www.woerterbuchnetz.de/DWB?lemma=anmut.

6. Friedrich Schiller, "On Grace and Dignity," in *Schiller's "On Grace and Dignity" in Its Cultural Context: Essays and a New Translation*, ed. Jane V. Curran and Christopher Fricker (Rochester, N.Y.: Camden House, 2005), 124; "Über Anmut und Würde," in *Werke und Briefe in zwölf Bänden*, vol. 8: *Theoretische Schriften*, ed. Rolf-Peter Janz (Frankfurt am Main: Deutscher Klassiker Verlag, 1992), 334.

7. Schiller, "On Grace and Dignity," 147; "Über Anmut und Würde," 364.

8. Brod, "Nachwort," 495, 496.

9. Of course, insofar as this absent grace is thematized, the novel contradicts its own premise. But this is only to reiterate the point that materiality in the literary work can only ever be the *evocation* of materiality, not materiality itself.

10. Franz Kafka, *Das Schloß*, ed. Malcolm Pasley, in *Schriften—Tagebücher: Kritische Ausgabe*, ed. Jürgen Born, Gerhard Neumann, Malcolm Pasley, and Jost Schillemeit, 15 vols. (Frankfurt am Main: Fischer, 2002), 154.

11. Franz Kafka, *Nachgelassene Schriften und Fragmente II*, ed. Jost Schillemeit, in *Kritische Ausgabe*, 32.

12. Robertson also notes the importance of the washing-up motif in *Das Schloß* (further suggesting the possible derivation of the name "Lasemann" from the Czech *lázen*, "bath"), though the interpretation he draws from this—that it functions as a symbol of "natural vitality and enjoyment" and a "domestic life pursued in accordance with Klamm's wishes"—is supported neither by the details nor by the mood of Kafka's novel. See Ritchie Robertson, *Kafka: Judaism, Politics, and Literature* (Oxford: Clarendon Press, 1985), 267.

13. Paul North, *The Yield: Kafka's Atheological Reformation* (Stanford, Calif.: Stanford University Press, 2015), 11.

14. Georges Bataille, "The Use Value of D. A. F. de Sade (An Open Letter to My Current Comrades)," in *Visions of Excess*, 93.

15. Friedrich Schlegel, Fragment 579, *Kritische Friedrich-Schlegel-Ausgabe*, ed. Ernst Behler, vol. 16: *Schriften aus dem Nachlaß: Fragmente zur Poesie und Literatur, Erster Teil*, ed. Hans Eichner (Paderborn: Schöningh, 1981), 133.

16. Kafka, *Das Schloß*, 293.

17. Kafka, *Das Schloß*, 138.

18. Theodor Fontane, "Unsere lyrische und epische Poesie seit 1848," in *Sämtliche Werke*, Edgar Groß, Kurt Schreinert et al. 24 vols. (Munich: Nymphenburger Verlagshandlung, 1959–75), 21.1:12.

19. Thus Fontane: "The world is tired of speculation and demands that 'fresh green field' that lay so near and yet so far." "Unsere lyrische und epische Poesie," 21.1:8.

20. Roland Barthes, "The Reality Effect," in *The Rustle of Language*, trans. Richard Howard (Berkeley: University of California Press, 1989), 147.

21. Jean-Paul Sartre, *Nausea*, trans. Lloyd Alexander (New York: New Directions, 2007), 127.

22. "I perceive the thing, the object of nature, the tree there in the garden. . . . If we now carry out the phenomenological reduction, every transcendent setting . . . receives its suspending bracket, . . . we allow no judgment that makes any use of the affirmation that posits a 'real' thing or 'transcendent' nature as a whole, or 'co-operates' in setting up these positions." Edmund Husserl, *Ideas: General Introduction to a Pure Phenomenology*, trans. W. R. Boyce Gibson (London: Routledge, 2002), §90, 189–90.

23. Edmund Husserl, *Logical Investigations*, vol. 1, trans. J. N. Findlay, ed. Dermot Moran (London: Routledge, 2001), 168.

24. Sartre, *Nausea*, 127.

25. Sartre, *Nausea*, 127.

26. Emmanuel Levinas, *Totality and Infinity: An Essay on Exteriority*, trans. Alphonso Lingis (Pittsburgh: Duquesne University Press, 1969), 256.

27. Jacques Lacan, "Variations on the Standard Treatment," in *Écrits*, trans. Bruce Fink (New York: W. W. Norton, 2006), 298.

28. Slavoj Žižek, *Looking Awry: An Introduction to Jacques Lacan through Popular Culture* (Cambridge, Mass.: MIT Press, 1991), 146.

29. Jean Baudrillard, *Fatal Strategies*, trans. Philippe Beitchman and W. G. J. Niesluchowski (Los Angeles: Semiotext(e), 2008), 84–85. Baudrillard acknowledges his debt to Sartre at the beginning of *Passwords*, trans. Chris Turner (London: Verso, 2003), 3–4.

30. See Schiller, "On Grace and Dignity," 126; "Über Anmut und Würde," 334.

WORKS CITED

Achinger, Christine. *Gespaltene Moderne: Gustav Freytags "Soll und Haben." Nation, Geschlecht und Judenbild*. Würzburg: Königshausen & Neumann, 2007.

———. "'Prosa der Verhältnisse' und Poesie der Ware: Versöhnte Moderne und Realismus in *Soll und Haben*." In *150 Jahre "Soll und Haben": Studien zu Gustav Freytags kontroversem Roman*, edited by Florian Krobb, 67–86. Würzburg: Königshausen & Neumann, 2005.

Adams, Marion. *Gottfried Benn's Critique of Substance*. Assen: Van Gorcum & Co., 1969.

Adorno, Theodor W. *Aesthetic Theory*. Translated by Robert Hullot-Kentor. Minneapolis: University of Minnesota Press, 1997.

Agamben, Giorgio. "In Praise of Profanation." In *Profanations*, translated by Jeff Fort, 73–92. New York: Zone Books, 2007.

———. "Nudity." In *Nudities*, translated by David Kishik and Stefan Pedatella, 55–90. Stanford, Calif.: Stanford University Press, 2015.

———. *Stanzas: Word and Phantasm in Western Culture*. Translated by Ronald L. Martinez. Minneapolis: University of Minnesota Press, 1993.

Alt, Peter-André. "Doppelte Schrift, Unterbrechung und Grenze: Franz Kafkas Poetik des Unsagbaren im Kontext der Sprachskepsis um 1900." *Jahrbuch der deutschen Schillergesellschaft* 29 (1985): 455–90.

———. *Von der Schönheit zerbrechender Ordnungen: Körper, Politik und Geschlecht in der Literatur des 17. Jahrhunderts*. Göttingen: Wallstein, 2007.

Anderson, Mark M. *Kafka's Clothes: Ornament and Aestheticism in the Habsburg Fin de Siècle*. Oxford: Clarendon Press, 1992.

Apter, Emily. *Feminizing the Fetish: Psychoanalysis and Narrative Obsession in Turn-of-the-Century France*. Ithaca, N.Y.: Cornell University Press, 1991.

Apter, Emily, and William Pietz, eds. *Fetishism as Cultural Discourse*. Ithaca, N.Y.: Cornell University Press, 1993.

Aristotle. *Physics: A Guided Study*. Translated by Joe Sachs. New Brunswick, N.J.: Rutgers University Press, 1995.

Arndt, Christiane. *Abschied von der Wirklichkeit: Probleme bei der Darstellung von Realität im deutschsprachigen literarischen Realismus*. Freiburg im Breisgau: Rombach, 2009.

Arndt, Christiane, and Silke Brodersen, eds. *Organismus und Gesellschaft: Der Körper in der deutschsprachigen Literatur des Realismus (1830–1930)*. Bielefeld: Transcript, 2011.

Arnold-De Simine, Silke. "Musealisierungsphänomene im Werk Adalbert Stifters." In *Ordnung—Raum—Ritual: Adalbert Stifters artifizieller Realismus*, edited by Sabina Becker and Katharina Grätz, 41–67. Heidelberg: Winter, 2007.

Ashton, E. B. Introduction to Gottfried Benn, *Primal Vision: Selected Writings*, edited by E. B. Ashton, vii–xxvi. New York: New Directions, 1971.

Auerbach, Erich. *Mimesis: The Representation of Reality in Western Literature*. Translated by Willard R. Trask. Princeton, N.J.: Princeton University Press, 1953.

Augustine. "On Marriage and Concupiscence." In *A Select Library of the Nicene and Post-Nicene Fathers of the Christian Church*, vol. 5: *Saint Augustin: Anti-Pelagian Writings*, edited by Philip Schaff, 257–308. Grand Rapids: Eerdmans, 1956.

Aurnhammer, Achim. "Inszenierung der Moderne im Traditionsbruch: Die lyrischen Anfänge von Benn und Brecht." In *Gottfried Benn, Bertold Brecht: Das Janusgesicht der Moderne*, edited by Achim Aurnhammer, 49–70. Würzburg: Ergon-Verlag, 2009.

Aus der Au, Carmen. *Theodor Fontane als Kunstkritiker*. Berlin: De Gruyter, 2017.

Aust, Hugo. *Theodor Fontane: "Verklärung." Eine Untersuchung zum Ideengehalt seiner Werke*. Bonn: Bouvier, 1974.

Axer, Eva. "'Zwischen Alt und Neu': Arno Holz's *Buch der Zeit* and his Concept of 'soziale Lyrik.'" In *Protest and Reform in the German Literature and Art of Modernity, 1871–1918*, edited by Godela Weiss-Sussex and Charlotte Woodford, 135–47. Munich: iudicium, 2014.

Bakhtin, Mikhail. *Rabelais and His World*. Translated by Hélène Iswolsky. Bloomington: Indiana University Press, 1984.

Bance, Alan. *Theodor Fontane: The Major Novels*. Cambridge: Cambridge University Press, 1982.

Barish, Jonas A. *The Antitheatrical Prejudice*. Berkeley: University of California Press, 1981.

Bartels, Adolf. "Die Ziele der gegenwärtigen Litteraturbewegung in Deutschland." *Die Grenzboten: Zeitschrift für Politik, Litteratur und Kunst* 52, no. 4 (1893): 131–38.

Barthes, Roland. "Objective Literature." In *Critical Essays*, translated by Richard Howard, 13–24. Evanston, Ill.: Northwestern University Press, 1972.

———. "The Reality Effect." In *The Rustle of Language*, translated by Richard Howard, 141–48. Berkeley: University of California Press, 1989.

Baßler, Moritz. *Deutsche Erzählprosa 1850–1950: Eine Geschichte literarischer Verfahren*. Berlin: Schmidt, 2015.

Bataille, Georges. "Formless." In *Visions of Excess: Selected Writings, 1927–1939*, edited and translated by Allan Stoekl, 31. Minneapolis: University of Minnesota Press, 1985.

———. "Materialism." In *Visions of Excess: Selected Writings, 1927–1939*, edited and translated by Allan Stoekl, 15–16. Minneapolis: University of Minnesota Press, 1985.

———. "The Use Value of D. A. F. de Sade (An Open Letter to My Current Comrades)." In *Visions of Excess: Selected Writings, 1927–1939*, edited and translated by Allan Stoekl, 91–102. Minneapolis: University of Minnesota Press, 1985.

Baudrillard, Jean. *Fatal Strategies*. Translated by Philippe Beitchman and W. G. J. Niesluchowski. Los Angeles: Semiotext(e), 2008.

———. *Passwords*. Translated by Chris Turner. London: Verso, 2003.

———. *Seduction*. Translated by Brian Singer. New York: St. Martin's, 1990.

Bauks, Michaela. "Nacktheit und Scham in Genesis 2–3." In *Zur Kulturgeschichte der Scham*, edited by Michaela Bauks and Martin F. Meyer, 17–34. Hamburg: Meiner, 2011.

Becker, Sabina. *Bürgerlicher Realismus: Literatur und Kultur im bürgerlichen Zeitalter. 1848–1900*. Tübingen: Francke, 2003.

———. "Nachsommerliche Sublimationsrituale: Inszenierte Ordnung in Adalbert Stifters *Nachsommer*." In *Ordnung—Raum—Ritual: Adalbert Stifters artifizieller Realismus*, edited by Sabina Becker and Katharina Grätz, 315–38. Heidelberg: Winter, 2007.

Begemann, Christian. *Die Welt der Zeichen: Stifter-Lektüren*. Stuttgart: Metzler, 1995.

Belting, Hans. "Macht und Ohnmacht der Bilder." In *Macht und Ohnmacht der Bilder: Reformatorischer Bildersturm im Kontext der europäischen Geschichte*, edited by Peter Blickle, Andre Holenstein, Heinrich Richard Schmidt, and Franz-Josef Sladeczek, 11–32. Munich: Oldenbourg, 2002.

Benjamin, Walter. "Franz Kafka: On the Tenth Anniversary of his Death." In *Selected Writings*, vol. 2: *1927–1934*, edited by Michael W. Jennings, Howard Eiland, and Gary Smith and translated by Rodney Livingston et al., 794–818. Cambridge, Mass.: Harvard University Press, 1999.

———. "Franz Kafka: Zur zehnten Wiederkehr seines Todestages." In *Gesammelte Schriften*, vol. 2.2: *Aufsätze, Essays, Vorträge*, edited by Rolf Tiedemann and Hermann Schweppenhäuser, 409–38. Frankfurt am Main: Suhrkamp, 1977.

———. *The Origin of German Tragic Drama*. Translated by John Osborne. London: Verso, 1998.

———. "Stifter." In *Gesammelte Schriften*, vol. 2.2: *Aufsätze, Essays, Vorträge*, edited by Rolf Tiedemann and Hermann Schweppenhäuser, 608–10. Frankfurt am Main: Suhrkamp, 1977.

———. "Stifter." In *Selected Writings*, vol. 1: *1913–1926*, edited by Marcus Bullock and Michael W. Jennings, 109–13. Cambridge, Mass.: Harvard University Press, 1996.

Benn, Gottfried. *Sämtliche Werke*. Edited by Gerhard Schuster. 7 vols. Stuttgart: Klett-Cotta, 1986–2003.

Bennett, Jane. *Vibrant Matter: A Political Ecology of Things*. Durham, N.C.: Duke University Press, 2010.

Benson, Peter. "Entering *The Castle*." *Journal of Narrative Technique* 23, no. 3 (Spring 1993): 80–91.

Benthien, Claudia. *Barockes Schweigen: Rhetorik und Performativität des Sprachlosen im 17. Jahrhundert*. Munich: Fink, 2006.

Bergson, Henri. *Laughter: An Essay on the Meaning of the Comic*. Translated by Cloudesely Brereton and Fred Rothwell. Rockville, Md.: Arc Manor, 2008.

Berman, Russell A. *The Rise of the Modern German Novel: Crisis and Charisma*. Cambridge, Mass.: Harvard University Press, 1986.

Bernheimer, Charles. *Flaubert and Kafka: Studies in Psychopoetic Structure*. New Haven, Conn.: Yale University Press, 1982.

Besançon, Alain. *The Forbidden Image: An Intellectual History of Iconoclasm*. Translated by Jane Marie Todd. Chicago: University of Chicago Press, 2000.

Beutel, Eckart. *Fontane und die Religion: Neuzeitliches Christentum in Beziehungsfeld von Tradition und Individuation*. Gütersloh: Kaiser/Gütersloher Verlagshaus, 2003.

Bischoff, Doerte. *Poetischer Fetischismus: Der Kult der Dinge im 19. Jahrhundert*. Munich: Fink, 2013.

Bittner, Michael. *Die Emanzipation des Fleisches und ihre Gegner*. Dresden: Thelem, 2016.

Blanchot, Maurice. *The Infinite Conversation*. Translated by Susan Hanson. Minneapolis: University of Minnesota Press, 1993.

Blankenship, Janelle. "Arno Holz vs. Thomas Mann: Modernist Media Fantasies." *Modernist Cultures* 1, no. 2 (Winter 2005): 72–109.

Blumenberg, Hans. "The Concept of Reality and the Possibility of the Novel." In *New Perspectives in German Literary Criticism*, edited by Richard E. Amacher and Victor Lange, 29–48. Princeton, N.J.: Princeton University Press, 1979.

Boa, Elizabeth. *Kafka: Gender, Class, and Race in the Letters and Fictions*. Oxford: Clarendon Press, 1996.

Böhme, Hartmut. "Erotische Anatomie: Körperfragmentierung als ästhetisches Verfahren in Renaissance und Barock." In *Körperteile: Eine kulturelle Anatomie*, edited by Claudia Benthien and Christoph Wulf, 228–53. Reinbek bei Hamburg: Rowohlt, 2001.

———. *Fetischismus und Kultur: Eine andere Geschichte der Moderne*. Reinbek bei Hamburg: Rowohlt, 2006.

Bölsche, Wilhelm. *Die naturwissenschaftlichen Grundlagen der Poesie: Prolegomena einer realistischen Ästhetik*. Edited by Johannes J. Braakenburg. Tübingen: Niemeyer, 1976.

Boscagli, Maurizia. *Stuff Theory: Everyday Objects, Radical Materialism*. New York: Bloomsbury, 2014.

Böschenstein, Bernhard. "Religiosität in Fontanes Verhältnis zur bildenden Kunst?" In *Religion als Relikt? Christliche Traditionen im Werk Fontanes*, edited by Hanna Delf von Wolzogen and Hubertus Fischer, 15–28. Würzburg: Königshausen & Neumann, 2006.

Böttcher, Philipp. *Gustav Freytag—Konstellationen des Realismus*. Berlin: De Gruyter, 2018.

Bowman, Peter James. "Fontane and the Programmatic Realists: Contrasting Theories of the Novel." *Modern Language Review* 103, no. 1 (January 2008): 129–42.

Bräutigam, Bernd. "Candide im Comptoir: Zur Bedeutung der Poesie in Gustav Freytags 'Soll und Haben.' " *Germanistisch-Romanische Monatsschrift* 35, no. 4 (1985): 395–411.

Bredekamp, Horst. *Kunst als Medium sozialer Konflikte: Bilderkämpfe von der Spätantike bis zur Hussitenrevolution*. Frankfurt am Main: Suhrkamp, 1975.

Brinkmann, Richard. *Theodor Fontane: Über die Verbindlichkeit des Unverbindlichen*. Tübingen: Niemeyer, 1977.

———. *Wirklichkeit und Illusion: Studien über Gehalt und Grenzen des Begriffs Realismus für die erzählende Dichtung des neunzehnten Jahrhunderts*. Tübingen: Niemeyer, 1957.

Brod, Max. "Eine Bemerkung zu Kafkas 'Schloß.' " In *Über Franz Kafka*, 371–74. Frankfurt am Main: Fischer, 1966.

———. "Nachwort." In Franz Kafka, *Das Schloß*, 492–504. Munich: Wolff, 1926.
Bronfen, Elisabeth. *Over Her Dead Body: Death, Femininity and the Aesthetic.* Manchester: Manchester University Press, 1992.
Brooks, Peter. *Realist Vision*. New Haven, Conn.: Yale University Press, 2005.
Brunetière, F. "La banqueroute du naturalisme." *Revue des deux mondes* 57, no. 83 (September 1, 1887): 213–24.
Burgard, Peter J. "Dead Metaphor Society? From Opitz to Hoffmannswaldau." *Neophilologus* 93, no. 2 (April 2009): 295–310.
Burns, Rob. *The Quest for Modernity: The Place of Arno Holz in Modern German Literature*. Frankfurt am Main: Lang, 1981.
Butler, Judith. *Bodies That Matter: On the Discursive Limits of Sex*. London: Routledge, 1993.
Calhoon, Kenneth S. *Affecting Grace: Theater, Subject, and the Shakespearean Paradox in German Literature from Lessing to Kleist*. Toronto: University of Toronto Press, 2013.
Calvin, John. *Institutes of the Christian Religion*, vol. 1. Translated by John Allen. New Haven, Conn.: Howe, 1816.
Campbell, Karen J. "Kafka's *Schloß* and the Subversion of Plot." *Journal of English and Germanic Philology* 85, no. 3 (July 1986): 386–403.
Chambers, Helen Elizabeth. *Supernatural and Irrational Elements in the Works of Theodor Fontane*. Stuttgart: Akademischer Verlag Hans-Dieter Heinz, 1980.
Chitnis, Rajendra A. "Putting Granny in a Home: Czech Writers and the Village in Kafka's Lifetime." In *Kafka, Prag und der Erste Weltkrieg / Kafka, Prague and the First World War*, edited by Manfred Engel and Ritchie Robertson, 107–25. Würzburg: Königshausen & Neumann, 2012.
Coetzee, J. M. *Elizabeth Costello*. New York: Penguin, 2004.
———. "The Harms of Pornography: Catharine MacKinnon." In *Giving Offense: Essays on Censorship*, 61–82. Chicago: University of Chicago Press, 1996.
Coppoletta, Friedmar. "*Und er bückte sich wieder und schrieb auf die Erde*": *Theodor Fontanes zunehmende Differenzierung der Bibel in seinem Romanwerk*. Potsdam: Universitätsverlag Potsdam, 2017.
Corngold, Stanley. *Lambent Traces: Franz Kafka*. Princeton, N.J.: Princeton University Press, 2004.
———. "Ritardando in *Das Schloß*." In *From Kafka to Sebald: Modernism and Narrative Form*, edited by Sabine Wilke, 11–26. New York: Continuum, 2012.
Corngold, Stanley, and Benno Wagner. "The Ministry of Writing (*The Castle*)." In *Franz Kafka: The Ghosts in the Machine*, 109–30. Evanston, Ill.: Northwestern University Press, 2011.
Cramer, Sabine. "*Grete Minde*: Structures of Social Disturbance." In *New Approaches to Theodor Fontane: Cultural Codes in Flux*, edited by Marion Doebeling, 136–57. Rochester, N.Y.: Camden House, 2000.
Crignon, Philippe. "Figuration: Emmanuel Levinas and the Image." Translated by Nicole Simek and Zahi Zalloua. *Yale French Studies* 104 (2004): 100–125.
Culler, Jonathan. *The Pursuit of Signs: Semiotics, Literature, Deconstruction*. Ithaca, N.Y.: Cornell University Press, 1981.
Däther, W. *Der Prozeß gegen Margarete Minden und Genossen: Ein dunkles Kapitel Tangermünder Stadtgeschichte*. Tangermünde: Friedrich Becker und Sohn, 1927.

Daub, Adrian. "The Ob-scene of the Total Work of Art: Frank Wedekind, Richard Strauss, and the Spectacle of Dance." *19th-Century Music* 39, no. 3 (Spring 2016): 272–89.

Davison, Carol Margaret. *Anti-Semitism and British Gothic Literature*. Basingstoke, U.K.: Palgrave, 2004.

DeJean, Joan. *The Reinvention of Obscenity: Sex, Lies, and Tabloids in Early Modern France*. Chicago: University of Chicago Press, 2002.

Deleuze, Gilles, and Félix Guattari. *Kafka: Toward a Minor Literature*. Translated by Dana Polan. Minneapolis: University of Minneapolis Press, 1986.

Delf von Wolzogen, Hanna, and Hubertus Fischer, eds. *Religion als Relikt? Christliche Traditionen im Werk Fontanes*. Würzburg: Königshausen & Neumann, 2006.

Delius, F. C. *Der Held und sein Wetter: Ein Kunstmittel und sein ideologischer Gebrauch im Roman des bürgerlichen Realismus*. Munich: Hanser, 1971.

de Man, Paul. "Anthropomorphism and Trope in the Lyric." In *The Rhetoric of Romanticism*, 239–62. New York: Columbia University Press, 1984.

Demetz, Peter. *Formen des Realismus: Theodor Fontane. Kritische Untersuchungen*. Munich: Hanser, 1964.

———. "Zur Definition des Realismus." In *Bürgerlicher Realismus: Grundlagen und Interpretationen*, edited by Klaus-Detlef Müller, 27–38. Königstein: Athenäum, 1981.

Derrida, Jacques. "Parergon." In *The Truth in Painting*, translated by Geoff Bennington and Ian McLeod, 16–147. Chicago: University of Chicago Press, 1987.

———. "Restitutions of the Truth in Pointing." In *The Truth in Painting*, translated by Geoff Bennington and Ian McLeod, 255–382. Chicago: University of Chicago Press, 1987.

———. "The Theater of Cruelty and the Closure of Representation." In *Writing and Difference*, translated by Alan Bass, 232–50. Chicago: University of Chicago Press, 1978.

Dierick, Augustinus P. *Gottfried Benn and His Critics: Major Interpretations, 1912–1922*. Columbia, S.C.: Camden House, 1992.

Döblin, Alfred. Introduction to *Verschollene und Vergessene: Arno Holz, Die Revolution der Lyrik. Eine Einführung in sein Werk und eine Auswahl*, 5–25. Wiesbaden: Steiner, 1951.

Dolar, Mladen. *A Voice and Nothing More*. Cambridge, Mass.: MIT Press, 2006.

Doppler, Alfred. "Hebbel und Stifter—Gegensätze und Gemeinsamkeiten." *Vierteljahresschrift des Adalbert-Stifter-Instituts des Landes Österreich* 34, nos. 1–2 (1985): 27–33.

Dore, Florence. *The Novel and the Obscene: Sexual Subjects in American Modernism*. Stanford, Calif.: Stanford University Press, 2005.

Douglas, Mary. *Purity and Danger: An Analysis of Concepts of Pollution and Taboo*. London: Routledge, 2002.

Downing, Eric. *The Chain of Things: Divinatory Magic and the Practice of Reading in German Literature and Thought, 1850–1940*. Ithaca, N.Y.: Cornell University Press, 2018.

———. *Double Exposures: Repetition and Realism in Nineteenth-Century German Fiction*. Stanford, Calif.: Stanford University Press, 2000.

Drux, Rudolf. "Über das anatomische Verfahren der Körperdarstellung in barocken 'Sprachgemälden': Am Beispiel der dekonstruierten Geliebten." *Deutsche Vierteljahrsschrift für Literaturwissenschaft und Geistesgeschichte* 83, no. 1 (March 2009): 88–102.

du Bois-Reymond, Emil. *Über die Grenzen des Naturerkennens: Ein Vortrag in der zweiten öffentlichen Sitzung der 45. Versammlung deutscher Naturforscher und Ärzte zu Leipzig am 14. August 1872*. Leipzig: Veit & Co., 1876.

Duttlinger, Carolin. *Kafka and Photography*. Oxford: Oxford University Press, 2007.

Dyck, Joachim. "Requiem—Es gibt keine Hoffnung jenseits des Nichts." In *Gedichte von Gottfried Benn*, edited by Harald Steinhagen, 13–18. Stuttgart: Reclam, 1997.

Eicher, Thomas. "Poesie, Poetisierung und Poetizität in Gustav Freytags *Soll und Haben*." *Wirkendes Wort* 45, no. 1 (1995): 64–81.

Eire, Carlos M. N. *War against the Idols: The Reformation of Worship from Erasmus to Calvin*. Cambridge: Cambridge University Press, 1986.

Emrich, Wilhelm. "Arno Holz und die moderne Kunst." In Arno Holz, *Werke*, 7:453–71. First published in Wilhelm Emrich, *Protest und Verheißung: Studien zur klassischen und modernen Dichtung*, 155–68. Frankfurt am Main: Athenäum, 1960.

Engel, Manfred. "Franz Kafka: *Das Schloss*." In *Klassiker: Neu-Lektüren*, edited by Ralf Georg Bogner and Manfred Leber, 177–95. Saarbrucken: Universaar, 2013.

Enzinger, Moriz. *Adalbert Stifters Studienjahre (1818–1830)*. Innsbruck: Österreichische Verlagsanstalt, 1950.

Eschenbacher, Walter. *Fritz Mauthner und die deutsche Literatur um 1900: Eine Untersuchung zur Sprachkrise der Jahrhundertwende*. Frankfurt am Main: Lang, 1977.

"Das Evangelium des Naturalismus." *Die Grenzboten: Zeitschrift für Politik, Litteratur und Kunst* 50, no. 3 (1891): 34–44.

Faber, Richard. "*. . . der hebe den ersten Stein auf sie*": *Humanität, Politik und Religion bei Theodor Fontane*. Würzburg: Königshausen & Neumann, 2012.

Fauser, Markus. "Die Kulturbedeutung des Alten in Adalbert Stifters *Studien*." In *Ordnung—Raum—Ritual: Adalbert Stifters artifizieller Realismus*, edited by Sabina Becker and Katharina Grätz, 17–40. Heidelberg: Winter, 2007.

Fenves, Peter. "The Kafka-Werfel-Einstein Effect." In Max Brod, *Tycho Brahe's Path to God*, translated by Felix Warren Crosse, vii–lviii. Evanston, Ill.: Northwestern University Press, 2007.

———. "Die Scham der Schönheit: Einige Bemerkungen zu Stifter." In *"geteilte Aufmerksamkeit": Zur Frage des Lesens*, edited by Thomas Schestag, 91–111. Frankfurt am Main: Lang, 1997.

Ferenczi, Sándor. "On Obscene Words." In *Sex in Psychoanalysis*, 132–53. New York: Brunner, 1950.

Fick, Monika. "'Komm, Schöpfer Tod': Zum Verhältnis von Biologie und Dichtung bei Gottfried Benn." *Deutsche Vierteljahrsschrift für Literaturwissenschaft und Geistesgeschichte* 81, no. 2 (June 2007): 282–314.

Finkelde, Dominik. "Tautologien der Ordnung: Zu einer Poetologie des Sammelns bei Adalbert Stifter." *German Quarterly* 80, no. 1 (Winter 2007): 1–19.

Finkielkraut, Alain. *The Imaginary Jew*. Translated by Kevin O'Neill and David Suchoff. Lincoln: University of Nebraska Press, 1994.

Fleishman, Ian. *An Aesthetics of Injury: The Narrative Wound from Baudelaire to Tarantino*. Evanston, Ill.: Northwestern University Press, 2018.

Fleming, Paul. *Exemplarity and Mediocrity: The Art of the Average from Bourgeois Tragedy to Realism*. Stanford, Calif.: Stanford University Press, 2009.

Fontane, Theodor. *Briefe*, vol. 1: *1833–1866*. Edited by Walter Keitel and Helmuth Nürnberger. Munich: Hanser, 1976.

———. *Briefe*, vol. 2: *1860–1878*. Edited by Walter Keitel and Helmuth Nürnberger. Munich: Hanser, 1979.

———. *Sämtliche Werke*. Edited by Edgar Groß, Kurt Schreinert et al. 24 vols. Munich: Nymphenburger Verlagshandlung, 1959–75.

———. *Schriften zur Literatur*. Berlin: Aufbau, 1960.

Forster, Chris. *Filthy Material: Modernism and the Media of Obscenity*. New York: Oxford University Press, 2019.

Foster, Hal. "Obscene, Abject, Traumatic." *October* 78 (Autumn 1996): 106–24.

———. *The Return of the Real: The Avant-Garde at the End of the Twentieth Century*. Cambridge, Mass.: MIT Press, 1996.

Foucault, Michel. *The Birth of the Clinic: An Archeology of Medical Perception*. Translated by A. M. Sheridan Smith. New York: Pantheon, 1973.

———. *The History of Sexuality*, vol. 1: *An Introduction*. Translated by Robert Hurley. New York: Vintage, 1990.

Frels, Onno. "Zum Verhältnis von Wirklichkeit und künstlerischer Form bei Arno Holz." In *Naturalismus/Ästhetizismus*, edited by Christa Bürger, Peter Bürger, and Jochen Schulte-Sasse, 103–38. Frankfurt am Main: Suhrkamp, 1979.

Freud, Sigmund. "Fetishism." In *The Standard Edition of the Complete Psychological Works of Sigmund Freud*, vol. 21: *1927–1931*, translated by James Strachey, 152–57. London: Hogarth, 1964.

———. *Jokes and Their Relation to the Unconscious*. Translated by James Strachey. New York: W. W. Norton, 1960.

Freymond, Roland. *Der Einfluß von Charles Dickens auf Gustav Freytag: Mit besonderer Berücksichtigung der Romane "David Copperfield" und "Soll und Haben."* Hildesheim: Gerstenberg, 1973.

Freytag, Gustav. "Ein Dank für Charles Dickens." *Die Grenzboten: Zeitschrift für Politik und Literatur* 26, no. 1.2 (1870): 481–84.

———. *Soll und Haben: Roman in sechs Büchern*. Bochum: Manuscriptum, 2007.

Fricke, Thorsten. *Arno Holz und das Theater: Biografie—Werkgeschichte—Interpretation*. Bielefeld: Aisthesis, 2010.

Fried, Michael. *Absorption and Theatricality: Painting and Beholder in the Age of Diderot*. Chicago: University of Chicago Press, 1980.

———. "Art and Objecthood." In *Art and Objecthood: Essays and Reviews*, 148–72. Chicago: University of Chicago Press, 1998.

Gailus, Andreas. "Brains: Forms of Life in Gottfried Benn's Rönne Novellas." *New German Critique* 45, no. 2 (August 2018): 1–32.

Gann, Thomas. *Gehirn und Züchtung: Gottfried Benns psychiatrische Poetik 1910–1933/34*. Bielefeld: Transcript, 2007.

Gelber, Mark H. "An Alternate Reading of the Role of the Jewish Scholar in Gustav Freytag's *Soll und Haben*." *Germanic Review* 58, no. 2 (1983): 83–88.

Geulen, Eva. "Depicting Description: Lukács and Stifter." *Germanic Review* 73, no. 3 (Summer 1998): 267–79.

———. "Tales of a Collector." In *A New History of German Literature*, edited by David E. Wellbery, Judith Ryan, and Hans Ulrich Gumbrecht, 587–92. Cambridge, Mass.: Harvard University Press, 2004.

———. *Worthörig wider Willen: Darstellungsproblematik und Sprachreflexion in der Prosa Adalbert Stifters*. Munich: iudicum, 1992.

Ghanbari, Nacim. *Das Haus: Eine deutsche Literaturgeschichte 1850–1926*. Berlin: De Gruyter, 2011.

Giel, Volker. "*Grete Minde*: Versuch einer Interpretation." *Fontane Blätter* 33 (1982): 69–73.

Gilpin, William. *Observations on the River Wye, and Several Parts of South Wales, &c, Relative Chiefly to Picturesque Beauty: Made in the Summer of the Year 1770*. London: Blamire, 1782.

———. *Three Essays: On Picturesque Beauty; On Picturesque Travel; and On Sketching Landscape: To Which Is Added a Poem, On Landscape Painting*. London: Blamire, 1792.

Globig, Klaus. "Theodor Fontanes 'Grete Minde': Psychologische Studie, Ausdruck des Historismus oder soziopolitischer Apell?" *Fontane Blätter* 32 (1981): 706–13.

Goethe, Johann Wolfgang von. *Faust: Eine Tragödie*. Edited by Albrecht Schöne. In *Sämtliche Werke*, vol. 7.1, edited by Friedmar Apel et al., 9–464. Frankfurt am Main: Deutscher Klassiker Verlag, 1994.

———. "Shakespear und kein Ende!" In *Sämtliche Werke*, vol. 11.2: *Divan-Jahre 1814–1819*, edited by Johannes John et al., 173–81. Munich: Hanser, 1994.

———. "Zum Schäkespears Tag." In *Sämtliche Werke*, vol. 1.2: *Der junge Goethe, 1757–1775*, edited by Gerhard Sauder, 411–14. Munich: Hanser, 1987.

Gombrich, E. H. *Art and Illusion: A Study in the Psychology of Pictorial Representation*. Princeton, N.J.: Princeton University Press, 1960.

Gorsen, Peter. *Das Prinzip Obszön: Kunst, Pornographie und Gesellschaft*. Reinbek bei Hamburg: Rowohlt, 1969.

Graevenitz, Gerhart von. *Theodor Fontane: Ängstliche Moderne. Über das Imaginäre*. Konstanz: Konstanz University Press, 2014.

Greenberg, Clement. "Modernist Painting." In *The Collected Essays and Criticism*, vol. 4: *Modernism with a Vengeance, 1957–1969*, edited by John O'Brian, 85–93. Chicago: University of Chicago Press, 1993.

Grom-Rottmayer, Hermann. "Bühne und Naturalismus." *Merker: Österreichische Zeitschrift für Musik und Theater* 11, nos. 19–20 (October 1, 1920): 474–78.

Grunert, Mark. "Lenore oder die Versuchung des Bürgers: Romantischer 'Zauber' und realistische Ideologie in Gustav Freytags *Soll und Haben*." *Monatshefte* 85, no. 2 (1993): 134–52.

Guarda, Sylvain. "Stifters *Abdias*: Kindheit in ästhetischer Spiegelung." *German Life and Letters* 61, no. 3 (July 2008): 297–310.

———. *Theodor Fontanes "Neben"-werke: "Grete Minde," "Ellernkipp," "Unterm Birnbaum," "Quitt." Ritualisierter Raubmord im Spiegelkreuz*. Würzburg: Königshausen & Neumann, 2004.

Gubser, Martin. *Literarischer Antisemitismus: Untersuchungen zu Gustav Freytag und anderen bürgerlichen Schriftstellern des 19. Jahrhunderts*. Göttingen: Wallstein, 1998.

Gutzkow, Karl. *Wally, die Zweiflerin*. Edited by Günter Heintz. Stuttgart: Reclam, 1979.

Hadot, Pierre. *The Veil of Isis: An Essay on the History of the Idea of Nature*. Translated by Michael Chase. Cambridge, Mass.: Harvard University Press, 2006.

Hahn, Marcus. *Gottfried Benn und das Wissen der Moderne: 1905–1932*. 2 vols. Göttingen: Wallstein, 2011.

Hamacher, Werner. "The Gesture in the Name: On Benjamin and Kafka." In *Premises: Essays on Philosophy from Kant to Celan*, translated by Peter Fenves, 294–336. Cambridge, Mass.: Harvard University Press, 1997.

———. *Pleroma*. Translated by Nicholas Walker and Simon Jarvis. Stanford, Calif.: Stanford University Press, 1998.

Hamilton, John. *Philology of the Flesh*. Chicago: University of Chicago Press, 2018.

Hanna, Christian M., and Friederike Reents, eds. *Benn-Handbuch: Leben—Werk—Wirkung*. Stuttgart: Metzler, 2016.

Hanstein, Adalbert von. *Das jüngste Deutschland: Zwei Jahrzehnte miterlebter Litteraturgeschichte*. Leipzig: Voigtländer, 1901.

Hart, Heinrich. "Die realistische Bewegung: Ihr Ursprung, ihr Wesen, ihr Ziel." *Kritisches Jahrbuch: Beiträge zur Charakteristik der zeitgenössischen Literatur sowie zur Verständigung über den modernen Realismus* 1, no. 1 (1889): 40–56.

Haubach, H. Josef. *Der strafrechtliche Schutz des Schamgefühls*. Würzburg: Memminger, 1917.

Hebbel, Friedrich. "Das Komma im Frack." In *Werke*, vol. 3, edited by Gerhard Fricke, Werner Keller, and Karl Pörnbacher, 684–87. Munich: Hanser, 1965.

———. *Neue Gedichte*. Leipzig: Weber, 1848.

Hegel, G. W. F. *Aesthetics: Lectures on Fine Art*. Translated by T. M. Knox. 2 vols. Oxford: Oxford University Press, 1998.

———. *The Difference between Fichte's and Schelling's System of Philosophy*. Translated by H. S. Harris and Walter Cerf. Albany: State University of New York Press, 1977.

———. *Differenz des Fichteschen und Schellingschen Systems der Philosophie*. In *Werke*, vol. 2: *Jenaer Schriften 1801–1807*, edited by Eva Moldenhauer and Karl Markus Michel, 9–138. Frankfurt am Main: Suhrkamp, 1970.

———. *Vorlesungen über die Ästhetik*. In *Werke*, vols. 13–15, edited by Eva Moldenhauer and Karl Markus Michel. Frankfurt am Main: Suhrkamp, 1970.

Helm, Anna H. *The Intersection of Material and Poetic Economy: Gustav Freytag's "Soll und Haben" and Adalbert Stifter's "Der Nachsommer."* Oxford: Lang, 2009.

Helmrich, Caspar. *Annales Tangermundenses*. In Küster, *Antiquitates Tangermundenses*, 1–64.

Henne, Helmut. *Sprachliche Spur der Moderne in Gedichten um 1900: Nietzsche, Holz, George, Rilke, Morgenstern*. Berlin: De Gruyter, 2010.

Hertling, Gunter H. "Kleists *Michael Kohlhaas* und Fontanes *Grete Minde*: Freiheit und Fügung." *German Quarterly* 40, no. 1 (January 1967): 29–40.

Hertz, Neil. "Medusa's Head: Male Hysteria under Political Pressure." In *The End of the Line*, 199–250. Aurora, Colo.: Davies, 2009.

Heym, Georg. *Dichtungen und Schriften: Gesamtausgabe*, vol. 1: *Lyrik*. Edited by Karl Ludwig Schneider. Hamburg: Ellermann, 1964.

Hnilica, Irmtraud. *Im Zauberkreis der großen Waage: Die Romantisierung des bürgerlichen Kaufmanns in Gustav Freytags "Soll und Haben."* Heidelberg: Synchron, 2012.

Hochreiter, Susanne. *Franz Kafka: Raum und Geschlecht*. Würzburg: Königshausen & Neumann, 2007.

Höcker, Arne. "Brainless: Scientific Observation and Literary Writing in Gottfried Benn." *Monatshefte* 105, no. 3 (Fall 2013): 458–71.

———. *Epistemologie des Extremen: Lustmord in Kriminologie und Literatur um 1900*. Munich: Fink, 2012.

Hoffmann, Christoph. "In der Prosektur: zwischen B. und Benn." In *". . . im Trunk der Augen": Gottfried Benn—Arzt und Dichter in der Pathologie Westend*, edited by Anne Marie Freybourg and Ernst Kraas, 35–44. Göttingen: Wallstein, 2008.

Hoffmann, Nora. *Photographie, Malerei und visuelle Wahrnehmung bei Theodor Fontane*. Berlin: De Gruyter, 2011.

Hofmannsthal, Hugo von. "Ein Brief." In *Sämtliche Werke*, vol. 31: *Erfundene Gespräche und Briefe*, edited by Ellen Ritter, 45–55. Frankfurt am Main: Fischer, 1991.

Hohendahl, Peter Uwe, ed. *Benn—Wirkung wider Willen. Dokumente zur Wirkungsgeschichte Benns*. Frankfurt am Main: Athenäum, 1971.

———. Introduction to *Benn—Wirkung wider Willen*, 13–86.

———. "The Loss of Reality: Gottfried Benn's Early Prose." In *Modernity and the Text: Revisions of German Modernism*, edited by Andreas Huyssen and David Bathrick, 81–94. New York: Columbia University Press, 1989.

Holmes, Tove. "'. . . was ich in diesem Hause geworden bin': Adalbert Stifter's Visual Curriculum." *Zeitschrift für deutsche Philologie* 129, no. 4 (2010): 559–78.

Holub, Robert. *Reflections of Realism: Paradox, Norm, and Ideology in Nineteenth-Century German Prose*. Detroit: Wayne State University Press, 1991.

Holz, Arno. *Briefe: Eine Auswahl*. Edited by Anita Holz and Max Wagner. Munich: Piper & Co., 1948.

———. *Werke*. Edited by Wilhelm Emrich and Anita Holz. 7 vols. Neuwied am Rhein: Luchterhand, 1961–64.

———. *Das Werk von Arno Holz: Monumental-Ausgabe in zwölf Bänden*, vol. 10: *Die Neue Wortkunst: Eine Zusammenfassung ihrer ersten grundlegenden Dokumente*. Edited by Hans W. Fischer. Berlin: Dietz, 1925.

Holz, Arno, and Johannes Schlaf. *Neue Gleise*. Berlin: Fontane & Co., 1892.

Horn, Anette, and Peter Horn. *Was aber neu ist, ist die Frage nach dem Satzbau: Die Gedichte Gottfried Benns*. Oberhausen: Athena, 2017.

Hsu, Linda C. "*Klamotten*: Reading Nietzsche Reading Kafka." *German Quarterly* 67, no. 2 (Spring 1994): 211–21.

Hückmann, Dania. *Rache im Realismus: Recht und Rechtsgefühl bei Droste-Hülshoff, Gotthelf, Fontane und Heyse*. Bielefeld: Transcript, 2018.

Hüffmeier, Wilhelm. "'Alles ist Gnade': Beobachtungen zu Kirche und Theologie bei Theodor Fontane." *Zeitschrift für Theologie und Kirche* 95, no. 2 (June 1998): 250–76.

———. "'Was ist, ist durch Vorherbestimmen': Spuren Calvins bei Theodor Fontane." *Zeitschrift für Theologie und Kirche* 107, no. 2 (June 2010): 239–60.

Hunfeld, Barbara. "Zeichen als Dinge bei Stifter, Keller und Raabe: Ironisierung von Repräsentation als Selbstkritik des Realismus." In Schneider and Hunfeld, *Die Dinge und die Zeichen*, 123–41.

Hunt, Lynn. Introduction to *The Invention of Pornography: Obscenity and the Origins of Modernity, 1500–1800*, edited by Lynn Hunt, 9–45. New York: Zone Books, 1996.

———, ed. *The Invention of Pornography: Obscenity and the Origins of Modernity, 1500–1800*. New York: Zone Books, 1996.

Husserl, Edmund. *The Idea of Phenomenology*. Translated by William P. Alston and George Nakhnikian. The Hague: Martinus Nijhoff, 1964.

———. *Ideas: General Introduction to a Pure Phenomenology*. Translated by W. R. Boyce Gibson. London: Routledge, 2002.

———. *Logical Investigations*, vol. 1. Edited by Dermot Moran and translated by J. N. Findlay. London: Routledge, 2001.

Huyssen, Andreas. "Benn in Occupied Brussels: The Rönne Novellas." In *Miniature Metropolis: Literature in an Age of Photography and Film*, 84–117. Cambridge, Mass.: Harvard University Press, 2015.

Ireton, Sean. "Between Dirty and Disruptive Nature: Adalbert Stifter in the Context of Nineteenth-Century American Environmental Literature." *Colloquia Germanica* 44, no. 2 (2011): 149–71.

Jameson, Fredric. *The Antinomies of Realism*. London: Verso, 2013.

Japp, Uwe. "Die Signifikation des Ästhetischen im Raum des Realen bei Adalbert Stifter." In Schneider and Hunfeld, *Die Dinge und die Zeichen*, 95–105.

Jay, Martin. *Downcast Eyes: The Denigration of Vision in Twentieth-Century French Thought*. Berkeley: University of California Press, 1993.

Jensen, Birgit A. *Auf der morschen Gartenschaukel: Kindheit als Problem bei Theodor Fontane*. Amsterdam: Rodopi, 1998.

Jeong, Hang-Kyun. *Dialogische Offenheit: Eine Studie zum Erzählwerk Theodor Fontanes*. Würzburg: Königshausen & Neumann, 2001.

Johnson, Barbara. *Persons and Things*. Cambridge, Mass.: Harvard University Press, 2008.

Jordanova, Ludmilla. *Sexual Visions: Images of Gender in Science and Medicine between the Eighteenth and Twentieth Centuries*. Madison: University of Wisconsin Press, 1989.

Kafka, Franz. *Schriften—Tagebücher: Kritische Ausgabe*. Edited by Jürgen Born, Gerhard Neumann, Malcolm Pasley, and Jost Schillemeit. 15 vols. Frankfurt am Main: Fischer, 2002.

Kant, Immanuel. *Critique of the Power of Judgment*. Translated by Paul Guyer and Eric Matthews. New York: Cambridge University Press, 2000.

Karlstadt, Andreas. "On the Removal of Images." In *A Reformation Debate: Karlstadt, Emser, and Eck on Sacred Images. Three Treatises in Translation*, translated by Bryan D. Mangrum and Giuseppe Scavizzi, 19–39. Ottawa: Dovehouse, 1991.

———. "Von Abtuhung der Bilder." In *Kleine Texte für theologische und philologische Vorlesungen und Übungen*, vol. 74, edited by Hans Lietzmann, 1–22. Bonn: Marcus und Weber, 1911.

Kehoe, Sean. "Cervical and Endometrial Cancer during Pregnancy." In *Cancer and Pregnancy: Recent Results in Cancer Research*, vol. 178, edited by A. Surbone, F. Peccatori, and N. Pavlidis, 69–74. Berlin: Springer, 2008.

Kendrick, Walter. *The Secret Museum: Pornography in Modern Culture*. Berkeley: University of California Press, 1987.

Kilcher, Andreas, and Detlef Kremer. "Die Genealogie der Schrift: Eine transtextuelle Lektüre von Kafkas *Bericht für eine Akademie*." In *Textverkehr: Franz Kafka und die Tradition*, edited by Claudia Liebrand and Franziska Schößler, 45–72. Würzburg: Königshausen & Neumann, 2004.

Kirchdörfer-Boßmann, Ursula. *"Eine Pranke in den Nacken der Erkenntnis": Zur Beziehung von Dichtung und Naturwissenschaft im Frühwerk Gottfried Benns*. St. Ingbert: Röhrig, 2003.

Kittler, Friedrich. *Discourse Networks 1800/1900*. Translated by Michael Metteer. Stanford, Calif.: Stanford University Press, 1900.

Kittstein, Ulrich. "Vom Zwang poetischer Ordnung: Die Rolle der jüdischen Figuren in Gustav Freytags *Soll und Haben* und Wilhelm Raabes *Der Hungerpastor*." In *Poetische Ordnungen: Zur Erzählprosa des deutschen Realismus*, edited by Ulrich Kittstein and Stefani Kugler, 61–92. Würzburg: Königshausen & Neumann, 2007.

Kleiner, Gerd. "Anmut/Grazie." In *Ästhetische Grundbegriffe: Historisches Wörterbuch*, vol. 1, edited by Karlheinz Barck et al., 193–208. Stuttgart: Metzler, 2010.

Kleinwort, Malte. *Der späte Kafka: Spätstil als Stilsuspension*. Munich: Fink, 2013.

Kleist, Heinrich von. "Über das Marionettentheater." In *Sämtliche Werke und Briefe*, vol. 2, edited by Helmut Sembdner, 338–45. Frankfurt am Main: Deutscher Taschenbuch Verlag, 2008.

Kopp, Kristin. *Germany's Wild East: Constructing Poland as Colonial Space*. Ann Arbor: University of Michigan Press, 2012.

Koppenfels, Martin von. *Immune Erzähler: Flaubert und die Affektpolitik des modernen Romans*. Munich: Fink, 2007.

Kornbluh, Anna. *The Order of Forms: Realism, Formalism, and Social Space*. Chicago: University of Chicago Press, 2019.

Kreienbrock, Jörg. *Malicious Objects, Anger Management, and the Question of Modern Literature*. New York: Fordham University Press, 2013.

Kremer, Detlef. *Kafka: Die Erotik des Schreibens*. Mainz: Philo, 1998.

Kristeva, Julia. *Powers of Horror*. Translated by Leon S. Roudiez. New York: Columbia University Press, 1982.

Küster, Georg Gottfried. *Antiquitates Tangermundenses*. Berlin: Auctor, 1729.

———. *Tangermündische Denkwürdigkeiten*. In Küster, *Antiquitates Tangermundenses*, 1–195.

Lacan, Jacques. "The Signification of the Phallus." In *Écrits*, translated by Bruce Fink, 575–84. New York: W. W. Norton, 2006.

———. "Variations on the Standard Treatment." In *Écrits*, translated by Bruce Fink, 269–302. New York: W. W. Norton, 2006.

Ladenson, Elisabeth. *Dirt for Art's Sake: Books on Trial from "Madame Bovary" to "Lolita."* Ithaca, N.Y.: Cornell University Press, 2007.

Lasker-Schüler, Else. "Doktor Benn." In Hohendahl, *Benn—Wirkung wider Willen*, 98.

Lawrence, D. H. *Pornography and Obscenity*. London: Faber & Faber, 1929.

Leitner, Ingrid. *Sprachliche Archaisierung: Historisch-typologische Untersuchung zur deutschen Literatur des 19. Jahrhunderts*. Frankfurt am Main: Lang, 1978.

Lenz, J. M. R. *Anmerkungen übers Theater*. In *Werke und Schriften*, vol. 1, edited by Britta Titel and Hellmut Haug, 325–62. Darmstadt: Wissenschaftliche Buchgesellschaft, 1966.

Leonard, Sarah L. *Fragile Minds and Vulnerable Souls: The Matter of Obscenity in Nineteenth-Century Germany*. Philadelphia: University of Pennsylvania Press, 2015.

Le Rider, Jacques. *Fritz Mauthner: Scepticisme linguistique et modernité*. Paris: Bartillat, 2012.

Lessing, Gotthold Ephraim. *Laocoön: An Essay on the Limits of Painting and Poetry*. Translated by Edward Allen McCormick. Baltimore: Johns Hopkins University Press, 1984.

Lethen, Helmut. *Cool Conduct: The Culture of Distance in Weimar Germany*. Translated by Don Renau. Berkeley: University of California Press, 2002.

———. *Der Sound der Väter: Gottfried Benn und seine Zeit*. Berlin: Rowohlt, 2006.

Levinas, Emmanuel. *Time and the Other, and Additional Essays*. Translated by Richard A. Cohen. Pittsburgh: Duquesne University Press, 1987.

———. *Totalité et infini: Essai sur l'extériorité*. Paris: Le Livre de Poche, 1990.

———. *Totality and Infinity: An Essay on Exteriority*. Translated by Alphonso Lingis. Pittsburgh: Duquesne University Press, 1969.

Levine, Michael G. "'A Place So Insanely Enchanting': Kafka and the Poetics of Suspension." *MLN* 123, no. 5 (December 2008): 1039–67.

Lonner, Alyssa A. *Mediating the Past: Gustav Freytag, Progress, and German Historical Identity, 1848–1871*. Bern: Lang, 2005.

Losch, Bernhard. "Widerstandsrecht bei Fontane: Grete Minde gegen Unterdrückung und Rechtsverweigerung." *Fontane Blätter* 67 (1999): 59–74.

Löwy, Isaak [Jizchak]. "Vom jüdischen Theater." In Franz Kafka, *Nachgelassene Schriften und Fragmente I*. Edited by Jost Schillemeit. In *Schriften—Tagebücher: Kritische Ausgabe*, 430–36.

Lück, Heiner. "Leben und Sterben am Abgrund: Das Schicksal der Grete Minde zwischen Patriziat und Bandenkriminalität." In *Tangermünde: 1000 Jahre Geschichte*, 256–74. Dössel: Janos Stekovics, 2008.

Ludwig, Otto. "Die Ideale der Gegenwart." In *Nachlaßschriften*, vol. 2: *Shakespeare-Studien*, edited by Moritz Heydrich, 351–54. Leipzig: Cnoblauch, 1872.

———. "Der poetische Realismus." In *Nachlaßschriften*, vol. 2: *Shakespeare-Studien*, edited by Moritz Heydrich, 264–69. Leipzig: Cnoblauch, 1872.

Lukács, Georg. "Der alte Fontane." In *Deutsche Realisten des 19. Jahrhunderts*, 260–305. Berlin: Aufbau-Verlag, 1956.

———. "Erzählen oder beschreiben?" In *Werke*, vol. 4: *Probleme des Realismus*, 197–242. Neuwied: Luchterhand, 1971.

———. "Expressionism: Its Significance and Decline." In *Essays on Realism*, edited by Rodney Livingstone and translated by David Fernbach, 76–113. London: Lawrence and Wishart, 1980.

———. "Franz Kafka or Thomas Mann?" In *The Meaning of Contemporary Realism*, translated by John and Necke Mander, 47–92. London: Merlin, 1962.

———. *The Historical Novel*. Translated by Hannah and Stanley Mitchell. Lincoln: University of Nebraska Press, 1983.

———. "Narrate or Describe?" In *Writer and Critic, and Other Essays*, edited and translated by Arthur D. Kahn, 110–48. New York: Grosset & Dunlap, 1971.

Lütteken, Anett. "'Ich sehe viele, die nicht da sind.'—Theodor Fontane und die Krise des Protestantismus." *Euphorion* 100 (2006): 395–426.

Macho, Thomas. "Stifters Dinge." *Merkur: Deutsche Zeitschrift für europäisches Denken* 676 (2005): 735–41.

MacLeod, Catriona. *Embodying Ambiguity: Androgyny and Aesthetics from Winckelmann to Keller*. Detroit: Wayne State University Press, 1998.

———. *Fugitive Objects: Sculpture and Literature in the German Nineteenth Century*. Evanston, Ill.: Northwestern University Press, 2014.

———. "The Indecent Body of Sculpture: Theodor Storm's Realist *Psyche*." In *Sculpture, Sexuality, and History*, edited by Jana Funke and Jen Grove, 105–24. Cham: Palgrave, 2019.

Maillet, Arnold. *The Claude Glass: Use and Meaning of the Black Mirror in Western Art*. Translated by Jeff Fort. New York: Zone Books, 2004.

Marcus, Steven. *The Other Victorians: A Study of Sexuality and Pornography in Mid-Nineteenth-Century England*. New York: Basic Books, 1966.

Marcuse, Ludwig. *Obszön: Geschichte einer Entrüstung*. Munich: List, 1962.

Marion, Jean-Luc. *The Erotic Phenomenon*. Translated by Stephen E. Lewis. Chicago: University of Chicago Press, 2007.

———. *In Excess: Studies of Saturated Phenomena*. Translated by Robyn Horner and Vincent Berraud. New York: Fordham University Press, 2002.

Martens, Wolfgang. "Klinische Lyrik." In Hohendahl, *Benn—Wirkung wider Willen*, 89–91.

Martin, Dieter. "'Ein Buch für Schwächlinge': 'Werther'-Allusionen in Dramen des Naturalismus." *Zeitschrift für deutsche Philologie* 122, no. 2 (2003): 237–65.

Martini, Fritz. *Deutsche Literatur im bürgerlichen Realismus 1848–1898*. Stuttgart: J. B. Metzlersche Verlagsbuchhandlung, 1962.

———. *Das Wagnis der Sprache*. Stuttgart: Klett, 1954.

Martyn, David. "The Picturesque as Art of the Average: Stifter's Statistical Poetics of Observation." *Monatshefte* 105, no. 3 (Fall 2013): 426–42.

Marx, Karl. *Capital: A Critique of Political Economy*, vol. 1. Translated by Ben Fowkes. New York: Vintage, 1977.

———. *A Contribution to the Critique of Political Economy*. Translated by S. W. Ryanskaya, edited by Maurice Dobb. New York: International Publishers, 1970.

———. *Zur Kritik der politischen Ökonomie: Erstes Heft*. In *Marx-Engels-Gesamtausgabe*, 2.2: *Ökonomische Manuskripte und Schriften, 1858–1861*, edited by Larissa Miskewitsch et al., 95–245. Berlin: Dietz, 1980.

Marx, Karl, and Friedrich Engels. "The Communist Manifesto." In Karl Marx, *Selected Writings*, edited by Lawrence H. Simon, 157–86. Indianapolis: Hackett, 1994.

Mauthner, Fritz. *Beiträge zu einer Kritik der Sprache*, vol. 1: *Sprache und Psychologie*. Stuttgart: Cotta, 1901.

———. *Erinnerungen*, vol. 1: *Prager Jugendjahre*. Munich: Müller, 1918.

McIsaac, Peter M. *Museums of the Mind: German Modernity and the Dynamics of Collecting*. University Park: Pennsylvania State University Press, 2007.

Meillassoux, Quentin. *After Finitude: An Essay on the Necessity of Contingency*. Translated by Ray Brassier. London: Bloomsbury, 2008.

Menninghaus, Winfried. *Disgust: Theory and History of a Strong Sensation*. Translated by Howard Eiland and Joel Golb. Albany: State University of New York Press, 2003.

Mertner, Edgar, and Herbert Mainusch. *Pornotopia: Das Obszöne und die Pornographie in der literarischen Landschaft*. Frankfurt am Main: Athenäum, 1970.

Metz, Joseph. "'Es ist ein seltsam, furchtbar erhabenes Ding, der Mensch': Verdinglichung, absoluter Mehrwert und das perverse Erhabene in Adalbert Stifters proto-benjaminischen Stadtbildern." In *Organismus und Gesellschaft: Der Körper in der deutschsprachigen Literatur des Realismus (1830–1930)*, edited by Christiane Arndt and Silke Brodersen, 49–67. Bielefeld: Transcript, 2011.

Michalski, Sergiusz. *The Reformation and the Visual Arts: The Protestant Image Question in Western and Eastern Europe*. London: Routledge, 1993.

Michasiw, Kim Ian. "Nine Revisionist Theses on the Picturesque." *Representations* 38 (Spring 1992): 76–100.

Mieszkowski, Jan. "Who's Afraid of Anacoluthon?" *MLN* 124, no. 3 (April 2009): 648–65.

Miller, Gerlinde F. *Die Bedeutung des Entwicklungsbegriffs für Menschenbild und Dichtungstheorie bei Gottfried Benn*. New York: Lang, 1990.

Miller, Henry. *Obscenity and the Law of Reflection*. Yonkers, N.Y.: Alicat, 1944.

Miller, J. Hillis. "Catachresis, Prosopopoeia, and the Pathetic Fallacy: The Rhetoric of Ruskin." In *Poetry and Epistemology: Turning Points in the History of Poetic Knowledge*, edited by Roland Hagenbüchle and Laura Skandera, 398–40. Regensburg: Pustet, 1986.

———. "*Praeteria* and the Pathetic Fallacy." In *Victorian Connections*, edited by Jerome McGann, 172–78. Charlottesville: University of Virginia Press, 1989.

———. "The Sense of an Un-ending: The Resistance to Narrative Closure in Kafka's *Das Schloss*." In *Franz Kafka: Narration, Rhetoric, and Reading*, edited by Jakob Lothe, Beatrice Sandberg, and Ronald Speirs, 108–22. Columbus: Ohio State University Press, 2011.

Minden, Michael. "Stifter and the Postmodern Sublime." In *History, Text, Value: Essays on Adalbert Stifter*, edited by Michael Minden, Martin Swales, and Godela Weiss-Sussex, 9–21. Linz: Stifter-Haus, 2006.

Mitchell, W. J. T. "Ekphrasis and the Other." In *Picture Theory*, 151–81. Chicago: University of Chicago Press, 1994.

———. *Iconology: Image, Text, Ideology*. Chicago: University of Chicago Press, 1986.

"Moderne Charaktermasken." *Die Grenzboten: Zeitschrift für Politik und Literatur* 8, no. 2.1 (1849): 241–49.

Mösender, Karl. "Stimmung und Erdleben: Adalbert Stifters Ikonologie der Landschaftsmalerei." In *Adalbert Stifter: Dichter und Maler, Denkmalpfleger und Schulmann. Neue Zugänge zu seinem Werk*, edited by Hartmut Laufhütte and Karl Mösender, 18–57. Tübingen: Niemeyer, 1996.

Müller-Seidel, Walter. *Theodor Fontane: Soziale Romankunst in Deutschland.* Stuttgart: Metzler, 1975.

Musil, Robert. "The Obscene and the Pathological in Art." In *Precision and Soul*, edited and translated by Burton Pike and David S. Luft, 3–9. Chicago: University of Chicago Press, 1990.

———. "Das Unanständige und Kranke in der Kunst." In *Gesammelte Werke*, vol. 2: *Prosa und Stücke: Kleine Prosa, Aphorismen, Autobiographisches, Essays und Reden, Kritik*, edited by Adolf Frisé, 977–83. Reinbek bei Hamburg: Rowohlt, 1978.

Nägele, Rainer. "Schloß ohne Schluß: Kafka, Benjamin und kein Ende." In *Lesarten der Moderne: Essays*, 149–75. Eggingen: Isele, 1998.

Nancy, Jean-Luc. "On Painting and Presence." In *The Birth to Presence*, translated by Emily McVarish, 341–67. Stanford, Calif.: Stanford University Press, 1993.

Nancy, Jean-Luc, and Federico Ferrari. *Being Nude: The Skin of Images.* Translated by Anne O'Byrne and Carlie Anglemire. New York: Fordham University Press, 2014.

"Die naturalistische Schule in Deutschland." *Die Grenzboten: Zeitschrift für Politik, Literatur und Kunst* 45, no. 2 (1886): 66–76.

Nebrig, Alexander. "Entbindung von der Disziplin: Arno Holz' Begründung des Lebenswissens in *Phantasus*." In *Das Wissen der Poesie: Lyrik, Versepik und die Wissenschaften im 19. Jahrhundert*, edited by Henning Hufnagel and Olav Krämer, 239–62. Berlin: De Gruyter, 2015.

Němcová, Božena. *Babička*. Toronto: Sixty-Eight, 1982.

———. *Großmutter: Bilder aus dem böhmischen Landleben.* Translated by Anton Smital. Leipzig: Reclam, 1885.

Neumann, Gerhard. "Chinesische Mauer und Schacht von Babel: Franz Kafkas Architekturen." In *Kafka-Lektüren*, 482–503. Berlin: De Gruyter, 2013.

———. "Kafkas *Schloß*-Roman: Das parasitäre Spiel der Zeichen." In *Franz Kafka, Experte der Macht*, 137–69. Munich: Hanser, 2012.

———. "Speisesaal und Gemäldegalerie: Die Geburt des Erzählens aus der bildenden Kunst. Fontanes Roman *L'Adultera*." In *Theodor Fontane: Romankunst als Gespräch*, 79–101. Freiburg am Breisgau: Rombach, 2011.

Ngai, Sianne. *Our Aesthetic Categories: Zany, Cute, Interesting*. Cambridge, Mass.: Harvard University Press, 2012.

Nitschke, Claudia. "Chaos und Form, Raum und Ethos in Stifters *Bunte Steine*." *German Life and Letters* 68, no. 4 (October 2015): 554–68.

Nordau, Max. *Degeneration*. Lincoln: University of Nebraska Press, 1993.

———. *Entartung*. Berlin: Duncker, 1896.

North, Paul. "Castle Logic: Hints in Kafka's Novel." In *1922: Literature, Culture, Politics*, edited by Jean-Michel Rabaté, 56–73. New York: Cambridge University Press, 2015.

———. *The Yield: Kafka's Atheological Reformation*. Stanford, Calif.: Stanford University Press, 2015.

Ohl, Hubert. "Bilder, die die Kunst stellt: Die Landschaftsdarstellung in den Romanen Theodor Fontanes." In *Theodor Fontane*, edited by Wolfgang Preisendanz, 447–64. Darmstadt: Wissenschaftliche Buchgesellschaft, 1973.

Osborne, John. *The Naturalist Drama in Germany*. Manchester: Manchester University Press, 1971.

———. *Theodor Fontane: Vor den Romanen. Krieg und Kunst*. Göttingen: Vandenhoeck & Ruprecht, 1999.

Ostmeier, Dorothee. *Poetische Dialoge zu Liebe, Gender und Sex im frühen zwanzigsten Jahrhundert*. Bielefeld: Aisthesis, 2014.

Pailer, Gaby. "Schwarzäugige Mordbrennerin: Fontanes *Grete Minde*, eine Tochter von Cervantes' *La gitanilla*." In *rebellisch. verzweifelt. infame: Das böse Mädchen als ästhetische Figur*, edited by Renate Möhrmann, 171–85. Bielefeld: Aisthesis, 2012.

Pastor, Eckart. "Das Hänflingsnest: Zu Theodor Fontanes *Grete Minde*." *Tijdschrift voor levende talen / Revue des langues vivantes* 44, no. 2 (1978): 99–110.

Pease, Allison. *Modernism, Mass Culture, and the Aesthetics of Obscenity*. Cambridge: Cambridge University Press, 2000.

Peters, Julie Stone. "Performing Obscene Modernism: Theatrical Censorship and the Making of Modern Drama." In *Against Theater: Creative Destructions on the Modernist Stage*, edited by Alan Ackerman and Martin Puchner, 206–30. New York: Palgrave, 2006.

Pfau, Thomas. "Metasprache und Bilderfahrung in *Der Stechlin*." *German Quarterly* 86, no. 4 (Fall 2013): 421–43.

Pniower, Otto. "Grete Minde." In *Dichtungen und Dichter: Essays und Studien*, 295–331. Berlin: Fischer, 1912.

Pohlmann, August Wilhelm. *Geschichte der Stadt Tangermünde seit Gründung derselben bis zu dem laufenden Jahre 1829, aus Urkunden und glaubwürdigen Nachrichten*. Stendal: Franzen und Große, 1829.

Porter, James I. "The Disgrace of Matter in Ancient Aesthetics." In *KAKOS: Badness and Anti-value in Classical Antiquity*, edited by Ineke Sluiter and Ralph M. Rosen, 283–317. Leiden: Brill, 2008.

———. *The Origins of Aesthetic Thought in Ancient Greece: Matter, Sensation, and Experience*. Cambridge: Cambridge University Press, 2010.

Powell, Larson. *The Technological Unconscious in German Modernist Literature*. Rochester, N.Y.: Camden House, 2008.

Preisendanz, Wolfgang. *Humor als dichterische Einbildungskraft: Studien zur Erzählkunst des poetischen Realismus*. Munich: Eidos, 1963.

———. *Wege des Realismus*. Munich: Fink, 1977.

Ragg-Kirkby, Helena. *Adalbert Stifter's Late Prose: The Mania for Moderation*. Rochester, N.Y.: Camden House, 2000.

Rajan, Tilottama. *Deconstruction and the Remainders of Phenomenology: Sartre, Derrida, Foucault, Baudrillard*. Stanford, Calif.: Stanford University Press, 2002.

Redfield, Marc. "*Lucinde*'s Obscenity." In *Rereading Romanticism*, edited by Martha B. Helfer, 103–30. Amsterdam: Rodopi, 2000.

Richards, I. A. *Practical Criticism: A Study of Literary Judgment*. New York: Harcourt, Brace & Co., 1946.

Riha, Karl. "Blechschmied Arno Holz: Zur Struktur des satirischen Monstredramas 'Die Blechschmiede.'" *Text + Kritik* 121 (January 1994): 74–83.

———. "Veränderung des Dramas in der Satire: Arno Holz, *Die Blechschmiede*, Karl Kraus, *Die letzten Tage der Menschheit*." In *Kritik, Satire, Parodie: Gesammelte Aufsätze*, 132–44. Opladen: Westdeutscher Verlag, 1992.

Rilke, Rainer Maria. *"The Duino Elegies" and "The Sonnets to Orpheus": A Dual Language Edition*. Translated by Stephen Mitchell. New York: Vintage International, 2009.

———. *Werke*, vol. 1: *Gedichte 1895 bis 1910*. Edited by Manfred Engel and Ulrich Fülleborn. Frankfurt am Main: Insel, 1996.

———. *Werke*, vol. 2: *Gedichte 1910 bis 1926*. Edited by Manfred Engel and Ulrich Fülleborn. Frankfurt am Main: Insel, 1996.

Rittner, Andreas. *Alt-Märckisches Geschichtbuch*. In Küster, *Antiquitates Tangermundenses*, 1–87.

Robbe-Grillet, Alain. "Nature, Humanism and Tragedy." *New Left Review* 31 (May/June 1965): 65–80.

Robertson, Ritchie. *Kafka: Judaism, Politics, and Literature*. Oxford: Clarendon Press, 1985.

———. "Myth vs. Enlightenment in Kafka's *Das Schloß*." *Monatshefte* 103, no. 3 (January 2011): 385–95.

Roche, Mark W. "Provocation and Parataxis." In *A New History of German Literature*, edited by David E. Wellbery, Judith Ryan, and Hans Ulrich Gumbrecht, 678–83. Cambridge, Mass.: Harvard University Press, 2004.

Ronell, Avital. "Doing Kafka in *The Castle*." In *Finitude's Score*, 183–206. Lincoln: University of Nebraska Press, 1994.

Rosenkranz, Karl. *The Aesthetics of Ugliness: A Critical Edition*. Translated by Andrei Pop and Mechtild Widrich. London: Bloomsbury, 2015.

———. *Ästhetik des Häßlichen*. Edited by Dieter Kliche. Stuttgart: Reclam, 1990.

Rothe, Wolfgang. Introduction to *Deutsches Theater des Naturalismus*, 7–39. Munich: Langen/Müller, 1972.

Rothfeld, Lawrence. *Vital Signs: Medical Realism in Nineteenth-Century Fiction*. Princeton, N.J.: Princeton University Press, 1992.

Roux aîné, H., and Louis Barré. *Herculanum et Pompéi: Recueil général des peintures, bronzes, mosaïques, etc., découverts jusqu'à ce jour, et reproduits d'après le Antichita di Ercolano, il Museo Borbonico, et tous les ouvrages analogues, augmenté de sujets inédits*, vol. 8: *Musée secret*. Paris: Didot. 1877.

Ruskin, John. *Modern Painters*. Edited by David Barrie. New York: Knopf, 1987.

Sachs, Hans. "Ein straffred Diogenis Philosophi, uber das viehische verkerte leben menschliches geschlechts." Nürnberg: Neuber, 1555. Staatsbibliothek zu Berlin. http://resolver.staatsbibliothek-berlin.de/SBB0001B15400000000.

Santner, Eric. "Kafka's *Metamorphosis* and the Writing of Abjection." In Franz Kafka, *The Metamorphosis*, edited and translated by Stanley Corngold, 195–20. New York: W. W. Norton, 1996.

———. *On Creaturely Life: Rilke, Benjamin, Sebald*. Chicago: University of Chicago Press, 2006.

Sartre, Jean-Paul. *Being and Nothingness: A Phenomenological Essay on Ontology*. Translated by Hazel E. Barnes. New York: Washington Square Press, 1992.
———. *L'être et le néant: Essai d'ontologie phénoménologique*. Paris: Gallimard, 2016.
———. *Nausea*. Translated by Lloyd Alexander. New York: New Directions, 2007.
Sawday, Jonathan. *The Body Emblazoned: Dissection and the Human Body in Renaissance Culture*. London: Routledge, 1995.
Scheler, Max. "Shame and Feelings of Modesty." In *Person and Self-Value: Three Essays*, translated by M. S. Frings, 1–85. Dordrecht: Martinus Nijhoff, 1987.
———. "Über Scham und Schamgefühl." In *Schriften aus dem Nachlass*, vol. 1: *Zur Ethik und Erkenntnislehre*, 53–148. Berlin: Neue Geist, 1933.
Schelling, F. W. J. *Über das Verhältnis der bildenden Kunst zu der Natur*. Edited by Lucia Sziborsky. Hamburg: Meiner, 1983.
———. "Über die Wissenschaft der Kunst, in bezug auf das akademische Studium." In *Werke: Auswahl in Drei Bänden*, vol. 2: *Schriften zur Identitätsphilosophie*, edited by Otto Weiß, 537–682. Leipzig: Eckart, 1907.
———. *Ueber das Verhältniß des Realen und Idealen in der Natur, oder Entwickelung der ersten Grundsätze der Naturphilosophie an den Principien der Schwere und des Lichts*. Hamburg: Perthes, 1806.
Scherpe, Klaus R. "Der Fall Arno Holz: Zur sozialen und ideologischen Motivationen der naturalistischen Literaturrevolution." In *Positionen der literarischen Intelligenz zwischen bürgerlicher Reaktion und Imperialismus*, edited by Gert Mattenklott and Klaus R. Scherpe, 121–78. Kronberg: Scriptor, 1973.
——— "Kafkas Poetik der Beschreibung." In *Kontinent Kafka: Mosse-Lektures an der Humboldt-Universität zu Berlin*, edited by Klaus R. Scherpe and Elisabeth Wagner, 88–102. Berlin: Vorwerk 8, 2006.
[Scheuermann], Julia Virginia. *Sturm und Stern*. Berlin: Schuster & Loeffler, 1905.
Schiewer, Gesine Lenore. *Poetische Gestaltkonzepte und Automatentheorie: Arno Holz—Robert Musil—Oswald Wiener*. Würzburg: Königshausen & Neumann, 2004.
———. "Verbales Verhalten im Horizont von Ethnologie und Psychologie: Zur 'Sprache des Lebens' in dem dramatischen Spätwerk von Arno Holz." In *Dialogue Analysis IX: Dialogue in Literature and the Media (Selected Papers from the 9th IADA Conference, Salzburg 2003)*, part 1: *Literature*, 99–108. Tübingen: Niemeyer, 2005.
Schiller, Friedrich. *Geschichte des Dreißigjährigen Kriegs*. In *Werke und Briefe*, vol. 7: *Historische Schriften und Erzählungen II*, edited by Otto Dann, 11–448. Frankfurt am Main: Deutscher Klassiker Verlag, 2002.
———. "On Grace and Dignity." In *Schiller's "On Grace and Dignity" in Its Cultural Context: Essays and a New Translation*, edited by Jane V. Curran and Christopher Fricker, 123–70. Rochester, N.Y.: Camden House, 2005.
———. "Über Anmut und Würde." In *Werke und Briefe in zwölf Bänden*, vol. 8: *Theoretische Schriften*, edited by Rolf-Peter Janz, 330–94. Frankfurt am Main: Deutscher Klassiker Verlag, 1992.
Schirmeyer-Klein, Ulla. "Realismus-Literaturprogramm für einen bürgerlichen Staat: Der programmatische Realismus in den 'Grenzboten' 1848–1860." Ph.D. diss., Ludwig-Maximilian-Universität (Munich), 1974.

Schlaf, Johannes. *Ein Dachstubenidyll*. In Arno Holz and Johannes Schlaf, *Papa Hamlet. Ein Tod*, 83–102. Stuttgart: Reclam, 1963.

———. *Noch einmal "Arno Holz und ich."* Berlin: Messer & Cie, 1902.

Schlegel, Friedrich. *Kritische Friedrich-Schlegel-Ausgabe*. Edited by Ernst Behler. Vol. 16, *Schriften aus dem Nachlaß: Fragmente zur Poesie und Literatur, Erster Teil*, edited by Hans Eichner. Paderborn: Schöningh, 1981.

Schleiermacher, Friedrich. *On Religion: Speeches to Its Cultured Despisers*. Translated by Richard Crouter. Cambridge: Cambridge University Press, 1996.

———. *Über die Religion: Reden an die Gebildeten unter ihren Verächtern*. Edited by Andreas Arndt. Hamburg: Meiner, 2004.

Schmidt, Arno. *Der sanfte Unmensch: Unverbindliche Betrachtungen eines Überflüssigen*. Frankfurt am Main: Ullstein, 1958.

S[chmidt], J[ulian]. "Die Märzpoeten." *Die Grenzboten: Zeitschrift für Politik und Literatur* 9, no. 1.1 (1850): 5–13.

Schmidt, Julian. *Geschichte der deutschen Literatur im neunzehnten Jahrhundert*, vol. 1: *Weimar und Jena in den Jahren 1794 bis 1806*. Leipzig: Herbig, 1855.

———. *Geschichte der deutschen Literatur im neunzehnten Jahrhundert*, vol. 3. Leipzig: Herbig, 1855.

———. *Geschichte der deutschen Literatur seit Lessing's Tod*, vol. 1. Leipzig: Herbig, 1858.

———. *Geschichte der deutschen Literatur seit Lessing's Tod*, vol. 3. Leipzig: Herbig, 1858.

———. *Geschichte der deutschen Literatur von Leibniz bis auf unsere Zeit*, vol. 5. Berlin: Hertz, 1896.

Schmidt, Julian, and Gustav Freytag. "Den Lesern der Grenzboten." *Die Grenzboten: Zeitschrift für Politik und Literatur* 7, no. 2.3 (1848): 1–4.

Schneider, Gesa. *Das Andere schreiben: Kafkas fotographische Poetik*. Würzburg: Königshausen & Neumann, 2008.

Schneider, Lothar. "Die Diätetik der Dinge: Dimensionen des Gegenständlichen in Gustav Freytags *Soll und Haben*." In *150 Jahre "Soll und Haben": Studien zu Gustav Freytags kontroversem Roman*, edited by Florian Krobb, 103–20. Würzburg: Königshausen & Neumann, 2005.

Schneider, Sabine, and Barbara Hunfeld, eds. *Die Dinge und die Zeichen: Dimensionen des Realistischen in der Erzählliteratur des 19. Jahrhunderts*. Würzburg: Königshausen & Neumann, 2008.

Schnitzler, Norbert. *Ikonoklasmus—Bildersturm: Theologischer Bilderstreit und ikonoklastisches Handeln während des 15. und 16. Jahrhunderts*. Munich: Fink, 1996.

Schopenhauer, Arthur. *On Will in Nature*. In *On the Fourfold Root of the Principle of Sufficient Reason; On Vision and Colours; On Will in Nature*, edited and translated by David E. Cartwright, Edward E. Erdmann, and Christopher Janaway, 303–448. Cambridge: Cambridge University Press, 2012.

Schor, Naomi. *Reading in Detail: Aesthetics and the Feminine*. London: Routledge, 2007.

Schorske, Carl E. *Fin de Siècle Vienna: Politics and Culture*. New York: Vintage, 1981.

Schrader, Hans-Jürgen. "Frühneuzeitliche Munizipien in religiös-sozialen Hassausbrüchen: Raabes 'Höxter und Corvey' (1874) und Fontanes 'Grete Minde'

(1879)." In *Metropole, Provinz und Welt: Raum und Mobilität in der Literatur des Realismus*, edited by Roland Berbig and Dirk Göttsche, 289–319. Berlin: De Gruyter, 2013.

Sebald, W. G. "Bis an den Rand der Natur: Versuch über Stifter." In *Die Beschreibung des Unglücks: Zur österreichischen Literatur von Stifter bis Handke*, 15–37. Frankfurt am Main: Fischer, 1994.

Servaes, Franz. "Arno Holz." In *Praeludien: Ein Essaybuch*, 71–105. Berlin: Schuster & Loeffler, 1899.

Shakespeare, William. *The Excellent History of the Merchant of Venice*. [London]: J. Roberts, 1600. Folger Shakespeare Library, Luna Digital Image Collection. https://luna.folger.edu/luna/servlet/s/241ms1.

———. *Hamlet*. In *The Arden Shakespeare Complete Works*, 291–332. Edited by Richard Proudfoot, Ann Thompson, and David Scott Kastan. London: Methuen, 2011.

Shapiro, Susan E. "The Uncanny Jew: A Brief History of an Image." *Judaism: A Quarterly Journal of Jewish Life and Thought* 46, no. 1 (Winter 1997): 63–78.

Sokel, Walter H. *Franz Kafka—Tragik und Ironie: Zur Struktur seiner Kunst*. Munich: Albert Langen Georg Müller Verlag, 1963.

Sontag, Susan. "An Argument about Beauty." *Daedalus* 131, no. 4 (Fall 2002): 21–28.

———. "The Pornographic Imagination." In *Styles of Radical Will*, 35–73. New York: Anchor, 1991.

Specht, Benjamin. "'Empirisierte Transzendentalpoesie': Wirklichkeits- und Subjektbegriff in Poetik und Lyrik von Arno Holz." *KulturPoetik* 17, no. 1 (2017): 62–80.

Spielhagen, Friedrich. "Ueber Objectivetät im Roman." In *Vermischte Schriften*, vol. 1, 174–97. Berlin: Janke, 1864.

Spies [McGillen], Petra. "A Creative Machine: The Media History of Theodor Fontane's Library Network and Reading Practices." *Germanic Review* 87, no. 1 (March 2012): 72–90.

Sprengel, Peter. *Darwin in der Poesie: Spuren der Evolutionslehre in der deutschsprachigen Literatur des 19. und 20. Jahrhunderts*. Würzburg: Königshausen & Neumann, 1998.

———. "'Hamlet' in 'Papa Hamlet': Zur Funktion des Zitats im Naturalismus." *Literatur für Leser* 84, no. 1 (March 1984): 25–43.

———. "Holz & Co. Die Zusammenarbeit von Arno Holz mit Johannes Schlaf und Oskar Jerschke—oder: Die Grenzen der Freiheit." *Text + Kritik* 121 (January 1994): 20–32.

Stadler, Ernst. "Lyrische Flugblätter (Sammelrezension)." In Hohendahl, *Benn—Wirkung wider Willen*, 95–96.

Steinberg, Erwin R. "K. of the Castle: Ostensible Land-Surveyor." *College English* 27, no. 3 (December 1965): 185–89.

Stifter, Adalbert. *Werke und Briefe: Historisch-Kritische Gesamtausgabe*. Edited by Alfred Doppler and Wolfgang Frühwald. 11 vols. Stuttgart: Kohlhammer, 1978–2020.

Stillmark, A. "Stifter Contra Hebbel—an Examination of the Sources of Their Disagreement." *German Life and Letters* 21, no. 2 (January 1968): 93–102.

Stöckmann, Ingo. "Über Fülle/Überfülle: Textverfahren der Copia um 1890." In *Entsagung und Routines: Aporien des Spätrealismus und Verfahren der frühen Moderne*, edited by Moritz Baßler, 319–34. Berlin: De Gruyter, 2013.

Strafgesetzbuch für das Grossherzogthum Hessen, nebst den damit zusammenhängenden Gesetzen. Darmstadt: Verlag der Invaliden-Anstalt, 1841. www.mdz-nbn-resolving.de/urn/resolver.pl?urn=urn:nbn:de:bvb:12-bsb10395527-6.

Strindberg, August. "On Modern Drama and the Modern Theater." In *Strindberg on Drama and Theater: A Source Book*, edited and translated by Egil Törnqvist and Birgitta Steene, 79–84. Amsterdam: Amsterdam University Press, 2007.

———. "On Realism: Some Views." In *Strindberg on Drama and Theater: A Source Book*, edited and translated by Egil Törnqvist and Birgitta Steene, 33–34. Amsterdam: Amsterdam University Press, 2007.

Strohschneider-Kohrs, Ingrid. "Sprache und Wirklichkeit bei Arno Holz." In *Poesie und Reflexion: Aufsätze zur Literatur*, 305–33. Tübingen: Niemeyer, 1999.

Strowick, Elisabeth. *Gespenster des Realismus: Zur literarischen Wahrnehmung von Wirklichkeit*. Munich: Fink, 2019.

———. "Poetological-Technical Operations: Representation of Motion in Adalbert Stifter." *Configurations* 18, no. 3 (Fall 2010): 273–89.

———, ed. *Wirklichkeit und Wahrnehmung: Neue Perspektiven auf Theodor Storm*. Bern: Lang, 2013.

Sussman, Henry. *Franz Kafka: Geometrician of Metaphor*. Madison, Wis.: Coda Press, 1979.

Swales, Martin, and Erika Swales. *Adalbert Stifter: A Critical Study*. Cambridge: Cambridge University Press, 1984.

Tatar, Maria. *Lustmord: Sexual Murder in Weimar Germany*. Princeton, N.J.: Princeton University Press, 1995.

Thompson, Michael. *Rubbish Theory: The Creation and Destruction of Value*. Oxford: Oxford University Press, 1979.

Thormann, Michael. "Der programmatische Realismus der *Grenzboten* im Kontext von liberaler Politik, Philosophie und Geschichtsschreibung." *Internationales Archiv für Sozialgeschichte der deutschen Literatur* 18, no. 1 (1993): 37–68.

Todorov, Tzvetan. *The Fantastic: A Structural Approach to a Literary Genre*. Translated by Richard Howard. Ithaca, N.Y.: Cornell University Press, 1975.

Tomkins, Silvan. *Shame and Its Sisters: A Silvan Tomkins Reader*. Edited by Eve Kosofsky Sedgwick and Adam Frank. Durham, N.C.: Duke University Press, 1995.

Travers, Martin. *The Hour That Breaks: Gottfried Benn. A Biography*. Bern: Lang, 2015.

———. *The Poetry of Gottfried Benn: Text and Selfhood*. Bern: Lang, 2007.

Twellmann, Marcus. "Das deutsche Bürgerhaus: Zum oikonomisch Imaginären in Gustav Freytags *Soll und Haben*." *Deutsche Vierteljahrsschrift für Literatur und Geistesgeschichte* 87, no. 3 (2013): 356–85.

Varone, Antonio. *Eroticism in Pompeii*. Translated by Maureen Fant. Los Angeles: J. Paul Getty Museum, 2001.

Varro, [Marcus Terentius]. *On the Latin Language, Books V–VII*. Translated by Roland G. Kent. Cambridge, Mass.: Harvard University Press, 1993.

Vedder, Ulrike. "Münzen, Bilder, Frauen, Romane: Fontanes Erbstucke." In *Realien des Realismus: Wissenschaft—Technik—Medien in Theodor Fontanes Erzählprosa*, edited by Stephan Braese and Anne-Kathrin Reulecke, 79–95. Berlin: Vorwerk 8, 2010.

Verbeek, Ludo. "Auswandern—Unnütze Prolegomena zu Kafkas *Schloß*." In *"Schloß"-Geschichten: Zu Kafkas drittem Romanplan—Eine Diskussion*, 11–64. Eggingen: Isele, 2007.

Vinken, Barbara. "Cover up—Die nackte Wahrheit der Pornographie." In *Die nackte Wahrheit: Zur Pornographie und zur Rolle des Obszönen in der Gegenwart*, edited by Barbara Vinken, 7–22. Munich: dtv, 1997.

———. "Pygmalion à rebours: Fetischismus in Zolas Œuvre." In *Pygmalion: Die Geschichte des Mythos in der abendländischen Kultur*, edited by Matthias Meyer and Gerhard Neumann, 593–621. Freiburg im Breisgau: Rombach, 1997.

———. "Zola—alles sehen, alles wissen, alles heilen: Der Fetischismus im Naturalismus." In *Historische Anthropologie und Literatur: Romanistische Beiträge zu einem neuen Paradigma der Literaturwissenschaft*, edited by Rudolf Behrens and Roland Galle, 215–26. Würzburg: Königshausen & Neumann, 1995.

Vismann, Cornelia. *Akten: Medientechnik und Recht*. Frankfurt am Main: Fischer, 2000.

———. *Files: Law and Media Technology*. Translated by Geoffrey Winthrop-Young. Stanford, Calif.: Stanford University Press, 2008.

Vogel, Juliane. "Stifters Gitter: Poetologische Dimensionen einer Grenzfigur." In Schneider and Hunfeld, *Die Dinge und die Zeichen*, 43–58.

Vogl, Joseph. "Lebende Anstalt." In *Für alle und keinen: Lektüre, Schrift und Leben bei Nietzsche und Kafka*, edited by Friedrich Balke, Joseph Vogl, and Benno Wagner, 21–33. Zurich: diaphanes, 2008.

———. *Ort der Gewalt: Kafkas literarische Ethik*. Zurich: diaphanes, 2010.

———. "Der Text als Schleier: Zu Stifters *Der Nachsommer*." *Jahrbuch der deutschen Schillergesellschaft* 37 (1993): 298–312.

Wagenbach, Klaus. *Franz Kafka: Eine Biographie seiner Jugend, 1883–1912*. Bern: Francke, 1958.

Waldron, Jennifer. *Reformations of the Body: Idolatry, Sacrifice, and Early Modern Theater*. New York: Palgrave, 2013.

Wandrey, Conrad. *Theodor Fontane*. Munich: Beck'sche Verlagsbuchhandlung, 1919.

Weber, Samuel. *Theatricality as Medium*. New York: Fordham University Press, 2004.

Wegener, Hanns. "Gottfried Benn: 'Morgue und andere Gedichte.'" In Hohendahl, *Benn—Wirkung wider Willen*, 97–98.

Weitzman, Erica. "'Ich, von dem du ausgingst?': Inheritance and Anamorphosis between Freytag and Kafka." *Monatshefte* 111, no. 1 (2019): 79–98.

———. "'An Injury to Shame': Obscenity and Affect in Nineteenth-Century German Aesthetics." *Orbis Litterarum* 74, no. 1 (February 2019): 3–17.

———. *Irony's Antics: Walser, Kafka, Roth, and the German Comic Tradition*. Evanston, Ill.: Northwestern University Press, 2015.

———. "Scham, oder die Metaphysik." In *Rücksendungen zu Jacques Derridas "Die Postkarte": Ein essayistisches Glossar*, edited by Matthias Schmidt, 329–40. Vienna: Turia + Kant, 2015.

Wellek, René. “The Concept of Realism in Literary Scholarship.” *Neophilologus* 45, no. 1 (January 1961): 1–20.
Wellershoff, Dieter. *Gottfried Benn: Phänotyp dieser Stunde*. Munich: dtv, 1958.
West, Paul. *The Very Rich Hours of Count von Stauffenberg*. New York: Harper & Row, 1980.
Wiedemann, Conrad. “Schwierigkeiten mit ‘Dafnis’: Gedanken zu den Barocknachdichtungen von Arno Holz.” *Text + Kritik* 121 (January 1994): 84–95.
Wild, Christopher J. *Theater der Keuschheit, Keuschheit des Theaters: Zu einer Geschichte der (Anti-)Theatralität von Gryphius bis Kleist*. Freiburg im Bresgau: Rombach, 2003.
Williams, Kirk. “Anti-Theatricality and the Limits of Naturalism.” In *Against Theater: Creative Destructions on the Modernist Stage*, edited by Alan Ackerman and Martin Puchner, 95–111. New York: Palgrave, 2006.
Williams, Linda. *Hard Core: Power, Pleasure, and the “Frenzy of the Visible.”* Berkeley: University of California Press, 1989.
Winkler, Michael. “Benn’s Cancer Ward and George’s Autumnal Park: A Case of Lyrical *Kontrafaktur*.” *Colloquia Germanica* 13, no. 3 (1980): 258–64.
Wölfflin, Heinrich. *Renaissance and Baroque*. Translated by Kathrin Simon. Ithaca, N.Y.: Cornell University Press, 1964.
Zilcosky, John. *Kafka’s Travels: Exoticism, Colonialism, and the Traffic of Writing*. New York: Palgrave, 2003.
Ziolkowski, Jan M., ed. *Obscenity: Social Control and Artistic Creation in the European Middle Ages*. Leiden: Brill, 1998.
Zischler, Hanns. *Kafka Goes to the Movies*. Translated by Susan H. Gillespie. Chicago: University of Chicago Press, 2003.
Žižek, Slavoj. *Looking Awry: An Introduction to Jacques Lacan through Popular Culture*. Cambridge, Mass.: MIT Press, 1991.
Zola, Émile. “The Experimental Novel.” In *The Experimental Novel and Other Essays*, translated by Belle M. Sherman, 1–54. New York: Haskell House, 1964.
———. *Nana*. Edited by Henri Mitterand. Paris: Gallimard, 2002.
———. “Le Naturalisme.” In *Œuvres complètes*, vol. 11: *Œuvres critiques II*, edited by Henri Mitterand, 288–91. Paris: Cercle du Livre Précieux, 1968.
“Zur Ästhetik des Häßlichen.” *Die Grenzboten: Zeitschrift für Politik, Litteratur und Kunst* 47, no. 2 (1888): 529–34.

INDEX